Essex County Council

ALL
ROADS
★
LEAD
NORTH

ALL ROADS ★ LEAD NORTH

AMISH RAJ MULMI

HURST & COMPANY, LONDON

First published in India by Context, an imprint of Westland
Publications Private Limited, in 2021

First published in the United Kingdom in 2021 by
C. Hurst & Co. (Publishers) Ltd.,
New Wing, Somerset House, Strand, London, WC2R 1LA
© Amish Raj Mulmi, 2021

All rights reserved.

Printed in the United Kingdom by Bell and Bain Ltd, Glasgow

The right of Amish Raj Mulmi to be identified as the author of this publication is asserted by him in accordance with the Copyright, Designs and Patents Act, 1988.

A Cataloguing-in-Publication data record for this book is available from the British Library.

ISBN: 9781787385399

This book is printed using paper from registered sustainable and managed sources.

www.hurstpublishers.com

Typeset by SÜRYA, New Delhi

To our parents
Bimala Hada Mulmi and Ananda Raj Mulmi
Pratibha Hardikar Paranjpe and Dilip Paranjpe

And to Neha,

without whom this book would not have been possible
'We can know the past but the present is hidden from us.'

– Jorge Luis Borges

CONTENTS

Introduction: A Fine Balance	xi
Part One: BORDERLANDS	
1. Traders on the Silk Road	3
2. Neither Nepal nor China	25
3. A Fence in the Himalaya	43
4. War and Peace	62
Part Two: IN THE SHADOW OF EMPIRES	
5. Communism Comes by Road	81
6. Ghosts: Tibetan Exiles in Nepal	101
7. Between Two Boulders	120
Part Three: STATUS UPDATE	
8. 'A Friendship Across the Himalayas'	145
9. Chinese Capitalism with Nepali Characteristics	173
10. All Roads Lead North	192
Epilogue: Future Tense	211
Notes	223
Bibliography	269
Index	277
Acknowledgements	287

INTRODUCTION
A Fine Balance

In the winter of 1898, Sylvain Lévi, a French Indologist, trundled up the steep mountain passes that connected the plains of Nepal to the Kathmandu valley, the capital, in a palanquin and with sixteen bearers. Levi was by then accomplished in the field of Indology, but he had always wanted to study Nepal, for he believed the country had been at a crossroads of South, Central and East Asian influences throughout its history.[1] Unlike other orientalists of the time, who had begun to emphasise the tradition of the Vedas as the fount of Indian civilisation, Levi believed in the historical process. He was of the opinion that India's history could not be examined in isolation, without looking at its cultures' interactions with other parts of Asia.[2]

Levi left Calcutta on 8 January 1898, and after changing three trains, disembarked at Sugauli, the site of the 1816 treaty between the Gorkhas and the East India Company. Five days later, he arrived at the summit of Chandragiri, the 2,500-metre hill that overlooks the entire Kathmandu valley from the south. 'Everywhere at the further end and on the slopes are the villages and cultivations and east to west above the encircling mountains, a continuous lines [sic], uninterrupted, without a breach, of white snow peaks. Here they are quite close, three or four valleys to cross and beyond on the other side, Tibet, a piece of China, *C'est le Tibet, un morceau de la Chine.*'[3]

At the time, Nepal was ruled by Rana Prime Minister Bir Shamsher, now accepted as among the more liberal-minded Ranas to rule the country. Within the first week, Levi was taken to court to meet the acting prime minister and commander-in-chief Dev Shamsher and questioned about his knowledge. '[Dev Shamsher] speaks to me of the *Sakuntala* in French. He asked me if I believe in the devas.' By the end of it, the commander-in-chief instructed his men to assist Levi in his search for manuscripts and inscriptions.

Over the three months he would stay in Kathmandu, Levi would note with derision the sanitary habits of the people who lived in the valley ('But if one's eyes are opened one's nose must be closed. Kathmandu deposits her filth in her courtyards instead of her sewers.'[4]), and the people's unwillingness to allow a foreigner insight into their past ('These wretched people conceal their antiquities.'[5]). Like most European explorers of the time, he regarded antiquities as a tradeable object. ('As the manuscript is of a beautiful palaeography, I shall take it if I can obtain it at a fair price, because each possessor of a manuscript believes himself, in principle, a possessor of a treasure.'[6]) He was a product of his times, carrying the impress of imperial superiority that was the hallmark of colonial explorers.

Leaving Kathmandu in March 1898, he would publish *Le Népal: Étude historique d'un royaume hindou* ('Nepal: Historical Study of a Hindu Kingdom') between 1905–08, a magnum opus that continues to guide modern scholars on Nepali history. Despite previous works by European scholars—including Brian Hodgson, the legendary naturalist-cum-British resident in Kathmandu—Levi's study stood out in one particular respect: he incorporated the historical views of Nepal through Tibetan and Chinese documents, going back all the way to the Tang dynasty annals from the seventh century CE. This was hitherto unknown in scholarship; Nepal had been viewed through the lens of India, as an offshoot of its dynastic histories or Indian cultures, and little attention was paid to its interactions with Tibet and China; a view that dominates popular discourse around the country even today.

Levi's view of history—as an evolving process influenced by several factors and cultures—is unfortunately less popular in the subcontinent, with history viewed through a linear and nativist lens as popularised by British colonialists. Imperialists often saw their subjugation of the subcontinent as a natural result of historical affairs, one which sought to 'bring' civilisation to 'Your new-caught, sullen peoples/half devil and half child,' as Rudyard Kipling wrote in 'The White Man's Burden'. Quasi-imperialist views dominate modern discourses as well, best illustrated by the Indian media's imagination of Nepal's modern-day relationship with China. Consider its coverage in the aftermath of the May 2020 India–Nepal dispute over the Kalapani road, and its firm belief that the only reason Nepal could have objected to the road is because China asked it to. Beyond the ridiculous and sexist falsehoods about the Nepal prime minister being 'honey-trapped' by the Chinese ambassador, headlines such as 'China Uses Nepal' suggest the Indian media's surprise at the possibility that South Asian countries could have relationships with nations other than India. It is also revelatory of the ignorance that Indian popular discourse about the subcontinent displays; anecdotal evidence would suggest the average Nepali knows more about contemporary Indian politics and society than vice-versa.

Such a narrow view of history leaves little room for the agency of other nations in the subcontinent, for history was not made overnight. Nepal's newfound affinity to the north is not the result of one disputed road or a new map; rather, it is a decades-long process in which India has continuously erred and lost focus on issues around Nepal, while China has steadily gained it. While it has come at the expense of India's political and economic ties with Nepal, there is little doubt even among the most nationalist of Nepalis that China will replace India in cultural, religious and social spheres. And yet, there is little evidence that Indian policy, or its media, which shapes the popular discourse, has attempted to understand the nuances that led the Nepali establishment to shy away from the corridors of Delhi. Instead, binary and outlandish views dominate, and because of India's overwhelming global influence in shaping the South Asian narrative, the Nepali perspective is lost amid the cacophony of Indian news channels and the assumption of quasi-imperial notions on how the rest of the subcontinent should respond to India.

✦

Levi's study of Nepal through Tibetan and Chinese documents begins with descriptions by the seventh-century Chinese Buddhist pilgrim Xuanzang, also known as Hiuen Tsang, who wrote that, 'The Kingdom of Ni-po-lo has a circumference of about four thousand leagues. It is situated in the heart of the snowy mountains. The capital has a circuit of about twenty leagues . . . the inhabitants are naturally hard and ferocious; they do not consider good faith and justice as worth having and have absolutely no literary attainments; but they are gifted with skill and dexterity in the arts.'[7] In all likelihood, Xuanzang based his descriptions on hearsay, since he only visited the plains of modern-day Nepal, but his records allowed Nepali historians to accurately place Amshuverman, a mahasamant of the Licchavi dynasty, who was the power behind the

Kathmandu throne in the sixth and seventh centuries. Thus, ancient Nepali history, as Nepali historian Vijay Kumar Manandhar has noted, proceeded from a 'matter of idle speculation' into recorded history.[8]

Buddhism was the locus of classical interactions between the three civilisations of Nepal, Tibet and China. A creation myth about Kathmandu reflects this: the bodhisattva Manjushri, who came from China, drained the primordial lake with his flaming sword and installed as king Dharmakara, who had accompanied him on his pilgrimage. 'Dharmakara organised Nepal with China as his model: sciences, knowledge, trades, culture, manners, commerce, all followed Chinese examples.'[9]

The Buddhist connection is invoked by modern leaders on both sides, the three primary figures being Buddhabhadra, a fifth-century monk who travelled to China; Bhrikuti, a seventh-century princess who is said to have married the Tibetan king Songtsen Gampo and taken the religion to Tibet; and Arniko, a thirteenth-century Buddhist sculptor and architect who rose at the court of Kublai Khan[10]. Nepal valley, as the Kathmandu valley was originally known, emerged as an important centre for Vajrayana Buddhism between the last centuries of the first millennium and the first centuries of the second. American anthropologist Mary Slusser wrote, 'Patan [one of the three cities of the valley], at least, with its interlocking web of viharas, had become essentially a Buddhist university center not unlike the celebrated ones of Bengal and Bihar. From Odantapuri, Nalanda, Vikramshila, and other Indian centers of Buddhist learning, knowledge and teachers streamed into the Nepalese viharas. Nepalese Buddhists went to the Indian centers to study, and from them teachers such as Atisa and Ratnaraksita came to Nepal. Moreover, the Valley viharas, no less than the Indian ones, were centers to which the Tibetans gravitated for Buddhist instruction.'[11]

Such cultural exchanges were the result of the confluence of several political factors. The Tibetan civilisation was taking shape; in China, the stability of the Tangs and the Yuans allowed for more exchanges with the south; and in Nepal, Hindu kings provided royal patronage to Buddhist monasteries. There were interregnums, of course: earthquakes, infighting and invasions troubled the Nepal valley, while Tibet began to fragment politically after the death of King Langderma in the ninth century. In China, too, the Mongols overpowered numerous fragmented kingdoms that had come to be after the decline of the Tangs to establish the Yuan dynasty. But these were aberrations in a by-and-large stable political landscape, which in turn inevitably led to greater exchanges across the Himalaya.[12] As Buddhism spread and scholars travelled far and wide in search of manuscripts, new political relationships followed in their wake.

In 644 CE, Tang dynasty army official Wang Xuance arrived in Nepal as part of a political mission, accompanying a Brahmin ambassador of the Indian king Harshavardhana who had visited the Tang court. The Nepal valley at the time was ruled by the Licchavi king, Narendra Dev ('Naling-ti-po'), who 'adorns himself with pearls, rock crystal, mother of pearl, coral and amber; he has in the ear rings of gold and pendants of jade, and a breloc belt ornamented with the figure of Buddha. He seats himself on a seat of lions.'[13] Xuance's journey has been largely forgotten today, but it encapsulates the fascinating balance of power between the various emerging political units in and around the Himalaya at this time.

Xuance returned to the court of Harshavardhana in 648 CE. But by the time the Chinese mission reached Magadha, Harsha was dead, and one of his vassals, Arunasva (Na-fu-ti O-lo-na-choen, according to Chinese sources) usurped the throne and attacked the mission. '[Xuance's] arrows were exhausted and [men] captured. Moreover, these barbarians plundered the tributes and gifts received from other countries. Then Hsuan-Tse stood alone and fled in the night.'[14]

Xuance made his way to 'Tu-fan', or Tibet, which dispatched 1,200 soldiers with him and his vice-envoy, Tsiang Cheu-Jean. The Nepali king provided him with 7,000 horsemen. Thus reinforced, Xuance returned to Magadha. He besieged the town of Tch'a-pouo-ho-lo (identified as somewhere in the Pataliputra region) for three days. 'Three thousand men were killed and ten thousand persons were drowned in the river and died.'[15] Arunasva was captured, 'along with 12,000 persons, men and women, and more than 30,000 animals, oxen and horses. India was thus conquered.'[16] Xuance took Arunasva back to the Tang court, where his victory was proclaimed, and the general promoted.

Xuance's mission led to further visits: Buddhist monks Hieun Tai, Tao Fang, Tao Cheng, Matisimha and Hieun Hoi, the last three dying in Nepal after crossing over the Gangetic plains in the seventh century. In 651 CE, Narendra Dev sent an emissary to the Tang court, but once the Tang dynasty collapsed in the tenth century, the great rush of exchanges was over—at least until the thirteenth century, when a young artist by the name of Arniko went to the court of Kublai Khan.

Post Arniko, Chinese missions erratically visited the now-fragmented Nepali hill states, but the Mallas, who had come to rule the valley states, would cement their relationship with Tibet through trade and religious exchange. With Tibet becoming the centre for Vajrayana Buddhism, Nepal and Tibet now experienced a reversal of roles. While earlier, Tibetan monks would come to monasteries in Nepal to study, by the seventeenth century, Nepali Buddhists were to be found in the Himalayan plateau, especially at Tashilhunpo monastery in Shigatse[17]. 'Tibetan Buddhism gradually came to be favored by the Nepalese merchants and artisans domiciled in Tibet because it allowed them far greater freedom than the closed system that had by this time fully evolved in Nepal,'[18] by which Mary Slusser meant the formalised caste structure in the Kathmandu valley. Tibetan monks would also take the lead in managing the upkeep of several monasteries in Kathmandu; in the nineteenth century, British resident Brian Hodgson remarked that the upkeep of the valley's two most famous stupas—the Swayambhu stupa and the Bouddha stupa—was 'almost exclusively in the keeping of the Tibetans, and Lamas are the permanent ministering functionaries.'[19]

In a sense, Nepal's relationship with Tibet and China, between the early years of contact in the first millennium and the annexation of the valley's city-states by the Gorkha Shahs in the eighteenth century, was largely apolitical, with trade and religion being the locus. While China figured in the imagination of Nepali rulers, contact between the two civilisations went through several periods of lapses. Tibet, however, was next door, and with Vajrayana and trade as spiritual and temporal connections, Tibet and the Nepal valley grew entwined with each other. Nepal itself drew closer to the Kagyu school of Tibetan Buddhism headed by the Karmapa; in particular, with the Shamarpa Lama associated with the Yangpachen monastery near Lhasa. Nepali historian Ramesh Dhungel traces this tradition back to the fifteenth century, when the fourth Shamarpa constructed a monastery near Swayambhu.[20] The eighth lama in the tradition was born in Helambu, a Himalayan valley east of Kathmandu, in 1695.

The relationship between Nepali traders and Tibetan Buddhist monks furthered this exchange. Even as late as 1956, a few years before the Tibetan Uprising, the sixteenth Karmapa, head of the Kagyu school, visited the home of Bhajuratna, a noted Newar trader, just before the latter's death. 'No one else was permitted to be present in the room during this [week] while they prayed and meditated together, except to bring in their meals,' a biography recalls.[21] The relationship between the trader and the teacher began in 1947 when the Karmapa desired a Rolex watch, which Bhajuratna imported into Lhasa via Kalimpong.

'The relations of Nepal with China and Tibet reflect, in their vicissitudes, the great events of central Asia. Nepal, in fact, marks the extreme limit where Chinese influence can reach, at the height of her expansion,' Levi wrote.[22] As he combed Chinese and Tibetan sources for any traces or records of contact with Nepal—'[n]ow interrupted, now taken up again, now held up to be again renewed'—Levi concluded that relations between the three had 'commence[d] from the very day that the tribes of Tibet emerge into civilization and become an organized state'. In doing so, Levi was perhaps the first European scholar to acknowledge Nepal's turn towards the north.

✦

Until the middle of the eighteenth century, Nepal was a collection of hill states. Then, Shah King Prithvi Narayan Shah, who hailed from a hill state known as Gorkha, embarked on an ambitious military campaign. By the end of the eighteenth century, Nepal—which until then signified just the valley that comprised the three city-states of Kathmandu, Bhaktapur and Patan—emerged as the modern polity it is today. While the 1814–16 war with the East India Company chipped away at its territory, domestic political squabbles eventually led to the emergence of the Rana dynasty under Jung Bahadur in the 1840s. For the next hundred years, barring one brief rule that ended in assassination, the descendants of Jung Bahadur's youngest brother ruled Nepal as prime ministers, while the Shah kings' authority was completely whittled away. With the British as allies, Rana authority was supreme. In 1950, however, the Ranas ceded power to Shah King Tribhuvan after a popular revolution. The king had been backed by independent India's first prime minister, Jawaharlal Nehru, while a motley group of idealistic revolutionaries that came to form the Nepali Congress had launched an armed struggle against Rana rule. Nehru then negotiated a settlement that allowed the king to return to power.

The key to understanding India–Nepal ties lies in how the British viewed Nepal, and also had a firm influence in the Kathmandu court by controlling Nepal's foreign and defence matters. The British first recognised Nepal as an independent nation via a 1923 treaty. Until then, the colonial authority's attitude towards the country could be surmised through Viceroy Lord Curzon's 1903 letter to the secretary of state: '[The British relationship with Nepal] approximates more closely to our connection with Bhutan than with any other native state . . . Nepal should be regarded as falling under our exclusive political influence and control.'[23] While the British guaranteed Rana rule over Nepal, the Ranas in turn supplied soldiers to the famed Gurkha regiments, and more than 250,000 Nepalis fought in the two world wars. The dynasty also built its fortune by supplying timber and other natural resources to British India.

The 1923 treaty was the basis for the 1950 agreement between India and Nepal—one that the latter continues to regard as unequal. A post-colonial India under Jawaharlal Nehru wanted a special relationship based on its security umbrella over all three of its Himalayan neighbour-states, Nepal, Bhutan and Sikkim. Although it insisted the three were independent and sovereign, there was a catch. Nehru, in the same 1950 speech to the Indian Parliament, in which he outlined the Himalaya as India's 'magnificent frontier', outlined his views on what an independent India's relationship with Nepal was to be like: 'We have been inheritors of many good things from the days of British rule, and many bad things also; and our relations with our neighbouring countries grew up sometimes in an expansive phase of British policy, of British imperialism . . . Naturally, and quite frankly, we do not like, and we do not propose to like, any foreign interference in Nepal . . . So our relationship is intimate, and no other country's relationship with Nepal can be as intimate, and every other country must have to realise and appreciate this intimate geographical, cultural and other relationship of India and Nepal. There is no way out except by realising this fact.'[24]

While the religious, cultural and economic ties between India and Nepal are, without doubt, the backbone on which the political relationship is built, it is this 'special' nature of the ties that Nepali leaders since 1950 have chafed at. Those who have ruled Nepal—although many have come to power because of Indian support—perceived India as a threat to their rule, and encouraged anti-Indianism to cement their positions in Kathmandu. India's argument—that if

Nepal wants special economic ties, it must acknowledge special political ties too—holds ground. Nonetheless, anti-Indianism has long been encouraged by Nepali monarchs and politicians as an effective and popular countermeasure against perceived Indian intervention in the country. While Delhi would accuse Nepal of playing the 'China card' as a counterweight to Indian influence, it was not until the first decades of the twenty-first century that the 'card' would deliver any real results.

Today, contemporary India's insecurities over losing its influence and primacy in Nepal and South Asia to China are well founded. While this is partially a result of China's new ambitions in its neighbourhood, Indian micromanagement of Nepali political affairs during the post-Maoist conflict transition, which peaked with the 2015 blockade, has been a key argument for Nepali leaders to look to the north. Through all these decades, China has been perceived as a 'better neighbour' in Nepal; leaders and ordinary people alike point to Beijing's respect for Nepali sovereignty and its aid and grant projects as the reasons why this is so. But a closer reading would suggest that Beijing has been beneficent when its own concerns have been addressed by Kathmandu. Nonetheless, the perception remains, built upon years of Indian political manoeuvres in Nepal as well as Delhi's own cultivation of a Kathmandu elite that has utilised anti-Indianism to consolidate power. Combined with the long-standing tendency of Nepali rulers to point to the 1950 treaty as the root of the unequal relationship between the two countries, China proves to be a natural alternative—a fact that Beijing has long understood, and is now capitalising on.

✦

Postcolonial Indian scholarship on South Asia has traditionally viewed the history of the subcontinent as the history of British-subjugated India, only turning its lens towards other nations on matters of security or politics. Such scholarship unconsciously borrows the hubristic imperial lens; it views the region from an 'India-first' perspective that ignores, for the most part, the nuances that give the country its cultural and economic importance in the region.

This book seeks to correct such a view by examining little-known histories of the Himalaya and South Asia with Tibet and China. The Himalaya themselves have been constantly fetishised through imperial ideas of exploration that do not acknowledge the dynamism of its many societies that have continuously interacted and traded with each other as seasons came and went, a pattern replicated to this day. Tibet was seen as a 'Shangri-la', mythologised and eulogised for its spirituality, but little more. Once Tibet was closed off after China's annexation in 1951, such Shangri-la fantasies shifted to Nepal, the closest replica available. As anthropologist Mark Liechty has documented, Nepal became a shadow-Tibet, a Shangri-la transposed to a more accessible side of the Himalaya.[25]

To counter such a narrative, this book studies two parallel narratives. First, it is a study of Nepal's history with China, especially since 1950. Second, it looks at how China has affected the lives of Nepalis since it emerged not as a faraway emperor but as a next-door neighbour in 1950, the year it entered Tibet. Lhasa's modern relationship with Beijing is fraught with polarised views from both sides, but what is important to our understanding of the Tibetan political status is that a series of troubles on the frontier, ending with the 1792 military campaign against the Gorkhas, led to greater Qing political control over Tibetan affairs. The ambans, Qing representatives in Tibet, were given a greater say in Tibet's foreign and domestic affairs (as we shall see in chapter four). By the middle of the nineteenth century, however, the Qing were preoccupied with both the Taiping rebellion and the aftermath of the Opium Wars to exert any sort of control over Lhasa. This was best seen in its inability to defend Tibet in its 1855–56 war against Nepal under Rana Prime Minister Jung Bahadur. By the dawn of the twentieth century, as the Qing dynasty collapsed and a republican China struggled to find its feet, Tibet assumed the powers of an independent state. This was the state of affairs until Chinese troops entered Tibet in October 1950. The seventeen-point agreement signed in 1951 affirmed Chinese sovereignty over Tibet, but Tibetans in exile argue that the CCP contravened its terms within the first decade itself.

The point I make here is that Nepal's primary connections with the north were derived from its political, economic and religious connections with Tibet until the pre-modern era. The fact of geography continues to make Tibet the primary window into China for Nepal. It was only after 1950 that China emerged as Nepal's immediate neighbour. Thus, any references to Tibet after 1950 follows the status quo as it is today.

It is against this background that the book begins.

This book is also an attempt to establish the many ways in which China has shaped, and continues to shape, Nepali lives. It is not intended to be a contrast to the relationship vis-à-vis India, but rather an insight into how Nepal and ordinary Nepalis view the north. While economic and socio-religious connections drove relations in pre-modern times, it is the political that has driven the relationship in the modern era. My intention has been to look at the parallel ways in which history shapes the present, and how states change the everyday lives, motivations and desires of ordinary people.

In doing so, the book seeks to reclaim histories of the global south that have thus far only been described from the vantage points of global powers. This is especially felt in South Asia, where most books on China, primarily by Indian authors, emphasise the security aspect of the India–China relationship because of the 1962 war.[26] This popular, security-oriented discourse has corroded a more objective analysis of the many ways in which China is connected to our part of the world. And, while it is difficult to escape the 'yam between two boulders' thesis of the Nepali viewpoint because of the role India plays in modern Nepal's view of China, I want to break free of nationalist tellings of histories, and instead bring to light a people's perspective, one that reveals as much about the past as it does the present.

At the same time, I do not attempt a comprehensive text on Nepal–China relations; far from it. China's aid programme and history has been dealt with cursorily, for I am driven by the argument that aid aligns itself to foreign policy goals. Nor do I dwell on China's economic engagements, particularly the mechanisms of infrastructure investments and the Belt and Road Initiative (BRI), focusing instead on a broader picture through select case studies to give a sense of how such engagements shape the Nepali view of China.

I will also attempt to nuance the modern narrative around China in the Anglophone world through the Nepali perspective. The global power contest leaves little room for smaller nations like Nepal, which are often engaged with on a pro tem basis, with ties being severed when they no longer serve the greater power's interests. Take, for instance, the American relationship with Tibet. The US first supported the Tibetan struggle against the PRC's annexation, even funding an armed resistance group, under the guise of fighting communism in the Cold War, and then conveniently withdrew when relations with the PRC normalised in the early 1970s. But this short-sighted view of international relations, in fact, often works against the long-term interests of big powers, as they shape the perceptions of local leaders and societies.

Also consider this: India has been at the heart of every major democratic change in Nepal, from the 1950 revolution onwards. Yet, it has failed to gain from any one of them, with the 2006 revolution paving the way for India's own weakening within Nepal. India blames Nepali leaders for ingratitude, absolving itself of responsibility for missteps and mistakes. But as long as Delhi sees Nepal from a security lens, and continues to cultivate a self-preserving Kathmandu elite, it will continue to lose further ground in the country.

Further, in writing this book, I have tried to steer away from the simplistic Manichaean view, primarily a Western one led by the United States in the contemporary era, that China is 'evil'. Here, I have learnt from residents of the Nepali Himalaya who are of Tibetan ethnicity, speak the language, have familial and other ties with Tibet, who acknowledge China's widespread subjugation of Tibetan culture and people, believe in the Dalai Lama and yet interact with modern China on their own terms (also because the alternatives are few). I do not absolve China for its human rights excesses in Tibet (and more recently in Xinjiang) and lack of transparency in dealing with foreign governments. In fact, how China views Tibet and its people is perhaps best understood, outside Tibet itself, in Nepal. While international human rights commitments still bind it to a degree, Kathmandu has entered into a quid pro quo relationship with Beijing over the issue of Tibetan exiles. In return for increased aid and security commitments, Nepal has suppressed all political expression and protest by Tibetan exiles, and has cracked down on their cultural expression too. Tibetan exiles today have few, if any, means of identification in the country. The Nepali popular discourse is silent about them—another Chinese 'success story' in Nepal. And yet, it is through the Tibetan geography that contemporary bilateral interactions are shaped, just as it was in the past.

But China also needs to be understood beyond the Tibet lens. Why is Beijing proving to be a more attractive alternative for political elites in developing countries like Nepal? And why are such countries willing to deal with China, despite its subversion of the Western liberal democratic order? Here, Beijing's rhetoric of respecting the sovereignty of countries holds an important lesson, especially with the sensitivities attached to foreign influence on domestic politics in countries in the global south. The international liberal order is being whittled by populism, while an increasingly unilateralist and isolationist foreign outlook in the US, the symbol of said international order, has weakened multilateral institutions like the United Nations. In contrast, Beijing's opacity, willingness to deal with non-democratic institutions, and its purported non-interference in domestic affairs make it as attractive to the global south's political elite as the economic transformations it promises.

This book was written in two phases during mid-2019 and early-to-mid 2020 in Delhi and Kathmandu. I travelled to Limi valley in western Nepal in the latter half of 2018, and to Mustang and Rasuwa in the first half of 2019. In between, I spoke to people in Kathmandu and Pokhara, both sites of historical documentation as well as contemporary analyses. My travels were interrupted by the COVID-19 pandemic, because of which I could not visit the Zhangmu[27]–Kodari border to the east of Kathmandu, an important site for contemporary China–Nepal interactions. (Several Tibetan names have been Sinicised by China—for example, Zhangmu is known as Dram in Tibetan; in this book, I've retained the Chinese names, but have also provided the original names in Tibetan and their Nepali variant wherever possible.) I also could not travel to China (except for a brief sojourn on Chinese soil in Gyirong[28]), and because of my unfamiliarity with the Tibetan and Chinese languages, have relied on sources in English, Nepali and Hindi. All the Chinese and Tibetan sources quoted in this text are translations. However, because this book is intended to be a Nepali view of China—rather than the other way around—I hope to have covered adequate ground through these sources.

As an independent researcher and writer, online resources such as the Central Intelligence Agency's (CIA's) declassified archives, the China News Analysis archives, the Wilson Centre's digital archives, the Wikileaks files, especially of the post-2006 period, and the Nehru Memorial Museum and Library's (NMML) and the Jawaharlal Nehru Memorial Fund's digital copies of Nehru's selected letters and writings were crucial to my primary research. I spent days at NMML in Delhi and the Martin Chautari Library in Kathmandu before the pandemic brought my visitations to a halt. But several online resources—the

Digital Himalaya collection, the People's Association for Himalayan Area Research database, Academia.edu and similar online journal sites—helped me create a historical narrative that will hopefully bring new light to the subject.

I have acceded to the wishes of individuals on whether or not to identify them by their real names. I have not identified several people I met during my travels; some of my anecdotes were picked up—as most are—over tea or an evening drink. As such, I have tried to independently verify these claims as best as I can. As a non-institution-affiliated writer, difficult questions rarely brought forth answers in sensitive zones such as the borders, but because this book is not about the border and its mechanisms as much as it is about the people who live on the Nepali side, I have intentionally not touched upon the security aspects of the relationship (which, in any case, are opaque). Even in Kathmandu, questions regarding the security relationship elicited vague or politically correct answers. As such, this asks for a deeper analysis by researchers more familiar with the subject.

✦

In October 2019, before Chinese president Xi Jinping visited Kathmandu on his way back from Mahabalipuram, India, an essay by him was published widely in Nepali newspapers. Xi's penchant for quoting from ancient Chinese texts is well known; in 2015, China's official state publisher, People's Daily Press, issued a book titled *Xi Jinping Cites the Classics*.[29] In the essay, Xi outlined four broad points along which Nepal–China relations would move ahead, but what was notable was his recollection of the ancient cultural contacts between the two countries. '[T]he Chinese and Nepali monks Fa Hien and Buddhabhadra visited each other's country and together translated Buddhist scriptures into Chinese. Their translation works have remained influential to this day.'[30] Xi went on to recall the princess Bhrikuti and the sculptor Arniko, two symbols of historical ties between the two nations.

Such classical ties must not be underestimated; they shape modern relations in many ways, not least because they provide a historical continuity. They also allow countries to ground mutual relations in spheres other than just politics. Beyond its political dimensions, Buddhism has been at the centre of modern Nepal–China ties since its early days, and by the look of things, will continue to shape the future too. There has been an emphasis on cultural and people-to-people interactions from the very beginning of ties between the two nations. For example, in November 1956, a delegation from China participated in the fourth Conference of the World Fellowship of Buddhists in Kathmandu. In its turn, a Nepali Buddhist delegation visited China in July 1959. Despite it being the early days of the bilateral relationship between the People's Republic of China (PRC) and Nepal, the president of the Chinese Buddhist Association told the delegation, 'Buddha was born in Nepal 2,500 years ago [and] China has received monks and artists from Nepal in the past.'[31]

Among the six Nepali Buddhist delegates was Satya Mohan Joshi, a Nepali writer and cultural historian. Joshi returned from China and wrote an article titled 'Nepali artist Arniko and his works', which established his reputation as an Arniko scholar and brought the thirteenth-century sculptor back into focus as a pillar of Nepal–China relations.[32] Joshi, who turned 100 in May 2019, was sprightly for his age when I briefly visited him one morning in Patan. His living room was filled with plaques and mementoes honouring him; books were strewn all around, and on one of the shelves, sat a prominent bust of Arniko. A few months previously, Chinese ambassador to Nepal, Hou Yanqi, had visited Joshi. 'Ambassador Hou also encourage[d] young generation to follow him as an example to commit to developing China-Nepal friendship from generation to generation,' the official statement from the Chinese Embassy read.[33]

From Buddhist monks and Tang generals to modern scholars, the past continues to shine a light on the present. Both nations understand that these cultural connections of the past will be the key to their emerging relationship in the twenty-first century. In modern times, it has been shaped in the shadow of geopolitics (Tibet, China's own Cultural Revolution, the post-1962 India–China rivalry and the Cold War). But to understand the Nepal–China relationship beyond the corridors of power, we must first turn to history.

– Kathmandu,
January 2021

Part One

BORDERLANDS

'Oh wife, I shall not stay long in Tibet. I shall return after staying only one or two years.'

'Don't go to Tibet, oh my husband! I see no good in it!'

'Oh wife, don't speak to hold me back! Let me first see, if I can get work in Tibet!'

– A Newar folk ballad

'As soon as a road is built, the kindness vanishes.'

– Ma Jian, *Red Dust*

1

Traders on the Silk Road

In 1952, a puritanical Indian minister, B.V. Keskar, decided that Hindi film songs were 'degenerate', and banned All India Radio from airing such songs. Instead, he said, Indian youth needed to listen to highbrow classical music.[1] The ban presented an opportunity for Radio Ceylon's newly launched Hindi service to start the iconic 'Binaca Geetmala' programme, a countdown show of Hindi film songs hosted by the legendary presenter Ameen Sayani.

Little did Keskar know that his priggish sensibilities would create lifelong memories for Pragya Ratna Tuladhar sitting in faraway Lhasa, for whom Wednesday evenings meant huddling around a vintage Phillips radio, listening to Sayani's inimitable baritone, and placing bets with other Newar men on which song would top the charts that week. It was 1956, and Pragya Ratna had just arrived in Lhasa as a fourteen-year-old boy, wet behind the ears. '*Aaj ka pratham paigaam*,' Pragya Ratna, now seventy-eight years old, says, imitating Sayani as he recounts his days as a Newar trader on the Silk Road. 'There was no electricity, so the radios were powered by batteries that were as big as today's car batteries.' Outside their 'kothis', or merchant establishments, Lhasa's cold winds howled. 'We'd shut our shops by six in the evening. Sometimes we'd go for a walk around the Barkhor [a street square near the centre of Lhasa, where most Newar stores were concentrated]. But Wednesday evenings were for Binaca Geetmala,' he recalls. A little later, as we take a break and sip on our tea in his living room, he brings out an MP3 player that resembles an old transistor. The device has over 5,000 classic Hindi film songs and recordings of 'Binaca Geetmala'. Tuladhar begins playing one of the episodes, looks at me, and says, 'I used to listen to this song in Lhasa.'

Pragya Ratna had grown up around brothers, cousins and relatives who had all been to Lhasa to trade. His cousins ran the Ghorasyar trading house from the corner of a Barkhor street square in Lhasa, dealing in everything from textiles to watches and Parker pens. Eventually, in 1956, he too went to Lhasa with a cousin. 'I was told going to Lhasa was one big adventure, and you didn't know whether you'd return or not,' he tells me. He is agile despite his age, and although there are moments where his memories take time to gather, it is clear that his time in Lhasa was a formative period, one that shaped Pragya Ratna's world view. In one old, grainy picture, now posted on a social media group, he stands on a roof in Barkhor, wearing a double-breasted cashmere suit, wide-legged pants fluttering in the wind. I struggled to find a resemblance between the confident man I met and the shy boy in the photograph, hands in his pockets and a curious look in his eyes.

✦

The Newars of Kathmandu (Newar is an anglicised spelling for the Newa people) have long practised a uniquely syncretic culture that merges aspects of Tibetan Buddhism, Vajrayana, with Brahminical Hinduism. Nepal valley—as the valley encompassing the three city-states of Kathmandu, Bhaktapur and Patan was known even as late as the middle of the twentieth century—was a complex society where Brahminical Hinduism, which had royal patronage, existed alongside Tibetan Buddhism, which gathered momentum as interactions with the Tibetan plateau continued to grow through trade,[2] particularly by those who belonged to the Newar Buddhist merchant caste of Urays.

Within the high-caste Uray group, multiple sub-castes find their origins in craftsmanship and commerce. Hence the etymology of surnames such as Tamrakar ('one who works with copper'), Kansakar ('one who works with metal'), and Tuladhars ('one who works with scales'), this last being the most dominant sub-caste in trans-Himalayan trade. It was primarily a family-based practice, with extended family members, cousins and relatives all incorporated under a single kothi, which is how Pragya Ratna ended up joining a relative's establishment.

While religion may have formed the crux of the socio-political relationship between Tibet and Nepal, trade was the backbone for cultural exchanges. With Hinduism's caste restrictions, which forbid social exchanges with outsiders, it is no surprise that the most enterprising trans-Himalayan traders were inevitably Buddhists. Further, trans-Himalayan trade was conducted at almost every possible geographical point along the Nepal–Tibet border. In eastern Nepal, the Arun valley, Olangchung village in the Tamur Koshi river valley and Namche Bazaar emerged as centres. In the west, Tukuche village in the Thak Khola valley connected traders from Baglung and Pokhara to Tibetan markets via the Mustang region, leading up to Mugu, Humla and Darchula in the far west. And in the centre, the mountain passes of Kerung and Kuti[3] connected urban centres like Kathmandu to Tibet. Much of this trade consisted of the transit of materials from the Indian plains to Tibetan markets, and vice versa. 'Kashmiri merchants carried their goods by Ladakh to the Kuti passes to procure wool from there', from whereon, the goods were sent to China, Tibet and even to Patna via Nepal.[4] Kathmandu was an entrepôt of sorts, with traders from across the subcontinent arriving there with their wares, among them Gosains, a wandering band of ascetics who have been described as 'trading pilgrims', and Kashmiri Muslim merchants.[5]

Nepal produced very little of her own to sell. However, by virtue of controlling the two major passes of Kerung and Kuti, and because of a seventeenth-century treaty that gave them access to Tibetan markets along with the exclusive right to mint coins for Tibet in exchange for gold dust and silver bullion, Newar traders emerged as one of the leaders of this trans-Himalayan network of commerce. They were subject to Nepali laws while in Tibet, and paid no taxes there, with all customs duties being paid to the thakali, the chief of the thirty-two Newar trading houses in Lhasa, who in turn kept a sixth of all proceeds for himself and transferred the rest to the Nepal government. The Nepali resident, called 'nayo' or 'vakil', would act both as an adjudicator in disputes between traders (and collect fines) as well as represent Nepali interests in Lhasa. As the traders returned, they had to pay 3 paisa each to the Nepal government. Customs duties were levied on all articles brought into Nepal from Tibet and vice versa.[6]

In the absence of roads in the plateau, long caravans of traders, either on foot or on horses and mules, carried 'cotton goods ... woollen goods, hardware, corals, precious stones, tobacco, dried fruits, sugar, molasses and various domestic utilities such as matches, needles and soap' from India, bringing back 'skins, musk and money', as well as Chinese silk and tea, thangkas and gold dust.[7] The routes were arduous, the altitude unforgiving and attacks from bandits frequent. 'People thought Lhasa merchants brought back loads of gold, but it wasn't like that,' Pragya Ratna said. 'I know of people who died on the way. Phari [in Tibet] was nearly 14,000 feet high. The thewa [caravan leader] would insist we stick to a timeline—we had to reach or leave a place by a certain time, else the wind would pick up, and we'd be stuck.'

The eighteenth-century Jesuit priest and traveller Ippolito Desideri wrote that the road from Lhasa to Kathmandu followed the Tibetan towns of Shigatse and Sakya. Travelling via Gyantse, his party crossed the Mahalangur Himalayan range, which also houses Everest (known as Sagarmatha in Nepali, Chomolungma in Tibetan and Qomolongma in Chinese). 'Everyone suffers from violent headaches, oppression in the chest and shortness of breath during the ascent, and often from fever, as happened to me . . . Many people chew roasted rice, cloves, cinnamon, Indian nuts, here called Sopari and Areca [to alleviate high-altitude sickness].'[8] Another account relates how traders would consume garlic and shallot for the same affliction. It took Desideri thirty-three days to arrive at Kuti from Lhasa, almost the same time it took trade caravans to make that journey.

The Kathmandu–Kuti route was called 'one of the most dangerous in the whole Himalayan range',[9] but despite this, traders preferred it to the one via Kerung pass to the west of Kathmandu, which usually took about two days more. A trader took ten days to walk to Kuti from Kathmandu in 1933: 'the way alternately ascended abrupt heights and descended to fearful currents or dry riverbeds strewn with huge boulders'.[10] There was a point where one used a rope bridge to traverse a 'roaring torrent'. Traders sometimes sat in a basket and were pulled across mountain streams, although this frightening medium was increasingly used for goods rather than people in later years. There would have been iron-chain bridges too, as Desideri described, along with wooden planks 'only the width of a man's foot' and wooden bridges that 'swayed and oscillated most alarmingly'. As Nepal bhasa (the Newar language) novelist Chittadhar Hridaya wrote, men occasionally fell into the gushing waters or deep ravines below. 'It must be for this reason that men are said to know no cremation ground.'[11]

However, two significant changes—one infrastructural, the other colonial—transformed the nature of this trans-Himalayan trade, and the Kathmandu valley slowly dried up as an entrepôt. The first was the introduction of railways in India by the British. With railheads reaching the Nepal–India border by the end of the nineteenth century, transportation within Nepal began to witness a distinct change. Historian Perceval Landon wrote in 1928, 'For any long distance, it is now easier and quicker and, it may be added, cheaper for a Nepalese to make his way either to one of the railway stations on the Indian border . . . and then join the Indian railway system for an excursion east or west even when his destination is in his own country.'[12]

The other transformative event was an imperial transgression, what historians have argued should be called the 'British invasion of Tibet'.[13] British colonial anxieties over Russian geopolitical manoeuvres in Tibet, combined with the more-than-a-century-old efforts to open up Tibet for trade and Lhasa's status as the 'holy grail' for colonial explorers, led to Colonel Francis Younghusband leading a military expedition into Tibet in July 1903. The defeated Tibetans were forced to accept an agreement that said Lhasa could not deal with any foreign powers without British consent, and a war 'indemnity' of 500,000 pounds was to be paid over seventy-five years, 'with the British occupying the Chumbi valley until the indemnity was paid in full'.[14] But more importantly, the British opened up trade stations at Gyantse and Gartok in addition to the earlier one at Yatung. A road had been opened up from Lhasa to Phari by 1892 CE; an earlier agreement between British India and Sikkim allowed for roads to be built inside the Himalayan protectorate. The new route between Calcutta and Lhasa that bypassed Kathmandu altogether began to worry Newar merchants in Lhasa, who petitioned the Nepal government in 1892: 'With 2/3 hundred thousand rupees supplied by various Tibetan monasteries, a new road has been built from Phādi [Phari] which never previously existed. Tibetans, sending (agents), have started to buy and sell goods regularly in Calcutta. Lord, if this continues on, Nepalese merchant trade is condemned to cease and your revenues will decline.'[15]

Despite the petition, the benefits of the Calcutta–Lhasa route were evident, and Newar traders now began to travel south from Kathmandu and cross the border to Raxaul, from where they took a train to Calcutta, reaching it 'five days after leaving Kathmandu'.[16] Calcutta had long been a source for many of the goods traded into Tibet, and it was more convenient to transport the goods from here to Kalimpong, Darjeeling and Siliguri, where some of these traders eventually settled. Via Gangtok, these traders crossed into Tibet through the passes of Nathu La or Jelep La to Yatung, Phari—today called Dromo and Pagri respectively—and eventually, Lhasa.

✦

'Fourteen or fifteen of us sat in the back of a truck, on top of bales of cloth,' Pragya Ratna remembered. 'It took us nine days to get to Lhasa from Phari.'

By the time Pragya Ratna left in 1956, China had already gravelled the road from Phari to Lhasa, substantially reducing the travel time. Tuladhar had flown from Kathmandu to Simara in the plains of Nepal ('the ticket cost me NPR 36'), and taken the Nepal Government Railway from Amlekhgunj to cross the border into Raxaul, and thereon a jeep to Kalimpong, where all the material from Calcutta would be collected, packed and loaded onto a mule caravan that would take them up to Phari.

Life in Lhasa seemed to follow a standard routine. There were about thirty to forty Newar establishments, he recalled. The stores would open at 7 a.m., with midday breaks, until the evening. Pragya Ratna learnt basic Tibetan, which allowed him to communicate with customers at the shop, but he hardly interacted with them otherwise. When he had time, he would read the Hindi novels his cousin had brought to Tibet. 'He had brought Devaki Nandan Khatri's *Chandrakanta*—all six volumes of it. But I couldn't read such long novels, so I started with the shorter ones.' He recalled the title of one such book—*Hum Aise Kaise Baney?* ('How did we come to this?')—which I could not identify. Otherwise, they would go for picnics. The nights were reserved for mah-jong, which the traders often played all night long.

At this time, Tibet had already come under the PRC, after the seventeen-point agreement signed between the Communists and the Tibetan government in 1951. Pragya Ratna remembers seeing no Chinese civilians. 'All of them wore military uniforms.' Relations between the Tibetans and the Chinese had not come to a head in Lhasa, although clashes had already broken out in Kham, and some of the Khampas had begun to stream into the capital. Pragya Ratna recalled that the Chinese soldiers had a fondness for watches. 'The best watches at the time came from West End and Roamer. I sold several to the Chinese, but I didn't see even one of them wearing them,' he chuckled. 'I don't know what they did with them.' The soldiers also came to ask for '51'—the Parker 51 fountain pen, billed as the 'world's most wanted pen'.[17] A scholar notes that demand for luxury products had swiftly risen after Chinese officials and soldiers were posted in Tibet, especially as prices in Lhasa were much lower than in Beijing. 'This allowed . . . [traders] to make unprecedented profits.'[18]

In Pragya Ratna's recollection, the Chinese did not bother the Nepali traders. Instead, they were invited to be part of Chinese celebrations and events. 'The Chinese invited all the traders to the founding anniversary of the PRC in 1957. They did their march-pasts, left-right-left. When they saw us Nepalis, they started to clap. One general gave a speech, which I didn't understand because it was in Chinese.' Newar traders also participated in public works programmes in Lhasa. 'The Lhasa river regularly would break its banks and flood the city. The Chinese asked us if we Newars could also help them build an embankment. We closed our stores for two days and went to work with the Tibetans and the Chinese. They were very pleased to see me use a shovel or lift a doko.'

Pragya Ratna's recollection of life in Lhasa at this time corroborates the precarious co-existence of Tibetans and Chinese that historians have suggested existed until 1959. Newar traders rarely interacted with outsiders because of linguistic barriers, and although Pragya Ratna had heard stories about clashes between the two groups, they had not affected trade. The 1892 petition, quoted earlier, also explains how trade was carried out on both cash and credit basis, and it was the women who mostly came to the shops. 'Lord, in Lhasa it is not men who come to purchase goods. We have to deal with women. Even though we do business with kājīs, it is their wives who visit our shops to carry away goods in the quantities they want. This is a long-standing tradition here.'[19]

But interactions between Newars and Tibetans were also shaped in ways other than commerce.

✦

Newar traders to Lhasa were men like Pragya Ratna: young, usually married (Pragya Ratna married an eight-year-old girl when he was twelve; child marriage was common even until the middle of the twentieth century among Newars), and who saw Lhasa as a trading outpost, rather than as a place to sink one's roots into. Several historical commentaries have noted that relations between Newar traders and local Tibetans bordered on civility, but often broke out into petty squabbles, with one particular episode in the late nineteenth century that almost led to war between Nepal and Tibet.

One of the key irritants in this relationship was the extraterritorial rights Newar traders and their half-Tibetan offspring, who have come to be known derogatorily as 'khacharas' — a term that comes from the Nepali word for mule — enjoyed in Tibet. These rights were emphasised by the Rana prime minister Jung Bahadur in his supposedly punitive 1855–56 war with Tibet and the subsequent Treaty of Thapathali. The fiduciary relationship between the two states had grown out of the seventeenth-century Malla treaty under which thirty-two Newar trading houses were permanently established in Lhasa, and Tibet was not to impose any customs duties on goods bought or sold by these merchants. Nepal minted coins for Tibet under the treaty's terms at least until the end of the eighteenth century, when a mint was established in Lhasa with Qing assistance.

The minting of such coins — called Mahindramalli, after a previous Malla king — was highly profitable, with profit amounting to 12 per cent of the total transaction, 'four per cent, being derived from the gold dust, and eight per cent, arising from the alloy of the mohur'.[20] Soon, it was not just the Kathmandu city-state that was minting coins for Tibet; 'coins were generally distinguished by a shell for [Bhaktapur], a trisul [trident] for Patan, and a sword for Kathmandu'.[21] As Tibet sent gold dust and silver bullion as payments for the coins, the Malla kings began to debase the currency under the financial pressure of their many internecine wars with the Gorkhas. Such debased coins were increasingly being circulated in Tibet.

By 1768, the three city-states of the Nepal valley were no longer independent, with the Gorkha territorial expansion continuing unabated. Trade suffered as a consequence; a Gosain trader, for instance, chose to return from Lhasa to Bengal via Bhutan rather than the Nepal valley, while the Panchen Lama at the time wrote to Gorkha King Prithvi Narayan Shah, 'Everybody is now afraid to enter your country and it will become poor and desolate.'[22] The Gorkhas demanded the circulation of their own coins in Tibet after taking over the city-states of the Nepal valley. But Lhasa refused to accept the newly minted coins, even though they were not debased, saying the new rulers of Kathmandu needed to 'take back all money of Nepal that is under circulation' before the new coins could be circulated.[23] This friction over the use of debased currency and its exchange rate became one of the primary reasons for Gorkha antagonism towards Tibet even after the death of Prithvi Narayan Shah in 1775. It would eventually lead to war in 1788, and force Tibet to pay a tribute to Nepal.

A second war in 1855–56, initiated by Jung Bahadur to supposedly protest the mistreatment of Nepali traders and Nepal's diplomatic mission to China, resulted in another treaty. Tibet now had to pay Nepal an annual sum of NPR 10,000 and Nepali citizens retained their extraterritorial rights. Most importantly, Nepal and Tibet promised to come to each other's aid in the event of foreign aggression, which Nepal chose not to do, a fact that soured the view of Tibet's ruling class towards Kathmandu. Charles Bell, British resident in Tibet in the 1920s, noted that a common view among Tibetans was that '[Nepal] did not help us during the British military expedition to the Chumbi Valley in 1888, nor during that to Lhasa in 1904; they did not help us in our recent contests with China [after a Qing reassertion of sovereignty around 1908].'[24]

Bell equated the relationship between Nepalis in Tibet and the local residents as 'neighbours but aliens'. He gave the example of local laws against hunting, which the Nepalis regularly flouted because of the privileges they enjoyed, besides other instances of impropriety towards Tibetan laws and customs: although smoking was forbidden on Lhasa streets, Nepalis smoked openly, while 'none of us in my Mission would have dreamt of [it]'; one individual was discourteous to the Dalai Lama; and, of course, Nepal had failed to come to their aid. When Bell hosted a play for his Tibetan friends, a judge in the play tells a Nepali trader, 'You have cheated many, charging exorbitantly for goods of small value,' a sentiment the British resident thought 'appears to reflect the opinion of Tibetans on many of the Nepalese traders in their country'.[25]

There are several records of scattered uprisings against Newar traders; sporadic incidents were recorded in 1854, 1862 and 1871. In 1884, however, things took a turn for the worse. In April that year, after a dispute between a Newar trader and two Tibetan women, all eighty-four shops belonging to Newar traders in Lhasa were plundered, with losses amounting to NPR 833,709. A merchant known as Harsapati

Udasa wrote to the Nepal government, 'For the whole night, starting from around 1–2 ghadis after sunset, these Bhotyās [Tibetans] looted the trading house from top to bottom, taking (everything) away; some ghadis before sunrise they set fire to the remaining goods and account books, rendering them useless. [Even] after they left, the smoke from the fire they had set burning badly affected the trading house along with the people (hiding) above the ground floor. Unable to find even a single vessel of water to extinguish the fire, and even though they asked neighbours for help with water, no one brought any water for fear of the outrageous Bhotyās.'[26]

Kathmandu was outraged and prepared for war; it was only after Tibet agreed to pay NPR 942,098 in instalments over seven years, and promised to punish the marauders and restore as much plundered property to their rightful owners as possible, that war was averted.[27] Another similar incident was reported in 1929; Gyalpo, a Tibetan-Nepali trader, was charged with trading in illicit goods such as tobacco and minting counterfeit coins. Diplomatic tensions between the two countries became charged when Gyalpo sought shelter in the Nepali legation, and over a thousand Tibetan police and soldiers stormed the place.[28]

Although Newar traders conducted business in Tibet, donned Tibetan clothes, spoke the language, worshipped at the same temples and celebrated the same festivals as the locals, and even entered into relationships with Tibetan women, they rarely assimilated into Tibetan society. The traders had organised themselves into seven different guthis, an informal social order; 'the Newars liked to remain within their little circles', a biography acknowledges.[29] Newar men lived in Tibet for years at a stretch; 'I knew some of the men who had stayed for eight–nine years,' Pragya Ratna said. Most stayed at least three years.

Having left their wives behind in Kathmandu, traders would often enter into relationships with Tibetan women. The Newar women had little choice; a woman married to a trader recounts a song commonly told to children at the time: 'The coral from Lhasa / brings a quarrel back home / ignoring the fights / the man hugs his second wife.'[30] Daughters from such relationships were considered to be Tibetan citizens, whereas the sons were considered Nepali citizens, with the same extraterritorial rights accorded to them as their fathers.

The sons often acted as local representatives in their father's trade. 'Nepalese traders relied on their half-Tibetan offspring to help them maintain a commercial presence in Tibet during their extended absences. While the Nepalese may have held children of these mixed marriages in contempt, they relied enough on the Khatsaras' [khacharas'] role as guardians of lucrative Nepalese business interests to jealously guard their legal status within Tibet.'[31] They also emerged as one of the most 'dominant foreign presence'[32] in Lhasa, a city teeming with traders from as far as Kashmir and Central Asia. Although few figures are available, a 1961 survey tells of their dominance within the Nepali trade. Among the seventy-four businesses owned by Nepalis in 1961, '[thirty-four] firms were owned by pure Nepalese', while the other forty were owned by Tibetan-Nepalis. Yet the financial disparity was clear: 92 per cent of all assets were owned by the 'pure' Nepali traders, and only five Tibetan-Nepali businesses had capital worth more than 10,000 yuan. On the other hand, twenty-seven of the thirty-four businesses owned by 'pure' Nepalis had capital worth more than 10,000 yuan.[33]

The ambiguous status of the half-Tibetan, half-Newar sons was one of the key points of tension between Nepali and Tibetan authorities, and as we shall see, with the Chinese too. Tibetan authorities regularly accused them of 'unfair business practices and the perception they were hiding behind their Nepalese foreign parentage'.[34] Further, the social exclusion and tenuous legal position they held in Nepal did not make it easy for the Tibetan-Nepalis. Although the sons were granted the same privileges as Nepali citizens, and were occasionally used by the Nepal government as spies, such as during the Younghusband expedition, 'the striking feature' of the government policy towards them was one of exploitation and lack of concern.[35] They were 'politically ignored, economically exploited and socially discarded by both Nepal and Tibet', with the Nepal government acknowledging them as citizens only 'to exact tax and free labour'.[36] Further, they were also not welcome in Kathmandu, where they could, under customary Nepalese law, claim a share equal to that of the 'pure' Newar sons from their father's estate.[37]

After China took over Tibet in 1950, it overturned the existing conventions and taxed Tibetan-Nepalis, even enrolling a few of them into its army, despite Nepal's protests. With the signing of a new Nepal–China treaty on Tibet in 1956, Tibetan-Nepalis were given a choice between Nepali and Chinese citizenship in 1962. According to anthropologist Dor Bahadur Bista, who was appointed as Lhasa

Consul General during 1972–75, a majority opted for the latter. Bista recorded the population of Nepalis in all of Tibet at approximately 500, a majority of them Tibetan-Nepalis. Most of them were 'illiterate' daily-wage earners, and a few were farmers.[38]

✦

Existing accounts on 'Lhasa Newars', as such traders are colloquially called, tend to gloss over the relationships between Newar men and Tibetan women. The reasons for why Newar women did not accompany their men tend to focus on the hardships of the journey, of how they were not up to it and the social taboos around women travelling. Folk literature also highlights the viraha, or pain of separation, between the Newar wife and husband. One of Nepali literature's epic poems, *Muna Madan*, tells the story of a newly married couple in which the husband has to leave for Lhasa to make money. The poem is based on a Newar folk song titled *Ji Waya La Lachi Maduni* ('It's not even been a month since I came') that begins with a newly-wed woman telling her mother-in-law, 'Not even a month has passed since I came to this house, and your son is already saying he will go to Tibet. Stop him just this once!' But Tibet is where fortunes are made, and the son replies, 'Oh wife, I shall not stay long in Tibet. I shall return after staying only one or two years.'[39]

Ji Waya is but a continuation of the literature that was derived from trade. The myth of Simhalasarthabahu, a legend often considered the figurehead of the Newar trade in Tibet, begins with a 500-strong caravan getting shipwrecked during a storm on the river Tsangpo, and arriving in 'Ratnapura', where beautiful young women seduce them: 'By our good luck we have taken sight of you . . . Please come to our Ratnapura and make love to us.'[40] The women are cannibalistic rakshasis in disguise, however, and the Buddhist deity Avalokiteswara appears before Simhala, our hero, to tell him the truth about them. His friends are unwilling to leave—'to have had the chance to enjoy sex and such lovemaking, etc.—how fortunate we are to have been so divinely blessed!'—but Simhala persuades them with a little divine help, and they cross the Brahmaputra on a flying horse. The divine horse warns them not to look back at the grieving women—predictably, everyone but Simhala turns around, only to fall to their deaths and be eaten by the rakshasis. Simhala is followed to Kathmandu by his demoness-paramour, where the local king begins to desire her. The inevitable happens, and Simhala finally gathers an army that subdues the demonesses and converts Ratnapura to Buddhism.

The subtext is obvious: an explicit warning to not fall for the wiles of foreign women. Tibetan wives were called 'sem', a derogatory term for 'low caste'. As for the other wife back in Kathmandu, her husband's Tibet journey represented jealousy and heartbreak, and often competition for the ancestral wealth. A song from the late eighteenth century begins, 'The man I love has abandoned me. He went to Tibet and has become a voluntary exile.' Another poem is more tragic: 'A letter was brought from Tibet . . . When I opened the letter, I saw: my husband had left us.' And in yet another song about the pain of viraha, a newly married wife laments, 'Why, oh lord, should I eat and adorn myself? My husband has gone to Tibet.'[41]

These folk songs portray an idyllic picture of tragic romance. The truth was simpler. Newar men often married young. The harsh travel conditions required to go to Lhasa—not to mention the stringent caste rules forbidding women from travelling—forced them to travel without their wives. But travel they must, for trade had built the fortunes of many. Many ended up living in Lhasa for years at a stretch. In the event, they often initiated relationships with Tibetan women.[42]

✦

'I remember my father as my mother's husband,' Prakash (asking not to be identified) told me one evening in Kathmandu. He was born to a Tibetan mother and a Newar father, the youngest of three children. Prakash runs a travel agency and lives in Kathmandu. His father had long passed away, and there was a stoicism to him that I found endearing. Outside, dark clouds gathered, threatening a downpour. We sat cross-legged in a Newari cafe and ordered a few beers.

I asked him if he knew the circumstances under which his parents had met. 'My mother was a street vendor, as far as I know,' he said. Several years later, after his mother and sisters died in an accident, Prakash travelled back to Lhasa to look for any connections from his mother's side. He had a vague notion of where she had lived, but when he arrived, he saw that a new building had come up in its place. 'My father should have told me more about my mother after she passed away and what her connections with Tibet were like.'

Prakash gave me a sense of what it was like to be born of an illegitimate relationship in a society obsessed with caste and purity. His father had insisted that his Tibetan family leave Lhasa once the troubles broke out in 1959, and so the four of them crossed over to Kalimpong, where Prakash later enrolled in a school for Tibetan refugees. 'As a child, I never really knew who my father was,' he said. It was only when he started coming to Kathmandu during his winter breaks that he realised he too was a Tuladhar, and that his father had another family already living in the city. Prakash and his two older sisters would wear bakkhus (a cloak-styled robe worn by Tibetans), which made them stand out. At family feasts, the three of them would sit at the far end, along with their mother. Because of her language, dress, background and the circumstances of her relationship, she was discriminated against not just by the extended family but also by Kathmandu residents at large. 'My mother and I once went to a newly opened five-star hotel, but the guard didn't let us enter because we wore bakkhus, and he thought we were Tibetan refugees.'

The discrimination he faced as a child gave Prakash an inferiority complex that took him a long time to shed. The family had moved to Kathmandu after Prakash finished school, and he would refuse to walk around town with his mother. They were called 'bhotes', a Nepali slur for anyone of Tibetan ethnicity. 'I didn't want to be known as a bhote. I wanted to be known as a Newar.' Prakash grew up to be a rebellious man; he just could not understand why he was treated differently by his stepmother and her children; why his siblings would get new clothes while all he got were hand-me-downs; why he was not allowed to touch his father's car. He demanded attention. He began to steal money and got clothes made on credit by the family tailor. 'My dad would call me a crook, a liar, but he never understood why I did the things I did.'

His two sisters, both considerably older than him, faced worse, he said, as did his mother. 'There were a lot of times my mother cried talking about the past.' In Asan, the town square where most Lhasa Newars had a home back in the day, Prakash lived in a house with his stepfamily. 'We had a two-room home. My father would sometimes tell me to sleep outside while he slept with my mother, and two days later, he would tell me to go back inside. I never understood these things at the time, but when I look back now, I am sure it must have pinched my stepmother too. It must have been difficult for her to accept a second wife. This was not what she wanted from her husband, but circumstances had forced her into such a situation. I feel sorry for her when I think about it today.'[43]

Prakash spoke of his past with surprising calm. I was making him dig out some bitter memories. Before he agreed, I had reached out to others with a similar heritage, but they had refused to speak to me. At the intersection of personal and communal histories often lie these bitter truths. But confronting the errors of the past could go a long way in addressing the discord of the present.

'My mother used to tell me I should not get too angry, that I should be calmer,' Prakash said, 'when I would complain about why I was treated differently than my other siblings. She said they were the first wife's children, and that I would not get the same rights and privileges as them. She would say we should be grateful to our father for bringing us out of Tibet. If we hadn't left, we would have been dead or killed by the Chinese.' When his mother and sisters died in an accident, however, the spiral of angst grew worse. Prakash felt that his father and stepmother did not respect their deaths, and he moved out. The already precarious relationship between father and son had reached breaking point. 'The real trouble began when my father started becoming prosperous. My stepmother would never leave me alone in a room with him. There was no question of me or my mother getting anything. Nobody wanted to spare anything for us.'

To be sure, it was not just the Newars who entered into relationships with Tibetan women. The foreign parentage of khaches (Tibetan-Muslim offspring) and kokos (Tibetan-Chinese) was equally an issue for Tibetan authorities. 'Combined with central Tibet's gender imbalance due to the large number of males joining monasteries, many of these foreign men formed relationships, and in some cases established households, with Tibetan women.'[44] But the rigid caste rules of Newar society, and the claim the male offspring could make on the wealth of their fathers, often made them outcastes in Kathmandu society, despite polygamy being legal and acceptable at the time: '[The sons] were of course not welcome in their father's Kathmandu homes or in the valley . . . They were not of acceptable status for marriage to proper Uray girls either.'[45] Tamla Ukyab, a former Nepali bureaucrat who was consul general in Lhasa in the 1980s, told me there were several legal disputes in Kathmandu after 1959, when the Newars' Tibetan families moved to Kathmandu.

That said, having a second Tibetan wife was not really considered a scandalous affair back in the day. 'It was common,' Pragya Ratna said. 'People didn't really care about it. The Tibetan wives were usually bought another apartment. The two families didn't live together. The husband paid the second wife's expenses. There weren't any issues in society, at least as far as I know.' There aren't any clear figures for how many half-Nepali children lived in Tibet at the time. A scholar suggests nearly a thousand Tibetan-Nepalis took up Nepali citizenship after 1959,[46] while British resident Charles Bell suggested there were 600–700 Newars in Lhasa in 1920, and 'over' a thousand with mixed parentage.[47] Another speculates that there were 'more than two thousand' such people in 1956.[48]

Prakash cut off ties with his father in the mid-1980s. 'I never called him. He never called me.' He thinks the family did not reach out to him because they thought he would make a claim on the property. 'Maybe if I had no other recourse, I would have asked him for my share of the property.' The situation did not arise, however. Prakash's travel business did well; he married, and had two sons, his relationship with them shaped by the lack of affection from his own father. Then one day, while his family was at Bouddha, the ancient stupa to the north-east of Kathmandu, his son told Prakash his father had passed away. 'He saw a post on Facebook about his death. Nobody informed me. Nobody called me.' He did not go for the funeral.

Prakash said he had no regrets now. Throughout our meeting, he insisted that others like him may not share his own story, but he did acknowledge there had been a lot of bitterness in the initial years when the Tibetan families first arrived in Kathmandu. He felt no love towards his stepmother and father, but there was no hate there either. 'Maybe they were not as bad as I thought they were. There was a solid wall between us, and I couldn't open a door to the other side.'

Most writing on the Lhasa Newars tend to focus on the romanticism of the trade: the long caravans, the difficult terrain, surviving bandits, cold winds and extreme temperatures; the imagery of the Silk Road, with merchants selling their wares from across the world in alien lands; the land itself a harsh mistress. Rarely is there an admission of the personal space; rarer still is the presence of women—either the wives the men left behind in Kathmandu, or the women they married in Tibet. The children are absent altogether. Perhaps one of the reasons for this is the ruling Shah–Rana emphasis on Hindu purity. 'Uray alliances with Tibetan wives and lamas, fundamental to their mercantile prosperity, lifestyle and spiritual inclinations involved major deviations from the norms of Brahmanical orthopraxy [of the Shahs and Ranas] . . . For the most part, the traders kept their twin families separated by the Himalayas, but occasionally half-Tibetan females returned to Kathmandu, where they married Uray boys and were absorbed into Uray patrilineages . . . with only minor status repercussions.'[49]

But these are all ex post facto explanations that do little to justify the uncomfortable histories of the Tibetan wives and their offspring. Further, there has been little acknowledgement that Tibetans had a role to play in the success of Newar traders in Lhasa—a prosperity that endured, as can be seen in the many businesses the descendants of Lhasa Newars have founded in Nepal. 'Even today, one can say Kathmandu's Newars are what they are because of Tibet,' Prakash said. 'At least they should acknowledge those links. They shouldn't ignore them completely.'

✦

The first gunshots were heard on the night of 19 March 1959. 'At 3.40 a.m., gunshots were suddenly heard from the river. These were heard very clearly all over Lhasa during the quiet night.'[50] Pragya Ratna had been sleeping when his brother woke him up to say the shooting had begun.

A few days earlier, on 10 March 1959, in front of the Norbulingka Palace in Lhasa, a massive demonstration of Tibetans attempted to stop Tenzin Gyatso, the 14th Dalai Lama, from attending a performance at the Chinese military headquarters. A week later, the Dalai Lama escaped to India at night. 'During the three days between when the Dalai Lama fled and when the battle for Lhasa started, the level of tension and anxiety in Lhasa was extremely high, with both sides believing that the other was on the verge of attacking.'[51]

The Newar traders in Lhasa had already barricaded themselves inside their homes in the preceding days. Pragya Ratna recalled seeing one of the biggest demonstrations of Tibetans ever on one of those days. He was not sure if it was one of the 10 March protests. 'They were all speaking in Tibetan, so I couldn't understand them, but that was the first demonstration by Tibetans I ever saw in Lhasa.' Tensions ran extremely high. At Ghorasyar, the Tuladhars had used the bales of cloth and whatever they could lay their hands on to fortify their doors and windows. The others had done the same. 'All of us Newars decided we would be responsible for our own protection, and we would not let any outsider enter.'

On the morning of 20 March, Tan Guansan, political commissioner of the People's Liberation Army (PLA) forces in Tibet and one of the leading officials of the Tibet Work Committee in Lhasa, asked Beijing for permission to attack Tibetan forces. The attack was to be carried out in three phases: the first would be to 'attack Jogpori hill and cut relations between it and the Tibetan forces' in the Potala Palace; the second would be to attack the Norbulingka Palace; and the third phase was to be a pitched battle in the city's streets.[52] When Tan did not hear back from Beijing by 10 a.m., he gave the orders to attack.[53]

Pragya Ratna and his brethren cowered inside their homes. 'We didn't step out anywhere, we did not even look out of the windows.' He thought the Chinese took care not to bomb the areas where the Newars lived. 'Instead, they kept firing from above our rooftops.' Even so, Nepali Consul General A.B. Basnyat found slugs and broken glass inside the consulate on 20 March. Telephone lines had been cut. 'Basnyat was convinced he had been in the way of PLA troops firing at Tibetans; the Chinese assured him that it could only have been rebels who attacked the consulate, not Chinese soldiers. Basnyat did not press the point—he knew that his country needed a friendly PRC—but he made it clear that he wished to be assured of safety for himself and the people he represented.'[54]

The excitable lad that he was, Pragya Ratna walked up to the roof. Bullets whizzed all around him. 'I took shelter behind the roof's walls.' That night, when he went to the toilet, which was inside the courtyard, the house shook from a frightening explosion. 'I peeked out the window, and saw that the pagoda of the Simhalasarthabahu temple in Barkhor street outside had collapsed,' he recalled with visible excitement. 'We got really lucky the bomb didn't fall on us.'

The Lhasa rebellion was quelled in forty-six hours and fifty minutes, but in that time, history had been made, for better or worse. 'We Newars left our homes after sixty to sixty-five hours. The Chinese had announced, "It is the duty and responsibility of the Chinese government to protect your life and property. Nothing will happen to you. We will stand guard. Please open your shops. Everything has returned to normal."

'They posted soldiers with sten guns at a distance of 30 metres outside our shops. The Newars quickly opened their stores. But the markets dried up after that. We went for a walk and saw several dead people—Tibetans, monks, but no Chinese soldiers. Some must have died, but the Chinese would have carried them away,' Pragya Ratna said.

What had once been a vibrant centre of trade quickly came under military occupation as China tightened its grip over Lhasa. Until then, it was not illegal to possess a gun in Tibet. Newar traders kept several guns at home, either to protect themselves while on the road, or because they had been given guns as barter by Tibetans. 'Our house had twelve or thirteen guns. Karuna Ratna Tuladhar [his uncle and the proprietor of Ghorasyar] had twenty-eight guns, including a German pistol he kept in his drawer. It held nine rounds. I remember being fascinated with it.' The Chinese had asked the Newars to surrender all guns after the uprising. 'I insisted the pistol not be surrendered. I wanted to smuggle it back to Nepal. But we had to give it up ultimately,' Pragya Ratna recalled. 'It was an excellent pistol, the magazine would slip out easily, and it was easy to handle as well.'

On 28 August 1959, Pragya Ratna wrote to Karuna Ratna in Kathmandu, 'Last month, the Sem's [Tibetan] currency stopped working. The Chinese exchanged the currency with their own at the rate of 40 to a 100.'[55] Even before the uprising, there were signs the Chinese wanted to incorporate the informal trade under a formal umbrella. Traders had traditionally used the hundi method to remit money back home and to their suppliers, but the Chinese asked them to start sending money via their banks.

A month later, Pragya Ratna packed up his bags and returned home the same way he had come three years ago. His Lhasa sojourn was over. He was seventeen at the time. 'Newars did not want to live in Lhasa any more. They started to return in numbers and bring back their wealth. The Chinese customs people did not stop us.' On the truck from Lhasa to Phari, Tuladhar lost a hand-stitched woollen cap. He had carried back some musk pods in a thermos. At Nathu La, Indian border guards first asked how much money he had brought back with him. Then one of them found the musk and took away two pods.

✦

The first telegram is dated January 1961: 'Am stayed in your shop and taking charge.'[56] Purna Man Tuladhar, an uncle of Karuna Ratna, took over Ghorasyar just as the India–China conflict began to peak, and tensions between the two giants had made trade across the Himalaya increasingly strained and full of uncertainties. Easy movement across the passes would soon come to a halt. With border tensions increasing, the PRC began to tighten its control over the Tibetan frontier, but it encountered difficulties on various fronts. Not only was the border undemarcated, but there was also a tendency among those who lived in these borderlands to cross over without documentation, and sometimes, to continue to live in Tibet for years. As the Tibet uprising fuelled unrest inside the plateau, the Chinese began to make claims of sovereignty on all those who lived in it. Under the rules of the new empire, the cosmopolitan Himalayan frontier could no longer afford to be ambiguous. 'When an empire goes heavy, it ceases to be tolerant of those who fall across its frontiers, illegible and undefined . . . For the Nepalis, Indians, Bhutanese, and Sikkimese who traded, worshipped in, and visited Tibet, 1959 brought hard choices about whether to stay or leave.'[57]

The signs had been visible for a while. After the 1956 Nepal–China agreement that abrogated all extraterritorial rights for Nepalis in Tibet, traders were required to hold a passport to cross the border. Nepal started issuing passports to traders in November 1958. Earlier, Chinese officials had begun insisting that Tibetan traders focus on 'internal trade' to 'lessen dependence on foreign trade',[58] and promised financial assistance to Tibetan-Muslim traders if they would 'challenge' Newar traders. The 'free-flowing' trade that had characterised Lhasa was beginning to give way to China's designs for the region. By August 1959, all Chinese officials and their families had to purchase commodities from state-owned shops, and they were forbidden from buying foreign products.[59] Although a few of them continued to sell luxury products, 'for the majority of the Nepalese traders who made their living selling essential goods, life was difficult given that the Chinese had banned the public sale of commodities. Even the sale of yak dung cakes and firewood was prohibited. "Pavement hawkers" too, who had plied their goods on the streets of Lhasa, were forced off those streets by a variety of tactics. As a result, Nepalese traders were increasingly closing their shops and returning to Nepal.'[60] A 1993 paper, in turn, calculated the revenue of Nepali-owned businesses in Tibet between 1960 and 1961, just before the trade finally came to an end. In 1960, the turnover for seventy-four Nepali-owned businesses stood at 2,573,000 yuan; the turnover had dropped sharply the next year to 531,000 yuan.[61]

Purna Man had his own kothi called 'Chhusingshar', but he was to oversee the closure of Ghorasyar. A collection of telegrams, today in the possession of his nephew, Kamal Ratna Tuladhar, gives us an outline of what the last days in Lhasa were like for Newar traders. On 29 January 1961, Purna Man wrote to Kathmandu, 'Taken charge whole from Ratna Bahadur'. A few days earlier, Ratna Bahadur, who worked at Ghorasyar, had sent a telegram confirming the handover. 'Handed over all accounts of shop to Purna Man stop already submitted my application for immediate departure so arrange to send man shortly if you wanted to do so.'

The trepidation in the telegrams from this time was notably absent in earlier correspondence. For example, a 1946 letter from Ghorasyar concentrates entirely on updates about the trade in textiles, but in the last paragraph, Pushpa Ratna Tuladhar, the younger brother of Karuna Ratna, says although previous issues of *Life* and *Time* magazines had reached him in Lhasa, the new issues had not. 'Why is that so?'

In 1959, there were over 1,500 Newar traders, Tibetan spouses and their children in Tibet.[62] Although Pragya Ratna recalled that the Chinese did not stop the traders from leaving Tibet, a historian suggests otherwise. The Nepali traders' insistence on retaining their own nationality and citizenship had afforded them a singular position among the Lhasa traders. But China became more stringent in its dealings with them. 'At the invitation of the local Chinese authorities, a growing number of Nepalese participated in the various cultural events and public rallies. Roundly praised by the Chinese officials at the time, the Nepalese were sorely disappointed when their participation had little or no effect on their status.'[63] China also began to impose stringent conditions on the Tibetan wives leaving the country, such as asking for a guarantee from the Nepal consulate that their husband's property would be inherited by the half-Tibetan children as well, an anathema as far as Nepal was concerned, both politically and socially.

At the heart of Chinese recalcitrance was the question of citizenship in Tibet, which could be ambiguous and perfunctory, as was the case with the Tibetan-Nepalis, just as the trade once was. 'What that meant was that it was no longer possible to be both Nepali and Tibetan, or to be a citizen of both Sikkim and China. Now was the time to stand up and be counted by a state, to declare your loyalty and the jurisdiction you fell under. The PRC was changing what life in the borderlands had historically meant. People would now have to be part of a state—one state and no more.'[64]

In May 1960, the Chinese finally issued passports and visas to the Tibetan spouses of Newar traders. By September 1960, 250 Newar traders, their Tibetan spouses and their children left for Nepal. In all, nearly a thousand half-Tibetan children of Newar traders opted for Nepali citizenship.[65] The millennia-old trans-Himalayan trade was finally coming to an end. In October 1962, PLA forces overran Indian positions in Arunachal Pradesh and Aksai Chin. The India–China war ended any hopes of the trade being revived, and the Nathu La Pass would be closed until 2006.

By June 1963, Purna Man had had enough. 'Better wind up shop considering situation whether I come winding up wire,' the somewhat confusing telegram reads. Within a year, he was out of Tibet. 'Coming on receive motor,' a cryptic June 1964 telegram reads. Kamal Ratna Tuladhar, the keeper of these letters and telegrams, told me he remembered going to pick up Purna Man from Bhaktapur by car. The last Newar trader in Lhasa had come back via Kuti, the centuries-old pass that had died out after Younghusband opened up Nathu La. The Lhasa Newars had come full circle.

2

Neither Nepal nor China

The blue tarp makes for a ramshackle bar, but a bar it is. There is a selection of liquor to choose from: Lhasa beer, Chinese Budweiser, Xian cigarettes and baijiu, a Chinese alcohol distilled from sorghum. I have inveigled my way into a Lhasa beer-drinking session with some locals in Waltse (Halji in Nepali), one of the three villages in the trans-Himalayan valley of Limi. On the shelves of this all-in-one shop-cum-bar, Chinese noodle packets with psychedelic wrappers scream for attention, while a packet of chicken feet hangs quietly next to them. Across the street, inside a centuries-old monastery, a cultural programme is in full swing, music blaring from speakers rigged to an amplifier powered by a solar panel. It is a night of celebration. A trade fair has just wrapped up, and the politicians have returned after making their customary speeches. There is an air of festivity all around, and the liquor has made us all garrulous.

Sitting with me are two truck drivers who drove us here from Nyalu Pass at 4,990 metres. The ride was a bumpy one, but with the truck weighted down by more than sixty people and luggage, the bumps did not really matter; there was no room to stretch one's legs anyway. Those who were standing held on for dear life; those who sat, remained seated through the four hours, backs touching, legs pinned beneath.

A trek to Limi via Simikot, the nearest airhead, usually takes six days. 'Hidden deep within the Himalaya is Humla: the highest, most northern and remote district of Nepal,' advertises one trekking agency. It took us two and a half days of strenuous walking in September 2018, with a four-hour horse ride to Nyalu Pass and another four hours in the aforementioned truck, to reach Limi. There was a particular stretch where the trucks had to cross the river that lends its name to the valley, which is home to 900 people living in three villages. As soon as the truck entered the river, calls of 'so-so' rang out—calls for good luck. When the driver whips out his smartphone at the bar and shows me the video of our crossing, I watch it with bated breath. The massive Chinese Dongfeng truck entered the Limi waters, and amid the swirling current, its wheels lurched from side to side, almost toppling, but somehow not, with the engine belching smoke all the while. The river was in spate; the monsoon rains have gone on for longer than usual this year.

I berate the driver for his bravado. The locals laugh. The Lhasa beer continues to flow. As snacks, we have Himalayan berries and wild rose buds, the skin of which tastes like something between cranberry and rose. A cold wind, typical of the mountains, slices the air outside. It is just another night in Waltse, a village at an elevation of 3,700 metres, nominally Nepal, but for all practical purposes, living outside it.

On the shelves of the bar-shop, run by the Limi Valley Youth Club, with profits flowing to the local primary school, is an array of goods that tells the story of a modern, consumerist economy, far removed from the malls in metropolitan cities, yet connected to them despite a lack of transportation and communication services. There is no road from down south in Nepal to this village, except the recent dirt track we travelled on. But the people of Limi are not looking to the south, no. They are turned to the north, towards China, which straddles their valley, a remnant of the Tibetan culture that was widespread across the Himalayan plateau before the arrival of the PRC in 1950. This is the Nepal–China border, the in-between land, neither here nor there. From Nepal comes the flag. The rest, from China.

An invading force would be hard-pressed to take on Waltse. The village is surrounded on three sides by a massif that is bare in the summers, but stacked with snow once October sets in. On the fourth side is the river Limi, a mad rush of white-water rapids. Perhaps that is why Waltse became a centre of the Drikung Kagyu sub-sect of Tibetan Buddhism, and why the eleventh-century Tibetan translator Rinchen Zangpo decided to build his 108th, and last, monastery here. Oral histories tell us the Rinchenling monastery was commissioned by King Yeshe during the revival of Buddhism in Tibet in the ninth century. 'Evidence from the hagiographies of Rinchen Zangpo, the royal chronologies of the Guge-Purang kingdom [of Tibet], and catalogues of Khojarnath, the main Rinchen Zangpo temple in Purang, suggests that a temple associated with Rinchen Zangpo was constructed in Limi during the 11th, or possibly 12th, century.'[1] The monastery's murals look ancient, and the basement holds a four-faced Vairocana statue in a dark room that has outlived the ages, a gateway to another time.

The Rinchenling monastery belongs to an era of fluid borders, when the primarily Western notion of fixed political boundaries had not yet left its imprint on our part of the world. The monastery's evolution tells us a story about the rising and ebbing fortunes in the Tibetan plateau. Founded under the then popular Kadam sect of Buddhism, the Rinchenling's allegiances later turned to the Sakyapa sect, and in the fifteenth century, when a Sakyapa monk killed one from the Drikung Kagyu sect, the local king awarded the monastery to the latter sect, which administers it still.

Oral histories suggest the Limi valley—and western Tibet—became a refuge for members of dissenting sects once the Yellow-Hat Gelugpas became more influential after the ordination of the Dalai Lama as the spiritual and temporal leader of Tibet. The three villages of Limi valley—Waltse, Til and Dzang—have come to be part of Nepal since the delineation of the Nepal–China border in the 1960s.[2] A curious tale is recorded about how Limi came to be included in Nepal. In early 1960, after the takeover of Tibet and the flight of the Dalai Lama, Chinese authorities invited Limi elders to a meeting in Burang (Purang in Tibetan, Pulan in Pinyin, Taklakot in Nepali), explaining the social benefits of Chinese rule and sending a gift of silver corn to convince them to join the PRC. The Limi oracle, however, recommended that the villages remain in Nepal.[3] The tale lends credence to the CIA's observations from the time that 'Tibetans acting for the Chinese' had been trying to persuade ethnically Tibetan communities living in Nepal's Himalaya 'that they owe allegiance to Tibet'.[4]

The people of Limi had been living under a dual system of taxation and governance until the modern political border unequivocally located them inside Nepal. They had, until then, paid their land taxes, sa khral, to agents of the Nepali state, and the mi khral, or personal tax, to Tibetan authorities.[5] The Rinchenling monastery was subordinate to the Gyangdrag monastery near Mt Kailash. The valley itself was at the centre of a barter economy that involved yak and sheep caravans carrying salt from the great salt pans of upper Tibet, crossing the 5,000-metre Lapcha Pass into Limi, and following rivulets into the lower hills of Humla, Accham and Bajhang, where traders would barter their salt for wheat or rice, which would be taken back to Tibet. 'In the autumn of 1972,' Austrian anthropologist Christoph von Fürer-Haimendorf wrote, 'I met a group of nine Purangbas from the village of Lokba, which lies near Kojernath and Kangdzu. They had come to Yari [Humla] with some 360 sheep and goats carrying salt as well as provisions and cooking utensils for the journey . . . All these Purangbas wore Mao buttons just as many of the Bhotias of Yari with whom they traded wore King Mahendra buttons.'[6]

Those who lived in the upper valleys of the Himalaya did not conform to the popular imagination of remote communities who lived in their own silos. 'The people of Limi have been highly mobile for centuries.'[7] The great salt caravans were not exclusive to this remote corner either. In fact, trade was one of the reasons why high-altitude areas, such as Khumbu, Limi valley in Humla and Dolpo, came to be inhabited—these regions 'might well have remained uninhabited or been visited only by herdsmen taking their flocks for a few weeks to lush summer pastures had it not been that they lie in the interstices of two complementary economic zones'.[8] These Himalayan regions, such as the Kathmandu valley, served as trade centres between the Indo-Gangetic plains and Tibet. The trade continued into the modern era because of the ethnic and familial connections between the people of Limi valley and Tibet, and because of the commercial networks they had developed in the lowlands. Across the Nepali Himalaya, with the exception of the Newars, trade was mostly pursued by ethnic groups that were culturally or ethnically closer to Tibet, with their own set of rituals that lay out the rules of the trade between them.

In Limi, for example, trading marts would alternate between Nepal and Tibet on a yearly basis. These tsongsas would be held in pastures that also served as grazing grounds for the pack animals. Limi valley herders would take their animals to Tibet during the winters, where the wind would leave the grass uncovered, and in the summers, Tibetan herders would come down to Limi's plentiful grasslands.[9] Tibet scholar Melvyn Goldstein wrote about Limi's trade with Tibet in 1975: 'Limi people purchase at least 40 items in [Tibet]. While most of these are manufactured articles such as cloth, matches, cigarettes, thermos flasks, soap, batteries etc., there are also other important non-manufactured products such as rock salt and Tibetan (brick) tea. In turn, Limi sells products such as mustard oil, butter, wooden items (bowls, beams, planks etc.), and animals (horses, hybrid dzo) to Purang.'[10]

Note that Goldstein was visiting Limi in 1974, after the Chinese had taken over Tibet and imposed restrictions on the Nepal–China border. The 1959 Tibetan uprising and China's increasing discomfort at the semi-sovereign nature of the Himalayan borderlands had made it imperative for the PRC to demarcate its borders, which it did in 1961. For the traders and nomadic pastoralists of the Himalaya, however, a fixed border rang the death knell, and created new economic struggles in a region that had sustained itself on cross-border trade. Although the delineation made space for traditional barter trade between Nepalis and Tibetans living within 30 km of the border, the agreement restricted the use of pasturelands in Tibet. The people in Limi were restricted to a pasture near Mansarovar that was of lower quality than what they had access to earlier. The agreement had to be revised every five years, until it lapsed in 1992, and many households sold off their livestock as a result.[11]

Although one imagines such an agreement would have brought movement of people and animals between the two countries to a complete halt, this was not the case in Humla, as Fürer-Haimendorf records in 1972 and Goldstein in 1974. Traders continued to cross the high passes, but it became less and less profitable, especially with the import of subsidised iodised salt from India.[12] The salt-grain caravans that once dotted the Himalayan trails are now a rarity. Even in Humla, where a scholar recorded a caravan as late as in 2011, it was obvious that they were a thing of the past. Only the stories remained: of how huge herds of sheep and chyangra, the mountain goat, would come down every summer, and of Limi villagers taking their herds across the Lapcha Pass into Tibet. Instead, the new global economy—spearheaded by an import of Chinese consumer goods via a recently built road from the border—had arrived in the valley.

✦

To call Limi remote would be an understatement, especially if one travels there from Nepal. In fact, it is far more accessible from China.

Tales of smooth, four-lane highways from Lhasa all the way to Kailash-Mansarovar are carried back by the hundreds of Limi locals who work in Burang—an urban dream with its high-rises, concrete structures and smooth roads.

It is perhaps these tales of concrete brilliance from China that make me imagine a smooth highway running almost parallel to Mansarovar when I finally see the lake from Lapcha Pass, the only place in Nepal from where one can view the holy duo of the Kailash mountain and the lake. The lake is an azure strip that colours the base of a mountain range a fair distance away, a child's landscape art come alive. Kailash, on the other hand, is obscured by clouds. While the Buddhists prostrate and light juniper branches as incense, the Hindus bring out their vermilion. I leave a fifty-rupee note under some rocks; faith has never been my strong suit, but even from this distance, the lake born of Brahma's mind conjures something magical.

Lapcha Pass is where Limi ends, and Tibet (or China, if you prefer) begins. We rode here on the same truck that took us to Waltse, with the same driver. It was just as crowded this time. Every mechanical part groaned as the truck strained to move in the thin mountain air, with regular halts to top up the water in the radiator. A twenty-litre gallon of water sat in the back for good measure, for water is scarce in this cold desert with its bare undulating ridges. About twenty minutes before the pass, our truck gave up the ghost. The altitude, the collective weight of the passengers and the condition of the engine all came together to bring it to a halt. As the wheels rotated hopelessly, those of us in the back brought out our masks. The dust, the pebbles, the smell of burning rubber, all of it disturbed the solemnity of this land. Only when a few of us got off did the truck move again.

A soup-bowl-like pass, Lapcha is beaten into submission by the elements. Grass barely grows higher than an inch here; instead, lichen creeps up the rocks, a grey moss-like being with alien bubbles sprouting on the top. There is a tug of war in the skies; the sun is losing its battle to dark clouds. A brief rumble of thunder can be heard in the distance towards Kailash. The wind is freezing cold and blowing at us from all sides. Within a month, all of this will be covered in snow. Altitude sickness is common here. For me too, every breath is an effort, and a twenty-minute walk to the 'viewpoint' feels like a marathon. On our way down, two police constables join us. Five police officials had travelled with us to the pass. The solitary police post in Limi, the last symbol of the Nepali state until the border, is a ramshackle concrete structure midway between Waltse and Dzang villages; it has no electricity, and a solar battery is used to charge the radio set, which had shorted itself a few days before we reached Waltse.

The two constables ask an old pilgrim who had travelled with us where the border lies. The old man points to the base of the pass on the other side. 'That's China,' he says.

'And where are the border pillars?' one of the officers asks, taking off his police jacket as he poses for a picture.

'There, behind that,' the old man says, pointing towards a crest to the left of the pass.

'And the other one?'

The old man turns around and points towards another crest. 'At the bottom of that.'

The officers seem satisfied. I don't think they have it in them to hike up to the spots where the pillars are said to be. I ask them if this is the first time they have come to the border. Both of them nod, yes. It has been four months since they were posted to Limi, and neither of them is from the district, let alone the valley. The cold, the culture, the language, the food, the people, the land—everything is alien to them. Their patrols are limited to the three villages, and to enquire whether any of the trucks coming down from Lapcha carry contraband or illegal migrants.

In September 2020, the Nepali state's limited capacity in the Himalayan borderlands was highlighted when local officials began to dispute Chinese construction near the pass. The local municipality chief argued that the Chinese structures lay at least 2 km within Nepali territory, but one of the two border pillars, number eleven, had gone missing, so no one was really sure where the border itself was. A team of security officials hurriedly investigated, and discovered the pillar buried under snow and rubble. Meanwhile, in Kathmandu, the foreign minister rushed to claim that the structures were built on the Chinese side. The controversy highlighted the asymmetry in border infrastructure on the two sides, and refuses to die out in an era when China's rise is contested. In Limi, once again, the question of where Nepal ends and China begins remained fraught with uncertainties.[13]

'This place, this is neither Nepal nor China,' the assistant sub-inspector who headed the police post told me the day before we drove to Lapcha pass. He hoped to be posted somewhere else by the end of the year, although the police post is manned only during the months the valley is not snowed in—just like the bare primary school here.[14] 'These people, they don't cooperate with us. If there are any troubles in their village, they resolve it themselves. Only when it's an outsider creating trouble do they call us,' he whispered to me as we sat in the sun. That night, he got drunk on Chinese beers and liquor, and insisted the monk who showed him to his bed also bring him a bottle of water. The monk asked him to lie down and disappeared. The cop soon began to snore.

The clash of cultures—and equally, how sovereignty is contested, negotiated and sometimes rejected in the borderlands—was evident in so many different ways at Waltse. The night before, a contingent of police officials had arrived at the village after a long hike from Hilsa, the other border outpost in Humla; a group of eleven had started at 5 a.m. and reached the village only at 9 p.m. 'We didn't see anybody to ask for directions, and got lost in the uwa, barley fields,' a constable told me, as we sipped black tea in the morning. The police contingent looked forlorn, waiting outside the monastery for someone to tell them what exactly they were supposed to do. The provincial chief minister was to come for the trade fair, and the police were there to coordinate the proceedings, including setting up a makeshift helipad out of white ribbons. A local was indignant when I asked him what the police did in Limi. 'Nothing, really, except give trouble.' Another told me the police had no work in Limi. 'They come for their patrols, we give them tea, vegetables, but that's about it.'

The presence of the police in Limi felt, for the most part, symbolic. Between the three villages, there are about 900 residents. The trucks that transport goods and people back and forth from the border and Simikot bear no Nepali licence plates; in fact, they had been driven here via Tibet. The entire district of Humla itself is not connected by road to the rest of Nepal. The idea of 'belonging' to Nepal, of relating to Kathmandu, was largely absent, except for the ward office of the rural municipality Limi is part of. 'The most immediate and pervasive source of power' that shapes the lives of Limi residents is 'the social sovereignty' of the community itself, made up of khrims, a set of community contracts that have evolved over time. 'Villagers explicitly see community and

Nepali law as being of equal importance, rather than the former being subordinate to the latter.'[15] Thus, even as Nepal imposes its sovereignty through instruments such as citizenship cards and other documentation that is essential for Limi residents, Limi is a place between nations and states, between state and non-state sovereignty, where the border itself is 'an economic resource'.[16]

As the Nepali state modernises and expands its reach into these borderlands, there is a conscious effort to incorporate its citizens into the state. 'We don't understand their language, they don't understand ours,' the assistant sub-inspector said. 'But there are orders from the top to promote the use of Nepali, at least in the schools.' The cultural programmes I witnessed in the villages had made that evident; it was clear the children were struggling while singing Nepali songs, even as their teacher, a non-Limi resident, prodded them on. Tsewang Lama, the local member of Parliament (MP), told me, '[Limi's] people, their psychology matches that of Tibet. Limi is disconnected from the rest of the district for more than half the year. If you need to go to Kathmandu, the easiest way is to go to Burang in China, cross back into Nepal using the Darchula border, cross over into India, then take the bus from the Mahendra Nagar border to Kathmandu. It's very difficult to connect with Nepal for people here. How can we have national unity if we don't even have roads to connect the country?'[17]

As is true in most of Nepal's Himalayan borderlands, a road did come to Limi, only it came from China. The present dirt track that connects Lapcha to Waltse began to be cleared sometime in 2010, with Tsewang Lama taking the lead and his cousin Mangal Lama coordinating the project.[18] China agreed to open the Lapcha crossing 'for limited local exchange and transportation of rice in the name of development aid'.[19] The track followed the old caravan route to Tibet, and excavators were transported from Kathmandu via Gyirong, the border point immediately north of the capital, and Lhasa.[20] The track has now been extended up to Simikot, nearly a hundred kilometres away. But even if the present dirt track is upgraded to a metalled road, the looming presence of China, and the opportunities it offers, stands in stark contrast to what Nepal can offer. Consider the issue of language: the Limi folk who work in Burang are able to do so because they can speak Tibetan. The few Nepalis who do not speak Tibetan but work in Burang reportedly earn less than their counterparts. And while most

Nepali migrants travel to the Persian Gulf countries or South East Asia to work as labour, for Limi locals, working in Burang makes much more economic sense.

There is also the elephant in the room: the people of Limi follow Tibetan Buddhism, and have familial relations with those living inside Tibet and in exile. Limi children study in Tibetan-run schools in India. Several people told me that, because their surname in official Nepali papers was 'Lama', they had been questioned by Chinese authorities until they could convincingly prove their Nepali citizenship. There is a curious situation here: the people of Limi regard the Dalai Lama as their religious head, but steer clear of the politics regarding Tibet. 'He is not our political leader. We are Nepalis after all,' one of them told me. None of the homes in Limi displayed a picture of the Dalai Lama; this came as a surprise to me, because he is very popular in Nepal.[21] As a scholar has noted, 'Citizenship in this border zone is often a multiple, rather than singular concept, with families and individuals making claims on, and maintaining allegiances to, both the Nepali and Chinese states, while simultaneously possessing a sense of Tibetanness.'[22]

Tsewang Lama, the MP, said something that struck me as a deep insight into the psyche of those who live here. Before making his move into politics, he was a research scholar who studied the many cultures of Humla extensively. Standing on the terrace of the Waltse monastery, he broke down Limi's issues and then moved on to the question of citizens' rights in a federal Nepal. 'Our rights, and the rights of the people of Limi, are two different ideas. Their basic right is the right to eat. For them, the right to eat, to clothe themselves properly, gaans, kapas, these are human rights. That is freedom for them.' For a culture that is far removed from the technological and material progress of the twenty-first century and suffered under the changing rules of the modern market economy, for a people whose agricultural output is not sufficient to last the year and are struggling to survive in a harsh environment, and for a region that in an age of 4G connectivity and electric cars has no access even to proper roads, let alone a public transportation system, what is likely to matter more?

This is not limited to Limi. All along the Himalayan borderlands, the imbalance between the slow pace of development from the Nepali side and the rapid push towards infrastructural transformation from the Chinese side means many of these communities have now come to depend on importing food and other necessities via or from China. During the COVID-19 pandemic, the northern parts of Humla district, including Limi, reported a food shortage because the border had been closed down. In October 2020, seven months into the shutdown, Limi locals bought 300 quintals of rice from a government depot in Simikot, and paid NPR 355,000 as transport charges to bring it to the valley.[23] The rice would only last them three months. Finally, in December, Chinese authorities opened the Hilsa and Lapcha border points for a day at the request of their Nepali counterparts. Sixteen Chinese trucks delivered daily necessities such as rice, blankets and flour to the region. In upper Dolpa, to the east of Humla, as elsewhere in the trans-Himalayan region, when the borders shut down during the pandemic, authorities wrote to Kathmandu to urgently supply them with basic necessities.

Liberal ideals of citizenly freedoms made little sense in a place like Limi, which was snowed in nearly half the year and had no economic opportunities. But even as development experts, policymakers and planners sitting in faraway Kathmandu thought of ways in which Humla can be connected to the rest of Nepal, it was abundantly clear that the people here had already thought of, and exploited, the opportunities that living on the border with China offered them. When the traditional way of life came to an end with the imposition of the rules of modern states, Limi residents suffered, as did the rest of Humla and other border districts. They began to 'use the border—and their ability to move across it—as a resource for their livelihoods'.[24] The road from the north had opened up new possibilities for the future, and infused a newfound confidence among the people, despite the asymmetries between industrialised China and backwater Nepal. Kathmandu was remote; China, and the dreams it promised, were much closer.

✦

For the most part of history, trade has been carried out on a small scale, between individuals rather than intangible corporate entities. Trade in its elementary form is built on a foundation of interpersonal relationships that lead to credit facilities and interdependence during travels back and forth, with trust being the most important element.

Trade in the Himalayan regions occurred along similar lines. 'Whether based on simple barter or on complex, multi-sided deals operated within a monetized economy, the trading activities of the societies here considered are normally the enterprise of individuals, or of small teams of friends or kinsmen pooling their resources for specific undertakings,' Fürer-Haimendorf wrote.[25] With the enforcement of modern border restrictions, such trade patterns came to a grinding halt. But obstacles may also provide for new opportunities, as academic Tina Harris writes, to gain 'more high-risk profits, such as through the transport of illicit or restricted goods'. At the same time, 'new roads and railways, while allowing for the easier and faster movement of goods and people on one level, may simultaneously obstruct, separate, or erase other existing places; the dividing of nomadic pastures, abandonment of other passageways, or relocation of communities are examples of this'.[26] Those who trade across borders constantly seek new means to circumvent or exploit existing policies. Harris quotes two cousins who began by supplying basic goods—'medicine, herbs, everything! [And] bricks also, cement. And sand also! [And] vegetables'—from Kathmandu to Lhasa in the 1980s, at a time when Tibet remained undeveloped. As competition grew and Tibet opened up to tourists, the cousins switched to Nepali handicrafts. Then, as construction began to boom in Lhasa, they supplied steel rods and cement, but even here, they began to face competition as China's domestic production capacity soon matched the demand.[27]

In 2002, Nepal and China began issuing 'border citizen cards' for those who lived within 30 km of the border on each side, classifying them as 'border inhabitants' and giving them special rights to travel and work within this 30 km region without a passport or a visa. It is on the basis of this documentation that the people of Limi trade, work and live in Burang for months at a stretch. Nepalis who work in China thus possess 'overlapping sovereignties'.[28] Sara B. Shneiderman, a scholar on citizenship in the Himalaya, writes, 'For several generations, border citizens have engaged with the policies of both Nepal and China, as well as the prerogatives of the Tibetan polity, to make claims on—not evade—the multiple states that constitute the border zone in which they live.'[29]

Further, new economic geographies are created as a response to new state policies. In the Himalaya, they have come about as a result of China's Great Western Development Strategy, *xibu da kaifa* ('open up the west'), which was launched in 2000 and intended to speed up development in six provinces, one municipality and five autonomous regions, including the Tibetan Autonomous Region, in the western region of China. 'Most of the investment has been dedicated to developing transportation, energy, communication, and irrigation and improving urban infrastructure in the interior regions.'[30] By all accounts, this has brought rapid economic change in Tibet, with its GDP 'quadrupling' between 1997 and 2007, and growth based on 'rapid tertiarisation and a construction boom alongside a small and constant GDP share of secondary industry'.[31] The highlight of this policy was the Qinghai–Tibet Railway, an engineering feat, but above all, the policy was 'a program of state and nation building, a renewed "civilizing mission" to more closely incorporate minority ethnic groups, and a reconsolidation of central state control after two decades of decentralization and localism'.[32]

Trade across the Himalaya would continue to evolve as new political realities took shape and brought these frontier lands under state sovereignty. The salt-for-grains barter trade began to collapse after the demarcation of the Nepal–China border. With the introduction of subsidised iodised salt from India, there was very little chance the caravan economy of the past would survive. In Limi, the alternatives had already been noticed as far back as 1974. When all unsupervised trade with their Tibetan counterparts halted after the border agreements, Limi's traders switched to the import of modern consumer goods, and exported, among other things, handicrafts to Tibet, the most profitable being wooden bowls called 'phuru'.

✦

I notice Palden (name changed) because of his fox-fur hat: it is straight out of a Mongolian epic. The fox tail droops down his left shoulder, while the fur sits snugly on his head. Palden's tent at the trade fair displays the traditional attires of the Limi people. There is a particularly striking blue robe with gold sequins and embroidery that is over eighty years old. Its craftsmanship is superb, and its worn-out edges betray its vintage. Phuru bowls banded with crafted silver sit alongside it. Palden's grandfather, too, sports a fur hat and has a moustache drooping down his lips, making him resemble a Tibetan Salvador Dalí. He animatedly explains to me the different implements that a Tibetan man carries in his robe: a knife with an ivory hilt to slice up meat, ivory chopsticks and a tobacco pouch. Their tent is tethered with ropes made of yak wool. An inebriated local explains how these ropes are better than the nylon more commonly used nowadays.

That evening, once the rush of the fair is over, I sit with Palden in an empty tent. He looks as if he is not yet twenty, but he is already married and has a child. He was sent to study in India in 2005, and returned in 2014 to Waltse to assist his parents. 'There was no road here, and things got difficult. We didn't have enough food to eat,' he tells me. So he did what most young men and women in Limi valley have been doing for the past two decades: he went across the border to Burang to work as labour on a construction site. He unloaded cement from a truck for an average wage of around 80 to 100 RMB a day, sometimes 150 RMB if the construction site was managed by a reputable company. It would take five of them to unload a truck in an hour and a half. 'You have to stack the cement sacks properly. It's not like here in Nepal, where you can just throw things around,' he says.

The border identity cards allow Limi (and Humla) residents to work and live in Burang. Everybody I met there had a 'working in Burang' story: the thirteen-hour shifts, with little time for breaks; the pay varying between 200 to 260 RMB a day, lower than official rates, but far higher than wages in Nepal. Men worked at the more physically demanding jobs, such as at construction sites, while the women worked in homes as housemaids or cleaners. One evening, I met a man who had come to Waltse to see if anyone was travelling onwards to Burang, where his wife worked as a cleaner in one of the housing projects. It had been several months since they had met. The previous year, she had given birth to their son in Dzang village in the winter, and it had been a complicated delivery. After she recovered, she returned to Burang, while he went to Kathmandu, where he owned a shop.

The difference in the material conditions between China and Nepal are clear for anyone to see. Hilsa, the Nepal border which you cross to go to Burang (and if you are a pilgrim, climb on to the jeeps that will take you to Kailash), is a near-desolate, dusty settlement with metal shacks that function as police posts. Across the river is the concrete behemoth that is the Chinese customs and immigration office. Burang is 30 km inland, sitting just on the edge of the radius where Limi locals are permitted to work. Like most Chinese cities, the construction looks relatively new from the many pictures on social media. Rows and rows of concrete structures, and the ease with which cars, motorcycles, trucks, buses ply here makes you forget that the town sits at nearly 4,800 metres. There is a steady inflow of Nepalis coming in from Humla here: more than a thousand in 2018 alone.[33] When the pandemic shut down the borders in March 2020, 148 Nepalis were stranded in the town.[34] There is significant competition in the labour market because of the increased number of Nepalis, so Palden decided he would take the plunge and start a business. Along with four other friends, he leased a store for 30,000 RMB, a significant investment. Familial connections help; his aunt lives in Burang, and he rents a room at her place for 2,000 RMB for the year. She helped them scope out a store, where they began to sell phurus, religious beads and clothing. With the profits of the first few years, the five then bought the lease of a smaller store, about five feet by five feet, where they now sell jackets. 'Northface,' he says, referring to the sportswear brand that has become eponymous with the down jackets that have replaced traditional Tibetan bakkhu robes at these heights. They have to pay a further rent of 2,000 RMB per month on the store. I calculate his costs, and ask whether they make a profit. 'About 500 RMB a day,' he says, 'which we split among the five partners.'

I want to know more about the phuru trade. The smooth maple-wood bowl is a must for any Tibetan ritual, and the more expensive ones have silver bands carved with various mythical figures and symbols. The bowls from Limi are known across Tibet; as a Lonely Planet guide says, 'Even in Lhasa, wooden bowls from Limi are prized over those made elsewhere.' But the bowls are rarely made in Limi anymore. Instead, Palden and other phuru traders like him go to Dehradun in India to source the maple burls required for the bowls. The bowls are shaped in India itself, and then brought to Kathmandu by bus, where they are polished and smoothened by hand. The bowls are painted in Limi, and taken to stores across the border. The larger the bowls get, and the more ornate the silver band engravings, the higher its price. A small bowl costs around NPR 3,000, whereas a larger one can cost up to NPR 11,000 in Burang. The margins are significant, but for Palden, there are also that many partners to split with.

Palden's annual schedule reminds me of the kora, the pilgrim's circumambulation of Mt Kailash. He is in Burang for a few months, and travels back and forth between Kathmandu and Delhi during the winter, returning to Waltse every spring. He is also an exemplar of Limi's modern-day relationship with China: negotiating the bureaucratic hassles that come with transporting products across borders, and ensuring he remains a model citizen in Burang so that he can carry out his trade without the Chinese authorities bothering him. At the same time, Palden, and others like him, symbolise the overlapping sovereignties they have to negotiate.

Palden informs me about how Chinese goods enter Limi: there are six individuals who represent the three villages of Limi in Burang, and who coordinate the requirements of their villages. Mangal Lama, the road contractor, explained how Chinese authorities in Burang assist Limi valley through an annual 300,000 RMB aid in kind. While China agreed to provide diesel during the construction of the road, the 'social sovereignty' of the Limi locals also kicked in, with every household paying for two bags of wheat and two bags of rice to raise the costs for additional fuel and the rent for the excavators that were clearing the road. Mangal also told me that, although security at the border remained the primary concern, the Chinese were willing to look into further collaborations between their districts. Since the middle of this decade, annual meetings between officials of both countries are alternately held in Humla and Burang.[35]

As with the products, so with the people. By 'experiencing development' from the Chinese side rather than the Nepali side,[36] Limi residents have learnt to be careful about potential irritants in the relationship. Palden tells me the Chinese regard the Limi folk as 'good people' because they live by the rules. 'The Chinese tell us don't get too drunk, don't go to discos. And that's right. If we die in China, it's their responsibility. We keep quiet and work by their rules. And that's why they like us.' The assistant sub-inspector tells me the Chinese authorities had asked their Nepali counterparts to not allow anyone under the age of twenty or over fifty to cross over as labourers. 'Nepalis, they get drunk and create ruckus in Burang. If they get arrested, it becomes a diplomatic hassle, so the two border authorities cooperate with each other.'

Further, as in the rest of Nepal, China imposes its will on the border as a prerogative. Beyond its increased pressure, both on authorities and residents, to deny Tibetan refugees an easy passage to Kathmandu or India, '[Limi residents] have been explicitly warned that they will no longer be permitted to do business or labour in Burang if they guide or shelter Tibetans seeking exile.'[37] In June 2019, after the murder of a Chinese woman by four Nepalis in Burang, local authorities closed off the border and sent back all Nepalis. The order was rescinded after the intervention of Kathmandu and Beijing authorities, but the episode showed that freedom of movement along the Nepal–China border would remain a prerogative of the Chinese state and its concerns. 'Many of the [people of Humla] expressed fear about how dominant the Chinese are, citing examples such as setting high prices, dictating that only one person may get one food item at a time, oppressing Tibetans, and even beating Humla traders if there was a mistake on their permit.'[38] However, there is no denying that, without China and its food exports, the residents of Humla, let alone of Limi, would find it difficult to sustain themselves. 'Humlis [people from Humla] are at the mercy of the Chinese, but it is precisely China's provider-ship that makes Humlis place great value on their relationship with China.'[39]

When I worked for a Kathmandu-based paper a decade ago, the few news reports that emerged out of Humla had to do with food insecurity and the UN agency World Food Programme's efforts to distribute rice in the district. Simikot, the district headquarters, is still years from being connected to the national road network. Humla is known to be Nepal's poorest district, even though it is not. The people of Limi valley, for that matter, are not poor by most standards; half of them own a home in Kathmandu, while several have migrated to New York. This is not a new phenomenon; Goldstein, who lived in Limi during his research in the 1970s, wrote, 'On the whole, Limi, as of 1974, was relatively successful economically. The various economic strategies employed by the inhabitants generated surpluses which allowed many of them to function *well above* [emphasis mine] subsistence levels.'[40] The irony is unmissable: under the caravan economy, western Tibet subsisted on food imports from the lower hills of the Himalaya, as a result of which Humla communities were relatively well off. But in the contemporary era, rapid infrastructure development across the border had 'completely reversed the former trade imbalance'.[41] Such a situation continues; while outward migration from the three villages has become a larger concern for the older generation, it is clear that the 'poverty' of Limi is only in Kathmandu's imagination. But the locals have had to negotiate several crossings to get to where they are today.

As modern geopolitics and consumerism made it infeasible for the barter economy of old to continue, some in Limi first took to means that broke existing laws. The Hilsa crossing emerged as a key site for illicit wildlife trade. 'With the salt trade reduced to a shadow of its former self and Tibetan antiques no longer readily available by the late 1980s, traders felt there was no other option than to tap the region's last remaining asset—its remoteness, which guaranteed a certain degree of invisibility. In the words of a local trader remembering the 1990s, "Many people did illegal business, but they had no choice."[42] One of the many anecdotes I heard relating to the wildlife trade that occurred through this remote but open border in the 1980s and '90s was that, while individuals from two of the villages made money, by the time those from the third village entered the trade, the state had begun to crack down, and several traders were imprisoned and suffered losses. The Dalai Lama's 2006 call to stop using tiger and leopard skin robes also had a significant impact on reducing demand. The shifting realities of the Himalaya was also made evident when better policing and expansion of state authority at crossings such as Hilsa resulted in more remote passes to the west, such as Urai in Bajhang, emerging as new hubs for illegal trade.[43]

Then, China's *xibu da kaifa* brought in rapid economic changes in the Ngari prefecture, and drew the people of Limi to Burang. Today, the region is an exemplar of life in the Himalayan borderlands. As the Chinese 'gift of development' continues to expand state authority in Tibet's once-hinterlands, the corresponding regions in Nepal are learning to exploit new economic potentials even without the assistance of their own state, through mechanisms that grant them a significance few other Nepalis possess. The 'in-between-ness' of Limi gives its people an advantage—the mobility created by a blurred citizenship and overlapping sovereignties an impossible scenario in any other region.

3

A Fence in the Himalaya

Pasang[1] and I are discussing the virtues of his 200cc Lifan Chinese motorcycle when really we should be worrying about frostbite. We are at a height of more than 4,000 metres, and all around us is a sea of white. Snowmelt is trickling down the drain that runs along the nearly 10-metre-wide gravelled road that is wider and smoother than any I have encountered on my journey north from Pokhara, nearly 200 km away. This road should not be here, I think to myself, even as I shoot a video on my phone, holding onto Pasang with one hand as we ride up. Nepal's new roads are notoriously dangerous, but this particular 16-km stretch, from Chhosar village in upper Mustang to the Nepal–China border at Kora La, is a dream. Built by a Nepali road construction company, it belies the popular narrative of Nepali contractors lagging behind their international counterparts in delivery and quality.

The road was widened and the gabion walls built a few months earlier, in December 2018. To the south are the magnificent ranges of Annapurna and Dhaulagiri, the narrow Kali Gandaki River severing them to create one of the world's deepest gorges. On all other sides are rolling mountains covered in snow, lower and less steep than the eight-thousanders, but imposing nonetheless. Pasang says most of these hills will be dirt-naked in the summer. We are on the Tibetan plateau geographically; politically, it is still Nepal. But this is not the 'green hills and mountains to the north' that Nepal is known for. Instead, this is desert country, with a fierce cold wind that blows in from the south every afternoon at speeds sometimes touching 100 km/h. Knee-high, thorny caragana shrubs populate the landscape, their thin succulent leaves providing fodder for the livestock; and carefully managed, traditional water-sharing irrigation methods allow the few villages in this bone-cold climate to survive. 'Mustang is as barren as a dead deer,' Tashi, French writer Michel Peissel's confidant in the latter's classic 1967 text on Mustang, declared.[2] But walk past the magnificently irrigated villages of Kagbeni, Tsarang and Ghemi, and one marvels at the traditional knowledge systems that allow a sea of green—barley, buckwheat, potatoes—to grow in patches in this cold, barren desert.

The winter has been one of severe discomfort. Snow fell heavier than in years past, and scores of livestock have died.[3] Conversations inevitably turn to the erratic weather patterns of the last few years, the dire warnings of climate change come to life. It begins to snow the April afternoon I arrive in Lo Manthang, the capital of the ancient Tibetan kingdom of Mustang, once a suzerain to the Nepali kings and located at the heart of the Himalayan salt trade. The snow continues to fall till late evening, the famous walled city turning silent as everyone is indoors, except a few horses perhaps. Coming from a place where the rain falls in sheets and is accompanied by thunder, the quiet of snowfall perplexes me. The next day, as I prepare for the ride with Pasang, he tells me to expect 'a lot of snow' on the border itself.

The road now turns into a river of white as Pasang and I go higher on the Nechung ridge. The surprisingly weak sun of an April morning does little to quell the chill in the air. I have forgotten to bring gloves, and Pasang is wearing gloves without fingertips. 'These are meant for the summer, you see,' he tells me. He did not expect it would be this cold—the winter's long shadow continues to throw a blight. I can only nod; riding pillion, I try to shield myself from the cold wind behind him. My jacket sleeves are now stretched to cover my fingers, but the cold still finds a way to chill my bones. The motorcycle seems to be doing much better than we are, so I ask Pasang its price.

'Brother, what do you think?' he asks me.

I attempt a guess. 'One lakh fifty?'

He laughs. 'Cheaper. Ninety thousand. That's what I paid.'

That is considerably cheaper than I had expected. Nepal's customs duties make buying a vehicle an expensive affair.

'How did you get it so cheap?'

'I bought it at the fair here on the border. I haven't paid duties on it, that's why it's so cheap. But that's also why I can't ride the bike beyond upper Mustang. But, brother, only Chinese bikes work up here in Mustang.'

'Really?'

'That's right. If you bring an Indian bike here, it won't start at all. There just isn't enough oxygen here for those bikes. But these Chinese, they've built bikes meant for these heights. They are no problem at all.'

Pasang is twenty-two, and finished his twelfth-grade exams in Pokhara; he does not want to study further. On most days, he paints the homes of Lo Manthang for NPR 1,500 a day. Pasang is terribly proud of *belonging* to Mustang. We stop for a break and admire the view to the south—one has to get used to the idea that the Himalaya are south of us here. He asks me several times, 'Isn't the landscape better here than in most of Nepal?' Or, 'Don't the mountains look better here than in Pokhara?' I nod in agreement; a jeep makes its way down from the other side. The folks inside are almost shocked to see the two of us in this vast expanse. (I'll meet the jeep driver later in the day; he will tell me he struggled with the vehicle even though it was a four-wheel drive. When I tell Pasang, he laughs as if to say, 'These outsiders, what do they know?')

The previous evening, he had seemed reticent when we discussed our two-person expedition to the border. But up here, in the emptiness that is the Tibetan plateau, in what was an ancient kingdom shaped by tantric Buddhism and trans-Himalayan trade, surrounded on all three sides by what is today a superpower, Pasang comes into his own. We continue discussing the motorcycle. It is a puny bike, belying its ability at these heights. It was bought at one of the two trade fairs that are held at the border here every year. But while barter-trade fairs were regularly held at several places across the Tibetan plateau and in the highlands such as in Limi valley, the trade fairs in Mustang today 'are mediated by cash, directed by Chinese administration, and take place only on the Tibetan side [at Lizi, or Likse in Tibetan] of the border each spring and fall'.[4] The fair was held alternately in Nepal and Tibet until a decade ago, when the Chinese unilaterally decided to hold it in Tibet.

I ask Pasang what else could one buy at the fair. 'Food items, biscuits, beers, TVs.' How does one buy a TV here? 'The same way as a bike. If a 40-inch TV costs you NPR 80–90,000 in Kathmandu, you can get it for around NPR 30–40,000 here.' No foreigners are allowed to go to the fair. Pasang says the road workers in Mustang, who are primarily from the western hill districts of Rolpa and Rukum, also come to the fair to buy cheap booze. Everyone has to abide by Chinese regulations. 'This includes entering China's Tibetan territory through the Kora La border gate at a specific and designated time, disclosing biographic data and being photographed for entry into a *tsongra*-specific [i.e. fair-specific] database, carrying a basic ID chit provided by Chinese border guards, and relinquishing any personal items such as necklaces and lockets that depict the Dalai Lama . . . By cooperating with these conditions, visitors without even a passport or any form of Nepali state identification can then enter Chinese territory, drive, ride, or walk the 10 kilometers from the Kora La border post to the *tsongra* grounds in Likse, and stay for the duration of the trade fair (up to several weeks at a time).'[5]

The transactions at these fairs are mostly one-way. Pasang struggles to recall any Nepali items that are sold to the Chinese. In August 2016, China closed down the fair three days early, citing low volume of trade. That same year, Nepali customs officials said Nepal did not export anything to China. The next year, Chinese authorities opened the border for ten days, during which locals rushed across to buy necessary goods. Although the opening up of a road from Pokhara has done much to remedy the dependence on China, it is evident locals still prefer to buy Chinese blankets, thermoses and bikes. 'Folks call their contacts across the border before the fair with their requirements,' Pasang says.

We are now at a gently sloping ridge that turns to the right. On our left are the ruins of an old chorten, traditionally considered the frontier between Tibet and the Mustang kingdom. The modern border sits about 1.5 km away. As we take the bend, in the distance, against a pristine white landscape, is a massive concrete structure that turns out to be the under-construction Chinese immigration and customs building.[6] I can make out a razor-wire fence running across the snow on both sides of the gatehouse. On this massive plain that is Kora La, not a pass in the traditional sense but at an elevation from the Nechung valley below, the concrete giant appears out of nowhere, a massive man-made aberration in a harsh-but-beautiful terrain. In form, it resembles the customs building the Chinese have built at Rasuwa. But at this altitude, it also appears symbolic of the Chinese intent to overcome the forces of nature, as was one of the earliest missions of the PLA in Tibet, with the setting up of the first state farms in what was once barren land.[7]

At 4,660 metres, Kora La is one of the lowest crossings in the Himalaya. Once central to the caravan trade that most Himalayan communities relied upon, it is where the Kali Gandaki corridor, one of the 'national pride' infrastructural projects for Nepal,[8] begins. The corridor, like other roads that come down from the Chinese border, intends to create a transit route between China and India through Nepal, but it will also sever the economic leverage New Delhi has over Kathmandu by opening up Nepal's northern frontiers to China. Kora La's relatively lower altitude, however, makes the Chinese state wary, for it is here that the weaknesses of Beijing's control over its frontier regions has been most apparent in the past.

✦

On the night of 30 December 1999, two SUVs raced across the Tibetan plateau towards Kora La in the darkness. In the early morning of 31 December, one of the vehicles drove past the border pillar at Kora La, crossing over into Nepali territory, and came to a halt. There were no roads at this time, so 'they left the vehicle in the care of a family on the Mustang side of the border, telling them they would come back for it in a few days'.[9] A documentary suggests Chinese border officials discovered the vehicle the next morning, drove it back to China and torched it.[10] In Nepal, a waiting party helped the escapees to travel to Lo Manthang. A week later, on the morning of 5 January 2000, the fourteen-year-old Ogyen Trinley Dorje, otherwise known as the Karmapa, the head of the Karma Kagyu sect of Tibetan Buddhism, appeared in front of media persons in Dharamsala, India, announcing that he had fled from Tibet.[11]

Dorje's escape was remarkable, for he had been the only high-ranking reincarnated Tibetan lama to be recognised both by the Dalai Lama and the Chinese Communist Party. According to his official statement, 'The decision to leave my homeland, monastery, monks, parents, family, and the Tibetan people was entirely my own—no one told me to go and no one asked me to come.'

The Chinese response was guarded at first. Beijing said he had left a note in his Tsurphu monastery saying he was leaving to bring back the 'Black Hat' crown, ritually important to the sect, from the Rumtek monastery in Sikkim. 'The Karmapa had made it clear, according to Beijing, that he did not intend to stay away or to "betray" the "motherland".'[12] At the same time, Chinese intelligence agents questioned 'people in Nepal' after his escape, while also arresting officials from the Tsurphu monastery.[13] Nepali officials also cracked down on Tibetan refugees in Kathmandu following his escape.[14]

Then, Indian authorities began to raise doubts. The sum of their fears was captured by B. Raman, a noted security analyst and ex-intelligence official, who wrote, 'Did [the Karmapa] really escape clandestinely after giving a slip to the Chinese as claimed by him or was it a choreographed escape organized by the Chinese intelligence to create a split among the followers of His Holiness the Dalai Lama, undermine his authority and project the Karmapa as the interim head of the Tibetan Buddhists after the death of His Holiness till the Dalai Lama's successor is chosen by the Chinese Communist Party, by stage-managing the identification of the child who is his incarnation?'[15] When a large sum of Chinese currency was recovered from his Indian monastery a few years later, the fears of him being an 'agent of Beijing' were revived.

The Indian establishment distrusts Dorje, alleging in 2018 that he had not informed New Delhi he would be taking up Dominican citizenship. Delhi officials have gone so far as to say, 'The government of India does not recognise Ogyen Trinley Dorje as the 17th Karmapa Lama. There are other contenders.'[16] There is little doubt among Tibetans and the Dalai Lama, however, about his background and opposition to China, and his photographs adorn walls in guesthouses, restaurants and homes across in Nepal (and in Mustang). But for the purposes of this book, what is important is that the flight of the Karmapa resulted in the wired fence that today stands ominously on the Chinese side of the border in Kora La.

In Mustang, the effects of the escape were clear. A Nepali journalist, who reached the border a few months after the escape, told me the fence had not come up when he had visited; however, by the end of 2000, it was ready. Today, the fence stretches between border pillars number 21 to 27, a total distance of 22.2 km. Across pillar number 24 stands the two-storeyed concrete structure that is the customs office. Solar panels are arranged to a side, and a CCTV camera looks on into Nepal. 'Both on land and from the sky, rather than open grasslands and alpine streams, it is concrete pillars, barbed wire, solar panels, and closed-circuit cameras that characterize the Mustang-Tibet border today,' wrote geographer Galen Murton, while conducting his research on the Mustang border in 2014–15.[17] Four years later, the Chinese predilection for massive concrete structures is the most visible presence on this trans-Himalayan flatland, a challenge to the brute forces of nature that have carved out this alpine plain.

✦

The Lifan's front wheel crosses over into no-man's land as Pasang parks the bike. He is as surprised as I am at the pace of work on the customs building. Construction had begun in 2017, and the shell of this massive complex was ready within a year. A few clothes dry on the fence. I ask Pasang if anybody lives here. 'Not here, their post is about four–five kilometres away,' he says. Later, in Lo Manthang, a police official confirms this. 'They halted the construction during the winter,' the official tells me. The fence-turned-clothesline suggests they have restarted the work, but there is no sign of any workers. 'They've built underground living quarters,' Pasang says when I ask him. I take this with a pinch of salt.

We pose for photographs, taking care not to seem overly curious about what the Chinese are doing. I have been warned 'they' do not take frolic on the border lightly. 'If they see something suspicious, they drive down from their border post,' the security official had told me. I proceed cautiously into the no-man's land and click a few pictures. I have no idea if the fence is electrified; I do not want to risk it. In my mind, a convoy of 4WD jeeps races up the plain from the other side to see what two fools are doing out here in the cold.

Border pillar number 24 is a concrete block, about knee-high. On the Nepali side, the Devanagari script reads 'Nepal', with the Bikram Sambat year 2016 carved in red. On the Chinese side are two characters that read 'Zhongguo', China's official Sinitic name, and the common era year 1962, when the border between the two countries was demarcated. This pillar marks the end of Nepali territory, a symbol of 'territorialisation' from Nepal's side.[18] The closest symbol of the Nepali state is a tourist signboard about 3 km away, which points the way to a glacial lake; the closest institution, a police post in Chhosar, is nearly 20 km away.

'Why can't Nepal build something like that too?' Pasang questions. I suspect he knows the answer, but the query is rooted in something deeper. Across upper Mustang, locals have told me the Chinese regularly come to visit their villages and monasteries (and eat dal–bhat!), but Nepalis are not allowed to cross over except during the fair. Pasang continues, 'Earlier, there was a Nepali border post about a kilometre away from the border. They set it up there because they had water there. What sense does it make for a border post to be away from the border?' I find no evidence of this post he is talking about; perhaps he meant the old chorten, near which a 'Nepal gate' had stood till 2015, when the locals demolished it.[19] A 2012 bilateral agreement deemed Kora La as one of the six 'trading points' that were to be upgraded into ports on the Nepal–China border.[20] In 2015, after the Indian economic blockade, the two countries signed another agreement to upgrade seven traditional trading passes by building customs offices. The Nepal government then acquired land in Chhosar—a village known for its ancient cave systems that had once housed monks—to build a customs and immigration office, which will also house police and Armed Police Force personnel, the latter responsible for security at the border. There are also ongoing discussions over a dry port in Kora La.[21] However, all that exists in Chhosar today is a police checkpost that simply forbids foreigners from travelling beyond the village.

The construction of a road to the border has allowed the Nepali state to 'territorialise' upper Mustang. The region was closed to outsiders until 1992, and state presence was limited. However, the number of times that I heard that the Chinese travelled this side with ease while Nepalis were forbidden from crossing over into 'their' side revealed a deeper concern about China and sovereignty. In Chhusang, the gateway to upper Mustang, locals spoke about the wealth of the Chinese ('Their border officials ride better cars than our president') and their forays into Mustang ('The border gates open only at their command, not ours') over liberal pourings of buckwheat liquor. In Lo Manthang, a local said they were afraid to go to the border. 'What if they shoot us?'

The image of trigger-happy Chinese security officials is an exaggeration,[22] but the fact that the Kora La border represents a restricted space—despite being earmarked for future connectivity—tells us how uneven the bilateral relationship currently is. Even the building of the fence was a unilateral action by the Chinese, which 'finally closed and divided a trans-border space according to the prerogatives of the Chinese side'.[23] While day visits by Chinese officials into Mustang may not always be transgressions, their officials can move in and out of Nepal with ease; Nepali officials and locals, on the other hand, cannot do so, which too is significant. A weaker, poorer state like Nepal does not have the resources to take charge of its sovereignty in the fourth-world spaces—traditional indigenous spaces that subscribe neither to modern cartographic traditions nor to modern state regulations—that are the Himalaya. Even as it strives to bring in a region like Mustang, which was once excluded from the national discourse of development, within the state's ambit through the building of roads and other institutions, it faces a global power on the other side—a behemoth with whom it attempts to carve out a relationship distinct from the one it shares with its giant neighbour to the south.

Consider the local police force in Lo Manthang. The highest-ranked officer at the moment is a sub-inspector, and they operate out of a building originally earmarked for the agriculture department. They do not have a vehicle of their own, so they borrow Chinese bikes from the locals (the police too swear by the performance of these bikes!). An official complained bitterly about the past winter, when livestock dropped dead like flies, and he and his team had to wade through knee-high snow to distant villages. 'If the state wants to maintain its presence here, it must provide us facilities,' he said. Much of the district, including the border pass, is snowed in for half the year. 'Is there a point of having a customs office if it is closed for six months of the year?'

I ask him about the stories of Chinese officials crossing over into Mustang. They do, he says, but only after taking permission from Nepali security officials. 'But there's no movement from our side.' Mustang residents should ideally be allowed to work in China, as is the case in Humla and other border districts. Here, on the other hand, the Chinese unilaterally decided this would not be the case. While no reasons are officially given, one presumes it is because of the sensitivity that comes with Mustang's history with the Khampas, Tibetan resistance guerrillas. 'Besides, the nearest big settlement is nearly sixty–seventy kilometres away from the border, and the Chinese don't allow us to travel till there,' the official said.

He tells me a story about a Chinese official who travelled to Lo Manthang without permission, and the local police detained him for about an hour before sending him back. There is a certain glee on his face as he narrates the tale—he enjoys the retelling, as if it is a form of victory over an obdurate China. 'Their border officials were afraid the matter would reach upper levels, so the official came back with an inspector to apologise and say they would take permission from now on. Then they said we needed to work together in the future.' We both laugh as we sip our sweetish black tea; in these little moments of schadenfreude, we are united as Nepalis.

✦

It is clear then that China considers the Kora La border an exceptional case, one that calls for different rules than other border crossings. 'Border citizenship at the Mustang-Tibet border is altogether different and largely a practice of containment rather than mobility,' argues Murton.[24] Such selective containment is the result of Mustang's modern history, and the unique challenges China faces in controlling its Himalayan borderlands.

In 1964, French writer Michel Peissel undertook an epic journey, trekking up to upper Mustang with his retinue. It was the peak of the armed Tibetan resistance movement, and Mustang was the guerrillas' base. 'Although the border between Chinese Tibet and Mustang is considered in Western circles to be a rigid barrier, to the inhabitants of Lo [Manthang], it is, in fact, only a vague notion. They circulate quite freely between Chinese territory and their own land; while the Khampas [Tibetan resistance fighters] and the Chinese sit on either side, armed and on the alert.'[25] The inhabitants of Mustang, Peissel wrote, were frightened by the Khampas, despite similar ethnicities. Trans-Himalayan trade had declined because of the Khampas' predilection for looting the caravans, even as magars, Khampa war camps, dotted the region. The Khampas answered Peissel's queries vaguely while pursuing him for medicines, mostly for stomach aches. The Khampas had also laid siege to village grazing grounds. Tsering, one of the porters with Peissel, complained angrily, 'They steal our cattle, take our wood, and stop us from grazing yaks on the high pastures—which they use for their own horses and yaks.'[26] Another historian, however, notes that the Khampas were supported by the Mustang king, and their relations with the locals varied. While the bridges they built over Mustang's rivers were welcomed, their demands for supplies and animals were a serious drain on local resources. But several Khampas also married Mustang girls.[27]

The first Khampas arrived in Mustang in early 1960, under the command of Baba Yeshi, a charismatic leader who would later break ranks with the movement. After escaping to Sikkim from Tibet, Yeshi flew to Calcutta to meet with CIA representatives, then went to Darjeeling and Siliguri, and thereafter, Nepal. The CIA, which had been assisting the armed resistance inside Tibet since the mid-1950s, supplied Yeshi with three radio sets in Kathmandu. 'The three radios arrived in Kathmandu in a diplomatic pouch' and were delivered to the first batch of twelve Khampa fighters who set off on foot for Mustang.[28]

By autumn 1960, several hundred resistance fighters had reached Mustang, although the CIA had only approved support for 400 fighters. In March 1961, the first airdrop was approved by then US president John F. Kennedy. Early next month, 29,000 pounds of arms and ammunition—'bolt-action Springfield rifles, plus forty Bren light machine guns and a mix of forty M1 Garands and carbines'[29]—was delivered via aircraft to Mustang. Peissel notes that the US had also attempted to set up several listening posts in Mustang, but Nepal was not in favour.[30] Khampa war camps were set up in several locations along the Nepal–China border, but Mustang was where the resistance was centred.

The choice of Mustang as the primary location for Tibetan armed resistance has long been explained as one of convenience, motivated by ethnic, cultural and linguistic similarities between upper Mustang residents, also known as Lobas, and Tibetans. Others have also argued that Mustang remained, at the time, an autonomous suzerain kingdom within the Nepali state, and 'poor transportation and communication networks severely curtailed the Nepalese government's extent of control'.[31] Such reasoning does not give a complete picture, however. It is inexplicable that Nepali authorities at the time would not know of the armed resistance, despite it being common knowledge that the Americans were airlifting supplies to the guerrillas from the Syuchatar airfield on the outskirts of Kathmandu. Tibet historian Carole McGranahan also writes that, although the Nepali government denied any knowledge of the Tibetan resistance operating from their territory, 'privately, however, the king of Nepal had first told the US government he was willing to aid the Tibetans in 1950'.[32] Tamla Ukyab, a former Nepal Home Ministry official who interrogated the Khampas after their surrender in 1974, told me some of the fighters had been in contact with Surya Prasad Upadhyay, a Nepali Congress leader who was home minister in the first elected government that was dismissed by King Mahendra in 1960.

King Mahendra was also far from unaware about the happenings in Mustang. He visited Tibetan refugee camps in several publicised visits, and even met with Baba Yeshi, the resistance commander, who 'presented the king with Tibetan ponies' at their camp. 'The King also made a speech urging the Tibetans to resist communism, which he described as the common aim of Nepal and Tibet,' writes Tibetan historian Tsering Shakya.[33] He also notes that the Nepali government had asked the Tibetans to help clear a landing strip at Jomsom, in lower Mustang, which to date serves as the only airport in the district.

Nepali anxieties at Chinese attempts to persuade ethnic groups along the border to declare for Tibet—as was seen in Limi—would have served to elicit support for Tibetan exiles.[34] An added impetus would be Chinese transgressions on the Mustang border in June 1960, when PLA soldiers shot at a Nepali contingent, killing one soldier and imprisoning ten others. The 'Mustang incident', as it came to be known, immediately made Kathmandu wary of China. Retired British General Sam Cowan points out that 'the first indication the Nepal government received of impending trouble on the frontier came from the Indian embassy on the evening of June 26'.[35] The message, radioed from an Indian Army outpost, called for troop reinforcements after the 'sudden appearance of a large number of Chinese troops on the border'.[36] On 28 June, a group of seventeen men, which included Nepali army personnel and a customs officer, left for Kora La: 'On approaching the frontier they saw what they claimed were up to 2,000 Chinese soldiers. Three hundred yards short of the border, they came under fire. Subedar Bam Prasad was killed and another man wounded . . . Ten men, including the wounded man, and the horses were taken into Tibet under PLA control, as was the body of the Subedar. Six members of the party fled the scene and were able to bring the news to the outside world.'[37]

The then Nepali Prime Minister B.P. Koirala wrote to his Chinese counterpart, Zhou Enlai, on 29 June, asking for an apology and the immediate release of the soldiers. Zhou's reply on 30 June tells us Beijing was not aware of what had happened, for Zhou wrote, 'The Chinese Government is much concerned about this and has immediately contacted the local authorities for finding out the truth of this matter . . . If the unfortunate incident of the killing of a Nepalese national referred to in Your Excellency's letter is true, the Chinese Government will express its deep regret.'[38]

At first, the Chinese ambassador to India (who was concurrently ambassador to Nepal), Pan Zili, asked Kathmandu, 'How could the Nepalis be sure that Chinese troops were responsible?', suggesting Tibetan 'bandits' could have been behind the attack.[39] China then shifted its position and argued the incident had taken place in Chinese territory, 'at about one kilometre north of the Kore Pass'. Nonetheless,

Zhou tried to mollify Koirala, saying Chinese troops had been 'careless' and expressed 'deep regret' at the incident. The presence of Chinese troops on the border was perplexing, especially as the Nepal–China agreement signed a few months earlier, in March 1960, had demilitarised 20 km of the border on each side. A declassified CIA report from the time suggests China had been extra-careful in its stance following the India–China border dispute. When troops complained, 'If the armed personnel of the neighboring country do not listen to our warnings and with great bombast and arrogance carry out aggression, what should we do?' Beijing asked them not to speculate, and if confrontations did occur, they were to 'await orders from a higher level'.[40] The incident in Mustang seemed to catch them on the backfoot, especially as Zhou wrote that they had learnt of it from foreign news reports. Further, Ambassador Pan, asking how Nepal could be sure that the Chinese were behind it, only revealed the eternal fog of uncertainty in the Himalaya, 'a neat position of defense'.[41] Beijing had information on Tibetan rebels being active in Nepal and on the Himalayan borderlands, but without any numbers. 'Such information kept trickling in from captured Tibetans . . . Whether it was exaggerated or not, this news was bound to make the soldiers nervous.'[42]

Koirala and Zhou continued to exchange letters, but the Chinese position remained unchanged: China would pay compensation for the loss of life and return the prisoners, but its troops had not crossed the border. The Chinese would not concede to crossing the border, the CIA wrote, because 'to have done so would have been tantamount to admitting that China had committed aggression',[43] an anathema to perceptions of the Middle Kingdom at a time it was accusing India of aggression on the Himalayan border. On the other hand, B.P. Koirala continued to maintain the incident had occurred within Nepali territory, and that 'nothing has given His Majesty's Government reason to change their stand that the incident took place on Nepalese territory'.[44]

Cowan argued that the Chinese account of the soldier being shot a kilometre north of Kora La was false, and that, in fact, going by photographs and maps of the terrain, the Nepali party was actually about 2 km inside of the traditional Nepal–China border at the time. The 1962 border demarcation pushed the border a further 2.77 km north of the pass.

The incident raised several questions in Kathmandu. What was the Chinese party doing so close to the border in violation of an agreement signed just a few months earlier? A scholar argued that the incident was a 'subdued but pointed reprimand' to Koirala, and 'a reminder of the ease with which China could create difficulties all along the border', as 'the Chinese had been irritated with B.P.' over his non-committal response to a Kathmandu–Lhasa road and his shoring up of his nationalist credentials by publicising the Everest dispute (see chapter seven).[45] But this may not be true, since both sides had tried to defuse the situation almost immediately, albeit in their own ways. Historian Sulmaan Wasif Khan instead suggests that Kathmandu acceded to Beijing's explanation that the PLA troops were forced to the border because of Tibetans, and told Ambassador Pan that 'they did not mind the Chinese approaching the border . . . All they asked was advance notification; they might even be able to help . . . Tibetans, by endangering Sino-Nepali friendship, had triggered diplomacy that would bring the two countries closer to one another.'[46] As we will see, this may not be entirely true either.

The Chinese explanation of Tibetan 'bandits' is not convincing, especially since Tibetan armed resistance troops had not begun arriving in Mustang in June 1960, although Kathmandu had been pinpointed as one of the centres of the resistance. However, there had been previous instances of Tibetan rebels using the Mustang route to escape, such as in 1959, after an aborted mission in Tibet.[47] Cowan argues that the deployment of troops could have been to 'secure and close the border areas as a means of signalling and establishing Chinese control'.[48] A March 1959 report by Soviet leader Yuri Andropov details Chinese fears clearly: China thought 'help to Tibet, including cannons and machine guns, is coming from India via Nepal'.[49] In the fog of the Himalaya, where borders were vague, the incident could simply have been a miscalculation by Chinese troops jittery on a border they had only come to claim a decade ago.[50]

Subsequent to the incident, however, Beijing backed down. Based on documents captured from PLA soldiers by Tibetans, the CIA wrote, 'The Mustang incident damaged Peiping's [sic] "foreign policy struggle" sufficiently to have stimulated the Chinese leaders to order the Tibet Military Region Command Headquarters to *intensify* [emphasis in original] troop indoctrination on the matter of avoiding border firefights . . . It was centered on the proposition that "defense along the Tibet border is, at present, primarily a political struggle and a struggle in foreign relations".' Beijing, the CIA wrote, argued that India would take advantage of such carelessness along the border to 'create a situation of crisis . . . develop pretexts, write many articles and whip up anti-Chinese and anti-Communist sentiment'. By exercising restraint along the border, the report said, China hoped for a 'definite foreign policy advantage' by making their 'provocations and tricks politically unfeasible'.[51]

The CIA's report, and Khan's analysis based on Chinese sources, implies that Beijing was struggling to assert its sovereignty in the Himalayan borderlands at the time of the incident. There is little to suggest China deliberately wanted to provoke Nepal; relations were stable and warm, and Koirala had recently returned from a grand state visit. Instead, the geography, a long history of fluid borders and citizenship claims in the Himalaya, and Chinese nervousness over the situation in Tibet, had forced its hand into an armed confrontation it had to back down from. 'In the Tibetan borderlands, the PRC found itself a weak state indeed—at least until 1961, when it began to cement its control over Tibet.'[52] Once Tibetan struggle against Communist rule erupted, Beijing began to increase troops and surveillance in the region, but also followed a policy of exclusion. In the Himalaya, identity had been fluid. One could be a Newar from Lhasa, a Tibetan from Mustang or simply a nomadic herder from Limi. Trade and pastoralism had followed traditional boundary markers and depended on the open borders that geography had naturally restricted to a few crossings. As Beijing's weakness in these regions became apparent, it began to clamp down on movement through the passes. The Mustang incident became a template for future Chinese operations in the Himalaya; 'the PRC was drawing a thicker, darker line of definition around itself'.[53]

Nearly forty years later, the escape of the Karmapa ensured China would continue to see Mustang as a zone of exclusion and containment, hence its unilateral prerogatives on a border area that has been, for Beijing, an irritant in its intent to secure the Himalayan frontier. Despite Chinese security concerns and unilateral moves that had disrupted traditional livelihoods in the region, however, a dirt track was brought down from Kora La to Lo Manthang on the initiative of Mustang locals in 2002, the same road that has now been widened for commercial traffic, and on which Pasang and I froze our fingers riding the much-vaunted Chinese bike. Just as in Humla almost a decade later, the first roads in Mustang did not connect to Nepal, but to China.

✦

In 1990, when King Birendra visited Lo Manthang, local villagers petitioned him for three things: 'a motorable road from Pokhara to Mustang, a public electrical scheme in Lo Manthang, and the end of the policy of restriction in upper Mustang'.[54] The villagers had asked for the same things on the king's visit five years earlier. Of the three, while the policy of restriction is still in play today—non-Nepalis have to pay a minimum of USD 500 for ten days if they wish to travel to upper Mustang—Lo Manthang was connected by a road from the south only after 2012, while China set up a 70 KW solar power plant as a grant in 2015.[55]

Between 2000–02, however, locals got together and built Mustang's first road, a 20-km dirt track to the border at Kora La, with six village development committees in the area contributing NPR 352,000 each.[56] Chinese trucks began to enter from the north, carrying construction material and consumer goods, while Nepali timber was smuggled back into Lo Manthang. 'The only tax the trucks will pay is the road toll that the DDC [District Development Committee] may soon introduce with powers from the Local Self-Governance Act.'[57]

This local initiative must be understood in the context of the semi-autonomous relationship Mustang has had with Kathmandu ever since its Tibetan kings became suzerain to the Gorkha Shahs in 1789.[58] The Mustang kings were tasked with protecting the borders with Tibet, their soldiers participated in the wars with Tibet and China and they could rule their kingdom autonomously as long as they sent their yearly tribute of NPR 929 and five horses.[59] At one point in the 1820s, Kathmandu wanted to exchange the Mustang kingdom for Burang in Tibet. Tibetan authorities were said to have considered the offer 'seriously and favourably', but the Qing in Beijing rejected the offer saying 'the territory of a kingdom cannot be exchanged'.[60] By the time the Shah kings returned to power in 1951, the Mustang kings had little authority beyond a few villages. It was only when the Khampas set up base there that Kathmandu woke up to Mustang, and forbade any foreigners from travelling to the district until 1992, when the restriction policy was modified to serve tourism goals, hence the USD 500 fee.

To be residents of such an in-between place—and not just in material terms but also geopolitically, tangled in Nepal's international forays while receiving nothing in return—is understandably frustrating. This disconnect from the larger Nepali scheme of things continues to the present day. 'What has Kathmandu done for us?' was the constant refrain I heard in Lo Manthang. One person pointed towards his solar power battery and said, 'China has done more for us than Nepal.' China also used the 2015 earthquake and blockade to deliver aid to Mustang. 'We received more sacks of cement than we had asked for. We are quite surprised by the Chinese generosity,' a government officer told a newspaper when reports emerged that China had delivered 7,800 sacks of construction material and food items against Nepal's request of 1,200 sacks.[61] Now, China's international development agency will finance fifteen pilot projects in thirteen Himalayan districts bordering Tibet, including Mustang, under the 'Northern Region Border Development Programme'. And while Kathmandu authorities are increasingly willing to accept more Chinese aid and investment in Nepal's bordering districts, 'the strings attached to Chinese aid are very much about social policies over identity, mobility, and containment that adversely and severely affect ethnically Tibetan populations', such as in Mustang.[62]

The stark difference between the outlook of Mustang residents and those from the Nepali 'mainland' was most apparent when a police official complained to me about his hardships in the district, and framed them in contrast to the supposedly easier lives of local residents. When I suggested the possibility of employing locals in the police force, he dismissed it as a bad idea. 'These guys, they will speak in their own language, and we won't even know what they are doing,' he said, referring to the use of Tibetan on both sides of the border. 'But yes, if the government can give us training in Tibetan, we can surely perform better here.' There was a similar disdain towards local residents when I asked him if Mustang residents worked in China. 'Even if they were allowed to, I don't think they will do so. There are a lot of foreign donations made to the district, and most people here work in tourism. When it's winter, they move to Kathmandu.'

Such perceptions among government employees who come to work in Mustang and other border regions like Humla underline the difference between how locals see themselves and how the Nepali state views them. For Kathmandu, Mustang is a sensitive border district susceptible to foreign manipulation, as it has been in the past. In 2009, a series of visits by the American, Chinese, Pakistani and Indian ambassadors to Mustang raised new questions about foreign interests in the district. These concerns have been heightened after uranium was discovered in the area recently.[63] But more immediately, Mustang is the site through which another Nepal–China economic linkage is to be developed, a vital cog in the quest for economic independence from India. The upshot of all this is that, although the district itself is becoming more important to the national development project, its people and their concerns remain peripheral to Kathmandu.

One evening, as it snowed outside, and the hotel owner dusted the many antiques and handicrafts in his store, we began to talk about bikas, development and the road from Pokhara. He reminisced about the years when he had to walk for a week from Jomsom with a donkey caravan to bring goods to Lo Manthang, and both of us agreed it would be a few years before the road is black-topped. A heavyset man, he had just returned to Lo Manthang after the winter in Kathmandu. 'Why should we pay taxes when the state does not provide us with anything?' he asked.

On the other hand, the police official thought the compensation that had been promised to those whose livestock had died was a terrible idea. 'Why should the state provide compensation if locals don't pay taxes on their livestock? What if the situation repeats itself next year? Can the state continue to provide compensation?'[64] But the official also acknowledged the weakness of his position when we began to talk about the bikes, and how they operated in the district without paying taxes. 'Locals are ready to pay taxes on the motorcycles. But they also want the requisite paperwork and services that come with the payment of taxes. If the state cannot provide those, how can we ask them to pay the duties?'

In Mustang and Limi, the fourth world that had been allowed to function autonomously until the early years of the twenty-first century is clashing with the objectives of the modern state. Kathmandu seeks to territorialise these border regions with direct or indirect assistance from China. In Limi, the locals negotiated their exclusive positions to subvert traditional norms of sovereignty and initiated new forms of contact with the north through trade and employment. In Mustang, on the other hand, the instruments of state authority are internationalist rather than local: a dry port, an inter-country highway and such like. The road from the south provides vehicular access to the people here, but it will affect tourism in the region, as well as the environment, and perhaps the culture too. The road from the north, despite China's policies of exclusion, reflects a propensity for modern consumption through products such as China-made bikes, TVs, alcohol, cigarettes and packaged food items. Besides, the asymmetry in bilateral relations means China will continue to hold the cards and drive home its prerogative. Despite that, infrastructure upgrades also allow locals to dream of a future when the district is vital to inter-country trade and connectivity.

At Kora La, while Pasang and I marvel at the under-construction Chinese building, we discuss what will happen when the border finally opens up to commercial and passenger traffic. 'During the 2015 blockade, LPG cylinders were selling for NPR 9,000 in Pokhara. But here, we could buy Chinese LPG for NPR 3,000 a cylinder.' Only, they could not exchange the empty cylinder for a new one—there are not very many LPG vendors around, nor was the purchase necessarily 'legal'. 'If this border opens properly,' he concludes, 'India will not be able to impose another blockade on Nepal.'

4

War and Peace

On 3 August 1792, Lord Cornwallis, governor general of the East India Company, received an urgent missive from the eighth Dalai Lama asking him not to heed Shah King Ran Bahadur's pleas. 'This man's father,' the Dalai Lama wrote, 'and he, have to this time reduced all the Rajahs round about Nepaul, and also Nepaul itself; and from his craving disposition, wants to engage in hostilities with others. Thus, in the year 1203 [1789], and the present, he has excited disputes with me.'[1]

War had broken out between Nepal and Tibet, a second time in three years, after a Qing-brokered treaty in 1789 that forced Tibet to pay tribute to the Gorkhas failed. The Gorkhalis attacked Tibet once again in 1792. 'But by the favour of God this country has the protection of the Emperor of China; accordingly, two deputies always remain here for my protection; they wrote information of this circumstance to the Emperor, who detached a large army under the command of his officers to this country . . .' the Dalai Lama wrote. 'It is the resolution of the officers sent from China, by the favour of God, to exterminate the Rajah of Goorkhali and the other chiefs.' The Company, which at the time was seeking trade routes to Tibet, was asked to refrain from assisting the Gorkhalis, 'for the Emperor is not hostile to any except the Goorkhali'.

Lord Cornwallis, in turn, wrote to Kathmandu, 'The English Company have for many years carried on extensive commercial concerns with the subjects of the Emperor of China by sea, and have actually a factory established in his dominions. I am confident that this argument will satisfy you that a compliance with your request, to assist you with a military force against the Rajah of Lassa, who is dependent on the

Emperor of China, would be not only an infringement on the general policy of the English government, but also a measure inconsistent with the connection that has so long prevailed between the Company and the Emperor.'[2] Instead, Cornwallis sent Colonel William Kirkpatrick to mediate in the dispute. But by the time the British diplomat reached Kathmandu, a treaty between the armies of the Qing and the Gorkhas had been signed near the confluence of the Betrawati and Trishuli rivers, today a dusty bustling town filled with English boarding schools, guest houses and travel agencies that advertise daily buses south to Kathmandu.

The Nepal–China war of 1792, part of the 'ten great campaigns' of the Qianlong emperor, was the fallout of a long-standing dispute over coinage and Gorkhali expansionism that spread itself over two conflicts. The war came to define the modern Himalayan political landscape in many ways. It was the first time China came to defend its outer Himalayan frontier, and reshaped the Qing view of Tibet 'from a frontier to be guarded against, or *fangbian*, to a frontier to be defended, or *bianfang*'.[3] Historian Matthew Mosca writes of the Qing government being unaware of Gorkha military expansion in Nepal at this time, believing the Malla kings continued to rule the Kathmandu valley.[4] After the war, the Qing strengthened their hold over Tibet under the amban, the Chinese emperor's representative in Tibet. 'He received full authority over all administrative, political, economic and financial affairs, and a legal status equal to that of the Dalai Lama and the Panchen Lama.'[5] Another fallout was the institution of the Golden Urn for choosing higher reincarnations, under which the amban drew the lots of the selected candidates.[6] The amban was also made responsible for Tibet's foreign affairs and correspondence with the Qing emperor. And although the authority of the ambans over Tibet gradually whittled away as Qing authority began to decline in the nineteenth century, and the twenty-nine-article ordinance that was imposed on Tibet after the war was 'observed only intermittently or nominally',[7] this reorganisation of Tibet became central to twentieth-century imaginations about the role of Tibet in the Chinese state, both to the Nationalists under Chiang Kai Shek and to the Communists under Mao.

For the Gorkhalis, the war with China marked the limits of territorial expansion to Nepal's north, a boundary that still stands. Nepal would engage in another war with Tibet in 1855–56, when the Qing, weakened by the Opium Wars and the Taiping Rebellion, were unable to come to Tibet's aid. The 1792 war would also result in eighteen quinquennial Nepali 'tribute' missions that left for Beijing until 1908, and allowed the Qing to claim Nepal as a suzerain state in 1910.[8] Nepal would reject that status, claiming the tribute missions were a sign of friendship that brought commercial benefits to the country. The East India Company's reluctance to take sides in the war made it no friends either; Tibetan markets were lost to the British until the Younghusband expedition, and the Gorkhalis refused to trust them.

The first war, between 1788 and '89, ended after China's mediation, while the second, Qing General Fuk'anggan's Nepal campaign, began in October 1791 after the Gorkhalis sacked Tashilhunpo monastery and took possession of Shigatse, Tibet's second-largest city. The conflict had begun with the issue of coinage. 'A very small quantity of specie, and that of a base standard, is current in Tibet,' wrote Englishman Samuel Turner during his stay in Shigatse in 1783–84.[9] 'It is the silver coin of Nepal, here termed indermillee.'

When Shah King Prithvi Narayan Shah conquered the valley kingdoms, he wanted to take the debased coins out of circulation in favour of pure silver coins. But the Tibetans did not accept this decision, and wanted the new coins to be circulated at par with the old ones. Negotiations had continued even after Narayan Shah's death in 1775, and while his successors inherited this problem, it was clear Lhasa was unwilling to negotiate.

By 1789, the year the Shahs decided to expand west of the Mahakali River into Kumaon, rapid Gorkhali military expansionism had brought the baise and chaubise hill principalities of western Nepal under the Shah umbrella. Under the regency of Bahadur Shah, the second son of Prithvi Narayan and uncle to the minor king Ran Bahadur Shah, the Gorkhalis had established themselves as a formidable military power in the Himalaya. When the Kathmandu court gave asylum to the Shamarpa Lama, the second-highest ranking monk in the Kagyu School after the Karmapa, 'war between Nepal and Tibet became inevitable'.[10] The Shamarpa had fled Tibet after he was denied a share of the wealth and property of the Panchen Lama, his brother, upon the latter's death.[11] 'Not only did he tell the Gorkhalis of the startling riches of Tashilhunpo to incite them to intervene in Tibet, but his very presence among the Nepalese as an honoured guest was considered an affront to . . . the regent of Tashilhunpo.'[12] But there were other longstanding irritants too. The Tibetans had been annoyed by the disruption of trade caused by the Shah expansion, as indicated in the Dalai Lama's letter, and the aggression towards Sikkim.

Kathmandu declared war on Tibet in 1788. The Gorkhalis had overrun the two key passes of Kuti and Kerung (now known as Nyalam and Gyirong, respectively, in China), and reached the outskirts of Shigatse, when Tibet sued for peace. Lhasa was aware that any Qing intervention would inevitably lead to further erosion of the Dalai Lama's authority, over and above the two ambans who 'showed neither the energy nor the desire to interfere in Tibetan affairs'.[13] But the ambans had already informed the Qianlong emperor of the Gorkhali invasion, and the emperor's aide-de-camp, Pa-chung, was sent to mediate. Accordingly, Pa-chung negotiated a treaty between the two parties that called for a new exchange rate between the old and the new coins to suit the Gorkhalis. Tibet was to continue using coins minted by Kathmandu and also pay it an annual tribute of NPR 50,001 (or 9,600 taels).[14]

The Gorkhalis were pleased. They had forced Tibet to yield to their terms. Furthermore, they had made contact with the Qing, and the first Gorkhali mission to the Qing court left that same year. But Pa-chung had deceived everyone. He had told the Qing court the Gorkhalis were sending a tribute mission when it was nothing of the sort; the Tibetans had not recognised the clause that forced them to send an annual tribute to Kathmandu; and Pa-chung had told the Qianlong emperor he had settled the incident without the loss of a single soldier. So, it was no wonder that the Dalai Lama refused to pay the second instalment of the tribute once the Qing envoy returned home.

Bahadur Shah, under whose regency the Gorkhalis would see their greatest territorial expansion, was not someone to take the insult lightly. The second Gorkhali attack began in October 1791, and while the first expedition was a punitive one, this one was intended to be definitive. The Gorkhalis would sack the Tashilhunpo monastery in Shigatse, looting its fabled gold. Two high-ranking Lhasa lamas were taken prisoner. When Pa-chung heard of the second invasion, he threw himself into the river and committed suicide, afraid his deception had now unravelled. The Qing empire knew little about the political realities south of the Himalaya, and up to the second war, only one Qing vice-commander had visited Kathmandu. Now, the Qianlong emperor sent out a large contingent of nearly 10,000 soldiers under the leadership of Fuk'anggan to push the Gorkhalis out, with provisions sufficient to feed an army of 15,000 for a year.[15] Fuk'anggan came with an impeccable military reputation; he had recently put down rebellions in Taiwan and Gansu. The very mobilisation of the troops was a massive operation, 'far more of an achievement than Hannibal's crossing of the Alps',[16] as the Qing forces entered Tibet via Xining and Sichuan in the winter of 1791. The Gorkhalis had lodged themselves at the border passes of Kuti and Kerung even as Fuk'anggan sent them terms: surrender the Shamarpa Lama, and return the two captured lamas. Kathmandu refused, and now war with the Qing was a certainty.

'The Chinese, they lost this war when they sacrificed a cow at the local Kali temple,' my hotel owner tells me in Kalikasthan. A steep climb from Betrawati, the confluence town where the Qing–Gorkhali peace treaty was signed, on a road that zigzags first through a forest of sal, then oak and finally pine, brings one to this hilltop town in Rasuwa, north of Kathmandu. Kalikasthan was earlier known as Dhaibung. This is where the Gorkhalis had maintained their position after a sharp battle at Kamaregadhi fort on a precipice to the west. 'Our troops won the battle and killed 40 or 50 of the enemy with shots and swords. A hundred or 150 (of the enemy) fell down the hill and died. The enemy then encamped at Ramche while our troops maintained position at Dhaibung,' King Rana Bahadur Shah wrote to his commanders in the west after the war.[17]

Memories of the war are now reinforced with tales of Nepali bravery and ingenuity. A popular folklore is that the Gorkhalis had attached flaming torches to livestock horns to overrun the Qing positions. While the story cannot be verified, what is certain is that the Qing army suffered massive losses this far inside Gorkhali territory. In classic mountain warfare strategy, the Gorkhalis would fall back to another higher position to the south as soon as the northern positions were overrun, while the Qing followed them. Despite overwhelming numbers, the Gorkhalis tested the enemy forces' perseverance and willingness to sustain the war, for they were in familiar territory.

Fuk'anggan's army attacked in mid-June 1792, just as the monsoons began, another home advantage for the Gorkhalis. The Qing commander centred his main attack on the route leading south from Kerung pass, while another detachment covered the Kuti pass to the east. About a thousand Gorkhali troops were centred in Kerung. 'For three days the Gorkhali defenses held out against repeated attacks, but just before dawn on the fourth day the Chinese stormed the fort, letting fly an astonishing volley of musket-shot, arrows, flaming torches and even bags of gunpowder.'[18] The Gorkhalis first withdrew to Rasuwagadhi, which today marks the international border between China and Nepal, then to Syabrubesi, where the two forces faced each other across the Trishuli river. 'There was an exchange of gunfire between the enemy and us from the two sides of the river,' wrote the king.[19] But the Qing superiority in numbers meant Fuk'anggan's forces finally crossed the river from an upstream position after nearly ten days of fighting. The Gorkhalis withdrew once more to Dhunche, where the Chinese attacked them in waves. Qing prints from the time portray their overwhelming numerical superiority against barefoot Gorkhali soldiers defending their positions. From Dhunche, the Gorkhalis withdrew to the steep outpost of Kamaregadhi, where several Qing soldiers died after falling off the hill. The Qing asked for a parley. A ceasefire was held, but the Qing overplayed their hand. They asked for talks to be held with the king himself at Nuwakot, closer to Kathmandu. 'They further wrote that if we did not allow them to come to Nuwakot and failed to withdraw our troops from the two fronts, they would come by force,' Ran Bahadur Shah wrote.[20] The Gorkhalis saw through their game and rejected the talks, preparing instead for battle. The order from Kathmandu said that the Chinese were not to cross the Betrawati river at any cost.

The Gorkhalis ensconced themselves in ridges that overlooked the Betrawati valley, while two other detachments waited downstream. As the Chinese advanced uphill, they fell into the trap. 'Rocks, boulders, logs and missiles of all kinds were thrown down the slope.'[21] Gorkhali troops then fell upon them from three sides, and the Chinese began to withdraw, much to the frustration of their generals, and 'the chief Chinese official began to kill his retreating troops'.[22] 'Of the Chinese that managed to escape across the river, two sardars had their noses cut, and they immediately jumped into the Betrabati river and were drowned.'[23] The Qing onslaught had failed, and 'the number of dead and wounded was very great', according to a Chinese chronicler.[24]

Fuk'anggan sued for peace once again, this time with finality. The war was over; Gorkhali forces had been stretched on three fronts, and they could now concentrate exclusively on military campaigns in the west.[25] Qing supply lines had been exhausted; when Gorkhali generals arrived in their camp for negotiations, they were shocked to see 'the Chinese troops were suffering from the scarcity of food'.[26]

The principal clauses of the 1792 treaty enforced the status quo that existed before the wars. Any disputes between Nepal and Tibet were now to be referred to the amban for settlement, and Nepal promised to send five-yearly missions to Beijing. Nepal returned the loot from Tashilhunpo, along with the remains of the Shamarpa Lama, who had died in the interim (some say killed). And China promised to come to Nepal's aid in the event of any foreign aggression.[27] Ran Bahadur Shah boasted to one of his chiefs before the treaty negotiations, 'The Chinese Emperor is not a small emperor but a great one. By the grace of the goddess, we could have completely driven them out this time, but we did not think it proper to create permanent conflict with the Emperor.'[28]

Conquest does not seem to have been one of the Qing objectives; in any case, it is doubtful they would have been able to hold the territory. No Chinese troops have crossed over into Nepal on a military expedition since then. It is widely believed in Nepal that the Chinese lost, conjoining it with the narrative of the war with the British, another block in the nationalist myth about bir, brave, Gorkhalis.

Today, a modern Chinese mythos is under construction in Rasuwa. One of the worst-affected districts during the 2015 earthquake, all land trade between Nepal and China shifted to the border here when the Tatopani border to the east shut down after the quake. The crossing had officially opened for commercial traffic in 2014.[29] China's infrastructural push into Nepal is best seen on the 24-km stretch between Syabrubesi and Rasuwagadhi, where China or its companies are building a border bridge, a dry port and a 110 MW hydropower project, besides paving it. Several Chinese hydropower investments are concentrated in the district, an echo of the promises of development highlighted by successive Nepali governments through hydropower generation. Men and women from Rasuwa cross over to Gyirong,[30] nearly 40 km from the border, to work, while Chinese engineers and heavy machinery operators wear masks amid the dust of the highway and go about their projects on this side. Nepali trucks wait their turn in a 3-km-long queue to cross over into China by the side of the one-lane highway. Chinese tourists walk across the bridge and jump into waiting jeeps that will take them to Kathmandu. A Nepali man runs a restaurant at the Chinese border checkpost; a Chinese departmental store owner conveys the price of walnuts in broken Nepali.

China's 'handshake across the Himalayas' has shifted the 'centre of gravity' towards Rasuwa: 'While the entry of Chinese investment and infrastructural development generates social transformation across many Nepali landscapes, the pace of Chinese intervention in Rasuwa is at an altogether different scale—largely in accordance with the accelerative thrust of hydropower and overland trade facilities taking shape throughout the district'.[31]

The memories of war are a distant remnant of the past, more folklore than history. China is the benevolent neighbour here today. It is from here that the much-vaunted railway from Tibet, should it come, will reach Kathmandu. Rasuwa is, in effect, a physical manifestation of Nepal's increasing proximity to China.

At Rasuwagadhi border crossing, which Chinese maps from the 1792 war call 'Resoqiao' or 'Iron Chains Bridge',[32] dust is the norm. The walls of the fort where Gorkhali soldiers held off the Qing army in a three-day battle were rebuilt by the Nepal Army after it collapsed during the 2015 earthquake. The region's delicate geology has been further destabilised by the earthquake. Landslides are commonplace; in Timure, about 3 km from the border, a yellow house is submerged in a sea of mud, a macabre memorial to the nine people who died in a landslide here in 2018.

The fragile geology has not stopped Rasuwa from turning into a construction hub. Land prices in Timure have shot up in expectation of the dry port that the Chinese government-owned Tibet Fuli Construction Group Company Limited plans to build here, at an estimated cost of 124 million RMB, and hand over to Nepal. Just 400 metres south of the border crossing, China International Water and Electric Corporation is the lead contractor for the 110 MW Rasuwagadhi hydropower project. The road to Syabrubesi is being built by Tibet Tinalu Company Ltd. At Rasuwagadhi itself, where the Lende River meets the muddy waters of the Gyirong Zangbo,[33] the Chinese are building a new 'friendship' bridge to replace the makeshift bailey bridge installed after the quake.[34] Just before the border post, a Chinese driver struggles to turn his excavator towards the parking bay; his gearbox is leaking oil, and every time he presses the accelerator, a cloud of dust envelops us. The sound of the river is drowned by the industrial hum of excavators, bulldozers and drills. Trucks wait their turn to cross the border into China, a queue that stretches for kilometres. 'They have to wait for days sometimes,' Krishna,[35] my driver, tells me.

We cross the border in a group of seven: a Nepali customs official posted in Timure is here with his two sons, two other locals and Krishna and I. As we walk across the bailey bridge, the difference between the two countries has never felt starker. While dust marks the Nepali side, an order fashioned out of concrete marks the Chinese one. The immigration centre and cargo terminal is new, built after the earthquake; as recently as 2006, a two-floored building marked the Chinese side.[36] 'The Chinese are able to build whatever they want to build,' Krishna says. If the Chinese intended to shock and awe, they have succeeded.

A Nepali armed police official assists us, and tells the Chinese immigration officer we are all going 'shopping'. Nepalis can cross the border to shop at the supermarkets on the Chinese side with documentation; if I had brought my citizenship card, I could get a twenty-four-hour pass that would allow me to go up to Gyirong town, about 25 kms away. But no such documents are needed here; instead, the Chinese immigration officer lines us up and clicks a picture. Once out of earshot, my driver tells me all seven of us now have to return together, else the Chinese authorities will detain us.

I take my first steps in China, marvelling at the sudden change in spatial realities. The dust and din of Nepal seems like a thousand kilometres away. Nepali trucks queue up on a massive four-lane concrete road, in a show of distinctly non-Nepali discipline. The rugged hills that are the bane of Nepali highways have been tamed by human engineering here. Behind the terminal is a three-storeyed building, the ground floors of which are taken up by departmental stores selling everything from mosquito repellents to Lhasa beer at wholesale prices, and restaurants advertising Chinese and Nepali foods. The smell of apples lingers in the air. At Bhrikuti Tara, a restaurant owned by a Nepali, I meet a few truck drivers who are bringing in the fruit from China. 'No apples are coming from India because of the Indian elections,' one of them tells me.[37]

The Rasuwa–Gyirong border crossing was the only inland trade route between Nepal and China between 2015 and 2019, when the Tatopani–Zhangmu[38] border crossing reopened after four years. While the Tatopani crossing may be closer to Kathmandu, the Rasuwa crossing allows for easier transport to Nepal's other cities. In 2018, Rasuwa exceeded its revenue collection target by 26 per cent, and at least 900 trucks carried cargo between Nepal and China. Even trucks that operated on the Tatopani border had shifted here. 'The Tatopani truck owners are ready to ferry goods for NPR 75,000–80,000 per trip because they do at least two to three trips per month. But Rasuwa locals have been demanding at least NPR 110,000 per trip,' Krishna, who also owns one container-truck, tells me. 'We've been negotiating fares. Let's see what happens.'[39] He is a part-time local politician who knows the inner workings of the system, comfortably disembarking to direct traffic at the border. He knows a Nepali woman who married a Chinese man and now lives in Gyirong, and asks me if he should buy some land in partnership with them and grow some vegetables to sell to the Chinese. 'I am sure the money will be good.' I know little about the sales potential of such a venture, but it seems like an excellent idea on paper, so I don't deter him.

The customs official who crossed over with us peeps into the shop and asks whether we intend to return soon. He is done with his shopping; he has bought walnuts, canned juice, noodles and a few things I cannot recognise. 'There's no rush. We can leave once you have finished up,' he says, and returns to his sons, who sit on the pavement outside.

Behind the shopping centre is a ridge dotted with lungtas, Tibetan prayer flags, strung up on rockfall fences. Just as we are ready to go back, Krishna rushes into a shop and emerges with a twenty-roll pack of toilet paper. 'It's much cheaper here,' he says. All of us begin comparing prices. The bag of walnuts, at NPR 400, is a steal; so is the beer at NPR 100 a can. Our little excursion into China comes to an end when the seven of us walk inside the departure building. Another official asks us to line up, looking carefully at her mobile phone, and instructs one of us to remove his cap. Once outside, we pull up our masks and cross the bridge back into dusty Nepal; almost immediately, a traffic jam greets us. A truck hired by the Nepal Army to bring back ammonium nitrate for explosives from Gyirong has blocked the way, and a police officer with greying hair is almost apoplectic with rage. As we park our vehicle to a side, one of the customs official's sons points to a Chinese man smoking by the roadside. 'Isn't he the same guy who refused us a lift yesterday?' he asks his brother.

✦

The life of a truck driver ferrying goods from Gyirong to Nepal is fraught with difficulties. The long queue of trucks waiting for their turn to cross over into China is just the beginning; the queue can take days, sometimes weeks, to clear, and drivers manage two to three round trips at most in a month. Traders, mostly Kathmandu-based, place their orders with Chinese firms based in other cities. Goods are then loaded onto Chinese trucks or a freight train that delivers them till Shigatse, currently the last railhead, and ferried to a Gyirong 'mess', where Nepali trucks take over. Once the goods are loaded, the drivers begin their long journey back home. Goods from China are said to reach Kathmandu within ten to fifteen days via the land route, while the sea route via Kolkata takes forty to forty-five days. A new freight service from Xian to Shigatse is expected to cost traders about the same as bringing in goods via Kolkata (and less time than the latter).[40]

Despite the potential of the land route via Tibet, there is much to be done before the dependence on Indian ports can be overturned. Beyond the fragile geology that disrupts traffic during the monsoons, the current road infrastructure from both Tatopani and Rasuwagadhi to Kathmandu is not conducive to the swift passage of container-trucks. Although an agreement to expand and upgrade the highway, replete with tunnels and intended to shorten the distance, from Kathmandu to Rasuwagadhi was signed during Xi Jinping's 2019 visit, the project has not seen much progress. Further, China also unilaterally disallowed the passage of goods during the COVID-19 pandemic.

When Chinese authorities shut down the border crossing due to the pandemic, nearly 1,500 containers of goods, including BCG vaccines, were stuck in Gyirong for eight months. When it did open up, Chinese contractors brought containers from Gyirong to the border in batches of five, and despite the Chinese ambassador's assurances that China had 'maintained the freight function at the border ports to our best',[41] Nepali traders were deeply frustrated at the delay in imports.[42] The costs of transport had also shot up, with traders having to pay NPR 3.5 lakh as freight charges per container between Gyirong town and the border, and each container cost anywhere between NPR 8–10 lakh to reach Kathmandu.[43]

The Tatopani crossing in the east, similarly, opened up in October 2020 after several months of shutdown, but here, too, traders reported similar problems as in Rasuwa. The closure of the borders—despite the damage wrought by the pandemic and because of China's insistence that Nepal had not established adequate screening procedures—once again highlighted the unequal nature of bilateral relations. Nepal was unable to convince China about its safety processes, and the latter ignored the fact that the Tatopani and the Rasuwa crossings had emerged as important trade routes for Nepali entrepreneurs and transporters in the aftermath of the 2015 Indian blockade.

Back in April 2019, however, these issues had not come to the forefront. At that time, when I visited Rasuwa, there was a newfound sense of importance attached to the Rasuwa crossing, especially because the Tatopani border was closed at the time. Those who drove goods back and forth from Gyirong were a busy lot; several locals, including my driver Krishna, had invested in container trucks. Through a few enquiries, I finally met with Rajesh[44] the evening before he was to leave for Gyirong. A soft-spoken man who was always brushing his curly hair away from his face, I struggled to imagine him negotiating the complications of a border crossing. 'There are regular checks on both sides of the border. I have to show my immigration pass that has full details of my residence in Rasuwa,' he said. The immigration pass is the same border citizen's card that allows residents of border districts to work and trade in China. At the Rasuwa border, only the district's residents are allowed to cross over, but 'drivers from outside have also been crossing illegally', Rajesh said.[45] China's largesse in Rasuwa is evident here too; while Humla folks can work for only six months in Burang, the Rasuwa border pass is valid for a year (although this could also be because the Rasuwa border crossing can be kept open all year-round).

Gyirong seems a world away from the dusty tracks of Rasuwa. 'After the earthquake, the Chinese have built new homes in Gyirong. It's a small town, not very big, but there are several Nepali-run hotels that are open twenty-four hours. I can drink and have fun as long as I don't create a nuisance. The Chinese prefer if we spend our money there,' Rajesh said. Cargo drivers could go till Bangxing, 5 km beyond

Gyirong, to collect goods. After Tibetan labourers loaded the trucks, the documentation was checked and the cargo sealed.

Rajesh told me China's border infrastructure was incredibly efficient. 'There's a two-lane road that easily allows two trucks to pass. They've built a proper highway with drains, walls and tunnels in sections where landslides are common.' The train is yet to reach Gyirong, but labourers have told Rajesh it would come in two years. 'No one talks about the train to Kathmandu in Gyirong,' he said. Reports suggest the Shigatse–Gyirong line will be built by 2022.

The Nepal Army has built a shorter route to Rasuwagadhi, but it is replete with stories of rocks falling on vehicles from above. I asked Rajesh about its usefulness, and he shakes his head vigorously. 'Not at all. It's a very risky road. There are rock falls through the seventeen-kilometre stretch, and there are no drains either.' Just the day before we left for the border, a truck had overturned and fallen into the river. 'The road is wider than the existing one. But they need to build drains and walls.'

Rasuwagadhi is also where the fabled train from Gyirong to Kathmandu will enter Nepal. The train, if it arrives, will render the road obsolete, but more importantly, it will signal China's ability to overcome the Himalaya as a strategic and economic barrier in the same way that the Lhasa–Kathmandu road did in the 1960s. When the Qinghai–Tibet Railway (QTR) opened in 2006, it was a huge accomplishment, a miracle of engineering with the world's highest altitude line built on permafrost. It used heat-regulating technology called thermosyphons, cooling sticks dug deep into the ground every few metres. Beijing's ambitions about a railway line in Tibet go back to the early days of the twentieth century, when Sun Yat-Sen thought a trans-Tibetan railway would strangle Britain's hold over Tibet. Mao's attempts to extend the line from Xining in Qinghai to Tibet in 1959 were interrupted by a shortage of funds and 'the Three-Year Disaster' between 1959–62, a famine that was the result of the Great Leap Forward.[46] It was not until the early years of the twenty-first century that Mao's dream would come true.

Economic considerations aside, the QTR is the culmination of more than half a century of Chinese ambitions on the Tibetan plateau.[47] When Communist forces occupied Tibet in 1950, Lhasa was better connected with India and Nepal (via the old trade networks) than with China, which galled the early leaders. They immediately went about severing the old connections in favour of the Chinese mainland, especially as the border dispute with India grew. The lack of infrastructure on the plateau limited Beijing's geopolitical ambitions in South Asia too. While Mao raised the matter of a train to Nepal during King Birendra's 1973 visit, in 1975, Deng Xiaoping, as vice-premier, told US President Gerald Ford and Secretary of State Henry Kissinger that China's role in Nepal was 'limited' at that time, but 'perhaps things will get better when our railroad into Tibet is accomplished'.[48] There is also a disconnect in how Kathmandu and Beijing each view the proposed cross-border railway. While the former sees it as a tool to extricate itself from the economic dependence on India, the latter sees it both as a tool of geopolitical power projection as well as an entry route into north India's populous markets for Chinese products. This disparity in how the two countries view the railway has been apparent since the opening of the QTR.

Kathmandu's gigantic pursuit of a train from Lhasa began in 2006. As the QTR bullet-trained its way to Lhasa, Nepal requested China to extend the QTR from Shigatse to the border in 2008.[49] However, a high-ranking Tibetan official called Nepal's request 'a beautiful dream in Nepali hearts', despite a new turn in bilateral relations post the declaration of the Nepali republic.[50] When the QTR line to Shigatse opened in August 2014, Nepali politicians continued to push China to extend it to the border and onwards to Kathmandu. By the end of that year, China agreed to extend the rail link up to the border, 'urging Nepal to conduct a feasibility study for the same within its territory'.[51]

While the April 2015 earthquake caused much of the talk between the two countries to shift towards relief and reconstruction, it was the September 2015 'unofficial' Indian blockade that gave the project a much-needed fillip. The blockade, during which China offered assistance despite logistical constraints, served as the final nail in deteriorating relations between Delhi and Kathmandu. Nepal immediately signed an agreement to import petroleum products from China, breaking India's monopoly over the supply. During Prime Minister K.P. Oli's 2016 visit to China, Nepal signed several agreements, including one to use China's ports and another to build an international airport in Pokhara. Oli pitched for Nepal's inclusion under the Belt and Road Initiative (then called 'One Belt One Road'), hailing the bilateral relationship as an 'all-weather' one. The visit ended with a joint statement that, among others, committed to 'constructing cross border railways and railways network in Nepal, and support enterprises to start related preparatory work as soon as possible'.[52]

But how much of this translates to action remains to be seen. When the first feasibility study was submitted by China CAMC Engineering Ltd in July 2016, it contained a study not just of the Gyirong–Kathmandu railway, but also one on Kathmandu–Pokhara railway. The former section was estimated to be 121 km in length, with nearly 80 km of bridges and 10 km of tunnels. In May 2017, Nepal formally joined the BRI. The train continued to remain high on the agenda of bilateral visits, especially as Nepal wanted it to come under the BRI initiative.[53] Nepali ambitions had grown; the Gyirong–Kathmandu stretch was to be linked with another proposed 945 km East–West railway network.[54] Oli's June 2018 visit then sealed an MoU on 'cooperation for railway connectivity', heralded as 'the most significant initiative in the history of bilateral cooperation' which would initiate a 'new era of cross-border connectivity between the two countries'.[55]

However, the question of funding continues to plague the project. A pre-feasibility report submitted in December 2018 estimated the train would cost NPR 3.55 billion per kilometre, or NPR 28.55 billion annually for nine years.[56] The detailed project report (DPR) itself would cost NPR 35 billion and take two years to complete. Nepal wants China to fund the DPR, but China wants it to split the bill.[57] And although the project is now one of nine listed under BRI in Nepal, there has been little progress since. There have been reports that China had offered Nepal NPR 2 billion as a grant to fund either the DPR for the Gyirong–Kathmandu railway or to fund two feasibility studies for the Kathmandu–Pokhara and Pokhara–Lumbini railways.[58] But much of the initial fervour around the train—Prime Minister Oli's primary election plank—has died down, among funding issues and worries of a 'debt trap'. There is also widespread agreement the project will not gain momentum until the Shigatse–Gyirong line is finished. What's more, the agreement to upgrade the Rasuwagadhi–Kathmandu highway is also an indication that, despite public bluster, the train to Kathmandu is not an immediate priority for Beijing.

On the Nepali side, there are a number of key issues. Apart from debt and infrastructural challenges, Nepal also has to negotiate the Chinese plan to extend the railway up to India's borders.[59] If China's end goals from the railway are to reach India's markets, a train through Nepal may not necessarily make economic sense, especially if relations between the two heavyweights continue to sour post the June 2020 Galwan violence. Further, even if a railway to Kathmandu is built, the question of what Nepal can export to China remains. And finally, as with many things related to China, the entire project hinges on Beijing's will. Nepal has admitted it does not have the requisite technical skills required to complete the project. If China believes Nepal's affiliations may be shaken by the US or by India's pushback, it may well step back and reconsider the project.

Back in Kalikasthan, Rasuwa, these intricacies of the power corridor seemed distant. Talk of the train was rather subdued. One evening, I sat with a group of locals drinking tea and asked them about it. 'We'll see when the train comes,' one of them said. 'If the Chinese build it along the river, it may be possible. Nothing seems to be impossible for them in any case.' My hotel owner, though, had other views. 'The Chinese will use the train to sell us their products and compete with India. What use will it be for us?'

In Rasuwa, the memory of a distant war has been replaced by dreams of a concrete-built and connected future. 'Bikas', a term that translates as 'development' but has come to hold greater symbolic value in Nepal as both material and physical progress, is manifested here with China's assistance. It is in Rasuwa that one witnesses the Nepali belief—that China is a 'better neighbour' than India—come true, for the infrastructure projects are framed in a narrative of overall Chinese largesse towards the country, and towards the district itself. China has opened up new economic possibilities for those who live here, and even for those who do not, like the young man in his twenties who worked at the Rasuwagadhi hydropower project and hitched a ride with us on the way back to his home in the plains—even if he did not seem too keen on returning to the job. And while the prospects of a train may excite those in Kathmandu, in Rasuwa itself, locals have already devised ways of negotiating with the economic powerhouse that is China, despite national and international concerns of the extraterritorial control Beijing may acquire through such infrastructure projects. After all, Nepal is no stranger to the promises of foreign aid. If anything, Chinese infrastructure development in Nepal has been successful even beyond the cities, as in Mustang and Rasuwa. So, as the common refrain goes, why should Nepal not accept Chinese aid if Beijing does it better than other countries?

But to understand how the two countries arrived at the modern bilateral epicentre of Rasuwa, one must turn back to the Cold War, when ideological frameworks dominated international relations, and Nepal became a battleground for various world powers, and Kathmandu began asserting its sovereignty vis-à-vis India under two successive monarchs. Nepal had to walk a geopolitical razor's edge during much of the period between 1960 and 1990: suspicions of communist infiltration; the politics around foreign aid; Tibetan guerrillas funded by the CIA operating out of its soil; India-based anti-monarchy movements; and the newfound Sino-American 'friendship' that drastically changed the South Asian worldview.

Part Two

IN THE SHADOW OF EMPIRES

'What has made it impossible for us to live in time like fish in water, like birds in air, like children? It is the fault of Empire! Empire has created the time of history. Empire has located its existence not in the smooth recurrent spinning time of the cycle of the seasons but in the jagged time of rise and fall, of beginning and end, of catastrophe. Empire dooms itself to live in history and plot against history. One thought alone preoccupies the submerged mind of Empire: how not to end, how not to die, how to prolong its era.'

– J.M. Coetzee, *Waiting for the Barbarians*

5

Communism Comes by Road

In January 1952, a ragtag group of Nepalis, led by a portly man with a walrus moustache, made their way up from Rasuwa into Tibet. The group was severely unequipped for the altitude; at least five would die before reaching their destination. Their leader, Kunwar Inderjit Singh — or Dr K.I. Singh, as he is known in Nepal — had just attempted a coup in Kathmandu. His followers had broken him out of jail and captured several government offices. A few years previously, he had obtained the moniker 'Robin Hood of the Himalayas' for redistributing land to peasants during the 1950 revolution. When Singh's coup failed, after the government refused to negotiate on his demands, he and his group of revolutionaries abandoned Kathmandu and took the road north.

Singh reportedly walked about town in Kathmandu carrying 'a pair of six-shooters and cradling a 12-gauge shotgun in his arms'.[1] Before the 1950 revolution, he had fought for the short-lived Indian National Army and been discharged, fleeing Burma to practise homeopathy in Nepal (hence the title 'Doctor'). He joined the Nepali Congress and participated in the 1950 revolution, commanding the assault around Bhairahawa, to the west of Kathmandu. When the revolution was called off after a tripartite compromise, known as the Delhi Agreement — negotiated by Jawaharlal Nehru between Rana Prime Minister Mohan Shamsher, Shah King Tribhuvan and the Nepali Congress–K.I. Singh refused to fall in line. 'I will not cease fire until I can fulfil my goal of taking Bhairahawa,' B.P. Koirala, Nepali Congress leader and ideological fount of the 1950 revolution, quotes him as saying.[2] Eventually, Singh was arrested in 1952 by Indian security forces sent into Nepal 'at the request of the Nepali government' and brought to Kathmandu, where he was imprisoned.[3]

The revolution, which marks the beginning of Nepal's modern political history, was at best an incomplete one. The Delhi Agreement had emerged out of a consolidation of external diplomatic support behind King Tribhuvan against the Ranas. The Nepali Congress had initiated an armed insurrection from India as Delhi turned a blind eye to its activities. Indian Prime Minister Jawaharlal Nehru, aware of the need for stability on newly independent India's northern frontier, wanted a peaceful resolution that suited his foreign policy goals. 'It is quite impossible for Nepal to continue under Rana regime as before,' Nehru wrote to V.K. Krishna Menon on 20 November 1950.[4] In another letter to Home Minister Govind Ballabh Pant, he wrote, 'We do not suggest that the entire structure of the Nepal government should be changed.' What he wanted was an 'interim arrangement', India's 'desire being rapid restoration of peace and stability'.[5] The Delhi Agreement thus retained a few of the older Rana autocrats in a power-sharing arrangement with members of the Nepali Congress, while the Shah king returned to his status as head of the country.

Such an unruly coalition as a government was never going to work. The disgruntled Ranas, who now had to share power with ordinary folks, formed their own political party called the Gorkha Dal, which staged numerous demonstrations and even attacked Koirala inside his own office. The Nepali Congress, in turn, organised its militia into an armed group called the Raksha Dal, but the disaffection that was the result of a fizzled-out revolution had already spread. A fringe group within the Raksha Dal stormed government offices, telecommunication authorities and artillery stores on the night of 21 January 1952, and released several Congress members, including K.I. Singh, whom they acknowledged as their leader. After Singh failed to convince the government to yield to him, the 'Robin Hood of the Himalayas' arrived in Tibet with thirty-seven of his followers, '19 rifles and 500 bullets', Zhou Enlai, the Chinese premier, told Jawaharlal Nehru in October 1954. 'We immediately disarmed them, gave them asylum according to international practice . . . But if he engages in any activity for overthrow of Nepal government we would not allow him to do so.'[6]

The Chinese were as surprised to see Singh, having arrived in Tibet a few months earlier themselves. The PRC had not even established diplomatic relations with Nepal yet, so when Kathmandu demanded Singh's extradition in February 1952, local authorities in Shigatse simply referred the case to Beijing. 'The Chinese seemed at a loss as to what to do about Singh and his men, particularly as the Nepalese government, still treating the Tibetan government as an autonomous entity, communicated only with Tibetan officials in their effort to locate and repatriate Singh.'[7] Nepal continued to regard Tibet as an independent nation; Lhasa had been sending a yearly tribute to Kathmandu under the terms of the 1856 treaty.

Why Singh chose to go to Tibet is still a mystery. But '[t]he sheer audacity of the escape combined with Singh's larger-than-life personality fueled wide-ranging rumors' about him attempting a revolution in Nepal with China's help.[8] Over the next five years, his career trajectory would see him being labelled as a revolutionary, a communist, a populist and a rebel, before he finally became prime minister of Nepal.

✦

For more than a hundred and fifty years after the 1792 war, Nepal's contacts with China were limited to five-yearly missions—interpreted as tributes by Beijing and trade missions by Kathmandu—that continued till 1906. In the next few years, the dying Qing empire resurrected its claims of suzerainty over Nepal on the basis of these missions, and the fact that most Nepali rulers had vied for Chinese titles. But British might was now the foremost power in Asia, and backed by Calcutta, Rana Prime Minister Chandra Shamsher successfully warded off such claims and asserted Nepal's independent status. Further, the British told the Qing in 1911 'they will be bound to resist any attempt on the part of the Chinese Government to impose their authority or in any way to intervene' in Nepal or Bhutan.[9]

With the fall of the Qing in 1911, and the 1923 treaty with the British that explicitly recognised Nepal's independent status, Kathmandu was more circumspect about dealing with republican China. Under the Guomindang regime, Nepal received four missions between 1930 and 1946, but these did little to update relations between the two countries. The October 1949 victory of the communists under Mao Zedong did not improve matters either; in 1939, Mao had listed Nepal among the states paying tribute to China and taken away 'forcibly' by Britain.[10]

Such claims fogged Kathmandu's views of Beijing under the communists. Both the democratic socialist Nepali Congress and the monarchy had a dim view of communism. Reports emerged that new

Chinese maps included Nepal as part of China. Within the subcontinent too there was distrust, with fears that Nepali communists had been trained by their Indian counterparts.[11] All of this fed into a larger paranoia against communism fuelled by Cold War geopolitical rivalries.

Nepal had been fertile ground for communist ideals since the 1930s. Pushpa Lal Shrestha, one of the country's pioneering communists, translated the *Communist Manifesto* into Nepali in 1949. Revolutionaries dissatisfied with the Nepali Congress's anti-Rana movement and their democratic socialism became the first communists; 'they discussed among themselves three possibilities for giving the idea an organised shape: work as a Left group inside the Nepali Congress; organise as a workers-peasants party; form a communist party in Nepal'.[12] They decided on the last tactic, and formed the Communist Party of Nepal in April 1949, and brought out their first publication, *Communist Pachik Prachar Patra* (Communist Fortnightly Bulletin), on 15 September 1949. The date was chosen to mark the anniversary of the Kot Massacre, which had brought the feudal Rana dynasty to power a century earlier. The communists, who opposed the Delhi Agreement and India's intervention, called for a constituent assembly, 'determined to defeat the conspiracy of the king who was bent upon consolidating his position'.[13] But the Nepali Congress had aligned themselves with the monarchy, and so, the communists came to be regarded as an anti-monarchy force. The spectre of communism came to haunt Nepali rulers. Singh's escape into Tibet even before China had established relations with Nepal would give birth to conspiracies about communist takeovers. His attempted coup would also result in the nascent Communist Party being outlawed for three years.

Rumours emerged of an insurrection headed by Singh and backed by Beijing; the *New York Times* reported he was 'formulating plans for 'liberation' of the kingdom.[14] A declassified CIA report on Pakistani newspapers tracked communist China's 'intentions' in the Himalaya between August and October 1952. *Tameer*, a Rawalpindi newspaper, had reported on the arrest of fourteen individuals in Nepal on charges of smuggling arms into the country. 'The men confessed that Dr K.I. Singh . . . had sent them on their mission . . . [T]he rebel band had a complete plan for establishing a separate government in the northern part of Nepal.'[15] By November 1953, according to the CIA, Singh and his followers were in a village near Tradum in Tibet, where 'the Chinese

Communists had established for him a headquarters where he could organize and train Nepali Communists' in two training camps, both headed by 'Chinese Communist army officers'.[16]

But Singh's communist credentials were, at best, a veneer. From Lhasa, he moved to Chengdu, Sichuan, where, 'according to Chinese accounts, he repeatedly compared his journey from Kathmandu to China as his own personal "Long March", asking on his arrival to be taken to Beijing to meet with Mao Zedong'.[17] The request would not be fulfilled. Singh would go to Beijing in May 1953, where he would meet with a few minor officials, the Chinese treating him as a political fugitive rather than a revolutionary. 'There also does not seem to be any evidence that they contemplated at any point benefiting from his presence in fomenting communist activity in Nepal.'[18] In 1954, after China had signed the Panchsheel Agreement with India, Zhou Enlai summoned Singh to Beijing and told him in no uncertain terms that China would not send any soldiers to Nepal. When Nehru returned from China in November, he said, 'I do not think K.I. Singh will function in future.'[19]

At the Bandung Conference in April 1955, when twenty-nine nations—including Nepal, India and China—of Asia and Africa came together in a rare moment of Third World solidarity, Zhou conveyed to the Nepalis that Singh was anxious to return to Nepal, provided he and his followers were not victimised. Shortly after Nepal and China agreed to establish diplomatic relations in August 1955, the Himalayan Robin Hood was pardoned by King Mahendra and returned home to a hero's welcome. An archival photograph of this return shows him standing tall in a Willys jeep amid a sea of supporters, with the caption noting 'a huge parade was held in [his] honor'.[20]

Mahendra would appoint K.I. Singh as prime minister in July 1957 and then casually dismiss him four months later, just as he did with Nepal's first elected government in 1960 to institute the autocratic Panchayat system of governance and consolidate power in the monarchy. Despite Singh's revolutionary antecedents, rather than being seen as a communist, he has come to perhaps symbolise the ideological fluidity that is the hallmark of modern Nepali politics. After being elected prime minister, he told the Americans he was not a communist, and that when he was in China, he had had to 'behave in a manner pleasing to his hosts'. Now he was anxious to keep the Russians and the Chinese out of Nepal.[21] While reassuring the monarch that China had no designs on Nepal, Singh now began to argue for closer relations with India—in direct contrast to his earlier opposition to Delhi. But Nehru would consider him 'a rather mysterious person [who] may create trouble',[22] and 'not a communist—just a freebooter'.[23]

Why China did not simply hand Singh back to Nepal when he first arrived in Tibet is puzzling. Was he to be a key as Beijing approached Kathmandu to re-establish diplomatic relations?

✦

Under Mao, China had two distinct approaches to South Asia, the change pivoting on the Tibet question. While pragmatism was the hallmark of China's 'grand strategy'—national objectives that are pursued via 'different forms of power'[24]—in the 1950s, the PRC followed a moderately internationalist foreign policy outlook as it sought to secure the new state. When the PRC was established, it was a country with few allies. The US did not trust it, especially when it entered the Korean War. '[T]he terror, the close alliance with the Soviets, and the sense of futility and loss in the American decade-long support for [republican] China came together to construct a view of the country as the most vicious son of the depraved Communist family of nations.'[25] Further, in a post-colonial world, the Americans thought China, as a non-white country, could influence newly independent Asian and African nations to the dark side of communism better than the Russians could. But the Chinese also did not want to be secondary to the Soviets. 'Mao sought to shift the basis on which communist countries related to the Soviet Union from one of subservience to equality.'[26] Mao wanted to break away; the death of Stalin, he said, was like getting out of a straitjacket.[27]

China was on the lookout for friends—not necessarily allies, but states it could reason with. 'Ideology only went so far; one could compromise on it to retain friendship in an important neighbourhood.'[28] This was evident in the early days of China's relationship with Nepal. Despite the hiccups posed by Singh's presence in Tibet, Beijing did not lose sight of the end goal, which was to reignite bilateral relations with a country that would be important in legitimising its rule over Tibet. After all, Tibet's treaties with Nepal could be interpreted as Tibet being a sovereign state independent of China. Thus, China acceded to Nehru's keen interest in keeping Nepal within India's sphere of influence. In October 1954, Zhou also agreed to Nehru's suggestion that the Chinese ambassador to Delhi would serve concurrently as ambassador to Kathmandu. A few years later, he would tell B.P. Koirala that China would not match India's aid grants in Nepal because it did not want to be seen as a competitor.

This measured approach, however, began to wither as China's mistrust of India on the question of Tibet grew. Even as India–China relations deteriorated, Mao and the Soviets began to quarrel. After the Dalai Lama found refuge in India and Nehru began to show intransigence on the border, China sought Soviet support on the impending clash with India. But Soviet premier Khrushchev pinned the conflict on the Chinese. 'If you will allow me to say what it is not permitted for a guest to say, the events in Tibet are your fault. You ruled in Tibet and should have had your intelligence agencies to know the Dalai Lama's plans and intentions . . . What do you want, that we approve your conflict with India? That would be stupid of us,' he told Mao and Zhou in October 1959.[29]

The Chinese bristled at this. The break between the two communist empires finally came on 16 July 1960, when Moscow withdrew all 1,400 Soviet advisors from China. Mao, who saw himself as the true heir to Stalin, chafed at Moscow's control over the international communist movement. As India–China tensions grew, China would grow magnanimous in the border demarcation with Nepal (and Burma) to show that it was India at fault on the contentious border. 'Nepal was accorded even more treatment as a completely independent country than ever before.'[30]

The 1962 India–China war came at a crucial period of international geopolitics: Moscow was in the thick of the Cuban Missile Crisis, and sought Beijing's support on the issue. And Beijing did align with the Soviets, but it also launched the war against India even as the Cuban stand-off continued. For Mao, it was about making Indians respect Chinese interests. 'Since Nehru sticks his head out and insists on us fighting him, for us not to fight him would be discourteous. Courtesy means reciprocity,' he said.[31]

By 1963, however, Mao's attention shifted to the assertion of China's claims over parts of eastern Siberia 'as part of his competition with Moscow within the international communist movement',[32] and to gaining the sympathy of communist parties across the Third World.

When the Soviets and the Americans signed the Partial Test Ban Treaty in July that year, China believed the treaty intended to oppose its pursuit of nuclear weapons. As Mao's China became increasingly inward-looking, isolating itself from international affairs, the ideological shift towards greater radicalism would manifest in China's foreign policy too. By 1965, Mao believed in exhorting left radicalism in other Third World countries to 'create a new centre in international affairs'. 'China would support revolutionary groups in other countries, but only if they recognized Mao's strategic genius first,' wrote historian Odd Arne Westad.[33]

In Nepal, the Chinese brand of communism would travel by road—perhaps not in a taxi cab, as king Mahendra had quipped, but travel it would.

✦

In 1976, Agni Sapkota was a teacher in a primary school in Bogchen village, near Tatopani on the Nepal–China border, five hours east of Kathmandu. Schoolteachers are usually respected authorities in villages across Nepal, and Sapkota, who neither drank nor smoked, was especially so. He had enrolled forty-six students at the primary school, an impressive number in view of the country's low school-enrolment rates at the time. Pleased by his performance, the education department called him to Kathmandu for a training programme. 'I was happy in Bogchen. I didn't want to go for the training. But my bosses said I'd lose my job if I didn't turn up,' Sapkota said.[34] As the training continued, the news of Mao's death broke. 'I remember we were all eating dal–bhat when we heard the news. Our hands stopped midway to our mouths; it felt as if the earth had stopped revolving. Although we respected all Chinese leaders from the time of Sun Yat-Sen, Mao commanded a deep reverence from us all.'

Sapkota would go on to join the communists in 1979. As Nepali communist parties underwent several splits over the years, the result of ideological differences, a strain was growing more radical, disappointed and disgruntled by how parliamentary parties had given in to constitutional monarchy after the 1990 revolution. On 12 February 1996, radical Nepali Maoists declared a people's war—Sapkota among them. More than twenty years later, he would be elected speaker of a republic Nepal's Parliament.

Sapkota, who was born in Sindhupalchowk, a district that borders China, had his first glimpses of Chinese communism during the construction of the road from Lhasa. 'The highway construction site wasn't too far away from my village. There was a place called Dumre near Balephi, where the Chinese would put up operas and theatre, with young Chinese actors performing in them. Those really touched me,' he said. Mao's brand of communism would leave its imprint on thousands of Nepalis across the country, and eventually spark the ten-year-long civil war, during which China would deride the rebels as bandits. But it was too late; Maoism had come to represent an egalitarian dream in an unequal nation as far back as the 1960s, when the road from Lhasa began to make its way down to Kathmandu.

The story of the Lhasa–Kathmandu road begins with Mahendra's seventeen-day state visit to China in September 1961. Just nine months previously, he had imprisoned the elected government of B.P. Koirala as well as the leaders of several other political parties, and assumed direct control under the Panchayat system. Communist leaders were a notable exception to the slew of imprisonments—a result of pressure from the Sino-Soviet bloc, according to the CIA,[35] and possibly as a hedge against the Nepali Congress, whose remaining leaders had initiated an armed rebellion in the south of the country from their base in India.

China had maintained a discreet silence on the coup. Its ambassador 'reportedly extended his government's congratulations' shortly after Koirala's ouster to 'take advantage' of Mahendra's suspicions of India and 'lack of sophistication in international affairs'.[36] Mao was happy to work with a feudal regime in Nepal. '[D]eferential treatment of the Nepalese was used to increase the degree of their anti-Indian sentiment, and several Chinese leaders indicated their awareness of the power of flattery. They made political gains by convincing Nepalese officials that only fair-minded leaders of a big country would respect the sensibilities of leaders of a small country.'[37] Beijing increased its aid to Nepal, with NPR 35 million granted in both cash and commodities to pay for Chinese projects in Nepal. Between the years 1956 and 1973, China would disburse nearly USD 98.7 million in aid to Nepal, 44 per cent of it as grants—the highest proportion among all Chinese aid recipients.[38] This aid was linked to reducing Indian influence, apart from other strategic interests. To this end, China delinked its aid from any overtly political gains—unlike Indian aid, which was perceived as likening Nepal to being a part of India. 'The Indian inability to think of Nepal as a separate entity with the desire to go its own way was at the heart of the resentment in Nepal that severely crippled the Indian aid programme.'[39] On the other hand, 'China rendered its aid with great fanfare and made the conditions of its grants as attractive as possible, without regard to what this might do to the economic utility of the aid.'[40] In choosing to build a cement factory, a paper mill and a shoe factory as part of one of its first-aid packages, China was also being seen as helping Nepal lessen its dependence on Indian imports.[41]

The most important of China's aid projects in the country at the time was the Lhasa–Kathmandu road, which Mahendra agreed to on the last day of his 1961 visit, and as significant a deal both geopolitically and infrastructurally as the now-proposed train to Kathmandu. While Liu Shaoqi, the third most powerful man in the Chinese Communist Party, told the Pakistani ambassador in September 1962 that Nepal had requested China to build the road,[42] most accounts suggest that it was China that first pushed for the road. Although Zhou had remarked at a reception in Kathmandu during his April 1960 visit about 'possibilities to establish direct traffic contact' between Tibet and Nepal, B.P. Koirala, in a May 1960 interview, denied he had received any proposals on the road. 'Such a project will be initiated when our trade with Tibet grows to such an extent as would justify a road,' he told a reporter.[43]

Rose argues Mahendra did not want to sign on the agreement himself because of the displeasure he knew it would cause Delhi, and because he wanted to show his 'dissatisfaction with the pressure tactics which, according to some sources, the Chinese had employed in obtaining his assent to the road agreement'.[44] China had allegedly sprung the road agreement on him just a day before, and Mahendra was in no position to refuse it. Beijing agreed to provide the money for construction, as well as the required experts, technicians and equipment.

Sulmaan Wasif Khan argues that the Lhasa–Kathmandu road was critical for China to ensure food security in Tibet, which depended on imports from India at the time, and had been facing crippling shortages because of Mao's disastrous economic programmes. India had put an embargo on all trade with China in 1960. 'With a bit of luck, some of the trade with India could be replaced by an increased exchange with Nepal.'[45] Beijing had been facing 'chronic difficulties' in maintaining supply lines in Tibet, with roads via Sichuan and Qinghai—already a geographical nightmare to build and maintain—under pressure from the armed Tibetan rebellion. Another road to Tibet, via Aksai Chin, crossed disputed territory with India.

There had been another Himalayan road in the works since 1959, when Pakistan drew up plans for a trans-Karakoram highway linking Pakistan-administered Kashmir to Xinjiang. However, work on it began only in 1967. When the highway opened in 1971, it became the second Chinese road to cross the Himalaya after the Arniko Highway, as the Kathmandu–Lhasa road came to be called in Nepal, named after the thirteenth-century Nepali architect who travelled to the court of Kublai Khan.

The Kathmandu–Lhasa road was initially meant to cross the Himalaya via Rasuwa. But Mahendra insisted on the longer Kodari route in the east. India was deeply troubled by the news, although it made no official protests. Speaking in the Rajya Sabha, the upper house of Indian Parliament, in December 1961, Nehru said that, when he heard about the road, 'we did not like it; it opened out possibilities which were not desirable, apart from everything else, from the point of view of smuggling goods from India via Nepal to Tibet, goods we had forbidden the export of but could go through Nepal. We pointed this out to the Nepal government, and there the matter stands. We cannot order them about in this matter, but to say that they have not consulted us is partly true and partly not so; that is, from time to time, they talk generally about these matters, but about these specific matters there was no reference to us.'[46]

For Mahendra, any initial hesitation about the road soon paled before the potential benefits it could deliver. For one, a highway independent of Indian control meant greater leeway in Nepal's traditional dependence on India. In interviews, however, he argued that the highway would be strictly an economic link: 'I do not understand the great importance attached to this road. There already are some 50 trails used by traders between Nepal and Tibet, using yaks and ponies or on foot. One of these is to be widened to take vehicles. One road will not make that much difference . . . China offered to help build the north-south road and I saw no reason not to accept.'[47] Mahendra expected the road would revive some of the older entrepôt trade between Nepal and Tibet, which did not happen, nor could Nepal supplement food supplies in Tibet as China had expected. But more than any economic linkages, what the road signalled was a shift in the geopolitical balance of South Asia, and China's abilities to cross the Himalaya. In essence, it was a counter to Nehru's ideal of the Himalaya being India's natural frontier. In November 1961, the *People's Daily* 'observe[d] with satisfaction' India's displeasure at the road; China would 'aspire to detach' Nepal from India.[48]

As for whether there would be any military advantages from such a road, a Chinese defector who had worked on the highway reported that, although the construction agreement had stipulated bridges that could bear loads of 15–17 tonnes, the bridges could bear up to 60 tonnes.[49] And even as other Chinese aid projects in Nepal floundered, the road moved ahead at an excellent pace. Chinese engineers began the survey in March 1962; by the end of the year, the team had almost finished. By May 1967, the highway was open for commercial traffic.

✦

Although Mahendra remained wary of China under Mao — 'We are a monarchy and believe in God. China is Communist and anti-religious,' he told a journalist in a February 1962 interview[50] — he encouraged Nepali communists to isolate the Congress in domestic politics. Further, he also encouraged their turn towards the CCP. In August 1964, Keshar Jung Rayamajhi, a communist leader with a pro-Soviet tilt who in the latter half of his career would grow close to the monarchy, complained to the Americans that 'the King was pressing him to support openly the CCP', with the Chinese ambassador himself telling Rayamajhi to abandon the Soviets.[51] Rayamajhi remained unmoved, but the Sino–Soviet break-up would split the communist movement in Nepal too. In early 1965, forty-five Nepali communists were trained for four weeks 'under cover of the Kodari road project'.[52] In 1968, Pushpa Lal Shrestha was elected secretary of the majority faction that supported the CCP line.[53] Those who followed him included future prime minister, Manmohan Adhikari, who had been released from jail after he took a pro-monarchy line. Despite several splits in the next few decades, Nepali communism continued to carry a strong strain of Chinese influence, especially the revolutionary side of it. Inspired by the 1967 Naxalite revolution in India, a group of communists would kill eight landlords in eastern Nepal in 1971. Among these revolutionaries was nineteen-year-old Khadga Prasad Oli, who would be imprisoned for fourteen years, until 1987. 'We were drawn towards the Naxalites, so a new movement in Nepal began in 1970. Also the Cultural Revolution had an effect on us. We hadn't studied Marxism. So we just followed the line of the Cultural Revolution, but it was a mistaken path,' Oli would later admit in a 2003 interview.[54]

Chinese communist literature had entered Nepal as early as 1950. Historian Julia Lovell quotes Comrade Rohit, a left politician since the 1950s, as saying that he read *The Life of Mao* as a child. 'I learned about Mao's love of serving the people, his patriotism, the way he brought China forward,' he told Lovell.[55] For Nepalis, caste-based hierarchies and inequalities came to represent the feudalism they had to battle, and India was the imperialist coloniser they must resist. Sapkota told me Chinese workers had distributed *Chin Sachitra* ('China Pictorial') and Mao's Little Red Book during the construction of the Arniko Highway.[56] A leading Nepali intellectual also recalled how, when he started a children's library in his school in the 1960s, he wrote to several embassies in Kathmandu asking them for reading material. 'Only the Chinese and the Soviet embassies responded, by sending us *China Pictorial* and *Soviet Union Illustrated*.'[57] Others have documented how translations of Maxim Gorky's *The Mother*, which remains one of the most widely available translated world classics in Nepali, and other revolutionary texts were widely available in Kathmandu during the days of the Panchayat.[58] 'For those who did not leave the country, but grew up under the Panchayat regime (1960-1990) it was often the visions of a communist alternative circulated in highly subsidized Chinese, Russian, and Korean imprints that were influential.'[59] One activist recalled that, until 1962, Soviet progressive writing was widely available in Nepal, but it changed thereafter. 'There wasn't much Chinese influence—that only really started after 1962.'[60]

Nepali Maoists like Sapkota came to regard the Cultural Revolution in China as 'a pinnacle of revolutionary achievement'.[61] '[T]he ideals of personhood among young guerrillas in Nepal as well as their understanding of how one becomes a genuine communist are rooted in the Maoist doctrine, in an ethical universe constructed several decades ago by Maoists in China.'[62] The old texts that encapsulated the Chinese revolution—*Bright Red Star* by Li Xintian primary among them—were held up as models of revolutionary ideals, and the longstanding cultural myth of 'bir Nepali' was incorporated within the guerrilla ethos. 'Maoists showed remarkable continuity with that part of historical discourse',[63] and incorporated similar propaganda tactics to win the support of locals to build their 'Martyrs' Road' in western Nepal, honouring fallen Maoist soldiers, as those used by the Chinese during the building of the Arniko Highway.[64]

By 1965, the CIA thought, the Chinese had 'infiltrated agents into key government positions' and 'expanded their control over the small and divided Communist Party of Nepal'.[65] A limited Chinese presence in Nepal was welcomed by several non-communist leaders as a way to limit Indian influence. On Mahendra's balancing act between India and China, the CIA report suggested that, although the king 'fears the Chinese', he 'probably feels' that both countries posed an equal danger to Nepal's independence. But the Chinese had acted with propriety, and China's industrial strength and intellect was considered 'superior' to the Indians. Relations between Nepal and China had stiffened after Kathmandu reneged on an agreement with China to build a USD 20 million highway in the south of the country after pressure from Delhi, instead handing over the project to India and the US in 1964. However, 'restraint and tact in dealing with the sensitive Nepalese' had won them friends.[66]

A second undated CIA report said the Chinese had spent money 'liberally' in making friends in Nepal; 'in this they have had the greatest success among the students, who number fewer than 10,000 but constitute a real political force'.[67] Mao badges were commonly worn by students at Tribhuvan University, Nepal's largest. Much to the chagrin of the CIA author, 'American officials here lack money to counter the propaganda' and 'when the American embassy turned down a request from the Nepalese government for grains on the grounds that Nepal is not a deficit country, the Chinese stepped in within six weeks with an offer of 20,000 tons of rice'.[68]

In 1967, construction of the Pokhara–Naubise Highway began; another Chinese aid project that would connect Nepal's second-largest town to the capital. Known as the Prithvi Highway today, during its construction, 'at night, with the day's work finished, the Chinese pack the ground in front of a stage with Nepalese from nearby villages. Dancers leap across the stage beneath a huge portrait of Mao . . . When it all ends, the Chinese, who live at the camp's rude barracks, circulate through the audience distributing Mao badges and Mao's sayings. When another length of the road is completed, the whole camp, including the theater, is dismantled and set up again at the head of the road.'[69]

The Cultural Revolution had arrived in Nepal. 'Nepali workers, it was claimed, were forced to salute Mao's portrait and chant slogans praising him before they received their wages.'[70] Mao badges were so ubiquitous on the Arniko Highway that 'even a beggar' wore them.[71] Communism was travelling down the road, with '10 to 15 bags of mail a day' coming through Kodari carrying CCP literature. At the inauguration of the Arniko Highway in May 1967, a Chinese newspaper claimed Nepalis had shouted praises of Mao. A Nepali newspaper countered, 'Nobody else heard the Nepalis present on the occasion praising Mao as the "red sun".'[72] Nepal then responded with its own 'Mahendra button', which the Austrian anthropologist Haimendorf saw Nepali trans-Himalayan traders wearing in Humla in 1972.

In June 1967, Chinese embassy officials and aid workers began shouting anti-India, anti-US and pro-Cultural Revolution slogans at the Kathmandu airport when a flight carrying two Chinese diplomats expelled from New Delhi was diverted. Nepal warned the embassy that their officials must abide by Nepali regulations if they wanted to remain in the country. The government encouraged the press to print articles critical of Chinese activities. The cult of Mao was to be censured. Next month, at a fair held to celebrate Mahendra's birthday, the Chinese stall was attacked by Nepali students who objected to the absence of Mahendra's portrait next to Mao's. The protestors stoned an embassy jeep and attacked the Nepal–China Friendship Library. 'One mob marched from the fairgrounds to the center of town, throwing books of quotations from Mao onto the street.'[73] With hardliners at the helm of foreign policy, the Chinese responded strongly, blaming the US, India and Nepal. It was not until mid-August that China's accusatory tones were subdued, and Zhou personally wrote to Mahendra. Nonetheless, Nepal set up a Foreign Ministry committee to oversee Chinese and Soviet officials in the country.

It was in the midst of this newfound Chinese aggression towards foreign powers that eleven foreign missions in Beijing (including Nepal's) were attacked by Mao's Red Guards between January and August 1967. In many ways, China's Nepal policy in these years paralleled its Myanmar policy. There too, 'ethnic Chinese students in Rangoon began wearing Mao badges and propagating Mao Zedong thought'.[74]

Chinese foreign relations 'came to a standstill' during the Cultural Revolution years, as the country turned more xenophobic and '[a]ll that was foreign was viewed with suspicion'.[75] The revolution was meant to be exported. 'Starting in the early 1960s and continuing through the 1970s, the CCP gave substantial material and political support to [communist-led revolutionary movements]: training, radio stations, sanctuary and refuge in China, declarations of support, propaganda about revolutionary successes, in some cases money, arms, and in one case, even Chinese volunteers.'[76] It also began providing support to the many insurgent groups active within India's volatile northeast, like the Nagas and the Mizos, just as it had done in Myanmar.[77] By the end of 1967, China supported or endorsed armed revolutions in twenty-nine countries. Indian revolutionaries also found support in China, with a most curious tale emerging from Kanu Sanyal, one of the founders of the country's Naxalite movement, that would see him travel from Calcutta to Beijing via Kathmandu. Once again, communism would ride the Arniko Highway.

✦

The Naxalbari revolution was born in 1967 when a group of peasants attacked a landowner in Naxalbari in West Bengal, India. China was pleased; an editorial in the *People's Daily*, the voice of the Chinese Communist party, said, 'A peal of spring thunder has crashed over the land of India . . . The spark in Darjeeling will start a prairie fire and will certainly set the vast expanses of India ablaze.'[78]

In September that year, Sanyal proposed that the Communist Party of India (Marxist–Leninist) seek Chinese support. 'Seeking military aid was never on our mind,' Sanyal told his biographer; they wanted 'advice' on how to proceed with the revolution in India.[79] They first approached the Chinese embassy in Dhaka, but failed to make contact. Thereafter, a team of four, led by Sanyal, crossed over into Nepal. On the third day of their arrival in Kathmandu, they approached the Chinese Embassy, only to be turned back at the gates. 'We had never expected such a rude treatment.' But guerrilla fighters are made of tougher resolve, and when they returned the next day, the guards finally let them in (perhaps the necessary intelligence checks had been carried out by then). They met a senior official who set up a meeting with the Chinese ambassador for the next day.

Sanyal went with his colleague Deepak Biswas to meet Ambassador Yang Gongsu, who offered them 'tea and snacks and asked if we needed money. Expressing our gratitude, we told him that we had not come for monetary aid; rather, we wished to visit China to meet Chairman Mao.' Sanyal and his crew waited anxiously in Kathmandu for a few more days before the ambassador told them Beijing would welcome them, and asked them to shift to the embassy.

Along with a twenty-seven-year-old Chinese guide, the four were then taken to the border and dropped off at a bridge that connected Nepal to Tibet. 'We realised it was an old, abandoned bridge; the wooden planks were missing at several places . . . We crawled ahead with utmost care.' When they crossed the bridge, they reached a tunnel dug through the mountains. Sanyal's biography is not clear about whether the tunnel was within Nepali territory, but the biographer notes that 'the remains of the cigarette-bidi butts' at the tunnel entrance assured the rebels the route 'was in regular use for secret trips to China'.

In Tibet, an armed party of five PLA soldiers escorted them first to Lhasa, and a week later, to Beijing to meet Mao. Their dream was coming true; they witnessed a grand assembly on the occasion of China Liberation Day on 1 October, and the next day, they briefly met with Mao himself. The rebels would eventually 'stay put in China' for three months, during which they would learn about ideology as well as military tactics. In December, they had another meeting with Mao and Zhou. 'Forget everything you have learnt here in China. Once back . . . formulate your own revolutionary strategies,' Mao told them.

The Naxalites were flown back to Lhasa, where after a military exercise, the rebels discussed future cooperation with the Chinese. PLA officers asked them to 'minimise the use' of the Chinese embassy in Kathmandu, and instead establish a secret transit route along 'the Nepal-Bhutan route to China'. The four were taken back to Kathmandu via the Arniko Highway, where the ambassador gave them INR 10,000 'towards establishing the secret transit camps to China'. The four left the very next day at dawn, crossing over into India by late afternoon. Sanyal does not clarify whether other Naxalites used Nepali territory to pass through to China after him, but Naga and Mizo revolutionaries also travelled to China in 1976 via Nepal.[80]

✦

By the end of the decade, the split between the Russians and the Chinese was complete, with border clashes over islands in the Ussuri river. China's isolation was dangerous, and in 1969, Mao asked his army advisors to prepare a roadmap. They wrote, 'Soviet revisionists have made China their main enemy, imposing a more serious threat to our security than the U.S. imperialists.'[81] The Sino–Soviet clashes 'helped catalyze the rapprochement, but the real change was in Washington, with the arrival of an administration willing to compromise with China'.[82] Nixon believed the US needed alliances outside Western Europe and Japan to beat the Soviets, so the Americans stopped funding the CIA's Tibetan resistance programme as a goodwill gesture, while paving the way for the entry of the PRC into the United Nations and recognising that 'all Chinese on either side of the Taiwan strait maintain there is but one China and that Taiwan is a part of China'.[83] But amity with the US came at a cost, for China abandoned its friends in South East Asia and in Pakistan, to whose defence it did not come during the 1971 war with India that severed the country.

For Nepal, this war was another sign of Indian expansionism and hegemony in the subcontinent. As the war ended, a new king was to take the throne; Mahendra had suffered a cardiac arrest and passed away in January 1972. His son, Birendra, considered a liberal because of his Western education, 'could present Mrs. Gandhi with an opportunity to increase Indian influence', wrote the CIA in its assessment of Indian foreign policy after the war, adding that if India pressed too hard, 'relations could quickly deteriorate'.[84]

Meanwhile, the war had eroded China's credibility among states in the subcontinent, but Beijing's overall goal of neutralising Soviet influence in the region remained the same. Besides, '[s]maller countries, particularly Sri Lanka and Nepal, were wary of India's increased willingness to flex its muscles and were receptive to ties with China warmer and broader than before the war'.[85]

This meant that the new king of Nepal was more open to Chinese overtures than his father. After the Tibetan resistance programme was shut down, China began to trust Kathmandu more. An electric trolley bus project upgrading Kathmandu's public transportation system was gifted in 1975 with a NPR 40 million grant.[86] Birendra became the first head of state to visit Tibet in June 1976. Beijing supported his government during the widespread student protests of 1979, and although it was wary about the call for a referendum in 1980, its engagement with the palace continued.[87]

In February 1978, Deng Xiaoping would visit Kathmandu, a trip intended to showcase Beijing's return to normalcy after years of seclusion under the Cultural Revolution and the post-Mao purge. He supported Birendra's 'Zone of Peace' proposal, but '[a]id recipients would have to be warned that China would be less generous than in the past . . . The spirit of the Deng era was China first.'[88]

Although the Chinese committed to gifting a paper mill, which would only begin production in 1986, there were no positive developments on the trade and tourism front. Nepal had sought to develop its waters with Chinese assistance, but Deng believed that '[i]t is a big question that involves a lot of aspects which are impossible to discuss in a few words'. Nepal also sought tourist access to Tibet, which Deng gently shot down because the access to Tibet was 'very difficult'.[89] But communism would no longer be exported either. The frantic years of the Cultural Revolution and China's seclusion from the world was a thing of the past. Under Deng, a new China was to be born. His comments on 'crushing' the gang of four after Mao's death, and on the 'continuous, gigantic efforts' China was making to capitalise on the lost years of the Cultural Revolution, were not really intended for Kathmandu, but the Americans heard him intently.[90] Most importantly, he said China was 'eager' to develop friendly relations with India; he was reaching out to New Delhi, hoping to pull it away from the Soviet embrace.

Although Deng's Kathmandu visit was high on symbolism, few of Nepal's expectations were met. It would, however, act as a counterweight to Delhi's pressures on Kathmandu post the Sikkim annexation and Indian displeasure at the Zone of Peace proposal. Nonetheless, Indian officials and media took a 'positive attitude' to Deng's visit, playing up his comments about improving relations.[91] On the whole, the Americans noted, Nepal was 'fully satisfied' with the results, the key takeaway being that 'he came'.[92]

From now on until the collapse of the monarchy, China's primary point of contact in Kathmandu would be the palace alone. But the ideals of communism had come to be imprinted on Nepali minds. Even if China rushed to erase the ills of Mao, the helmsman continued to inspire Nepali revolutionaries. Nearly two decades after Deng's visit, in February 1996, a group of rebels would raid a police post in Rolpa in western Nepal. Among their homemade pistols and explosives was a rusty .303 rifle that had been part of the arsenal given to the Tibetan Khampas by the CIA. The ideological document adopted by the rebels declared, among other things, their 'eternal commitment to the theory of people's war developed by Mao as the universal and invincible Marxist theory of war'.[93]

The Communist Party of Nepal (Maoist) had just launched their People's War.

6

Ghosts: Tibetan Exiles in Nepal

The riverside is where wraiths roam in Nepali folklore. It is where the dead are cremated and where those who cannot be cremated, such as children, are buried. The souls of those who cannot escape are believed to be trapped between the gorges, and children are told that visiting a riverbank after sundown is an invitation to these spirits.

I walk down one such gorge by the Seti Gandaki river, which runs lazily along Dulegauda town, a nondescript highway settlement an hour's ride out of Pokhara towards Kathmandu. The homes here are laid out across the two sides of the Prithvi Highway, which splits the town. Across the gorge is the Jampaling Tibetan Settlement Camp. Its residents settled here in 1974 after the disbanding of the Chushi Gangdruk Tibetan armed resistance in Mustang.

A faded board first points the way, then a signboard with a relatively fresh coat of paint. The land for the settlement was donated by the Nepali government, 'unwanted by locals because it was believed to be haunted'.[1] Inside a sprawling compound where the grass is overgrown and a few oaks provide a semblance of shade, old sheds with crumbling roofs share space with new concrete stupas. Lungtas, literally meaning 'windhorses', are strung across trees; the breeze carries the prayers printed on them to the gods. An old woman laboriously performs a kora around a stupa, her curved back almost parallel to the ground. Dorje,[2] the Central Tibetan Administration (CTA) representative at the camp, tells me that while Tibetan youth may no longer be strongly religious, the older ones staunchly maintain their faith.

Dorje leads me to a dormitory-like building built around a lawn. I can hear noises from the mess, and the smell of freshly cooked rice and meat curry wafts in the air. Outside the mess, on a wooden bench, three old men watch the setting sun. There are a few young people around, but I can see no children. Dorje introduces me to the group; I catch 'Chushi' a few times, and the old men nod. Barely a few hundred veterans of the resistance force are alive today. Most of them live in Jampaling, while a few more live in the centre of Pokhara, where few are aware of them.

The story of the Chushi Gangdruk is one wrapped in Buddhist romanticism, CIA intrigue and anti-communist struggle at the peak of the Cold War. Yet, it is a story as much hidden by the fog of war as by an unwillingness to dig up old secrets, not just about the resistance itself, but also about superpower complicity and abandonment. It is telling that there was not a single document on Project ST Circus (as the covert operation was titled by the CIA) among the 13 million documents declassified in 2017. In Nepal, the story of the Chushi Gangdruk is one painted in banditry and villainy, which clouds the ordinary Nepali's perception of Tibetan exiles.

The story of armed resistance also did not suit the larger narrative of Tibetan exile, constructed as that was on Buddhist nonviolence. 'The claim that the Tibetan struggle is and has been nonviolent is as much a direct product of forgetting violence as it is a claim staked to a certain view of Buddhism,' historian Carole McGranahan writes.[3] That said, existing historical accounts are framed within the romanticism associated with these Tibetan anti-communist warriors who operated in collaboration with the CIA; consider titles such as *Orphans of the Snow* or *Buddha's Warriors*. Tibetan historian Tsering Shakya's denunciation of Western exoticisation of the Tibetan struggle through 'the myth of Shangri-la' is equally valid in the histories of the Chushi Gangdruk veterans.[4]

The first wave of Tibetan exiles arrived in Nepal in the aftermath of the fourteenth Dalai Lama's escape from Lhasa in March 1959, and the subsequent violence as PLA troops rushed to secure the country and put down the rebellion. Mao wrote, 'If the situation continues like this, we may be compelled (such "being compelled" is very good) to solve the Tibetan question earlier than expected . . . It would be the best if ten to twenty or thirty to forty thousand lamas and other reactionaries flee abroad. Such a situation would of course become unbearable to India, Bhutan, and maybe also Nepal. But, whereas Bhutan and Nepal are different, India will have brought this onto itself and cannot blame us.'[5] As word spread in Tibet of the Dalai Lama's escape and China's military crackdown, thousands fled the country, among them Senge, one of the three old men on the bench. Hand trembling and wrinkles webbing his face, Senge recounts his escape from Kham Nangchen to Mustang. 'I don't remember how long it took us to reach Mustang from Kham.' We speak through an interpreter. He joined the Chushi Gangdruk when he was twenty-seven because his mother asked him to, and stayed with the force for fourteen years until it disbanded. Dorje, the CTA representative, and I calculate the dates and conclude that Senge would have been part of the first wave of fighters. The varnish on his memories has faded, and there are few details he recalls with accuracy. 'We had to sleep under pine trees. We had no food; we sometimes had to wait for a month before supplies reached us on donkeys brought from Kagbeni. We cooked and ate leather at times.'[6]

Pema, a tall man with a narrow face furrowed with lines, who stood upright despite his advanced age and who had been quiet so far, said they had to perform military exercises in the morning and religious activities in the evenings. Combat operations were few and far between; two notable ones were the capture of Chinese PLA documents that told the Americans about the failures of the Great Leap Forward very early on in October 1961, labelled as 'the best intelligence coup since the Korean War',[7] and the filming of a raid on Chinese forces in June 1964, after Scottish missionary-turned-Tibet-sympathiser George Patterson convinced a group of fighters in Tsum, to the east of Mustang, to 'stage a raid for the cameras' in order to internationalise the Tibetan cause.[8] The film aired two years later, and the CIA was furious the Mustang operation had been compromised. Patterson's romantic (mis)adventure led to the CIA cutting off funds for half a year, and eventually sowed the seeds of division between different factions.

We are sitting around the courtyard, waiting for lunch, as the stories tumble out, some made mouldy by the passage of time. We talk about the myths around the Khampas (as the Chushi Gangdruk fighters were also known, since a majority of them came from the Kham region of Tibet). Dorje tells me that, when he was young, he thought the 'Khampas had courage'. He recalls many legends around the fighters: 'I heard the bunkers built by the Khampas still stand; they are difficult to destroy. I also heard the roads and embankments they built in Mustang continue to exist.' Yet, he doubts the resistance would have been successful even if American support had continued. 'We may have had short-term victories, but we couldn't succeed in the long run. Our population was a big negative factor. There were 2,000 Khampas at the most fighting the PLA, which was a million strong.'

Chushi Gangdruk veterans, however, see it differently. Pema, who arrived in Pokhara in 1959 and went up to Mustang to join the force, says they believed military action could win Tibet back. 'But we were asked to surrender. If Nepal hadn't asked us to put down our weapons, we would have continued fighting as long as we could.' Another veteran, Nyima, who had been sent to a Kathmandu carpet factory to work, said that, when he heard of the surrender, the first thing that came to his mind was, 'Now it's all finished!'

The 1974 Nepali military operation to overpower the resistance was conducted with the help of Baba Yeshi, an ex-Chushi Gangdruk commander who fell out with Gyato Wangdu, a charismatic man whom Jampaling veterans remembered as a 'good man' (the men I spoke to were not Yeshi loyalists). Following Patterson's film, the CIA wanted to replace Yeshi, against whom there had been allegations of misappropriation of funds. Wangdu was first sent as an assistant to Yeshi, but when the latter was asked to transfer to Dharamsala in 1969 and the former to lead the Mustang forces, Yeshi 'wanted none of it.'[9] He asked his loyalists to break rank and moved east from Mustang to Manang, then eventually surrendered to the Nepali government, relocating to Kathmandu by 1972.

On the other hand, by the end of the 1960s, even the Americans had begun to believe the resistance force was 'ineffective' and an 'unsuccessful irritant' to US attempts at rapprochement with the Chinese. The US began to gradually whittle down its covert support—financial and material—with funds now being directed towards rehabilitation. The programme had cost approximately USD 2.5 million a year; in 1971, the CIA's suggestion that costs be cut and the number of men reduced from 1,800 to 300 was accepted. 'Under the revised plan, after a resettlement payment of $2.5 million spread over a number of years, the costs of maintaining 300 guerrillas would be $100,000 per year and non-guerrilla operations would be reduced from $500,000 in FY 1970 to $363,000 in FY 1971 and $263,000 in FY 1972.'[10] The first of the rehabilitation funds in 1970 were spent on two carpet factories and a thirty-room budget hotel in Pokhara.[11]

The Americans thought the guerrillas had delivered little by way of action. There had been few successful military operations like the one that brought in intelligence on the PLA, and the US thought 'elimination of the intelligence collection operations [by the Tibetans] would not seriously diminish coverage of Western China for U.S. needs'.[12] Combined with new foreign policy goals of isolating the Soviets by opening talks with the PRC, and the fact that the Mustang operation was not really a covert one—the Chinese knew about it as early as 1961—the course of action was clear: the US was pulling out of ST Circus.[13]

With this development, Nepal was in a better position to act against the Chushi Gangdruk forces. The administration was weak in the northern regions—one of the reasons why the Chushi Gangdruk could operate undisturbed—and it was not until 1972 that a committee was set up to administer the Himalayan districts. Kathmandu had also been stretched by the Nepali Congress's armed insurrection in the Terai plains. In 1963, the Nepal Police chief admitted to British authorities in Kathmandu, '[The] Nepalese government did not have the security forces to deal with [the Khampas] and the situation was becoming difficult.'[14] China had been protesting about the Khampas in Mustang since 1963 at least; in September that year, Nepal received a 'sharp protest' about Khampa raids 'for the first time'.[15] By 1964, the Chinese were also distributing pamphlets urging the Khampas to desert: 'No questions will be asked of those returning to their former allegiance about the magnitude of their past evil deeds, nor will there be discussion of what their positions were; it is laid down once for all that that what is past is past.'[16] The Chinese embassy also offered the Nepali intelligence chief the use of Chinese troops.[17] But as bilateral relations soured during the Cultural Revolution, the question was put on the backburner, until Chinese premier Zhou Enlai 'expressed deep interest in the question of the Khampas' during King Birendra's late-1973 China visit.[18]

Birendra, who became king in 1972, was noticeably less enamoured by the Tibetans than his father was. On his return, he convened a meeting of security officials. Birendra wanted the Khampas disarmed before his coronation in 1975 through negotiations and a surrender, rather than an armed conflict. Tamla Ukyab, a Home Ministry official present at that meeting, told me the first step was a reconnaissance mission to areas occupied by the Khampas.[19] Ukyab and another official went to Mustang, via Dolpo to the west. They reached Kaisang, to the east of Jomsom, where the largest Khampa war camp had been set up at an inhospitable height of 3,510 metres, with the aid of a local. 'They had full-fledged barracks. Locals weren't allowed to enter. Although we didn't see any foreigners, it looked like they had been there—there was a nine-hole golf course on the grounds!'

Ukyab returned to Kathmandu with this information. Nepali forces decided to concentrate on disarming the Mustang camps first. A public relations campaign began. Newspapers denigrated the Khampas as 'idol lifters, inborn dacoits and callous mercenaries' who were allied with 'self-exiled Nepali anti-nationalists' and served the interests of 'Nepal's next-door neighbour', i.e. India.[20] Yeshi was brought to meet the king, where he and his followers were promised Nepali citizenship and social security in lieu of assisting Nepali forces. He acquiesced and participated in the operation, after which he established a camp in Jorpati, Kathmandu; exiles from Yeshi's breakaway Chushi Gangdruk group remain the only Tibetans to be officially granted citizenship by Nepal.

On 15 June 1974, nine units of the Royal Nepal Army based out of Pokhara, led by then Lt. Colonel Sachhit S.J.B. Rana, moved up to Jomsom. The American Embassy in Kathmandu sent a telegram to the State Department: 'GON [Government of Nepal] actions are designed to establish control over a hitherto unruly and autonomous element of the population, to defuse an issue of periodic dispute in their relations with the PRC and to preempt the Nepal Congress party from obtaining Khampa arms for political ends. There is, however, serious risk GON will miscalculate the Khampa response, and this in turn holds potential for an embarrassing armed conflict in which the Royal Nepalese Army might suffer casualties and in which extended guerrilla action might ensue.'[21]

The army walked to Jomsom in the rain; all equipment was carried on horseback. Three different rounds of negotiations began, Ukyab said: one with the war camp, one with the Dalai Lama's representative in Kathmandu, and one between the Dalai Lama's brother, Gyalo Thondup, and the Nepali ambassador in Delhi.[22] The government offered refugee status, loans, land and education for the fighters' children.[23] 'The Khampas wanted to stretch the negotiations until winter. We couldn't allow that,' Ukyab said. After multiple rounds of talks failed, the Nepal Army surrounded the camp and fired Howitzer rounds to show they were serious about military action. Undeterred, the Chushi Gangdruk forces fired back a round from a recoilless rifle. Nepalese soldiers withdrew; the Tibetans 'had better weapons than we did',[24] an official would later concede. Worried that an armed confrontation between Nepal and the Chushi Gangdruk forces was in the making, the Dalai Lama sent a taped message with his brother-in-law asking them to put down their arms. Most of the militants surrendered—barring one who shot himself, two who jumped to their deaths in the Kali Gandaki river below, and one notable individual: Wangdu. Along with eighteen others, Wangdu had taken the road north, towards the wild landscapes of upper Mustang, even more sparsely populated than the Jomsom region. In Ghami, a village just outside the famed Dhakmar cliffs of upper Mustang, Nepal Army officers found that Wangdu's posse had slaughtered a yak and carried its meat as food.[25] Without adequate high-altitude clothing and gear, the soldiers returned to Jomsom, and Wangdu's trail went cold.

Nearly a month later, on 7 September, the army received a report from far-west Humla that a group of Khampas had attacked a police checkpost in Muchu and was heading towards Yari.[26] Within two days, most exit points had been sealed off. On 9 September, Wangdu's group walked into a trap at Tinkar pass, further west of Humla, where the modern borders of China, India and Nepal converge (and near the site of the disputed territory between India and Nepal). Six Chushi Gangdruk fighters died in the shootout, Wangdu among them. Yeshi was brought in by helicopter to identify his body. The others managed to escape to India.

An exhibit of the Chushi Gangdruk weapons was put up in Kathmandu. The Americans were instructed to deny any involvement. Only if the Nepal king asked, the Kathmandu embassy was instructed, was he to be told that 'the United States government is not now involved in any way with the Khampas. Any supply which was provided by USG ended a number of years ago.'[27] To the rest, the embassy was to say, 'It is our practice not to comment on any charges of this sort.'[28] A few months later, the Nepal government informed the United Nations High Commissioner for Refugees (UNHCR) that they wanted to resettle 6,000 Khampas at a cost of USD 1.5 million,[29] and discreetly enquired whether the US would be receptive to 'fund resettlement' as 'some countries' had a 'moral' responsibility.[30] The State Department replied, 'Both the GON and the UNHCR are likely to continue to believe that we have a "moral" responsibility for Khampa resettlement. This is clearly not the case, particularly when [the] current problem was generated by unilateral GON action about which we were not consulted in any way. We have, therefore, no obligation, moral or otherwise, to participate in UNHCR's efforts.'[31] Finally, in January 1975, the US State Department wrote to its embassies in Delhi and Kathmandu, conveying that the US was 'not interested in contributing to proposed UNHCR Khampa assistance proposal although we wished them well . . . Accordingly, while we of course maintain continuing sympathetic interest in UNHCR activities and initiatives, Dept would prefer to let this particular matter rest.'[32]

The Mustang episode was over for the Americans. The secret war in the Himalaya had come to an end with Kissinger's ping-pong diplomacy. But keeping the peace can be more difficult than playing war.

✦

Loden Chokse was eight years old when his family decided to leave Tibet. Nomads from the far west of Tibet, now in Ngari Prefecture, they walked for seven days to reach Kora La in Mustang. 'I remember it was around October,' he tells me, sitting in his one-room office in the Tashiling settlement on the outskirts of Pokhara. Loden has a large photograph of his meeting with the Dalai Lama that has pride of place on the wall. There is also a poster with the Dalai Lama's words: 'Every day, think as you wake up, today I am fortunate to be alive, I have a precious human life, I am not going to waste it'. Also on the wall is a picture of the Karmapa. The shelves are full of mementos and trophies; Loden has been an active member of the Lion's Club in Pokhara.

'[When we first arrived in Mustang] I worked in Thakali homes for a few years in Lete, below Jomsom,' Loden says. 'We did not leave Tibet because of the Chinese, although my wife is from the east [where the armed rebellion against Chinese rule had first broke out]. We heard that Lhasa had been captured by the Chinese, and the Dalai Lama had escaped. We were nomads, so we didn't really think much about where we were going. Only when we walked for days at an end did I realise this was something different.'

In Pokhara, like in Kathmandu, Tibetan refugee camps were set up on the outskirts of the town, what was once the fringes but has now been subsumed within the urban sprawl. Camps were also set up in sparsely populated hills, such as Chialsa in Solukhumbu district in the east and Dhorpatan in the west, when it became apparent that the Tibetans would not be able to return home any time soon. 'By 1961, many of the refugees faced serious food shortages and suffered from a lack of adequate shelter and healthcare.'[33]

King Mahendra asked Nehru if some of the refugees could be resettled in India, which the latter thought 'inappropriate and unacceptable':[34] 'It is true that the Dalai Lama is, at present, residing in India. But that does not impose on us any obligation to invite other Tibetans to do the same.' Instead, Nehru pointed to the international aid Nepal had been receiving, primarily from the International Committee of the Red Cross, USAID and the Swiss Red Cross, and suggested Nepal use the funds for resettlement. The land for Tibetan settlements was bought by the Nepal Red Cross as an intermediary, as Tibetans could not (and still cannot) legally own property in Nepal. 'It also enabled the Nepalese government to disavow any direct support for the refugees in order to avoid jeopardizing its tenuous relationship with China.'[35]

In 1964, Loden's family moved to Pokhara after hearing that Tibetans were being resettled in camps. They lived in a temporary camp for about nine months before the Nepal Red Cross bought the land in Chhorepatan where the Tashiling camp stands today. 'Life was unimaginable back then. It was difficult on all fronts, and different too. In Tibet, we didn't have a culture of eating vegetables. When we saw Nepalis eat greens here, we cried to ourselves, "Now we have to eat grass as well!"' Loden remembers with a chuckle. But there were few moments of levity. The refugees had to rearrange their lives to suit a new geography and culture. 'We were all uneducated, so there's no history of our lives from back then. We had to bring salt and oil from Butwal [a southern town 160 km away from Pokhara] and carry it back to camp ourselves. People didn't know how to carry the doko,[36] and the straps would cut into our skin,' Loden recollects.

The Siddhartha Highway, which was to connect Pokhara with Bhairahawa in the plains, was under construction at the time with Indian assistance, and Tibetans worked as road workers on the project. A hydroelectric project was being constructed at the Fewa Lake, and refugees who worked there received NPR 2.5 as daily wage. Loden joined a school and cleared his tenth grade in 1970, following which he quit intermediate studies to teach other Tibetan children. 'Three of us had been sent to the government school to study, and whoever finished the SLC[37] first had to teach for three years at the camp. As I had cleared the SLC first, that task fell to me.' Loden fulfilled his commitment and taught for three years before taking up a job at a nearby hotel.

I ask Loden if he thought about joining the armed resistance in Mustang. He thinks for a bit before replying candidly, 'I didn't want to join them because it was an impossible situation, really. It's not that those who didn't join them weren't patriots. We were patriots, but they were hardliners. Only those who believed in violence wanted to fight the Chinese.' The year 1974 was a tense period for Loden and others like him who had not joined the resistance, especially when military operations commenced against the Chushi Gangdruk. 'We were also Tibetans. We were worried what the locals would think of us.'

Because they had been set up far away from urban centres, Tibetan settlements established micro-economies for long-term sustainability. With the help of Swiss Aid workers, they also set up handicraft industries within these settlements, primarily dealing in carpets. 'By the late 1980s, it had become the largest handicraft industry and the second-largest earner of foreign currency in Nepal.'[38] Despite a bar on ownership of property, several Tibetans could open restaurants, hotels and private shops until the 1980s. Tibetan entrepreneurs moved into the nascent tourism industry too. One of these hotels was the Annapurna Guest House in Pokhara, built with the help of CIA rehabilitation funds and opened to the public in November 1973. Loden worked there for seventeen years, rising up the ranks to become general manager, before leaving in 1994 to start his own hotel.

In many ways, Loden's story parallels the larger story of Tibetan exiles in Nepal. In the early years, they were settled away from town, and there was a certain laxity in how Nepali authorities approached the issue of their presence in the country. At this time, although relations between Nepal and China were cordial, there is little evidence that China pressured Nepal too hard on Tibetan issues. Only after the internationalisation of the Tibet issue in the late 1980s, followed by a declaration of martial law in Tibet in March 1989 and the arrival of new refugees in Nepal, did China begin to exert greater pressure. In

1986, the two countries updated the agreement on border inhabitants and restricted their movement to border districts. As the Tibet Justice Center's 2002 report explains:[39]

> Before 1986, the Nepalese government also tended to tolerate the arrival of new refugees for several reasons: It lacked the practical ability to enforce a strict border-control policy; fewer new refugees arrived during China's Cultural Revolution (approximately 1966-1979) because the Chinese government then maintained strict control over the movement of the Tibetan population; and in any event the Nepalese government did not perceive the number of newly arriving Tibetan refugees as a threat or a diplomatic liability during these years . . . The Nepalese government's *laissez-faire* approach toward Tibetan refugees began to change and tighten in 1986 . . . In 1989, pressure from the Chinese government and the growing number of new arrivals led Nepal to initiate a strict border-control policy.

When I ask Loden about his thoughts on Nepal's policy towards Tibetan exiles, he refuses to tell me, and instead refers me to the CTA website. 'We've stopped the Tibet movement in Nepal because we don't want to make life difficult for Nepalis. After all, we are grateful for what Nepal has done for us. It had no compulsion to keep us; it can still ask us to leave. But they haven't.' It is a tricky position for Loden, to be publicly visible while being a Tibetan in Nepal. It has been difficult for me too, to convince Loden to trust and open up to me, especially with deepening Nepal–China relations and the Chinese asking for Nepal's commitment to the 'one-China' policy, not just in words but also through action. 'We know the Chinese embassy is watching us,' Loden says. 'We know China is behind the crackdown on Tibetans in Nepal.'

✦

Once upon a time, the statue of King Prithvi Narayan Shah, hailed as the 'unifier' of Nepal, stood at one of Pokhara's busiest junctions. Next to the statue was a concrete signpost that proudly proclaimed 'Nepal-China friendship', marking the beginning of the Prithvi Highway. The statue, in keeping with the old king's popular portrayal across Nepal, depicted him holding up a finger, a symbol of how he had brought the country together. In 2006, however, as popular sentiment began to turn against the monarchy in the second Jana Andolan, the old king at the junction bore the brunt of it. Agitators tore down the statue and the pedestal stood empty for a few years, until a local group replaced it with a bust of Lakhan Thapa, a revolutionary who had dared to raise his banners against Jung Bahadur, the first Rana prime minister. Prithvi Chowk is now officially Lakhan Thapa Chowk; time will tell whether the name catches on colloquially, but the junction is busier than ever.

A little to the west, after a row of shuttered shops selling saris, Chinese bags and other knick-knacks, is a faded green gate. Inside, the hustle and bustle of Pokhara still loud enough to be heard, are several decrepit one-storeyed single-room apartments, the green-and-white paint peeling off the walls. A tall flagpole proudly displays the five colours of Tibetan Buddhism next to a tree bereft of leaves. A blue door opens. Inside, a single room about ten feet by ten feet in size. Two beds and multiple carpets take up the corners; I am directed to a small diwan on which lies a school bag full of books. All sorts of colourful mementos adorn the walls and shelves. Another door opens out to the back. A goldfish swims about lazily in a makeshift aquarium built out of a two-litre plastic Coke bottle. In the middle of this cornucopia is a small shrine where a lamp has been lit in front of a portrait of the Dalai Lama with his impish smile.

The Paljorling Camp is quite unlike the other Tibetan refugee camps in the country. Just outside is a loud and vibrant market; across its gates is a carriageway that is Pokhara's most expensive piece of real estate, courtesy the financial institutions on both sides of the road. Rents in this area are among the highest in the city, which throws the decrepitude inside the camp into sharp relief. 'We Tibetans, we look satisfied from the outside, we wear good clothes, we look happy,' Rinchen tells me, 'but that's not true at all.'

Rinchen has just returned from the local transportation office. The two of us sit cross-legged next to the divan while he opens a bag and pulls out some documents. 'My son needs a motorcycle licence,' he says. Rinchen has two sons; the older one has only recently cleared his tenth-grade examinations, and is now eligible for a motorcycle licence. But there are issues. He shows me two cards that have been carefully laminated; these cards are the only official identity his children have inside Nepal. They note down the dates and places of birth, parents' names and identity numbers. The title in Nepali reads: 'Documentary evidence of children born to Tibetan refugees'. An official has signed the cards, but there are no photographs of his sons. 'I carried the SLC marksheet along with this card to show the transport officials that it's *my* son who has applied for the licence. There's no photograph on this "identity card". There's no official stamp. How can anyone believe this is an original document?'

It is a complaint I hear across all the three camps: most Tibetan refugees under the age of forty have no documentation available to them from official channels. Nepal has not signed or ratified the 1951 Convention Relating to the Status of Refugees and its 1967 Protocol Relating to the Status of Refugees. Nor does it have its own legislation dealing with refugees. As such, 'Tibetans residing in Nepal are essentially stateless. They are neither citizens nor refugees under the law, and they possess neither the legal status nor the rights with which to improve their welfare.'[40] Tibetans who arrived in Nepal before 1989 and their children are provided with a 'refugee certificate', while those who came to Nepal after 1989 cannot remain in the country and are expected to transit to India via an informal agreement, known as the 'gentleman's agreement', between Nepal and the UNHCR. Although the agreement allows refugees to safely seek assistance from the CTA in India, several human rights groups have alleged that Nepal (and its security forces) have ignored the agreement over the past years, and have refouled refugees to China from the border itself.[41]

Rinchen shows me his 'RC', as the refugee certificate is called. It is a booklet with a blue cover, and the first page reads, 'Rinchen is a Tibetan refugee. He is permitted to stay in Nepal in accordance with laws and regulations. He will enjoy freedom of movement within the territory of Nepal with the exception of areas forbidden to foreigners, unless his habitual residence is located in such area.' This flimsy little document is precious to those who own it, but increasingly, it is proving to be worthless. 'What's the use of this RC now?' said my interpreter at the Jampaling Camp in Dulegauda, livid when I suggested that at least he had one. 'The RC should have a value. In Kathmandu you can no longer get a driving licence even with an RC. It's not so bad in Pokhara yet, but I am sure the problems will come soon. Forget bank accounts, shopkeepers ask us for a citizenship certificate even for a SIM card. We can't receive money sent from abroad because banks tell us the RC no longer work; we have to show them citizenship certificates.'

It is a view Rinchen shares. His children should technically qualify to receive RCs, but they are, in essence, without documentation. 'We aren't allowed to work in government jobs. Even in the private sector, we can only be employed informally. Although I got a PAN [permanent account number for taxation] for my business, I've heard of several instances where, despite possessing an RC, Tibetans have not been able to get PANs. It gets worse if we have to go to India. The Indian police don't accept the RC as a valid travel document, and ask us to get one. But to get a travel document is a long bureaucratic process in Nepal.'

The community faces issues on several fronts. While it could be argued that those with an RC are less affected, many Tibetan children born in Nepal before 1989 do not have one either, as Nepal stopped distributing RCs to Tibetans in the mid-1990s.[42] Fewer than 25 per cent of the nearly 20,000 Tibetans in Nepal today own valid RCs.[43] Beyond the documentation, there is the fact that Tibetan refugees feature high on the Nepal–China agenda; one of the most visible outcomes of the deepening relationship is Nepal's response to Tibetan exiles. The situation has worsened in the years since 2008, when Tibetans in Nepal protested the Beijing Olympics for several months. The number of refugees entering Nepal has declined significantly since then too. Until 2008, almost 2,200 refugees crossed over annually; in 2013, only 171 did.[44] In 2015, only 85 refugees applied for an exit permit to India, less than a tenth of the 1,248 who applied in 2010.[45]

Although the reduction in refugee numbers is also because of increased Chinese vigilance on the border and new economic opportunities inside Tibet, there are allegations that the Armed Police Force (APF), the Nepali security agency responsible for border security, deports refugees to Tibet at the border, such as in September 2019 in Humla.[46] When I asked a retired senior APF official whether such reports were true, he denied them, saying the APF follows all formal protocols with respect to refugees. 'Tibetan refugees enter Nepal through hidden routes, making themselves public only about 20–30 km inside Nepal. At that point, we can't afford to send them back,' he told me. He suggested that it was China's responsibility to stop Tibetan refugees from entering Nepal. 'We are strapped for resources, and we cannot patrol the entire border. China insists we must do more both formally and informally, but we do the best we can.'

The Nepali authorities' crackdown on all forms of political, even religious, expression by Tibetans in Nepal has been attributed to China's increasing formal and informal pressure, with its increasing investments and aid activities being seen as quid pro quo. Instances of preventive detention on the eve of important dates—10 March, the anniversary of the 1959 Lhasa uprising; the Dalai Lama's birthday on 6 July; or before the visits of Chinese dignitaries—are common in Kathmandu's Tibetan settlements.[47] All the Tibetans I spoke to agreed that, although the issues with documentation existed before 2008, Nepali authorities were not as stringent as they are now. Sudheer Sharma, geopolitical analyst and editor of *Kantipur*, agreed that Chinese engagements in Nepal had increased after the 2008 anti-China protests in Kathmandu. But there had been earlier indications too. In his memoir, Vivek Kumar Shah, the ex-military secretary at the palace during King Gyanendra's tenure, wrote that, at a dinner reception held for a Chinese PLA delegation in 2001, a Chinese general enquired about the Dalai Lama, and was 'particularly interested' in Mustang.[48] 'During discussions, the Chinese general said China was ready to provide logistical and communications equipment to the Royal Nepal Army.'[49] The Chinese had backed the palace during its war with the Maoists, and Nepal had cancelled three different events in Kathmandu that were being held to mark the Dalai Lama's birth celebrations in July 2002—the first time it had been known to do so.[50] In October that year, the then prime minister, Sher Bahadur Deuba, confirmed to US Ambassador Michael Malinowski that Nepal 'was under pressure from China about the Tibetans'.[51]

This had begun to show. In 2003, then Nepali foreign secretary, Madhu Raman Acharya, told US embassy officials that 'it is difficult to go against strong Chinese interests . . . not that we like it, but we could not resist it'.[52] In 2005, consul to Lhasa (and later ambassador to China), Leela Mani Paudyal, confirmed to the US that the Tibetan Refugee Welfare Office had been closed down in Kathmandu on Beijing's instructions.[53] That same year, Nepal rejected a US plan to resettle 5,000 refugees in the US, allegedly because of Chinese pressure.[54] Yang Jiechi, then Chinese foreign minister, told the US ambassador in Beijing that 'China hopes the United States will not go further in permitting Tibetans who live in Nepal to resettle in the United States'.[55] China also provided weapons and ammunition to the Nepal Army at a time when the US and India had halted all military supplies after the royal takeover by Gyanendra. 'It is not by choice but by compulsion,' Paudyal told the Americans, by way of explanation.[56]

✦

Two incidents in the Khumbu region near Everest in 2002 and 2006 showed the gravity of China's intention with respect to escaping Tibetans.

In September 2002, two American climbers were shot at in the Khumbu region by two assailants in combat gear: 'One of the assailants reportedly identified himself as "Chinese military".'[57] The climbers were acclimatising by walking up to Nangpa La, a pass at 19,000 feet on the Nepal–China border, when they met a man carrying an automatic weapon who 'appeared to be of Han Chinese ethnicity and showed them what he claimed was his Chinese military uniform under his black jacket'. They offered the man some food and water, while the soldier enquired whether anybody was coming after them. The two climbers then spotted another man after an hour's climb, 'wearing the same type of ski hat as the first man they encountered'. They decided to return, and met the first soldier on their way down. Then suddenly, they heard a shot, and two or three minutes later, another that 'just missed us—we heard the bullet go right past our ears'.

The climbers threw off their backpacks and ran downhill, hiding behind rocks to catch their breath. Three more shots were fired at them, and so they hid behind another rock for three to four hours. Further investigation revealed that the two were clearly in Nepali territory, and that, on the morning of the incident, a group of thirty-five Tibetan refugees had crossed into Nepal.[58] The incident came as a surprise to all involved, including Nepali security officials who were 'clearly very concerned' that it took place in their territory. After talks with the UNHCR, the US embassy later confirmed that 'several members of a Chinese security force entered Nepal in pursuit of Tibetan refugees'.[59] It emerged that a group of refugees had earlier had an altercation with Chinese soldiers, during which they had overpowered the soldiers and escaped with 'two of their weapons'.[60] The embassy concluded 'a highly unusual series of events may have led Chinese military personnel to enter Nepal and fire on American citizens . . . [We] can only speculate that the soldiers had expected their movement would go unnoticed in the extremely isolated area around Nangpa-La, and were startled by potential witnesses.'[61]

The second incident, in September 2006, however, would be witnessed by several mountaineers from the 8,201-metre high Cho Oyu's advanced base camp. Seventy-six Tibetan refugees were crossing the pass into Nepal when four shots rang out, and the mountaineers saw a figure slump in the snow. One of them captured footage of the killing, while another clicked a picture of the fallen figure, a seventeen-year-old nun called Kelsang Namtso.[62]

While the incident occurred in Chinese territory, the brazenness of the shooting shocked the world. 'The seemingly indiscriminate shooting of Tibetans attempting to cross into Nepal is a potential embarrassment to China,' the US embassy in Kathmandu noted.[63] While several survivors would record their accounts with international organisations, Beijing itself remained silent at first.[64] A few weeks later, the official response would be that the soldiers shot in self-defence. 'When the video footage of the shooting was posted, press statements from the [Chinese] Ministry of Foreign Affairs dropped the "self-defense" explanation and began to refer to the incident as 'normal border management activity".'[65]

✦

The key issue today for Tibetan exiles living in Nepal is their de facto statelessness. 'Today, even if Nepal wants to do something for us, it cannot do so because of the geopolitical situation,' Loden tells me. But the statelessness—because of denial of RCs to eligible Tibetans, the lack of rights attached to the RCs themselves, and the socio-legal fallout of the lack of identity papers—is galling to them. 'The municipality gives us a birth certificate, so the children can study. But what beyond that? They can't get any permanent jobs, they can't open bank accounts. There is no future for the children in Tibetan communities across Nepal,' Loden says.

In my conversations with them, many Tibetan exiles spoke of Nepal's humanitarianism in allowing them to live in the country despite the lack of a legal framework or compulsion for doing so, but they were despondent about the recent crackdown on their communities. 'Tibetans and Nepalis have a long relationship that predates the Chinese presence in Nepal,' Dorje, the CTA representative, tells me in Jampaling. 'Let's not forget thousands of years of history [with Tibet] for a sixty-year-old friendship [with China].'

Today, nearly three-quarters of the Tibetan refugees here have no documentation at all. Non-RC holders do not qualify for travel documents either, which are difficult even for RC holders to obtain. Some even risk fraudulently obtaining Nepali passports to travel, like the Tibetan woman who was deported by Switzerland and arrested upon arrival in Nepal in 2017 for not being a genuine Nepali citizen.[66]

In Jampaling, an old woman who brewed tea told me that possessing an RC issued in Kathmandu was no guarantee of security. Although she lived in the settlement camp outside Pokhara, she had to return to the same administrative office in Kathmandu every year to renew the RC. The addresses on the RCs could not be updated to reflect her current residence, and she had to appear in person to renew the document. She pointed to her weak knee and said she had not been able go last year. 'The CDO office tells us to get a medical certificate if we are ill and cannot come to renew the RC. My Nepali is terrible, so I have to bribe someone if my work needs to be done.' I asked her if she planned to go again. 'What can I do?' she said, shrugging.

While the widely polarising issue of Tibet's political status and history vis-à-vis China is beyond the scope of this book, Nepal's official position is clear: its One-China policy does not support any separatism or activity that can affect bilateral relationships. As such, Nepal has used its many wings—sometimes in conjunction with the Chinese—to clamp down on Tibetan political expression and the movement of refugees into the country. Many in the Nepali establishment feel that the issue of Tibet has been restricted to the question of human rights on the plateau and little beyond. As a counterpoint, they present the economic development of Tibet. Their belief is that Tibet has primarily become a pressure point that those opposed to China (i.e. Western governments) raise through their supposed agencies (such as human rights groups) to hinder the evolution of Nepal–China relations and to block China's rise on the global stage. A foreign policy advisor to two previous prime ministers wrote, 'China is concerned about the possible plays by Western powers on the Tibet issue from Nepali soil.'[67] China has also pushed its narrative of Tibet's economic development through soft diplomacy that emphasises its sovereignty over the region. For instance, a photo exhibit was arranged in Kathmandu to commemorate 'the sixtieth anniversary of the campaign of democratic reform' in Tibet. Similarly, a biennial 'China's Tibet–Nepal' trade fair takes place in both countries. The old linkages between Nepal and Tibet—art forms such as thangka and paubha, or invoking Bhrikuti's marriage to a Tibetan king—are also co-opted by China in this cultural diplomacy.

Nepal has told other countries, primarily the US, that it will uphold the 'gentleman's agreement' and protect the rights of Tibetans in the country.[68] But increasingly there are worries that China's reported attempts to undermine international systems through which multilateral human rights agencies operate will have consequences on how Nepal views its commitments.[69] In October 2019, while an extradition treaty with China was nipped in the bud, two other agreements—one on mutual legal assistance and the other on border management—were signed that will make it harder for Tibetans to cross over into Nepal in the coming years, especially since the border agreement makes it easier for Nepal to hand back Chinese citizens who have crossed the border 'illegally'.

Those who are part of the Nepali establishment like to say that Tibetans live in Nepal on humanitarian grounds, and that, as such, they cannot do anything that hinders bilateral relations with China, such as by participating in protests. But as relations with China deepen, it is increasingly clear that the future of Tibetans in Nepal is bleak. They are stateless, lacking identification, the ghosts of our society: the nameless people who speak another language, who live on the outskirts of our towns and whose presence on our lands is why we cannot embrace China fully (though many are well-integrated, like Loden, despite the odds).

Back in Paljorling, I asked Rinchen whether he had ever thought about going to Tibet. 'I've only heard what Lhasa looks like. It must be beautiful.' His mother, who sat across from us, said, 'If things aren't fine there, why should we go back?' Rinchen listened thoughtfully and agreed. 'The environment in Tibet has to be more welcoming for us to return.' When his son entered to pick up a few books, I asked Rinchen if he had told his children about Tibet. 'I've kept a few books on Tibet for my children. I want them to know where they come from. I tell them their first country is Tibet, and that we are refugees in Nepal.' Did his sons ask him about Tibet? He laughed. 'They rarely do.' After a while, he said, 'It's very difficult for them to identify with Tibet. It's difficult for *us* now [after so many years]. We look at photos and we imagine Tibet in our minds. We have to be satisfied with that.'

7

Between Two Boulders

In 1955, the Chinese Foreign Ministry prepared two sets of documents for the Bandung Conference, which brought together twenty-nine Asian and African countries in a rare expression of postcolonial solidarity. Mao's forces had defeated Chiang Kai Shek's Guomindang to establish the People's Republic, but the Americans had sided with Chiang, and the PRC was not represented at the United Nations. It was now imperative for the PRC to establish diplomatic relations with as many countries as possible to negate the American encirclement. 'The eight-item agenda put forward by India [at the Bandung Conference] confines the colonialist issue to the specific colonies and trustee territories, which seems to have an attempt to absolve US from the blame. We should still take US as the main target of attack,' read the first document, outlining China's position.[1] It then slotted participating countries according to their outlook towards the PRC: 'Peace and neutral' countries like India and Burma; 'Close to peace and neutral', such as Nepal and Pakistan; 'Anti-peace and anti-neutral' countries like Thailand and the Philippines; and 'Close to anti-peace and anti-neutral' countries such as Japan and Iran.

A second document highlighted China's specific issues with these countries. With Nepal, there were three outstanding issues: the establishment of diplomatic relations; the existent Tibet–Nepal treaty; and the presence of renegade Nepali politician K.I. Singh in Tibet.[2] Of these, the treaty was a clear priority. Talks to establish diplomatic relations with Nepal had begun, and Singh was not as urgent an issue (he'd return to Nepal by August the same year). But China's claim on Tibet needed to be legitimised. Although the seventeen-point agreement between the Dalai Lama and China provided Tibet a measure of autonomy, it also said 'the Tibetan people shall return to the big family of the motherland—the People's Republic of China'.[3] The abrogation of Tibet's previous bilateral treaties was crucial, for they were a de facto recognition that Tibet had held an independent status in the past—a claim both the PRC as well as the Guomindang regime had rejected.

In Nepal, the emergence of a communist China as a northern neighbour was a matter of concern in a number of different ways. For instance, Nepali traders in Lhasa soon found they now had to relinquish their extraterritorial rights. Beijing also informed Kathmandu it could not receive the tribute missions that Lhasa had been sending under the 1856 treaty. 'Any country receiving such illegal missions will be regarded as harbouring hostile intentions towards the People's Republic of China,' a 1950 missive stated.[4] The PRC knew its position in Tibet was shaky; even Mao desisted from sending PLA troops to Xizang, or Tibet, until the UK, Pakistan and India had recognised Beijing's suzerainty over the region.[5] And as Liu Shaoqi told the Soviet ambassador, 'With a population of two million Tibet cannot put up any serious resistance to the PLA . . . But if Nepal, a country with a warlike [. . .] population of five million that serves in the Indian and other armies, interferes in the Tibetan question, the matter could become complicated.'[6]

Even so, the Dalai Lama's emissary arrived in Kathmandu in 1952, bearing the annual tribute of NPR 10,000 along with a note from the young Tibetan leader: 'I have every hope that there will be no hindrance to continuing the age-old relations between my Government and yours. I pray to God that our relations may become stronger than ever.'[7] But this was not to be. No tributes came the next year, as China informed the Tibetan government that the tributes had to stop. Nepali traders who were earlier judged in Nepali courts in Tibet now found themselves facing a Chinese court. Passports would soon be required to travel between the two countries. 'The Chinese acts were intended to serve notice to Nepal that the Tibetan situation was no longer the same.'[8]

✦

The 1856 Tibet–Nepal treaty had tenuous origins. With the Qing dynasty weakened by the first Opium War (1839–42), and the Taiping Rebellion eating away at their foundations, China did not come to Tibet's aid when Jung Bahadur, the first Rana prime minister, decided to launch his war against Lhasa. 'The 1855-56 war was . . . an unprovoked act of aggression on Nepal's part.'[9] The resultant treaty forced Tibet to send an annual tribute to Kathmandu, but more importantly, it removed all duties levied on Nepali traders, while the country's vakil, representative, in Lhasa was given jurisdiction over all Nepalis involved in disputes with Tibetans or others. Nepal assumed the role of 'protector' in Tibetan affairs, supplanting China. The Chinese amban had protested at the time, asking for a change in the treaty's language that made both countries defer to the Qing. Nepal then agreed to an amendment that said both Tibet and Nepal respected the Qing emperor, but the clause about coming to Tibet's aid was kept vague enough ('Gorkha would give as much assistance as possible') to suit its interests.[10]

When the PRC established control over Tibet in 1951, Nepal at first refused to acknowledge the new ground reality. In April 1954, Nepali Prime Minister Matrika Prasad Koirala said, 'Nepal even now acknowledged the Dalai Lama as the sovereign of Tibet.'[11] But India had already recognised Chinese sovereignty over Tibet, and now Jawaharlal Nehru expected Nepal to follow. 'You know also that we have been having long talks with the Chinese government in Peking in regard to Tibetan matters. It is important, therefore, that there should be the closest coordination between India and Nepal so as to avoid any differing approach, which may lead to complications,' Nehru wrote to Koirala on 23 March 1954, a few days before India signed the Panchsheel Agreement on Tibet.[12] Nehru said he had been 'favourably impressed' by Zhou Enlai. 'He is by no means the narrow-minded person that communists often are.'[13]

The close coordination between the Nepali and Indian governments at this point was not novel; in fact, Delhi's view of Kathmandu is best explained through these early years of cautious overtures towards China. Nehru believed the traditional people-to-people relationship, the close British involvement with the ruling Ranas and their control over Nepal's foreign relations, and India's support to the 1950 democratic movement gave the India–Nepal relationship a 'special' character. Further, there was Nehru's assumption that Nepal's foreign relations were closely linked with India's, and 'much as we appreciate the independence of Nepal, we cannot risk our own security from anything going wrong in Nepal which permits either that barrier [i.e. the Himalaya] to be crossed or weakens our frontier'.[14]

In 1950, India became the first non-communist nation to establish diplomatic relations with China. Kathmandu was expected to follow. B.P. Koirala, the Congress leader who led the 1950 revolution, wrote that politician Tanka Prasad Acharya, under whose prime ministership diplomatic relations between China and Nepal would restart in 1956, told him the Chinese were 'pressuring' him on the matter of not continuing the traditional extraterritorial rights of Nepalis in Tibet and halting the Tibetan tribute mission. Acharya said, 'India is also applying pressure on this.'[15] Koirala, a self-confessed socialist, supported Tibetan independence. After the 1954 India–China agreement, he told Nehru that the latter had 'gifted Tibet to the Chinese on a silver platter'. According to B.P. Koirala, Nehru had 'provided international legitimacy and recognition to the takeover of Tibet. You are also asking us [Nepal] to unilaterally let China have what it wants.' Nehru explained, 'When all is said and done, [Nepal] will not be able to maintain [her traditional] rights in any case . . . Renouncing your rights, on the other hand, will send a positive message to the Chinese.'[16] Elsewhere, Nehru wrote that the 1954 agreement was inevitable. 'It was a recognition of a certain factual situation which we could not possibly change.'[17]

India and China signed the Panchsheel Agreement that outlined their respective positions on Tibet in April 1954. Two days later, Nepal King Tribhuvan and Foreign Minister D.R. Regmi flew to New Delhi. A Nepali weekly later published an *aide-memoire* handed to Regmi in Delhi. Apart from Nehru's insistence that the two countries coordinate their foreign policy, a key point stated, 'in particular, in matters relating to the relations of Nepal with Tibet and China, consultations will take place with the Government of India'.[18] Nehru wrote to Tribhuvan in September 1954, 'This is the basis of our relations, that is, a common foreign policy and defence, and any relations with other countries have to be governed by this factor.'[19]

Nepal now began to give serious thought to establishing relations with China. Nehru said India was 'glad' about the development, and flagged Zhou about the American presence in Kathmandu during the Chinese premier's visit to Delhi in October 1954. 'America . . . is creating a lot of trouble [in Nepal]. Although America has no embassy in Kathmandu, the American ambassador in India is credited to Kathmandu . . . [Lot] of money is thrown about. Nepalese are easily bribed and they are thus inducing Nepal to allow America to establish an embassy there, but on our advice they postponed. The main difficulty is that if China opened an embassy there, America will also do likewise.'[20] Zhou agreed to appoint the Chinese ambassador in Delhi as concurrent ambassador to Kathmandu in deference to Nehru's wishes. 'We can consider Nepal's difficulties and not allow US to have any excuse.'[21]

Nehru's idealism made him believe India and China could forge a future together in a postcolonial world. Zhou concurred. 'Increasing the contacts between individuals is beneficial for the peace of Asia and the world at large,' he told Nehru.[22] This synchronicity in their worldview was seen in their conversations around Nepal. After his return from China, Nehru noted, 'I told [Zhou] that the Nepalese government had kept us informed of [Chinese desire for relations with Nepal]. The king of Nepal had been ill and had gone to Switzerland for treatment. On his return they would no doubt take up this matter. So far as we are concerned, we would welcome friendly relations between Nepal and China . . . it was desirable that they [Nepal and China] should settle such problems as existed in regard to Tibet.'[23]

Unfortunately for Nehru, King Tribhuvan of Nepal would not return from Switzerland. He died in Zurich on 13 March 1955, and his son, Mahendra, became king. Nehru would soon realise father and son were not alike—for all of Nehru's insistence that Nepal's foreign policy continue to be coordinated with India's, he would find that Mahendra had a mind of his own. Soon after, the bonhomie between Nehru and the Chinese too would dissipate, and Nepal would find itself sandwiched between two bigger neighbours who would eventually go to war.

✦

Mahendra, a literary man, wrote very little about himself. Reams have been written about him, though, both hagiographical as well as critical. And yet, they offer little insight into a king who shaped modern Nepal's worldview. While much of Mahendra's rule was focused on building the governance system that was the Panchayat, it was during his reign that Nepal effectively moved away from the heavyweight influence of Nehru and New Delhi.[24] His disdain for democracy was visible even before he dismissed B.P. Koirala's elected government in December 1960. In 1955, he had said, 'It's shameful that even four years after the introduction of democracy, we are struggling to identify four achievements. If democracy is a child, it has all the faults a child shouldn't possess: selfishness, greed and jealousy.'[25] But Mahendra was perhaps most wary of Koirala's grassroots popularity. 'Mahendra's [December 1960] action probably was . . . due to his fear that the popular Koirala, if he remained in office long enough, threatened the king's position as the dominant force in Nepal,' the CIA said.[26] Mahendra imprisoned the elected government on charges that it was colluding with 'anti-national elements and had acted against the interests of the nation, the sovereignty and national unity'.[27] Nehru wrote that he had been expecting Mahendra to take such a step. '[Mahendra] has repeatedly mentioned to me about his dissatisfaction with the Ministry.'[28] The king himself wrote to Nehru that the coup was 'finally adopted after all other efforts had failed to avoid this situation'.[29]

It is doubtful these charges had any element of truth—for the Nepali Congress (NC) government, despite its ideological roots in India and its discomfort over the Tibet issue, had taken forward relations with China. Nepal and China had initiated diplomatic relations on 1 August 1955. Adhering to Nehru's wishes, the Chinese ambassador in New Delhi was made concurrent to Nepal, and so no embassy was set up in Kathmandu. A second treaty on Tibet, similar to the one India had signed in 1954, was signed in September 1956, abrogating all past agreements between Nepal and Tibet. This was preceded by the first Chinese aid package to Nepal: 'Rs. 20 million [in Indian rupees] in cash and Rs. 40 million in "machinery, equipment, materials and other commodities during the next three years," to be used for the construction of a cement factory and a paper mill.'[30]

By the time the B.P. Koirala government took office, India–China tensions had flared up after the Dalai Lama's escape as well as disagreements over the border. Two senior NC leaders questioned China's actions a month after the 1959 revolt had broken out in Tibet. The NC then adopted a resolution that said, 'It is a breach of the Chinese promise of autonomy that has caused the Tibetans to rise in a national revolt and as such it is the duty of China to satisfy them by giving them what they want.' Koirala was quick to clarify his party's position was not the same as his government's.[31] Under Koirala, Nepal even opposed the 1959 draft resolution on the question of Tibet and human rights that had been tabled at the United Nations General Assembly on the grounds that, although China had been accused of military suppression and human rights violations in Tibet, the PRC 'still remains unrepresented in the United Nations'.[32] Its delegate, Surya Prasad Upadhyaya, said, 'If we speak of human rights and their suppression in Tibet, we should first try to find out what human rights the Tibetan people have enjoyed through the centuries and which of these human rights have been denied to the people of Tibet today . . . For these and many other reasons, we believe that no useful purpose has been served by bringing the Question of Tibet before the United Nations.' Nepal would continue to argue for the PRC's inclusion in the UN through the 1960s.

But in 1959, after the Lhasa uprising, more worrying for Nepal were reports that Nepalis had been arrested in Tibet after the uprising and denied the right to meet the consul-general. These reports, along with the news that the Nepali consulate in Lhasa had also been attacked, unnerved the NC government, despite its stand at the UN. China tried to ameliorate Kathmandu's concerns, but two incidents in 1960 served to make Koirala more circumspect about Chinese intentions in the Himalaya.

In April 1960, during the course of the border demarcation, a dispute arose over where Mt Everest lay. Two months later, Chinese troops shot dead a Nepali soldier in Mustang.

The controversy over Everest, known as Chomolongma in Tibet and Sagarmatha in Nepal,[33] began after Koirala returned from his state visit to China in March 1960, where he discussed the peak with Mao. Chinese maps had showed not just the peak but the entire Mahalangur range, which Everest is a part of, as part of China.[34]

During their talks, Mao told Koirala, 'Let Mount Everest remain a common summit, and let us call it a friendship summit.' Koirala did not agree, arguing that the entirety of the peak fell within Nepal:

> [Mao] said, 'But you do not even have a name for it in your language, and you call it "Mount Everest".'
> I remembered at that time, or someone had reminded me, that it was known as 'Sagarmatha'.[35] Even though I was new to that term, I replied, 'You do not have a name for the peak either. "Chomolongma" is a Tibetan name.'
> Mao replied, 'Tibet is China.'[36]

B.P. Koirala dismissed China's claim on Everest as 'ordinary' upon his return, but public opinion was whipped up sufficiently for the first anti-China demonstration in Nepal on 20 April 1960. The world's highest peak had been summited only a few years previously in 1953, and it had brought tremendous exposure to Nepal. After utterances from both sides about coming to a friendly solution on the issue, the Chinese eventually 'presented a *fait accompli* and put the Nepalese government in a dilemma' after its first expedition climbed the peak from the Tibetan side in May, and the expedition leader referred to Everest as 'the highest peak of the fatherland'.[37]

The Nepalis were in a bind. In a press conference held after the expedition, Koirala maintained Everest belonged to Nepal and 'to Nepal alone'. However, the claim, scholars suggest, was more for public opinion. 'Gradually it veered round to the view that the peak . . . had to be shared, without ever publicly stating so.'[38] The issue was not referred to the Joint Boundary Committee that had begun delineating the border between the two countries; instead, it was to be resolved politically. Finally, during Mahendra's state visit to China in 1961, a one-on-one discussion with Zhou yielded a resolution that eventually led to sharing the peak. 'A compromise was inevitable.'[39]

✦

Mt Everest apart, Koirala had brought back fond memories from his March 1960 visit to China. It was, by all accounts, a successful one. Zhou presented the Nepali prime minister with an overcoat, and he was taken to the newly established communes and factories. He was not impressed with the communes. 'I noticed that the children were indeed doing well, but felt there was too much control over the people.' Koirala acknowledged that his visits may have been useful for propaganda purposes. When his wife Sushila entered the kitchen of a home that was not on their official schedule, 'the condition inside was not as good as the outside indicated'.[40]

Zhou and the Nepali premier shared a comfortable relationship; Koirala says he knew 'few people as cultured and civilized' as Zhou, who was 'more accomplished' than Nehru. Mao met him at 11 p.m. Their conversations were fruitful. Although the Everest issue was contentious, the discussions on the rest of the border were successful. China's magnanimous attitude towards the border with Nepal, and with Burma earlier, has been interpreted by scholars as a signal to India, where the border talks would fail (and lead to war). The CIA wrote:[41]

The Chinese tried to make the impression of their willingness to negotiate a settlement even more credible by acting quickly to sign a border agreement with Nepal. . . .the Nepalese were used in roughly the same manner as the Burmese; that is, they were persuaded to settle their border differences with China in a two-step process, first agreeing to principles and the establishment of a joint commission and then working out a final treaty. The 21 March agreement provided for the mutual cessation of armed patrolling within a 12.5 mile (20 km) zone from the border—a proposal for a quasi-demilitarized zone similar to one made by Chou earlier and rejected by Nehru for the Sino-Indian border.

A second agreement increased Chinese aid to Nepal during Koirala's visit, leading to a Chinese aid mission in Kathmandu. When he asked Zhou why China did not match the Indian grant amount, the latter said, 'That may not be good for you or for us . . . India may become wary if we give you too much assistance . . . the international community would take it that we are trying to compete with India.'[42] Perhaps the Chinese thought a peaceful solution to the dispute with India could still be found.

Koirala travelled to Guangzhou on Mao's train, which had 'a library, a table for playing cards, a chessboard . . . Attached was the living room, and next to it my bedroom. There was a double bed, a porcelain bathtub . . . Every car was served by hostesses, and the arrangement was like that of some five-star hotel.'[43] Although he had reservations about the 'grandeur amidst which the Chinese leaders were living', his sense was that the visit had been successful. 'They had probably believed that we were completely biased towards India, and I believe we were able to change that view.'[44]

Zhou had proposed a mutual non-aggression pact while Koirala was in China. Delhi was not pleased. After rumours that the pact would be signed during Zhou's April 1960 visit, Nehru wrote to Koirala, 'We do not know what the terms of such an agreement are likely to be, but if the agreement with Burma is any guide, Nepal will undertake not to commit aggression against China and not to take part in any military alliance directed against China . . . The obvious implication of any such provision in a treaty would be that China wants to safeguard herself against hostile action by India . . . Indeed, this would be against

Nepal's dignity and self-respect, as the other party to the agreement would be a country which has already signed military alliances ... You will appreciate my concern over this matter because this will naturally affect the relations between Nepal and India.'[45]

In another letter to Bidhan Chandra Roy, the then chief minister of West Bengal, Nehru was blunter. 'No question arises . . . of Nepal going out of its way as probably suggested by the Chinese and make a treaty of this kind. Such a treaty would be definitely an unfriendly act to India . . . I am writing all this to you because perhaps you might have a talk with the King while he is in Calcutta about this matter and point out to him the consequences of any such treaty . . .'[46]

We do not know whether Nepal turned down the non-aggression proposal because of Nehru's concerns, but such a scenario is quite possible, especially because Nepal was still quite tentative about China at this time. Beyond Everest and Mustang, Kathmandu would also have heard of China encouraging people of Tibetan ethnicities living in the borderlands to join the PRC, as they did in Limi Valley. A *People's Daily* issue in September 1959 said 'a day may come when more "progressive people" in Sikkim, Bhutan or Nepal—a good number of them are of Tibetan origin—will claim their "peaceful liberation" and then Peking would be forced to help'.[47] In any case, the two countries signed a treaty of peace and friendship based on the Panchsheel terms of the 1956 treaty instead of a non-aggression pact.

Under B.P. Koirala, Nepal had attempted a precarious balancing act between the two giant neighbours at a time of rising tensions. He saw in China a diplomatic heavyweight that could offset New Delhi's pressures on Kathmandu, as well as shore up his government's credentials at a time when he faced domestic opposition on several fronts. A Chinese embassy opened in Kathmandu in August 1960, and a joint boundary commission was set up the next month. While Koirala's efforts were directed at maintaining a neutral foreign policy, Mahendra evidently did not think his government had performed well enough. On 15 December 1960, Koirala and his ministers were arrested while attending the first annual convention of the Tarun Dal, the Youth League. Koirala would later write in his memoir, 'That day, had we had some sub-machine guns in our hands, under no circumstances would the king have acted. But we were not prepared with guns, nor would it have been appropriate. We had already entered the constitutional process . . . That action by the king has failed to deliver peace up to this day [i.e. 1981]. In other words, it was not a sustainable action on his part.'[48]

✦

The royal takeover realigned Nepali foreign policy, bringing it closer to the Kathmandu ideal of an equidistant relationship with China and India. But relations between India and Nepal had begun to sour. While Delhi was peeved at the agreement on the Lhasa–Kathmandu highway, Mahendra in turn was displeased by the presence of NC exiles on Indian soil. When a twenty-two-year-old NC activist threw a bomb at Mahendra's motorcade in Janakpur, close to the Indian border, in January 1962, massive anti-India demonstrations took place in Kathmandu, with the king saying the anti-monarchists were operating from 'the sanctuary of a foreign power'.[49] To Nehru, Mahendra wrote, '[T]he unbounded feelings of wrath and contempt naturally welled up in the hearts of the Nepalese people against those who have fled away from Nepal into India and taken shelter there, and are currently engaged in criminal acts against their motherland from across the Indian territory.' The anti-India demonstrations, the king said, were 'to checkmate and keep within bounds . . . the feelings of suspicion of our people', and that they should not be taken as 'expressions of anti-Indian feeling'. And finally, indirectly suggesting Nehru was complicit in Nepali Congress activities, he said, 'Please, therefore, give your serious consideration to these real and honest facts, so either stop them [Congress activists] from doing any harm to Nepal and the Nepalese from Indian base or ask them to quit India at once.'[50]

Nehru's reply was blunt. 'It is stated in your letter that this [Janakpur] attack was organised and encouraged by Nepalese who are in India . . . I do not know what proof you may have about this matter. We have seen none and this has been denied by [Nepali Congress] leaders . . . We have told these leaders that they cannot use India as a base for any armed operations in Nepal. We have denied them access to arms or money . . . certain statements criticising the present regime in Nepal have been made by these Nepali Congress leaders in India. Such criticism is permitted by our law . . . We have been completely quiet in India and are friendly to Nepal, and this torrent of abuse from ministerial quarters and newspapers, without any facts to support it, has pained me greatly.'[51] Nehru evidently did not think much of the young king, calling him a 'foolish and conceited person' who was in the hands not only of 'bad advisers, but a palace clique that is anti-India' after India was blamed for allowing arms to be smuggled across the border.[52]

China watched these developments keenly. The Chinese embassy in Delhi noted, 'After the Nepali king took the throne, India not only publically [sic] criticized Nepal's royal family and meddled in Nepal's internal affairs and relations with China, it harbored and actively supported anti-king fugitive elements in using India as a base for armed subversion against the royal family . . . Nepal has strengthened its guard against India; it continuously resists all kinds of pressure from India, and develops relations with China despite various obstructions from India.'[53] In September 1962, India imposed an 'unofficial and undeclared' economic blockade on Nepal—similar in semantics to the 2015 blockade. The following month, at a banquet in Beijing, Chinese Foreign Minister Chen Yi said, 'In case any foreign army makes a foolhardy attempt to attack Nepal . . . China will side with the Nepalese people.'[54] The message was meant for New Delhi. If China had known war with India was inevitable by this point, the message also implied China did not want to extend hostilities to other neighbouring states, and it did not want India to do so either. Nehru told reporters Chen was 'showing off', but, privately, he was disturbed by the extent of pro-China coverage in Nepali newspapers, and Kathmandu's tilt to the north.[55]

The 1962 India–China war was fought over several issues, but key to understanding the Chinese position was that India's insistence over the McMahon Line as a boundary marker was rooted in a fallacy: it was borne out of the 1914 Simla Convention between British India, Tibet and the Republic of China, which historian McGranahan has labelled an act of 'imperial statemaking', and one that China has never officially recognised as the Chinese representative Chen Yi-fan did not sign the final treaty. The bifurcation of Tibet into Inner and Outer Tibet was intended to turn it into a buffer state, and while the borders in the northeast of India were demarcated by the former British foreign secretary, it was British imperial might that would keep the peace.[56] But now that the British had withdrawn, the border as delineated by McMahon was not acceptable to China.

Nehru, however, believed the Indo-Tibetan frontier was a 'settled one' and 'not open to argument or discussion, except perhaps with regard to minor tracts here and there which might be doubtful'.[57] But

China's position would also change. During Zhou's visit to India in early 1957, he told Nehru that 'I knew nothing about the McMahon Line until recently when we came to study the border problem after liberation of China . . . And now that it is an accomplished fact, we should accept it.'[58] As tensions rose, Zhou wrote to Nehru in January 1959, 'The "McMahon Line" was a product of the British policy of aggression against the Tibetan region of China . . . Juridically, too, it cannot be considered legal.'[59]

This change in the Chinese government's attitude was precipitated by the question of Tibet. As the Dalai Lama escaped and large-scale rebellions began against Chinese rule in Tibet, Zhou offered Nehru a territorial swap: 'Chinese sovereignty over the disputed western sector (Aksai Chin) and Indian sovereignty over the eastern sector.'[60] Nehru refused. As the Chinese saw it, one of the reasons behind Nehru's anti-China approach was that 'the Indian media and Parliament spread rumors about China's border conflicts with Nepal, Sikkim, and Bhutan and claim that China is encroaching upon small nations'.[61]

Thus, the two Asian giants fell out, and with it, the camaraderie between Nehru and Zhou also vanished. A discord between the two countries suited Nepali interests, especially for those who believed it was time to move away from Indian, and Nehruvian, influence. The 'China card', which Nepal has been alleged of playing in times of strain, was born.

History offers the advantage of retrospection. Nepal's leaders were at first wary of a communist China at their doorstep. It was Nehru's standing in the minds of early Nepali leaders, and Indian influence on the country's foreign policy then, that had paved the way for China in Nepal. But Nehru's short-sighted understanding of what Tibet meant for China resulted in the deterioration of what had until then been a fairly warm understanding between Beijing and New Delhi.

Meanwhile, Kathmandu too was chafing at the dilution of its sovereignty through the 'special relationship' with India. Under the proactive Mahendra, who had fewer ties with Nehru than his father, Nepal was newly assertive. When anti-monarchy activists began using India as a base, Mahendra was convinced he needed a future beyond Delhi.

When the India–China war began on 20 October, Kathmandu was spared the need to act strongly. Delhi immediately backed down on the blockade. Now that the stakes were higher, it also asked all NC activists to halt their armed movement and increased aid to Nepal. Mahendra was worried about the implications of an aggressive China ready to use force against its neighbours. If it was India today, why not Nepal tomorrow? But when Indian defences were quickly overrun by the Chinese before the latter withdrew to erstwhile positions, New Delhi's loss was also felt by its neighbours. 'If India could not even defend its own borders, how could it defend Nepal against China?'[62]

✦

'It is a fact of geography,' Mahendra once said, 'that [Nepal] cannot exist without being friendly to our neighbours.'[63] The 'king for the people', as the *New York Times* called him in 1960,[64] had offered his own take on his ancestor Prithvi Narayan Shah's famous dictum of Nepal being a 'yam' between two boulders. The road from Lhasa had established his credentials as a monarch who had successfully pulled Nepal out of the overbearing Indian embrace, but as we have seen, it also brought new headaches as China began to export its revolution to Nepal. By the time he died of a heart attack in January 1972, the Cultural Revolution had tempered Kathmandu's view of Beijing. But larger developments beyond its control meant Nepal once again danced on the razor's edge.

Beijing began to develop a rapprochement with Washington once Nixon came to power and Mao broke off with the Soviets. Meanwhile, an Indo–Soviet friendship treaty was signed in 1971 as a prelude to the Bangladesh war. This put Nepal right in the middle of two Cold War alliances. As the war unfolded, Nepal keenly watched India's military belligerence under Indira Gandhi and China's failure to prevent the dismemberment of its strategic partner, Pakistan—a sign of the limitations of Chinese capabilities and influence in South Asia.

Chinese foreign policy in South Asia had begun targeting the Soviets from the late 1960s onwards to create 'a belt of friendly states free from Soviet influence if not wholly amenable to that of China', according to the CIA.[65] Beijing believed a reconciliation with India 'would trigger an adjustment in big power interests in the region', and made 'overt gestures of friendship' towards Delhi in 1970, before the 1971 war threw all such calculations into the sink and complicated its position. India did not trust China enough to allow it to mediate in the Bangladesh war. Besides, a forceful Chinese response would give the Soviets grounds for increasing their own influence in the region. This would explain Beijing's decision to counsel restraint. 'Chinese policy during the war in December was basically defensive; through diplomacy and propaganda, but little else, Peking sought to confine the war in time and space, to avoid any possibility of Chinese military involvement, to save as much of Pakistan's West Wing as possible.'[66] Beijing's target during the war was Moscow, on whose doorsteps it laid the blame for the Indian aggression.

China's desire to improve relations with India, however, did not mean a shift away from its policy of engaging with smaller South Asian neighbours to extricate them from India's sphere of influence. Reaffirming its ties with Pakistan post the war, China continued to cultivate and play on fears of Indian expansionism. With respect to Nepal, although a 'mutual distrust of India' brought them together, 'the Chinese have taken care not to give India cause for alarm and have not fundamentally altered Nepal's status as a Himalayan buffer state'.[67] Further, Beijing had a new security calculus to worry about: the Soviet effort to set up a 'system of collective security' that encircled China.[68]

India, of course, did not trust the Chinese. 'The Chinese policy in respect of South Asia is to walk on four legs, if one may say so, namely Pakistan, Sri Lanka, Nepal, and Bangladesh,' then Indian Charge d'Affaires L.L. Mehrotra wrote to Delhi in April 1975. 'Any suggestion on our part to look at the Asian Collective Security proposal with respect rather than circumspection would enhance China's capability to play our neighbors against us and shout us out of our present status in the non-aligned world.'[69] Further, India's nuclear test in May 1974, followed by the annexation of Sikkim in April 1975—which Beijing did not officially recognise until 2003—increased China's discomfort. 'With Sikkim securely in India's grasp,' a CIA study concluded, 'Sino-Indian rivalry in the Himalayas is likely to center on Nepal.'[70]

The Republican government in the US was reaching out to Mao's China. In November 1974, American Secretary of State Dr Henry Kissinger met with Deng Xiaoping in Beijing. After the annexation of Sikkim ('I haven't understood Sikkim. It is incomprehensible'), Kissinger believed that India's 'immediate intention is in Nepal'. Deng agreed, saying, 'It is the dream of Nehru, inherited by his daughter, to have the whole South Asian subcontinent in their pocket.'[71] In a second conversation in December 1975, then American President Gerald

Ford asked Deng whether there was any threat of an Indian invasion of Nepal post-Sikkim. Deng replied, 'Nepal itself feels the threat, but at the moment there are no indications that India will make open military actions . . . As a land-locked country, Nepal has all its communications through India. This is the greatest practical difficulty for Nepal. And I believe that you can do more things with Nepal. We are doing what we can with our capability. We have established good relations with Nepal—we have mutual confidence—but what we can do is quite limited. Perhaps things will get better when our railroad into Tibet is accomplished . . . It is necessary to help Nepal. The Nepalese are a nation that can fight. Nepal isn't Sikkim or Bhutan.'[72]

While the Cold War had brought erstwhile enemies into a new alliance, in Kathmandu the spotlight now was on its new king, the young Birendra, who gave 'the impression of being a serious, rather lonely man, filled with a sense of mission to modernize' Nepal.[73]

✦

The CIA believed King Birendra, Mahendra's oldest son, could serve 'as a link between traditional and modernizing forces'.[74] 'Haunted by the fate of the Shah of Iran', Birendra's legacy in Nepal is that of a modernist king who wished well, but was beset by domestic political disturbances and external pressures that did not allow him to deliver. His foreign policy would follow a template similar to that of his father's—to pull Nepal away from India's bear hug—but with Deng's China reducing aid as it accelerated reforms to pursue growth, Birendra would have to make do with little more than moral support from its northern neighbour for the most part.

His rule began on a sour note with India. In August 1972, NC activists attacked a police station in the Terai, and in June 1973, an aircraft was hijacked. In both instances, Birendra saw Indian unwillingness to crack down on NC activists operating out of its territory. As early as his coronation in February 1975, when he announced Nepal would be declared a Zone of Peace, Birendra's desire to break away from the Indian security umbrella was clear. India's military adventures in the region—the annexation of Sikkim, the creation of Bangladesh and Delhi's newfound nuclear capability—were all worrying signs to him. India was immediately disturbed; its then ambassador, M.K. Rasgotra, wrote: 'I advised the [Indian] government to neither accept nor reject the Zone of Peace proposal and keep asking the Nepalese what its implications will be for India–Nepal relations, to the rights Nepalese nationals enjoy in India in matters of residence and employment and to India's security and other interests.'[75] When China and Pakistan supported the proposal without much ado, Delhi perceived it as a slight, and believed Kathmandu had consulted with the two before announcing the proposal. Could China's support be another means of curbing 'Indian expansionism', as Chinese President Li Xiannian had suggested?[76] Delhi was equally worried that the Soviet Asian Collective Security scheme would be 'flexible enough to adjust to twists and turns of the Asian environment', and thus South Asian concepts such as Nepal's Zone of Peace could be brought under it, reducing Indian influence in the region.[77]

The Zone of Peace proposal was indeed intended to shift Nepal away from India's security umbrella. And, ironically, nowhere was this more visible than in Birendra's commitment to acquire more arms. The degree to which India understood what the 'special relationship' meant, and equally Nepal's opposition to Delhi's interpretations of the 1950 terms combined with the 1965 defence agreement, would initiate further strain in ties between the Nepali monarchy and India.

In 1965, Kathmandu had negotiated a secret agreement with India to supply it military equipment after considering China's willingness to use force against its neighbours. 'American and British assistance would be sought only when India was not in a position to supply the necessary equipment.'[78]

In September 1975, General Arjun Rana, the then director general of military operations, informally followed up with US officials in Nepal on an earlier request to acquire 'twin 40s [40 mm guns], quad 50s [50 calibre machine guns], and smaller missiles such as Red-Eye', a handheld surface-to-air missile that was a precursor to the Stinger, made famous by the mujahideens during the Soviet occupation of Afghanistan.[79] 'Gen. Arjun stated requirement was to have a modest or minimum air defense protection of Kathmandu international airfield, one or two other airfields, and a "couple of key installations",' a cable dated 29 September 1975 read.[80] Rana explained to the US official that Nepal's concern was the lack of any air defence against 'raids, highjackings (sic) or other aerial attack'. India was unwilling to replace the existing equipment; Delhi would be approached in 1972, 1976 and in the early 1980s with a similar request, but all of them would be denied.[81] Rana was also concerned about Indian aerial reconnaissance during the 1974 operations against the Khampas, which he regarded as 'a blatant infringement of sovereignty that they would like to be able to counter, even if only facesaving in scope', the cable read.

The US was cautious; its Kathmandu embassy thought the US 'should not engage in new aid programs or sales that supplant traditional Indian relations'. Although Nepal could acquire such weapons elsewhere, the political impact of an American arms sale to Nepal outweighed any commercial gains. 'While adverse Indian reaction is quite predictable, even the PRC may view such a US action as an effort to increase US influence along their Tibetan flank,' the embassy concluded. The State Department concurred. India would 'question our motives', and as there was 'no likelihood' of military assistance for Nepal, the Nepal Army was to be 'discouraged' from submitting a formal request.[82]

Nonetheless, Nepal was not deterred. It would continue to look outside India for its weapons supply. Kathmandu would find a willing, and unexpected, ear to the north, especially given the fact that the next low in Nepal–India relations came at a time when Beijing was reaching out to New Delhi.

With Mao's death in 1976, Chinese leaders who had been purged during the Cultural Revolution began to make a comeback. Simultaneously, Beijing began to back down on damaged relations with almost all Asian powers. In South Asia, it focused on repairing the relationship with India, which had been disrupted once again by its war with Vietnam, especially as India's foreign minister, Atal Behari Vajpayee, was in China on an official visit when the war began.

To signal its intent, Deng once again informally proposed Zhou's 'east-west swap solution', which India rejected.[83] In the 1980s, China extended an invitation to the newly elected prime minister, Rajiv Gandhi, to visit China, reopened consulates and gave in to India's demands that a border settlement be negotiated 'sector by sector'.[84]

The Indian establishment still had a way to go before it could trust the Chinese, with its officials saying China had changed the rules by asking for 'mutual concessions' for the sector-by-sector negotiations. 'As a result, a stalemate has developed, with China maintaining that, as long as India refuses to make concessions in the east, the Chinese will concede nothing in the west.'[85] Despite a brief but tense confrontation at Sumdorong Chu in 1987, border talks between the two countries continued. Meanwhile, the Soviets signalled they wanted to normalise relations with China, and asked India to do the same. 'By the time of the Rajiv Gandhi–Deng Xiaoping December 1988 summit, India's global geopolitical position had actually weakened with China no longer perceiving India through a triangular Sino-Soviet lens.'[86]

In Kathmandu, Birendra had become unnerved after India's military intervention in Sri Lanka. Fears of Indian assertion, especially over the Madhes population, which Nepalese officials likened to the Sri Lankan Tamils in conversations with US officials, drew Kathmandu closer to Beijing. 'The Nepalese expressed concern that India could violate Nepal's territory as easily as it did Sri Lanka's.'[87] Although Birendra cancelled a contract with China in 1985 to build a section of the highway close to the Indian border and accepted Delhi's offer, he grew convinced that a security relationship with China would be a deterrence for India to use their 'Sri Lanka tactics in Nepal'.[88]

Note that this was a period of intense regional adventurism for India: apart from the Sri Lankan intervention, there was also a brief military operation in Maldives at the request of the latter's government. Birendra was also beset by domestic political difficulties. Opposition to the Panchayat system was growing, despite a 1979 referendum (which many believe was rigged) that voted in its favour. In June 1985, a series of bomb blasts across the country killed seven.

It was against this background that Nepal decided to import weapons, including sixteen anti-aircraft guns, from China in March 1988. 'The first consignment of arms — 500 truckloads worth $20 million — began arriving in June over the Lhasa–Kathmandu highway.'[89] The convoy reportedly travelled in secrecy, and civilian traffic was restricted over the highway. India, as expected, took serious umbrage; it considered the import a violation of the secret clauses of the 1950 treaty. In a secret letter made public only later in 1959, it was stipulated that 'any arms, ammunition or warlike material and equipment necessary for the security of Nepal that the government of Nepal may import through the territory of India shall be so imported with the assistance and agreement of the government of India'.[90] India argued that this agreement, coupled with the secret 1965 agreement, meant that Nepal had contravened the treaty by importing arms from China.

Kathmandu, on the other hand, argued that the 1950 agreement pertained only to arms being imported via India. Responding to New Delhi's argument that India had not been 'consulted', Kathmandu said Delhi had not consulted with it either on the decision to go to war with China and Pakistan. When India asked Nepal to no longer import arms from China and not use the weapons against India, 'Birendra refused to give any such assurances'. Instead, the king suggested India's belief that the 'Himalayas were India's vital defense barrier' was 'out-of-date' thinking.[91]

The reasons for China's decision to sell arms to Nepal while it was cultivating India are not known. Garver suggests NORINCO, the Chinese state arms marketing firm, saw the Nepal sale as a purely commercial one-off, a relationship it had exercised with other countries in South Asia. It is unclear whether the sale had the approval of higher authorities. If anything, 'Beijing's extremely low-keyed reaction to the India-Nepal confrontation precipitated by the arms sale may be interpreted as a sign of Chinese embarrassment, as tantamount to admission that someone on the Chinese side messed up . . . My own best guess is that the sale did not have higher level clearance, and that what we have is a case in which bureaucratic politics initiated moves having disastrous consequences for China's long-term relationship with Nepal'.[92]

Kathmandu had upended a delicate, if unequal, cart. Efforts to renew the trade and transit treaties between Nepal and India, which phased out in March 1989, failed. A number of factors influenced this outcome: Nepal had decided to impose work permits on 150,000 Indians living in the country, it showed preferential treatment to Chinese commercial products and it continued lobbying for the Zone of Peace proposal. Subsequently, India closed down nineteen of the twenty border points, and Nepal now had to pay increased customs duties on products entering the country via India.[93] 'If it wants special trade and transit facilities, New Delhi has told Kathmandu, it must take Indian sensibilities into consideration,' a report from the time said.[94]

The semantics of the decision aside, it was clear India was willing to use its economic leverage with Nepal, just as it had in 1962, and would do again in 2015. 'Lines at gas stations are long, straining tempers. The streets of Katmandu, the capital, are nearly devoid of cars, and travel around Nepal by air or bus is becoming more difficult. Forests are being stripped for cooking fuel,' read a 1989 report, uncannily similar to 2015.[95] In both blockades, New Delhi refused to delink the insecurities of Kathmandu's ruling class (and its anti-Indian propaganda) and the 'special relationship' between the Indian and Nepali people.

The biggest difference between 1989 and 2015 was China's reaction.

Faced with a domestic rebellion that led to the Tiananmen Square massacre, a foreign policy that looked to better ties with India and a 'primitive transportation system' between Lhasa and Kathmandu, China could do little in 1989 except offer 'low-key political support' and 'modest assistance' through shipments of fuel and food items. 'To Kathmandu, Beijing's advice apparently was to come to the best terms it could with India . . . China was simply not in a position to provide assistance adequate to Nepal's needs.'[96] A Nepali official returned from China with three messages: China would not be seen as siding with Nepal at the expense of other relations during its quest for growth; Nepal could not afford to spoil relations with India expecting China's support; and a request for a private meeting with Birendra to discuss future road openings with Tibet, which at the moment was too poorly connected for China to send petroleum products to Nepal.[97] The most prominent show of support, in fact, came with Li Peng's November 1989 visit, which Nepal arranged at the last moment as an addition to his tour to Pakistan and Bangladesh.[98] But little else was forthcoming, 'yet another demonstration of China's inability to act as an effective counterweight to India in South Asia'.[99]

China's vocal but limited support for Nepal continued into the 1990s, as the country institutionalised a constitutional role for the monarchy after the 1990 revolution that brought back parliamentary democracy. Beijing reached out to parties such as the Nepali Congress, which was seen as the primary political force at the time, to ensure that Nepal's commitment to the One-China policy would not waver under the new political system. In 1991, the Dalai Lama cancelled a proposed visit to Lumbini after China objected to it. Despite political instability marking the decade, successive Nepali governments reassured China of its interests, particularly related to the movement and activities of Tibetan exiles. The highlight of the decade was President Jiang Zemin's short 1996 visit to Kathmandu, but as China continued to focus on economic growth, Nepal had to make do with limited aid grants during this decade, which also saw the emergence of the Maoist civil war. It was not until 1999, when Jiang announced the ambitious *xibu da kaifa* campaign, that China could finally signal an intent to overcome its infrastructural and security limitations in the Himalaya. Beijing would pour billions into infrastructural development in Tibet, Xinjiang and Qinghai, among other regions, subsidising the cost of economic growth. This was accompanied by the attempt to bring restive minority regions in these frontier areas under state control. As China scholar Fravel writes, 'Paradoxically, the need to quash internal unrest required external peace, forming the basis for China's diplomatic engagement of the region.'[100]

This 'Open up the West' campaign resulted in greater infrastructural capabilities across the Tibetan landscape, without which China could not have come to Nepal's assistance in the aftermath of the 2015 Indian blockade. For the first time, it informed Nepal that 'if India continues to inflict hardship on Nepal, China is ready to come to Nepal's rescue— provided Nepali leaders come up with clear, long-term partnership plans with China'.[101] Such a statement was in stark contrast to 1989, when India was aware of Chinese limitations in assisting Nepal, and Indian force deployments along the border with China remained unchanged.[102] Such a statement also reflected a shift in China's own ambitions in the neighbourhood and globally.

The modern history of Nepal–China relations is, thus, equally a story about the triangle between Nepal, India and China, for the two neighbours are always in Kathmandu's calculus. The seas were calm as long as the two giants did not quibble, but the calm also meant Nepal could not exploit its position as a 'strategic buffer'. When the quibble turned into war, historically, any outreach Kathmandu made with the north depended on how India perceived it—seen in the cancellation of Chinese aid projects, for instance. China, too, did not consider it important enough for Beijing to risk its amity with Delhi. But come 2015, and China no longer saw Nepal as being under the Indian umbrella. Whether Indian foreign policy mandarins failed to see this, or whether China just decided to press its tactical advantage home in a deeply polarised time, the outcome was the same: the road to the north was being widened.

Part Three

STATUS UPDATE

'*A great sorrow it is to bid adieu;*
A great joy it is to make friends anew.'

– Qu Yuan, quoted by Mao to Nehru in October 1954

8

'A Friendship Across the Himalayas'[1]

Fifty-five-year-old Tibetan-American Penpa Tsering was in for a surprise when he handed his passport to the immigration official at Tribhuvan International Airport, Kathmandu. It was Saturday, 22 June 2019, and Tsering had just arrived from Delhi by the 1 p.m. flight. The officer scanned his passport, and printed out a letter. 'The letter contained Chinese characters at the top with some English characters below,' Tsering told me over email a few months after the incident. Then, a most curious question was thrown at him.

The officer asked him if he was the former speaker of the Tibetan Parliament in Exile, the legislative body of the CTA that oversees Tibetans in exile. The former speaker's name, it turned out, was also Penpa Tsering. Tsering said no, he was not. The officer told him the letter on his screen was from the Chinese government. Tsering repeated he was not the man the officer was looking for. The officer took him aside, asked him to wait and went away. Tsering tried to call the US embassy; a police officer snatched his cell phone away. 'They didn't even let me use my iPad.' When he tried to get up and walk a few steps to stretch his legs, the officer shouted at him to sit down.

Four hours later, Nepali officials told Tsering he was to be deported back to the US. He insisted they had the wrong man, but to no avail. Although he had arrived from Delhi, Tsering was booked on a flight to New York via Doha. He was made to pay USD 700 for the ticket.

It emerged that the Chinese embassy in Kathmandu had written to the Nepali Ministry of Foreign Affairs, asking them to disallow a man named Penpa Tsering, said to be a 'campaigner for the Free Tibet movement as well as a strong advocate' of the Dalai Lama, from entering the country.[2] Tsering had worked for the CTA for twenty years, so I asked him if he had been confused for the former speaker anywhere else. 'No, not at all,' he wrote.

A note on the deportation, later reprinted in a newspaper, read, '*Nijalai Nepal aauna nadine vanne Chinese Embassy ko letter 6*' (There is a letter from the Chinese embassy asking that the said individual not be allowed to enter Nepal).[3] Nepali immigration officials were not sure whether the man they had deported was the right one or not, but chose to be on the safe side by deporting Tsering, an official later said. The Home Ministry confirmed that the Chinese embassy had instructed Nepal to refuse entry to people 'China finds suspicious'.[4] News reports suggested there were calls from the Chinese embassy to the Immigration Office and Home Ministry to detain Tsering.

Tsering, who was born to Tibetan refugees in Nepal, had returned in 2013 on a pilgrimage for his departed father. There had been no issues then. In 2019, after he was deported from Nepal and returned to Albuquerque, New Mexico, where he lives, he wrote to his local senator, Tom Udall, who then wrote to the State Department. Its Capitol Hill Liaison Office wrote back, 'The consular chief is particularly concerned because consular notification did not occur while Mr. Tsering was in detention before his deportation. Officials from different offices in the Embassy have discussed this case with the Government of Nepal, so they are well aware of our interest and concern in how it was handled.' The US embassy in Nepal formally asked the government for clarification on the issue, but it is not known whether a response was elicited.[5]

The deportation of Tsering, an American national, captures the dynamics of the new Nepal–China relationship in the 21st century. China's newfound economic and geopolitical strength in the new millennium has allowed it to become more assertive and vocal about its expectations from other nations. In Nepal, this new relationship was founded on resolving China's security concerns about the exiled Tibetan diaspora, which peaked with the 2008 protests against the Beijing Olympics and three self-immolations in Kathmandu.[6] The relationship has undergone several changes in the past two decades, starting with the 2006 People's Revolution in Nepal, which forced Beijing to recalibrate its traditional position of dealing only with the monarchy in Nepal. With the abolition of the monarchy, Beijing now needed to find new allies within the cacophonous Nepali political sphere, where the Maoists had arrived as a mainstream political force.

For Kathmandu and its political elite, Beijing had turned into an alternative beyond the 'China card' for those chafing at micromanagement of Nepal's internal affairs by India. These actors—particularly those belonging to the left—saw a convergence of their own interests with Beijing's new assertiveness amid a domestic political atmosphere polarised by ethnic demands around issues of identity and federalism.

Analysts often point at the 2015 unofficial Indian blockade as the turning point in the Nepal–China relationship. However, 2015 was just the endgame. It was the culmination of several years of courtship between Beijing and Kathmandu, which began in 2005, when the erstwhile king Gyanendra decided to close down the office of the Dalai Lama's local representative as well as the Tibetan Welfare Office.

✦

In May 2002, days before King Gyanendra dissolved the Nepali Parliament and extended the state of emergency as the Maoist insurgency intensified, the Chinese ambassador to Nepal, Wu Congyong, told American Ambassador Michael Malinowski that 'international cooperation' was required to end the Maoist 'anti-government forces'.[7] Earlier, in a press conference, Wu had condemned the Nepali Maoists' 'violence and terrorist acts'.

Then in 2005, a few days after he shut down the Tibetan exile offices, Gyanendra announced a royal takeover, just as his father Mahendra had done in 1960. India, the US and the UK—Nepal's primary defence suppliers—halted all military assistance to Nepal. This time, China stepped in with military aid worth USD 1 million, calling the takeover an internal matter, and welcoming the decision to close the Dalai Lama's offices. Beijing insisted its Nepal policy had not changed; its ambassador, Sun Heping, told the Americans that China 'still wanted to see "cooperation and understanding" between the King and the political parties'.[8] But as eighteen truckloads of military shipment from China arrived in November that year and Gyanendra attempted to bring China into SAARC as an observer, Nepal began cracking down on Tibetan refugees by refusing to issue exit permits for transit to India.[9] The then Nepali consul general in Lhasa (and later ambassador to China), Leela Mani Paudyal, told the US embassy that 'forty years ago, Nepal had more leverage with China, then isolated and in need of allies'. But the geopolitical situation had changed, and 'it [was] not by choice but by compulsion' that Nepal had suppressed Tibetan activities in Nepal, closed down the Tibetan exile offices, and accepted Chinese military aid.[10]

By 2006, as Nepal descended into political chaos, China wanted to cooperate with the US to stabilise the country. It continued to have a policy of no contact with the Maoists unless they 'put down their guns first'.[11] But Beijing had begun thinking of alternatives, and already viewed Maoist leader Prachanda (as Pushpa Kamal Dahal is popularly known) more optimistically than it made public. After the Maoists signed an agreement to lay down their arms in June 2006, a Chinese Foreign Ministry official told the Americans that 'determining China's next step [in Nepal] is a very sensitive issue . . . If the Maoists are part of the political mainstream and a potentially dominant factor in Nepali politics, then China cannot maintain an "ostrich policy", keeping its head in the sand, oblivious to the realities.'[12] Beijing now saw Prachanda as a dynamic leader who 'frankly outperformed' representatives from the other political parties,[13] and recognised that its policy of non-interference in Nepal's affairs and its interest in maintaining stability on the border were inherently contradictory.[14]

China's warming up to the Maoists in the years after 2006 is the first key to understanding Nepal's contemporary turn to the north. It was no coincidence that it came just as the monarchy was abolished, nor that it occurred just when China's global ambitions had begun to soar (the 2008 Beijing Olympic games has been called China's 'coming out party' by many).

China's *xibu da kaifa* campaign had already led to increased engagements with its neighbours, with border security and consolidation one of the programme's intended goals. The 1990s had seen high-level bilateral exchanges, but despite Nepali aspirations for increased engagement, its slide into civil war pushed all relations to a minimum engagement. As discontent against the monarchy became widespread over Gyanendra's clampdown on civilian rights, and it became clear the king's attempts to put down the Maoist insurgency militarily were a failure, Beijing recognised the tectonic shifts that were occurring in Nepali society and decided to play its cards carefully, watching how the situation would unfold.

By May 2007, the second People's Revolution was over, and the Maoists had come into the mainstream. The Chinese embassy in

Kathmandu established informal contact with them. By March 2008, a month before the first Constituent Assembly (CA) elections, China's links with the Maoists had become 'strong'.[15] American officials in Beijing quoted the septuagenarian Wang Hongwei, a political scientist who would emerge as a key informal link between China and the Maoists, as saying 'he doubts the Maoists would take up arms again, even if they fare poorly in the upcoming Constituent Assembly election'. As luck would have it, the Maoists established themselves as Nepal's largest political force in the first CA elections. Professor Wang himself would tell the Americans that Beijing 'has reacted slowly to the increasing influence of the Maoists'. To illustrate his point, he said that in the past he was 'academically isolated' and 'encountered difficulties' with Chinese authorities because he did not to adhere to the official position that the Maoists were 'an anti-Government armed group' that was 'misusing the name of Chairman Mao'. However, Beijing had now begun to seek his advice.[16]

✦

The Nepali Maoists first reached out to China towards the end of 2000, when Manoj Thapa, a party official, visited China on a tourist visa.[17] Thapa's visit had been arranged by a former professor associated with the China Study Centre, a think tank in Kathmandu. Although he met a few intellectuals close to the CCP, nothing came of the meeting, however, and there was no further contact until 2005. Relations improved visibly after Professor Wang visited a PLA camp in July 2006.[18]

Agni Sapkota, former Maoist leader and current speaker of the Nepali Parliament, told me that a team of Chinese officials led by Wang had met with them at Dhulikhel, east of Kathmandu, and thereafter stayed at a Maoist camp for a week. A photo of Wang in PLA combat uniform, sitting in the sort of plastic chair that is ubiquitous in South Asia, was published in a magazine a few months later. Wang holds his collar and is looking outside the frame, while Barsaman Pun 'Ananta', the current energy minister, looks on. Several male PLA combatants stand at attention behind them, while a few women combatants sit holding their SLRs and shotguns in front.

The Chinese ambassador told the Americans 'neither Beijing nor his Embassy had approved' Wang's visit,[19] with Beijing saying that Wang had met the Maoists in his personal capacity.[20] Nonetheless, the visit acted as a catalyst. A few weeks later, Ananta flew to Shanghai via Bangkok. The doors had been opened.

China had not trusted the Maoists because they had made India their base when they launched the war. Also, China had fewer links with Nepali political actors because of its policy of regarding the monarchy as Nepal's permanent power centre. '[The Chinese] didn't want the monarchy to end at first. But when the people didn't want it, they did not support it either,' Sapkota told me. Similarly, Sudheer Sharma, editor of *Kantipur*, said the Chinese had limited relations with Nepali political forces other than the monarchy before 2008, unlike the Indians or the Americans. When the republic was declared, the Chinese 'felt a sort of vacuum', and reached out to both the Maoists as well as the Nepal army. 'But they didn't get very far with the army at the time.' As for why the Maoists, Sharma said, 'The Congress had an excellent legacy through B.P. Koirala, and the Chinese thought the Congress was a trusted force. But they believed the Congress' orientation was largely inclined towards India. The UML [Communist Party of Nepal (Unified Marxist Leninist)][21] at this time was a weak force, despite old relations with them. The Maoists won the first CA elections and established themselves as a new force. They had been trying to establish relations with China for a while, and the Chinese gave them space.'

China's erstwhile policy of dealing only with the monarchy had served it well, if not consistently, over the years. In a volatile scenario, when the Maoists were still armed and other parties (and countries) did not trust them fully, the Chinese preferred to let India and the US take the lead in post-conflict management while Beijing quietly worked its channels. A sore point in the Nepal–China relationship was that Beijing had always been seen as a 'card' against India. So, it took a 'wait and see' approach before it would trust the Maoists.

After the Maoists emerged as the leading party in the 2008 CA elections, Prachanda's first visit as prime minister was to China—meant to underline the fact that the Maoists were unlike conventional Nepali political forces. The unspoken tradition had been for new Nepali prime ministers to visit Delhi first. But Prachanda decided he would attend the closing ceremony of the Beijing Olympics in August 2008, despite messages from both Indian diplomats and politicians that it would send the wrong signal to Delhi.[22] Although he maintained that his first 'political' visit would be to India, Delhi was not too convinced.

'A Friendship Across the Himalayas'   151

The *Indian Express* wrote a scathing editorial: 'The Maoist emphasis on "equidistance" between China and India is diplomatic code in Kathmandu for an end to the very special relationship with New Delhi . . . India can no longer sustain its primacy in Nepal by merely proclaiming it.'[23]

In Beijing, Prachanda was received warmly. Then president Hu Jintao told him that China was ready to assist Nepal, and he was effusively welcomed in Lhasa and Chengdu. Although no bilateral agreements were signed, the visit provided international legitimacy to the Maoists as an above-ground political force. It also fulfilled Prachanda's long-held personal ambition to visit Mao's homeland. He, in fact, broke protocol and visited Mao's *hutong* home in Dongcheng, Beijing. A Nepali report read: 'As soon as one enters the home, one can listen to Mao's voice on an old telephone set. Dahal listened to it keenly, but could not understand it as it was in Chinese . . . He was taken aback to see his own interview and portrait on the wall. A museum official told him it was the practice to put up portraits of all leaders associated with Maoist parties across the world . . . Dahal also tried the red-braised pork (Mao Shi Hong Shao Rou), Mao's favourite dish. A small bust of Mao sat in the middle of the plate . . . At Mao's mausoleum, Dahal got emotional and was silent for almost a minute after laying a wreath at his statue. When he saw Mao's embalmed body, he looked like he could not say anything even if he wanted to.'[24]

On 6 April 2008, as observers from across the world descended on Kathmandu to oversee the first Constituent Assembly elections of a republican Nepal, two French members of Parliament (MPs), Thierry Repentin and Yvonne Colleen, along with then French ambassador to Nepal, Gilles-Henri Garault, visited the Tibetan refugee camp in Bouddha, Kathmandu. There, they met with the Dalai Lama's Nepal representative, Thinley Gyatso, and presented him with a flag of Tibet, along with assurances of support within France.[25]

Two weeks later, an American mountaineer, William Brant Holland, was deported from Nepal after a flag saying 'Free Tibet' was found in his bag at the Everest Base Camp.[26] Nepal banned him from climbing Everest for two years.[27] The two incidents cemented the view of Nepali (and Chinese) officials that the Tibetan protests that had been rocking

Kathmandu—and the world, including Tibet, where they began—since March 2008 were being fuelled by outside actors, especially those from the US and Europe.[28]

The second key to understanding the new Nepal–China relationship is the latter's vulnerability in its soft spot of Tibet. The 2008 protests marked a turning point in how China viewed Tibetans in Nepal. The protests caught Beijing off guard, and it thought the interim NC-led government under Girija Prasad Koirala had been lenient on the protestors. Therefore, it consciously reached out not just to the political class but also to the security establishment. 'The Chinese strategy, according to the Nepalese, is to establish a series of concentric "security rings" around Lhasa, with the outermost running through Nepal.'[29] Sudheer Sharma said he felt the Chinese were worried that protests similar to the 2008 ones could erupt in Kathmandu again.[30] 'In Nepal's context, one Chinese commentator told me they weren't as worried about the Tibetan community in Nepal as they were about Tibetans who come in from India or outside. The Chinese feel even the 2008 protests in Kathmandu were directed from outside.' China's concerns particularly relate to the separatism advocated by Tibetan exiles, which they feel will lead to the break-up of the PRC.

While one of the intentions of *xibu da kaifa* was to ameliorate dissent in China's restive western regions through economic development, Tibet has always been more than a border territory for Beijing. Beyond its vast natural resources, control over Tibet is vital both for its national sovereignty project and to bolster a weak Himalayan border, militarised after the 1962 war. It was to address its own security interests in Tibet that Beijing began to court the Nepali establishment more actively after 2008; the closure of the Dalai Lama's office under the king in lieu of military equipment had already provided it with a template. China was willing to go the distance. Now, it began to assert itself more volubly.

In 2008, the American embassy in Beijing was told by a Chinese Ministry of Foreign Affairs official that, while 'it would be stupid' for China to attempt to contain India's influence in Nepal, they would 'intervene' in China's core interests of Tibet. 'China will be involved in individual cases if they affect China's Tibetan interests,' the official confirmed.[31] The same official also outlined why Nepal remains key to China's control over Tibet: 'Nepal has the second largest population of "overseas Tibetans" and Nepal's support of China's stance on Tibet is "very important" to China.'

China has three primary goals to this end: putting an end to Tibetan border-crossing, enforcing a de-facto ban on Tibetan political mobilisation in Nepal and close cooperation with Nepal's security agencies to 'monitor and infiltrate Tibetan communities'.[32] With Tsering's deportation, a fourth objective can be added: to discourage Tibetan activists living abroad from entering Nepal.

While border crossings have reduced significantly over the years—both as a result of increased vigilance by both sides and Tibet's economic growth—increased cooperation with Nepali authorities was achieved through bilateral visits and aid agreements. Events such as the French MPs' visit to Bouddha, the American and Indian ambassadors' 'personal' visits to the sensitive border of Mustang in the summer of 2009 (which the Chinese ambassador counteracted with his own visit), and Madhesi MPs meeting the Dalai Lama who pressed to reopen the representative's office in Kathmandu that same year, made Beijing extremely suspicious, and thereby willing to exert more pressure on Nepali authorities.[33]

China now began to interact closely with Nepali security agencies, first providing material worth NPR 2 crore, which included metal detectors, bulletproof vests, passport-reading machines and X-ray machines, to be installed at Nepal–China border crossings. China also proposed a joint intelligence-sharing mechanism on Tibetan crossings with Nepal.[34] Nepal mobilised its Armed Police Force as a border security force, and a Nepali police official told a Chinese news agency that the absence of demonstrations that year was the result of 'cooperation' between the two governments and 'a major crackdown' by Nepali authorities.[35]

China's template for how it dealt with Nepal under royal rule was now transplanted to the republic. It announced three important aid packages between March 2011 and January 2012. First, General Chen Bingde, chief of general staff of the PLA, the highest-ranking PLA officer to visit Nepal, announced a military package to the Nepal army worth USD 19 million. Beijing allegedly wanted Chinese and Nepali officers to have reciprocal rank, similar to the arrangement the Nepal army shares with India, but this was blocked by Delhi.[36] In August 2011, China's domestic security chief, Zhou Yongkang, promised aid worth USD 50 million. Finally, in January 2012, Chinese Prime Minister Wen Jiabao offered USD 113 million in aid and a USD 20 million special grant during his brief stay in Kathmandu.

Such high-level visits were as much a signal of intent as they were a display of increased bonhomie. But of equal importance were several low-level training programmes and disbursement of aid and equipment to Nepali security officials and local authorities at border districts. Intelligence-sharing mechanisms were put in place, and several agreements that 'enhance[d] the capacity' of Nepali forces and 'bolster[ed] border control' were signed.[37] China's largesse towards Nepali security forces included several public 'gifts', such as the NPR 3.6 billion handed over to the National Armed Police Force Academy in 2017. That year, its authorities proposed a border security mechanism at a meeting of district officials that would have entailed joint patrols. The Nepali authorities referred the matter to the Home Ministry. The Chinese then said the Tatopani border would open only if the proposal was approved.[38]

In 2019, during Xi's visit, a proposed extradition treaty was quashed, but two separate agreements—a Mutual Legal Assistance treaty and a Boundary Management System treaty—were signed.[39] The two countries will now hand over citizens who have illegally crossed the border within seven days of being detained, while citizens charged with crimes could also be 'temporarily transferred' upon request by the other country. The fear among Tibetans is that these two treaties could be used to deny the movement and activities of refugees in Nepal.[40]

Several reports have emerged in recent years that Chinese security officials work in close cooperation with Nepali authorities who have felt the pressure to deliver, especially when China expects a quid pro quo in lieu of the material and financial aid it provides.[41] Surveillance cameras are now common across Tibetan residential areas in Kathmandu. Reports have also contended that Chinese officials have collaborated with Nepali police officials at Tibetan demonstrations, 'directing them, positioning them, [and] telling them to remove people'.[42] Human rights organisations have alleged intimidation and threats against Tibetans and activists inside Nepal.[43] And, while previously, human rights groups would publish regular reports on Tibetans inside Nepal, no new report has been published since 2014.

In my conversations with Nepal government and security officials, they consistently maintained that, as non-citizens, Tibetans do not have the right to any political activity inside Nepal, and that any act that infringes on Nepal's One-China policy will be deemed illegal. 'As refugees, Tibetans cannot indulge in political activities in Nepal. They try to do events or conduct protests at select dates, but the Home Ministry sends us instructions to stop them,' a retired security official told me. Further, some officials even deny that Nepal is bound by the 'gentleman's agreement' to send new Tibetan refugees to India. Former foreign minister Ramesh Nath Pande wrote in his memoir that Nepal 'did not have any records of such an agreement'.[44] However, Nepali authorities have repeatedly told the US that they will uphold the 'gentleman's agreement'.

Nepal's commitment to the One-China policy is invoked in all joint statements and declarations, while transgressions are highlighted: examples include the May 2019 participation in a Tibet convention in Latvia by two Nepali MPs, one of whom was suspended by his party, and a 2016 meeting between a former Nepali prime minister and the Tibetan prime minister-in-exile. Although China has grown more confident of its ability to restrict Tibetan activities in Nepal over the years, Tibet remains 'the number one issue for them', Sudheer Sharma told me. He thought Nepal would not extradite any Tibetans already living in the country, but it would be 'very difficult' for the refugees to hold any anti-China protests in Nepal.

Coverage on Tibetan issues has also trickled down to a bare minimum, despite a vibrant media that regularly comments on global issues. Reporters are directed to not cover protests or anything relating to Tibetans in exile. The most recent example of this is the case of three journalists at the Rastriya Samachar Samiti, a state-run news wire service, who were investigated for publishing news of the Dalai Lama being released from an Indian hospital. A journalist was quoted as saying 'China sponsors junkets for Nepalese journalists' and 'that's why probably we don't see lots of criticism' about China in Nepal.[45] In its more combative foreign policy approach post the COVID-19 pandemic, the Chinese embassy in Kathmandu issued a scathing statement against the *Kathmandu Post* and its editor in early 2020. While the statement was met with widespread condemnation by other Nepali editors, it was most unusual for a diplomatic mission that had prided itself on quiet diplomacy. In fact, it was the first on-record castigation of a Nepali media outlet by the embassy.

The silence of the Nepali establishment—political and bureaucratic—appeared to endorse what was a clear overreach by a diplomatic mission.

✦

Beijing's new approach in Nepal must also be understood in the context of the larger strategic contest between Beijing and New Delhi in South Asia, as well as the strain of the Nepal–India relationship. This is best highlighted by the acrimony between the Maoists and India that set in during Prachanda's first term. Perhaps Delhi felt the Maoists owed it for bringing them above ground;[46] perhaps the Maoists felt they needed to tell the Nepali public they were not burdened by India even though its leaders were based in the country during the insurgency. As such, it did not want to be termed a 'pro-India' party, a hugely negative connotation in Nepali politics.

But the former rebels made a mistake even before they took oath as the Nepali republic's first elected government, as Sapkota emphasised when I met him one cold and rainy winter evening.

Sapkota had been suffering from a cold; he was tightly bundled up in woollens and cleared his throat regularly as he reflected on the Maoists' errors in their first term. 'We forgot we had come into the mainstream through an agreement. If we had recalled the [12-Point] agreement and kept that in mind while moving ahead, things would have been a lot better today. After the first CA elections, we had given a green signal to Girija Prasad Koirala becoming president. But we backed out once we thought of the issues regarding identity and ideology. We shouldn't have done that. It would have been better if we hadn't gone back [on our decision]. If he would have become president, Prachanda would have been prime minister, and it would have been far easier to institutionalise the changes [we sought].'

Not electing Koirala, the patriarch of the 2006 revolution and of post-1990 Nepali politics in general, as the first president was a grave error on part of the Maoists, for the former rebels were still viewed with suspicion, despite their majority in the 2008 CA elections. The decision eroded the politics of consensus that had governed the former rebels' entry into mainstream politics, partly because Koirala, whom former Indian prime minister Manmohan Singh had once described as one of South Asia's greatest leaders, threw his weight behind the 12-Point agreement.

The Maoists erred a second time when Prachanda attempted to fire an army chief a few months before the latter's retirement, a decision his coalition government presented as one of asserting civilian control over the armed forces.

The Nepal army, at the time, was seen as an institution that could play counterpoint to the eagerness of the former rebels to 'capture the state'. Already, the Indian establishment was suspicious of Prachanda's intentions after his visit to the Beijing Olympics. A series of high-level Chinese security officials visited Nepal during his tenure, while the Nepali defence minister, a former Maoist, undertook a clandestine visit to Tibet in a Chinese embassy vehicle.[47] There was also an audacious proposal by Beijing to revise the 1960 Peace and Friendship Treaty in the early part of 2009. Although the official line was that the rapid political change in Nepal necessitated a new treaty, the primary motivation was that China required a more stringent response on the Tibetan issue from Nepal.[48] Prachanda was quoted as saying the Maoists had a 'tactical relationship' with the Indians, but a 'strategic one' with the Chinese.[49]

India's unease had been apparent; Prachanda had 'tried to be a ruthless maximiser, opening multiple fronts, and slowly burning bridges' with New Delhi.[50] When the prime minister moved to dismiss Army Chief Rookmangud Katuwal, it was the final straw. New Delhi isolated the Maoists; Prachanda was forced to resign after President Ram Baran Yadav refused to endorse Katuwal's firing.[51] India then cobbled together a broad anti-Maoist coalition of twenty-two parties, and by August 2009, when the India-aligned CPN-UML leader Madhav Kumar Nepal took oath, the American embassy in New Delhi noted, 'the GOI is generally relieved to deal with a garden variety communist leader rather than a revolutionary Maoist'.[52]

India was convinced that, in Prachanda, they had a Maoist leader who was willing to move Nepal closer to China and damage ties. 'In the past, [India] supported Maoists thinking that Prachanda would take a neutral line between India and China. These hopes are elusive. Should we facilitate the Chinese designs in Nepal by bringing about a political compromise which would enable the Maoists to continue in power or has the time come to work for a non-Maoist alternative?'[53] wrote a former chief of the Research and Analysis Wing (R&AW), India's external intelligence agency, just as Prachanda announced his resignation. The India–China relationship had already been fraught with tension as New Delhi perceived the newly assertive Chinese policy in South Asia intended to replace its regional hegemony. 'It's not just about Nepal . . . It's how it fits into a broader pattern of worrying behaviour,' an Indian diplomat said at the time.[54] Prachanda flew to China a night before Indian Foreign Secretary Nirupama Rao arrived in Kathmandu to resolve the differences with the Maoists, further alienating Delhi.[55]

As the Maoists tried to regain control of the government in 2010, a tape leaked by the R&AW began to make its rounds in Kathmandu. A Maoist leader, Krishna Bahadur Mahara, had been caught on tape asking for NPR 500 million from a purported Chinese businessman (who has to date not been identified), leading to the perception that Beijing had upped the ante and moved to support Maoists in Nepal. The Maoists were kept out of power till 2011, despite Prachanda's incessant wooing of Delhi in the interim. When Delhi remained unconvinced, he steered the discourse towards a favourite of out-of-power Nepali politicians: he accused the ruling regime of being Indian 'puppets' and India of conspiring against his party. The Maoist leader then exploited internal divisions within the UML and lent his support to another UML leader, Jhalanath Khanal, who became prime minister in 2011.

Prachanda's support for Khanal, who had been among the primary Chinese interlocutors in the UML, gave credence to the idea that the government had been engineered by Beijing.[56] A massive USD 3 billion-development project in Lumbini backed by a Chinese NGO with dubious links engendered fears in Delhi that China indeed had a strategy to 'encircle' India. The Khanal government quickly moved to reassure China about its security interests, as seen by the high-level visits that took place during this term.

Although India's peak foreign policy failure in Nepal was the 2015 blockade, it was this tricky period between 2009–11 when Delhi failed to understand the new political atmosphere in Kathmandu. The Indian policy of isolating the Maoists had been successful, but it had come at a cost. The hardline faction among the former rebels had gained traction, while others bristled at India's management of Nepali political affairs. The Madhesi parties from the Terai plains, who had been campaigning for proportionate representation on an identity-based agenda, began to be portrayed as Delhi's stooges. India had alienated Nepalis across the board, including the influential Kathmandu media. It had manipulated, coerced, forced and convinced Nepali politicians to align with its interests.[57] While such policies had succeeded in the past because of the lack of an alternative, Delhi failed to read the changed circumstances. In stark contrast to Delhi's high-handed approach, Beijing's subtle diplomacy, respectful of protocol and Nepali sensitivities, won it several allies. China exploited the resentment against Indian political management, and finally turned into the alternative that Nepali leaders had always wanted it to be. Although India had remarkable leverage in Nepal through economic, cultural and social ties, it was in the process of losing all political credibility. Indian interests in Nepal came to be identified with a narrow section of the population in the Terai plains, where the Madhesi movement, based on federalism and identity politics, had already antagonised the traditional hill elite. Wily Nepali politicians now brought the two issues together in a broader anti-federalism sentiment based on anti-Indianism even as Nepali lawmakers rushed to promulgate a new constitution in the aftermath of the 2015 earthquake. The endgame would be seen in September 2015, when the unofficial blockade—India's brahmastra, as *Kantipur* editor Sudheer Sharma would tell me—was imposed, necessitating a frantic discussion among Kathmandu's corridors that Nepal's economic dependence on India must be halted.

The first three trucks entered Kathmandu on Monday, 1 November 2015, with 36,000 litres of petrol from China, escorted by various security agencies. With such fanfare, the trucks made it to the front pages of newspapers. Although the move was mostly symbolic, the petroleum tankers became a symbol of Nepali resistance, with Chinese assistance, against Indian interventionism. It was the third month of the Indian blockade, one which the then prime minister, K.P. Oli, had described as 'cruel, inhumane and beyond imagination', cementing his position as a Nepali nationalist who would not give in to Indian bullying tactics.

Oli's political trajectory is unique even in the landscape of Nepal's opportunistic politics. In 1971, along with a bunch of other radicalised youth, he was part of an anti-landlord campaign in eastern Nepal, modelled on the 1967 Naxalite uprising in West Bengal, India. After the 1971 war, Oli said, he came to support 'the most extreme opponents of the Indian government', the Naxalites, although he would later say he did not support the violence. In 1973, Oli was arrested in Rautahat, and over the next fourteen years, he would be shifted from one jail to another, spending four years in solitary confinement, until he was pardoned by the king in 1987.[58]

His next moment in the political limelight would come in 1996, when he backed the Mahakali water-sharing treaty between India and Nepal—an agreement that remains a sore point in Nepal. After this point, Oli became a strident monarchist, once comparing Nepal's attempts to become a republic as trying to reach 'America in a bullock cart'. After he lost his seat in the first CA elections, Oli turned into a vocal opponent of the peace process, arguing against the integration of the Maoist PLA with the Nepal Army. His position within the UML appeared to be eroding with the emergence of Khanal as prime minister, but he made a comeback to Parliament after the second CA elections in 2013. Oli capitalised on his gains by taking a strident anti-Madhes position and becoming chair of the UML in 2014. After the 2015 blockade, many Indian commentators were surprised at Oli's anti-India turn, since he had been known to work 'most consistently towards strengthening ties with India'.[59]

The arrival of the three trucks carrying Chinese fuel were the first signals not just of Nepal's intent under Oli's prime ministership, but also a newfound determinism to decouple the Nepali economy from India's. Economic life across the country had come to a standstill under the blockade; LPG cylinders were in short supply, and firewood was being sold in the markets as an alternative fuel source. The country had just suffered two massive earthquakes, which had killed and displaced thousands and rendered many more homeless, and Delhi's brazen attempts to coerce Nepali lawmakers was the last straw for the people.

The constitution-making process had its flaws, especially the decision to 'fast-track' its promulgation after the April 2015 earthquake. The sixteen-point agreement that decided to fast-track the statute was pushed ahead by four major parties without consultations on several issues regarding federalism, provincial boundaries, electoral representation and women's citizenship rights. The statute was immediately rejected by several ethnic groups, primarily in the Terai, where violent protests started from the far west and carried over into the central plains adjoining India.[60] Delhi was concerned, and sent its then foreign secretary, S. Jaishankar, who advised Nepali leaders to delay the promulgation and initiate dialogue with the opposing groups. But when Nepali leaders did not heed Delhi and went ahead with the statute, India simply 'noted' its adoption. 'We are concerned that the situation in several parts of the country bordering India continues to be violent . . . We urge that issues on which there are differences should be resolved through dialogue in an atmosphere free from violence and intimidation, and institutionalised in a manner that would enable broad-based ownership and acceptance,' India said in a statement.[61]

Delhi's decision to not back the constitution stood in stark contrast to the responses from the US and China, as well as other multilateral partners, most of whom acknowledged the issues in the process and privately urged Nepali leaders to address the dissent, even as they positively acknowledged the adoption of the statute: 'Western donors have felt hobbled in recent years by criticism that they promoted culturally inappropriate liberal values and muddied the waters in the first CA. They have also been under pressure to channel development funds through the government and to show results via spending, so are loath to give further offence. There is fatigue with the seemingly endless post-conflict transition, feckless politicians and the global proliferation of far more deadly conflicts. Most donor countries and the UN welcomed the sixteen-point agreement, despite clear signs there was no buy-in from Madhesi and other marginalised groups.'[62]

When the constitution was adopted in September 2015, protestors in the Terai began to blockade the Raxaul–Birgunj border crossing, Nepal's largest trade and transit point, as well as other crossings with India. Even as India did not officially declare a blockade, it halted the movement of cargo and fuel trucks, citing violence on the Nepali side. 'Madhesi protestors' efforts were bolstered from the Indian side by bureaucratic foot dragging, new complications for transit and customs procedures and suddenly absent officials,' an International Crisis Group report said.[63]

In Kathmandu, the narrative put blame for the blockade squarely on Delhi. This highlighted an urgency among Nepali lawmakers—especially among the UML–Maoist coalition that was in power under Oli—to break away from India's intractable economic hold. A petroleum agreement with China, cancelling India's monopoly over supply, was only the first of several agreements. The massive assistance provided by China after the earthquake had been significant in emphasising their status as a friendly country, ready to help a neighbour in a time of dire need. Now, their assistance during the blockade, even if symbolic, convinced Kathmandu to turn to the north. In March 2016, along with a USD 215 million loan deal to build an international airport in Pokhara, Oli signed an agreement to use China's ports. But the fractious nature of Nepali politics meant his coalition government would soon be toppled by none other than Prachanda himself.

✦

No other Nepali politician has come to represent the opportunism — some would say survivalist skills — of the post-conflict era than Prachanda. Born into a poor rural household on the outskirts of Pokhara, to the west of Kathmandu, he had once wanted to join the Nepal army, but instead enrolled himself in an agricultural college in Chitwan to the south, where he became initiated into the communist movement. In one of history's many ironies, Prachanda found himself a job at a USAID-sponsored rural development project. It was he who, with two other comrades, went to Manang to pick up the first two .303 rifles airdropped by the CIA for the Khampas before the Maoists declared their People's War. For many years during the insurgency, Prachanda himself was a myth; all that existed was a sketch, and then a blurry photograph of a bearded man. Nobody knew who he really was. It was not until 2006, when the Maoists emerged above ground, that Prachanda would burst on to the Nepali political scene, a revolutionary who had succeeded in bringing the Nepali monarchy to its knees.

Prachanda's organisational skills and his rhetoric helped establish him as a leader, but what consolidated his position was his flexible approach to ideology. Such flexibility meant Prachanda also attempted power grabs with the unlikeliest of alliances. When he was kept out of power after the army chief affair, Prachanda grew desperate enough to try and cobble together a 'nationalist alliance' with his former enemy Gyanendra in 2010.[64] With the Maoists increasingly becoming irrelevant and beset by internal splits after the party lost heavily in the second Constituent Assembly Elections in 2013, Prachanda lent support to Oli's government during the blockade. Then, in May 2016, he decided to withdraw the support. The very next day, he changed his mind, allegedly after the Chinese put pressure on him to continue with the alliance of the Left parties, especially as Oli had just signed key agreements with Beijing. But 'Delhi kept nudging and encouraging Prachanda to think of where his interests lay'.[65] Prachanda characteristically saw an opening and, backed by the Nepali Congress and the Madhesi parties, took his chance. He pulled the plug on Oli's government in July.

China was displeased. A proposed visit by President Xi Jinping was postponed. The party tabloid, *Global Times*, ran an op-ed that said the bilateral relationship had 'fallen into low ebb'.[66] Another was more scathing, and highlighted Chinese concerns about being treated as a 'card' only when Kathmandu's relations with New Delhi are at a low: '[. . .] China feels tricked. When Kathmandu needed Beijing to relieve pressure from New Delhi, it got close to China and signed a series of crucial agreements with Beijing which would help Nepal get rid of its reliance on India. But once India's attitude toward Kathmandu relaxed a bit and the former made some promises to the latter, Nepalese politicians immediately put the nation's ties with China on the back burner.'[67]

The critique seemed to have made its point. During Prachanda's second stint as premier, an 'impromptu' meeting between Xi Jinping, Narendra Modi and him took place in October 2016 on the sidelines of the BRICS dinner in Goa, where the three leaders discussed 'trilateral cooperation', a concept Prachanda had first pushed in 2013.[68] But Delhi remained cool to the idea. Nepal went ahead and signed up to the Belt and Road Initiative (then known as One Belt One Road) in May 2017 under his premiership, even as India expressed its reservations on Xi's much-vaunted transnational initiative.

A month later, Prachanda resigned as part of a power-sharing agreement to make way for Sher Bahadur Deuba of the Nepali Congress, the tenth prime minister in ten years of the republic. That September, the rail agreement between Nepal and China was signed. The fabled train from Lhasa entered the public's imagination, and it ignited K.P. Oli's electoral pitch for the first parliamentary elections in the new republic that December. He took the credit for both the promised train and for standing up to India, projecting himself as a nationalist leader who would transform Nepal if elected.

Just before the elections, the Maoists decided they would fight the elections in an alliance with Oli's UML. The UML would emerge as the party with the highest number of seats, while the Maoists came in third. After the elections, the two parties would merge to become the Nepal Communist Party (NCP). Once again, Prachanda had surprised everyone.

✦

On the morning of 24 September 2019, as Prachanda and Oli looked over their shoulders, Song Tao, head of the CCP's International Liaison Department (ILD), and Madhav Kumar Nepal, whose 2010–11 prime ministership was encouraged by New Delhi, exchanged a bilateral agreement that formalised relations between the CCP and the NCP. The leaders looked pleased, no hint of their previous acrimony evident. The NCP would now be trained in 'Xi Jinping Thought', the political doctrine popularised by the Chinese president.

The ILD was 'probably' formed in the 1950s, according to a 1971 CIA study, and remained behind the scenes until the end of the 1960s, tasked with 'finding, investigating and eventually supporting pro-Chinese splinter groups and malcontents, encouraging them to form so-called "Marxist-Leninist" parties in opposition to pro-Soviet "revisionist" parties'.[69] Many of its leaders were purged during the Cultural Revolution, but once re-admitted, the ILD began to play an active role in 'the overall formulation of foreign policy'.

In recent years, the ILD has developed ties with over 600 foreign political units across 160 countries and is the key unit responsible for advocating Xi's 'new type of political party relations', which explains CCP policies to foreign political parties, think tanks and media. 'CCP wishes to use ILD diplomacy to not only urge acceptance of its domestic policies—the traditional goal of external propaganda—but also to spread its ideas about good governance to receptive policy actors around the world.'[70]

For Nepal, the tie-up between the CCP and NCP signals further Chinese integration into the Nepali political set-up. International relations scholar Pramod Jaiswal told me the highest level of engagement from the Chinese perspective comes when 'China begins to provide "political advice", where the CCP engages with parties. In Nepal, Chinese engagement has reached this level . . . One would earlier hear it was not China's policy to support internal politics, but that no longer exists. Beijing doesn't call it political "interference" but "advice".'

While China's role in encouraging the merger of the two leading communist parties is still unclear, Beijing's interest in keeping the NCP intact was made apparent in the series of meetings its ambassador conducted with Nepali political actors in 2020 when Prachanda and Oli began to bicker about their power-sharing arrangement. In December 2020, Guo Yezhou, a vice-minister in the ILD, arrived in Kathmandu to conduct several meetings with a wide range of Nepali politicians after Oli dissolved the Parliament. The NCP, despite China's attempts, split vertically. Guo is said to have been instrumental in bringing the two communist parties together in 2018. Reports suggested Guo's task was to assess the new political realities in Nepal, and whether Beijing needed to recalibrate its approach. Guo's team is also said to have explored whether another pre-poll alliance between the two communist factions before the mid-term elections called by Oli in April–May 2021 was possible. 'China had been looking for a reliable and trustworthy partner in Nepal since the fall of the monarchy. It found one in the Nepal Communist Party,' an NCP official said. Guo's visit reaffirmed the belief that China had preferred a government under an unified NCP; with new political calculations, however, China is now keen that it remains assured of its key interests in Nepal.[71]

The CCP–NCP tie-up, although said to be a party-to-party relationship, forms part of the larger bilateral ties between the countries. An NCP official told me that the Chinese ambassador took part in NCP meetings as a CCP representative. At the peak of the pandemic in June 2020, a virtual meeting between the NCP and CCP raised several eyebrows. The Nepal–India border dispute was still ongoing, while India–China border clashes had recently led to the death of several soldiers on both sides. In October 2020, another virtual interaction was held between the ILD and several other Nepali political parties, including the chief opposition, Nepali Congress. Then Guo's December meetings confirmed the belief that the CCP–NCP tie-up was in fact an extension of China's larger Nepal policy.

Such tie-ups also fit in with a more expansive neighbourhood policy as outlined by Xi Jinping in 2013, under which China was to pursue a policy of 'common destiny' with neighbouring countries. '[T]he strategic goal of China's diplomacy with neighbouring countries is to serve the realization of the two "centenary goals" and the great rejuvenation of the Chinese nation . . . China needs to develop closer ties with neighbouring countries, with more friendly political relations, stronger economic bonds, deeper security cooperation and closer people-to-people contacts.'[72]

While the popular perception is that China prefers a Communist government in Nepal, analysts believe it will engage with any party that shows similar electoral dominance. 'China prefers a government that is stable and powerful—and the Communists currently fall under that category . . . If Congress wins tomorrow, there will be similar engagement with the Congress,' Sudheer Sharma told me. Xi Jinping also emphasised the Nepali Congress's historical role in shaping bilateral relations in a meeting with Deuba during his state visit. 'No matter which Nepali party is in power, the two countries will maintain stable and friendly relations,' the Foreign Ministry announced.[73]

All of this has led to an elevation of ties. Oli's June 2018 visit to China was termed a 'turning point', and during Nepali President Bidhya Devi Bhandari's April 2019 visit, Nepal signed a long-pending protocol to the transit and transportation agreement to use four Chinese sea ports (in Tianjin, Shenzhen, Lianyungang and Zhanjiang) and three land ports (in Lanzhou, Lhasa and Shigatse). Then there was the diplomatic coup: Xi Jinping's short but highly effective visit in October 2019.

Xi's Kathmandu stay was notable in many ways. It marked the first visit by a Chinese president in more than two decades, and elevated bilateral ties to one of 'strategic partnership'. All the analysts I met said the visit would imbue a new dynamism to the bilateral relationship which, although marked by several agreements, had failed to see any movement. The visit also signalled China's satisfaction with how the relationship had progressed since the political transition. Among the messages Xi's visit sent was one on the train: the focus was on the Kathmandu–Pokhara–Lumbini line rather than the Gyirong–Kathmandu line. Work on the latter has been stuck not only because of funding, but also because Beijing would like the line to extend to the Indian border, giving it access to Indian markets—a distant possibility at this juncture.

Above all, Xi's visit meant while the India–Nepal relationship could continue to be 'special', the southern neighbour would no longer be Nepal's primary bilateral partner. Apart from the Tibetan issue, Beijing wishes to increase connectivity—not just through physical infrastructure but also through more people-to-people engagements—and to negate the ambitions of any other country in Nepal, barring India and China.

On the other hand, after the 2015 blockade, New Delhi has taken a low-key approach to Nepal, and its diplomats have mostly been quiet on issues. There was cautious optimism during the Indian Foreign Secretary Harsh Vardhan Shringla's November 2020 visit, which occurred in the aftermath of the Kalapani territorial dispute. What was evident was New Delhi's attempts to distance itself from the everyday political affairs of Nepal, with a focus now on issues around connectivity and economy, and an emphasis on civilisational people-to-people ties. India's statement that Oli's December 2020 Parliament dissolution was Nepal's 'internal matter' is also another indication Delhi is rethinking ties with Kathmandu and visibly stepping away from its neighbour's domestic political affairs. Although there are suggestions that Delhi no longer sees Nepali engagements with China as being against Indian interests, the key question really is how far India would be willing to accept Chinese presence and influence in Nepal. If India has accepted that China is here to stay, what are the new 'red lines' for them?

✦

Beijing's biggest challenge in Nepal in recent years, however, did not come from India, but from thousands of miles away in Capitol Hill.

Although the US–China geopolitical contest is now being felt across the world, it had been played out publicly in Nepal much before the war of words during the COVID-19 pandemic. The roots of their tussle in Nepal go back to 2018, when Foreign Minister Pradeep Gyawali was put in a spot after US Secretary of State Mike Pompeo said Nepal was part of the Indo-Pacific Strategy (IPS), an American foreign policy objective in a region where, according to its National Security Strategy 2017 document, 'a geopolitical competition between free and repressive visions of world order is taking place'.[74] The IPS has its roots in Donald Trump's November 2017 visit to Asia. Nepal's alleged participation in the IPS comes from agreeing to be part of the Millennium Challenge Corporation (MCC), a US government foreign-aid agency 'given to low-income and lower-middle-income countries selected through competition'.[75] It signed the MCC compact in 2014, under which the US would grant Nepal USD 500 million for infrastructure projects—particularly electricity transmission lines and maintenance of highways—while Nepal would put in USD 130 million. The MCC did not generate any controversy until Pompeo's statement. Subsequently, even as Gyawali refuted the fact that Nepal was a part of the IPS, visiting American assistant secretary for South Asia at the US State Department, David J. Ranz, said in May 2019 that the MCC was a crucial part of the IPS. A US government report too confirmed that the MCC was part of the IPS.[76]

The tussle now played out in Nepali domestic politics. The prime minister blamed the speaker—none other than Mahara, the Maoist politician close to China—for delaying the ratification of the treaty through Parliament. In February 2019, Joe Felter, US Deputy Assistant Secretary of Defense for South and Southeast Asia, compared MCC to BRI and said that Chinese investments in Nepal must serve Nepali interests, not Chinese, offering the now-infamous Hambantota Port deal in Sri Lanka as proof of the latter. A day later, Chinese Ambassador Hou Yanqi shot back that Felter's comments were 'irresponsible'. In the June 2020 virtual meeting with CCP, Prachanda said Nepal would not accept any support that comes with a security alignment. ILD vice-minister Guo Yezhou's series of meetings with Nepali politicians in December 2020 was also said to have elicited responses on Nepal's position on the MCC after the dissolution of Parliament.

The MCC treaty comes with its own set of rules—for example, the Republican agenda that Nepal could not use any of the MCC funds 'to pay for the performance of abortions as a method of family planning' or 'to pay for the performance of involuntary sterilizations as a method of family planning'[77]—that have created deep suspicion in Kathmandu about its implications. The Chinese have begun to see it as another element of American obstructionism to Beijing's rise. 'The doubt among the Chinese in Nepal today is whether Kathmandu has tilted towards the US through the IPS or not. They feel those who believe in such a tilt are in dominant positions in government,' Sudheer Sharma said.

Nepali analysts believe the key objective of Nepali foreign policy should be non-alignment, and that Nepal should be able to utilise both the MCC and the BRI. But it now looks like the two powers will demand to know where Kathmandu's allegiances lie, with the US ratcheting up its engagement with the Nepali political establishment in recent years. With Nepal being a vocal supporter of the Chinese position on the pandemic, its new Hong Kong laws and the increased interactions between the two ruling parties, it seems as if Beijing has found a willing ally in Kathmandu's current political establishment. But domestic political squabbles often find a way of manifesting in foreign policy.

The flurry of visits by members of the Indian establishment in October–November 2020, followed by a short day-visit of the Chinese Defence Minister Wei Fenghe at the end of November and Guo

Yezhou's December visit, was another reminder of the geopolitical tussle Nepal had found itself in. What was significant about these visits, however, was also that they came during a period of domestic political turbulence, with effects of the NCP split now conspicuous on foreign policy. 'The big question is how far will this domestic dynamic intersect with changing regional and global geopolitics,' wrote Akhilesh Upadhyay, a senior geopolitical analyst and former editor of *The Kathmandu Post*.[78]

Once again, geopolitics and domestic politics had become entwined with each other in Nepal, leading to perceptions about Nepali political actors becoming proxies for foreign players. One of the key markers of the post-1990 Nepali establishment is that a number of institutions have pursued their own goals that are separate from a national foreign policy objective. This has created a dissonance in how Nepal engages with the outside world, which has led to an inconsistent approach towards foreign or security policy, which is then driven by personal or partisan interests. One of the best examples of this is the Nepal army, which is viewed as a permanent establishment in the fractious nature of Nepali politics, and is an important contributor to UN peacekeeping missions. Yet, it waded into controversy by pulling out of the multilateral BIMSTEC military exercise in September 2018, even as it participated in another exercise with China that same month. Days after Xi returned to Beijing, China announced a NPR 2.5 billion aid package for the Nepal army, and yet, 'even the Americans have a strong relationship with the Army—and in fact it might be the closest', Sudheer Sharma said.[79] Wei's November 2020 visit also indicated the Chinese now wanted a relationship with the Nepal army that was as close or even closer than it shared with the US and Indian armed forces.[80]

The China–Nepal relationship is asymmetric, as all big power–small nation relations tend to be. Since 2008, China's ambitions in Nepal can be outlined as: securing the border to halt Tibetan refugee crossings, silencing Tibetan activism, eroding Indian influence and restricting other powers' engagements, and improving connectivity that allows for increased economic engagements and expands China's influence in South Asia. Among these, China has succeeded in quelling Tibetan activism and refugee movement, and the influence of other nations, especially India, has been reduced. But it has also been caught on the backfoot by domestic squabbles, which it had not expected. Nepal has also not been able to convince China it has the capacity to deliver on the many projects and agreements. Frustrated by the clamour over the train to Kathmandu, the Chinese ambassador publicly said the train would not be built 'overnight'. In a November 2020 interview, the ambassador also suggested more importance be given to road connectivity 'while advancing the railway project'.[81]

And despite Nepal whittling down the list of projects under BRI from a massive thirty-five to just nine upon Chinese insistence, there has been little movement on any of the projects.[82] There are also reports of inadequate planning and preparation on Nepal's part; during Xi's visit, Nepali officials asked their Chinese counterparts whether assistance could be forthcoming for the Kimathanka–Leguaghat border crossing. It was the first time the Chinese were hearing of such a proposal.

Further, Nepal's inability to negotiate with Chinese authorities was highlighted during the COVID-19 pandemic, when the Rasuwagadhi and Tatopani borders were shut down for more than eight months in 2020. More than 1,500 containers carrying goods to Nepal were stuck in transit, including a shipment of critical BCG vaccines, after China closed down the border citing the spread of the virus in Nepal. It was only after sustained queries that the two border points came back into operation by late 2020, but only a few containers were allowed to pass every day.[83]

There are also rumours of partisanship within key ministries leading to delays in project execution. Agni Sapkota put the blame on the bureaucracy's inefficacies when I asked him why we had seen such little movement on the agreements with China. 'We needed to prepare a bureaucracy who could implement the projects . . . We still haven't been able to do so. None of the involved ministries have done their homework properly. The bureaucracy hasn't been prepared. Our current state structure is extremely poorly prepared. Our development trajectory will be dislodged if there isn't a transformation in the way we do things. Smaller projects will continue on an as-is basis, but this is not a *kaamchalau sarkar* (temporary government). This is history's strongest [elected] government . . . but our way of thinking remains the same. Our bureaucracy is still the old one. Obviously the ministries handling the bureaucracy are also to blame, because there is a lack of leadership. It is difficult to move ahead in a new way if the bureaucracy continues to think in the old way. We needed a few bold decisions, and that has not been possible.'

The irony here is that, while other powers already perceive Nepal as being within Beijing's sphere of influence, Nepal itself has gained little out of the relationship. Domestic politicking and partisan interests are a key feature of the relationship from Kathmandu's side. For instance, Nepal recalled its ambassador to China a few months before his tenure was over at the peak of the COVID-19 crisis. The ambassador had negotiated the return of Nepali students in China without consulting Kathmandu, which annoyed the powers that be, but he was also a victim of internal NCP dynamics. Or take this case: the state airline has not been allotted a slot to fly to China, while a private Nepali airline whose management is close to Oli has been granted routes to five Chinese destinations. During the COVID-19 crisis, Nepal failed to activate its newfound bonhomie to source high-grade medical equipment from China, once again relying instead on a private supplier with dodgy links to Nepal's ruling party.

Similarly, very little Chinese investment has materialised, despite the hype, and most of it small, opaque investments restricted to tourism. While these are oriented towards the increasing number of Chinese tourists, they have also been detrimental to Nepali interests, as we shall see in the next two chapters. Nepal has also not been able to reduce the burgeoning trade deficit with China. And finally, Chinese nationals have taken advantage of the free visa regime to conduct criminal activities in Nepal, such as the gang of 122 Chinese who were duping women on Chinese dating websites by luring them into online gambling, and were extradited in November 2019 on shadowy terms. Several reports have also emerged of Nepali women being trafficked to China under the guise of marriage to Chinese men.

On other hand, Beijing's hold over Nepali institutions and political parties is now conspicuous. Nepali officials rushed to China's defence over reports of border encroachment in Limi valley, Humla, in September 2020. Inexplicably, a district official was asked to clarify why he raised the issue of unauthorised construction in the media.[84] The Nepali ambassador to China, in turn, blamed 'fake' Indian media reports as trying to harm bilateral relations between Nepal and China. A sitting Nepali Congress MP from Humla, who insisted China had indeed encroached upon Nepali territory, said he felt threatened by the Chinese embassy's letter to his party, which had been denounced as a 'pro-India' party by the state tabloid, *Global Times*. 'I want to reiterate that China will be responsible if anything unfortunate happens to me,' the MP said.[85] Most surprisingly, there was little reaction to his allegations either in the Nepali media or by other politicians. The Chinese embassy's letter to the Nepali Congress had referred to B.P. Koirala's efforts to resolve Nepal–China border issues in the past, and rejected all claims of border encroachment as well as of assaulting Nepali forces and officials at the border. The letter also emphasised that Nepalis had benefited from China's infrastructure development in Tibet.[86]

Nepali officials and politicians are also orienting themselves to Chinese governance methods through training programmes and scholarships. Kathmandu will also see more CCTV surveillance in the coming years, while new laws intend to give overarching powers to Nepali intelligence units. China's open castigation of a newspaper—and Nepal's silence on the issue—has engendered fears about the freedom of the press. The tie-ups between CCP and NCP and the adoption of 'Xi Thought' also suggests a Sinicization of Nepali political parties through the import of CCP models.

Despite Nepal's pretensions to non-alignment, there is indeed a convergence between Oli's anti-Indian nationalism and China's ambitions in South Asia. Its China policy—if one exists—is hostage to Nepali partisan interests in the absence of a larger national strategy. But while Beijing has secured its larger interests in Nepal, Kathmandu has failed to see beyond the 'China card'. It has not improved its capacity to negotiate for better deals, nor has it built non-partisan institutions that work towards national interests. Above all, Nepal has not been able to extricate itself from the aid-beneficiary mentality and come up with a strategy that can take advantage of China's economic and infrastructural progress on its own terms.

Beijing has engaged with Nepali political and government actors on a variety of issues; it has projected itself as a friend who will assist when the need arises. Its goals and methods significantly differ from the other powers that have engaged with Nepal in the past, and that today have their own goals within Nepal. That, ultimately, will be Kathmandu's test: can it deliver on Beijing's expectations without eroding its own sovereignty, and can it walk the tightrope that the future demands?

9

Chinese Capitalism with Nepali Characteristics

The Xinzhi Bookstore in Kathmandu's tony shopping district, Durbar Marg, is easy to miss if you don't know where to look. The Kathmandu outlet of China's biggest private books retailer, the Kunming Xinzhi Group, is off the tourist grid. It is set up in a basement-like space, and from the outside, is unimposing. There are a few notices on its walls, mostly for Mandarin language classes (coaching for clearing the HSK, or the Chinese Proficiency Test). Inside, one first finds shelves full of Chinese food products and ingredients—soy sauce, fruit vinegars, Sichuan pepper—and in one corner, sacks of Chinese rice. Thereafter, shelves full of books in Mandarin and Nepali, and some in English. Xi Jinping's *The Governance of China* takes pride of place, in Mandarin, Nepali and English. The two-volume text, a collection of Xi's speeches since 2012, has been called the literary successor to the Little Red Book. A review stated, 'Both volumes emphasize one central theme: China is poised to regain its stature as a great country. To do this, page after page implies or states, it needs stability, unity and a strong leader in control.'[1]

The bookstore is one of the many new avenues in which Chinese entrepreneurs are engaging with Nepal as bilateral relations deepen. Although Nepal and China may be culturally and socially distant, such engagements create a template for future interactions. Throughout my travels, I met with Nepalis who worked at Chinese-owned businesses or petroleum exploration projects, those who left their jobs at a Chinese-developed hydropower company, and those who were trying for employment in one. I also met with Chinese nationals who had made Nepal their home, either because of their jobs or their entrepreneurial spirit—noodle makers from Lanzhou, restaurant owners from Yunnan and farmers from Sichuan. At a 'China's Tibet trade fair', held in late 2019, Tibetan and Chinese sales representatives tried to sell Nepalis bottled mineral water from a glacier below Everest (on the Tibetan side), pitched for real-estate construction projects or simply sold various herbal medicines intended to soothe or invigorate, depending on what you needed just then.

In a space like Xinzhi, a fevered pitch accompanies the Chinese state's attempts to win friends and influence people. True to the spirit of the people-to-people exchange that Xi called for, these new spaces ground high-level political discussions at the local level: by inviting local customers, employing local people and invoking the Chinese worldview within a Nepali environment. Although this is seen most prominently in how the tourist trade has reoriented itself towards the Chinese visitor, it can also be seen in the mom-and-pop stores of the tourist district's lanes, the more organised retail spaces such as Xinzhi, and in high-profile companies such as Hongshi Shivam Cement, Nepal's largest cement manufacturer.

Nepal's tourism-oriented economy has regularly invoked the semiotics of Western consumerism. But this is different. Chinese-owned businesses incorporate a 'Chinese' identity in their operations, wherein the language of expression is inaccessible to a majority of the Nepali population (yet), since everything—from the labels, the items and the transactions—are conducted in Mandarin. What is also noticeable is the import of the cult of Xi Jinping in spaces such as Xinzhi. *The Governance of China* was translated into Nepali by a Kathmandu-based think tank and 'enable[d] the Nepalese politicians, intellectuals and policy makers to correctly understand the Chinese dream, its governance system and socialism with Chinese characteristics'.[2]

✦

Kathmandu's Xinzhi store, set up in 2014, is the seventh international outlet of the Kunming retail group. Sitting amid its many shelves are English-language classics, such as *Alice in Wonderland*, and a few Shakespearean plays published by Chinese publishers. One shelf is dedicated to Chinese-language dictionaries. The bookstore's Chinese-language classes are quite popular. I asked a Nepali girl who worked at the store whether a primary school text would be suitable for me to start with the language. She said the text would give me an idea, but I would not learn the language until I took the classes. To illustrate her point, she began enunciating the same character and how they are pronounced differently.

I looked around further, and picked up *Key Concepts in Chinese Thought and Culture*,[3] a bilingual volume in English and Nepali, and Xi Jinping's stories for young adults translated into Nepali.[4] The latter is an abridged version of *Narrating China's Governance*, a selective collection of Xi Jinping's speeches in which he outlines key elements that 'convey the essence of China's history and culture',[5] where each passage is accompanied by commentary that provides the context to the references. Each section broadly outlines 'Xi Thought'. There is the story of Yang Zhen, the honest bureaucrat from antiquity, who refused a bribe of gold at night, when nobody would know, by invoking the 'four knows'—'The heaven knows, the earth knows, you know and I know'—which Xi termed the 'consciousness of incorruption', a theme he has invoked repeatedly in his tenure. The text also refers to China's 'century of humiliation', between the mid-nineteenth century and mid-twentieth century, after the Opium Wars, when China's 'self-sufficient natural economy gradually disintegrated, and . . . [it] missed the opportunity of the Industrial Revolution'.[6] At the 18th CPC Central Commission's third plenary session in 2013, Xi extended the period to two centuries, calling it the 'lost 200 years', blaming the Qing dynasty's 'sheer parochial arrogance' for missing out on the industrial revolution's gains, and the West for making China 'a semi-colonial and semi-feudal country'.[7]

I had come to Xinzhi to understand why a Kunming-based group would open a Chinese bookstore in Kathmandu, and who its customers were. Yang Hua, the smartly dressed local manager, was busy speaking with a few Chinese customers. He told me that, because most of the books were about China, it was hard to pitch them to local customers, which is why they had also brought in books on Tibet and stationery products. The Kathmandu store was also the only Xinzhi outlet to retail food and FMCG products, purchased mostly by Chinese expats and a few high-end Chinese restaurants in Kathmandu.

I visited the store a month after Xi Jinping's brief visit to Kathmandu, and Yang thought Chinese investments and tourists would increase because of it. 'Of course the number of tourists will increase. But Nepal needs to improve its infrastructure,' he said, 'starting from the very basics like twenty-four-hour hot water in hotel rooms. Also, why do tourists have to pay different prices for flights, hotels and tourist spots? In China, everything is priced the same.'

I asked Yang, as he frequently wiped the sweat off his brow, about doing business in Nepal. 'It's been alright—neither too easy nor too difficult.' He did not know Nepali, and we conversed in English. Language was not a problem for doing business, he said. 'In any case, we are not competing with Nepali stores. We are selling to a different crowd.'

✦

Two hundred kilometres west of Kathmandu, I stood on a vast stretch of land that would soon turn into a 2,500-metre-long runway for a new airport. A short distance away, I could see the shell of a new terminal building coming up. By 2021, the international airport at Pokhara would be ready, nearly five decades after it was first proposed in 1969.

A Japanese company first wanted to expand the existing domestic airport in 1970.[8] After much lobbying by local business owners and travel operators,[9] the process of acquiring land began in 1974, but construction did not begin until 2016, when Nepal signed a USD 215.96 million soft loan agreement with China EXIM Bank to finance construction by China CAMC Engineering.[10] This too was the result of a decade of negotiations, with Oli's turn to the north and the 2015 Indian blockade acting as catalysts. The airport is meant to be handed over to Nepal's civil aviation authority on 10 July 2021; several news reports before the COVID-19 pandemic highlighted the possibility that the airport would finish earlier than expected, but that looks unlikely now.

Pokhara is a city ringed by water on all sides—lakes, rivers and streams—and even underground. The soil is particularly amenable to sinkholes; in the monsoons, after a bout of heavy rains, they open up regularly in farmlands surrounding the city, and sometimes inside the city itself. The land where the new airport will come up was once populated with rice fields, irrigated by the waters of the Bijayapur stream and the Seti Gandaki river. Growing up in Pokhara in the 1980s and early 1990s, for me, this was the edge of the known world (or at least the town, as it was then). Kundahar, as the area is known, was desolate; rarely did anybody venture there, except during the rice-planting season in June–July and the harvest in November. The land acquired for the airport straddles the exit route out of Pokhara towards Kathmandu. For years, I noticed the board that demarcated the airport land slowly rusting away. The board itself was in despair, bent, with one of its legs withered away, eroded by the elements. The project did not look like it was going anywhere, until Oli triumphantly arrived in China in May 2016 and signed the deal to finance its construction. Since then, the area has become a hub of construction activity, heavy earthmoving equipment rattling the two-laned highway as it enters the gates.

Pokhara's business owners and travel operators have long privately believed that an international airport in the city was being blocked by the Kathmandu hotel-and-travel lobby. As of now, every international visitor flying into Nepal must land in Kathmandu, automatically creating a market for overnight stays. 'Pokhara was seen as a competitor destination,' Basu Tripathi, a former member of the Nepal Tourism Board who now runs Adam Tours and Travels in Pokhara, told me. 'But now that the airport is coming, Kathmandu hotel owners have begun to buy land and invest in Pokhara.' I was told repeatedly that the project was expedited because of the politician Rabindra Adhikari, who was elected as MP from Pokhara and was tourism minister until his death in a helicopter crash in February 2019.

When I visited the site of the airport one afternoon in June 2018, construction was in full flow. A neat row of prefabricated structures—now a marker for Chinese projects in Nepal—functioned both as office space and residential quarters for the more than fifty Chinese engineers. Safety instructions in English and Mandarin were splashed across the walls, including a no-smoking notice for the dormitory and another warning that sufficient ventilation must be ensured if using a heater. A makeshift badminton court was painted on the courtyard outside the living quarters. Besides the site of the under-construction terminal building, a neat row of Chinese-built Shacman Delong F3000 dumper-trucks stood parked. The runway had been flattened, and by the end of 2019, it was ready. The runway, 2,500 metres long, can handle medium-range jets like Airbus 320s and Boeing 737s if a small, forested hill to the east were completely levelled. One prominent local businessman told me they had been lobbying for the runway to be expanded to 3,000 metres, allowing the airport to handle longer-haul aircraft, but had not really insisted on it because they wanted the airport itself to come up first.

These massive infrastructure projects are held up by analysts as a measure of Chinese influence in Nepal—and with good reason, for there are massive sums involved and their sheer physical presence is considerable. But this focus does not account for the larger ecosystem that develops around such projects, which is what has also happened in Nepal. Infrastructure investments often generate a local economy around their project sites. The airport, too, has created new opportunities, and Chinese entrepreneurs such as Xiang Shaohua have capitalised on them due to their familiarity with the language, culture and people, but primarily due to their nous to work in Nepali conditions.

When a Pokhara businessman introduced me to 'Sandesh', it took me a while to gather he was referring to Xiang's chosen Nepali name. When he first came to Pokhara as a tourist in 2009, Xiang did not think he would stay back and grow Chinese vegetables and rice to supply to the international airport's canteen and to the many Chinese restaurants that dot Lakeside, Pokhara's tourist district that straddles Fewa Lake. 'I'd met a Chinese restaurant owner here, and I asked him whether there were any opportunities to explore in Pokhara. He told me he didn't get proper vegetables here for his restaurant,' Xiang told me in Nepali with a distinct Chinese lilt. He started out by leasing half a hectare on the northern outskirts of the city. Eight years later, he was able to lease nearly two hectares across the under-construction airport, in an area called Chauthe.[11]

Meeting Xiang was a revelation. His story is a testament to the entrepreneurial spirit of the Chinese people, and to the transformations that have come with the new Chinese presence in Nepal. It is also a story that hints at, depending on how you look at it, profiting from the Chinese predilection for nativism, or a deep assertion of their identity in foreign lands through habits familiar to them—in this case, culinary.

Xiang used to run a business in Zhangmu, a Chinese town across the border at Kodari, but grabbed the opportunity that presented itself. He did not attend any Nepali classes; instead, he learnt the language over the years through conversations and practice. 'It was very difficult in the beginning as I didn't know any English either,' he told me, as we sat down to drink some tea at a restaurant conveniently named Sichuan Chinese. I was meeting him a day after he had sown rice in his new farm. Xiang came from a village near Chengdu, he said, and his two children—a son and a daughter—were still back home. 'I didn't know anything about Pokhara before coming here,' he said. For the first two years, there were no profits. But demand was increasing because more Chinese were visiting Nepal and the airport construction started, and that was how he leased a larger farmland. 'I could have earned more in China, but one can earn anywhere. I like Pokhara—the climate is great for farming, and I wanted to live in a nice place with good weather.'

I asked Xiang what it was like doing business in Nepal—in a foreign land, with a language barrier and without any visible social networks. Did he not want a Nepali business partner to ease things out? 'I thought it was easier to work on my own,' he said, 'I was twenty-two when I came here. I hadn't decided on any path. I gave myself three years in Pokhara. Now, I have Nepali friends too.'

What was the most difficult bit about doing business in Nepal? He thought for a bit, and said, 'The most difficult thing here is that things take time.' In what way—was it just the bureaucratic hassle, or was there more? He said it was difficult to import material from China, and there were lots of delays. The road from Zhangmu had been shut after the 2015 earthquake, and when I met him in 2018, only the Rasuwagadhi road was in use. 'It takes nearly a month and a half to bring in smaller farm equipment. If products can reach here quicker, it's much better for business.' But he had great hopes of the airport. 'I can leave Pokhara in the morning and reach home by the afternoon. Increased contact between two cultures is always better.'

Xiang's modest success from farming would not have been possible without the rising people-to-people exchanges between the two countries. Supplying to the pantry at the international airport may have allowed him to scale up, but it is the presence of several Chinese restaurants, and the tourists who patronise them, that gave him the confidence to start a business in Nepal without any local connections, without even knowing the local language. He also had to adapt to Nepali work cultures and norms. 'In Nepal, it doesn't matter if work is delayed. People like to take it easy. In China, it's the opposite. People are always in a rush and things get done quickly,' he told me, then he added, 'but it's okay if work gets delayed a bit. The tension gets reduced then, which is always a good thing.'

✦

Chinese investments in Nepal are prioritised in three areas: tourism, transportation and construction. Within these, Leela Mani Paudyal identified 'water and power utilities, infrastructure and mining' sectors as open to investments from the north.[12] In recent years, Chinese investments have also been concentrated in tourism, construction and the cargo handling sectors. Large-scale investments, however, are difficult to come by in Nepal in general. Of the 227 new FDI projects approved in 2019–20, only nine were in the large category, i.e. more than NPR 250 million.[13]

The road for large Chinese economic investments has also not been half as smooth as the newly expanded Kathmandu ring road built with Chinese grant assistance worth USD 33 million. In September 2018, the China Three Gorges International Corporation, whose parent body constructed the world's largest hydropower project, the 22,500 MW Three Gorges Dam, pulled out of the 750 MW West Seti hydropower project in western Nepal, worth USD 1.5 billion. The company found the project to be unfeasible because of 'the steep resettlement and rehabilitation costs', even though Nepal lowered the generation capacity to 600 MW and extended the power purchase agreement to twelve years.[14]

Then the USD 2.5 billion 1,200 MW Budhi Gandaki project, which was awarded to another Chinese contractor, the China Gezhouba Group Corporation (CGGC), fell into shambles. It was first awarded to CGGC in June 2017 under a government headed by Prachanda, then rescinded under an interim government headed by Nepali Congress leader Sher Bahadur Deuba because the agreement was found to be 'irregular and thoughtless', and once again restored to CGGC in September 2018 after the NCP was sworn in. But the momentum had been lost; the government failed to hold talks with CGGC, and now Nepal will build the project on its own.

With both hydropower projects, there were questions about whether the strategic tussle between India and China was manifesting through Nepali political actors. There was a lack of transparency in the awarding of contracts; CGGC, for instance, did not have to go through a tender process. But it is clear that Chinese companies—even if they are state-backed—have not fully understood the Nepali culture of prevarication and red-tapism, and thus are not quite able to navigate the Nepali environment. 'Smaller Chinese companies have not delivered on projects in Nepal because of lack of skill and corruption. But even the bigger construction companies have not been able to deliver, which in my opinion is because these companies have not understood Nepal's societal complexities and problems,' Sudheer Sharma said. 'They think if the government takes a decision here, things will be done as in China. But it doesn't work like that in Nepal. Here, there is no movement despite the government's approval. There are factions within the ruling party that will oppose a project; the local population will sometimes protest. I don't think the Chinese fully understand that.' He cited the ring road expansion project: 'Because the Nepal Electricity Authority did not shift the electricity poles, the project was delayed by three–four months.'

While Chinese companies and investors pay lip service by saying that Nepal is a good investment destination, and China leads the way in investment pledges in the country, the fact is that Nepal has not shown it is ready for foreign investment. The foreign investment threshold was raised to USD 500,000 from USD 50,000 in May 2019, barely two months after a much-hyped Investment Summit inviting foreign businesses.

Amidst all this, one Chinese company made the headlines in 2015 with its pledge to invest USD 251 million in a cement factory in Nepal—the largest foreign direct investment (FDI) in the country's manufacturing sector.

✦

I reached Hongshi-Shivam Cement's Kathmandu office one morning in 2018, a year after its plant in Nawalparasi district in the plains started production. Offices in Kathmandu usually open around 10 a.m.; by 9 a.m., however, the Hongshi office was busy. There was a buzz about the corporate office that was unusual for Nepal, and in the boardroom, I awaited Vikas Agrawal, the young chief financial officer.

Construction has been one of the fastest-growing sectors in the Nepali economy, fuelled by post-earthquake reconstruction, the growth in remittance incomes leading to increased home-building and the push towards physical infrastructure by successive governments. The sector contributed 7.8 per cent to Nepal's GDP in 2018–19, while a slowdown in the sector along with lower remittances in 2019 reduced GDP growth targets from 8.5 per cent to 7 per cent. Nepal's reliance on cement imports has been steadily declining, not just because Hongshi's plant, Nepal's largest, can supply 25 per cent of the total demand, but also because of a host of new manufacturers in the country. Cement imports declined by 13 per cent in 2019, and domestic production today accounts for 70 per cent of the total demand, which is expected to rise by 10 to 15 per cent every year, according to the manufacturers.

'Hongshi saw Nepal as a good market because, although the volumes are low, the margins are good here, better than in China,' Agrawal told me over tea, upending the popular notion that Chinese companies operate on scale in Nepal. 'Of course, in other countries like India, they look at volumes, but when you come to a country like Nepal, you can't do that.'

The venture between Hongshi Holdings, China's largest cement manufacturer, and Shivam Group came after several rounds of discussions between the two companies. With a total investment of USD 359.2 million, Hongshi owned 70 per cent of the venture, and Shivam the rest. Hongshi conducted in-depth research into the Nepali market; into limestone mines and their availability (limestone is a key input in cement production), quality and locations; and finally, into the choice of local partners. The partnership with Shivam Cement was a 'win-win' for both, according to Agrawal, since the company already had a significant share of the domestic market, and Shivam wanted to grow. 'Their technology, their production process, everything was quite low, so it was an excellent learning process for us to understand how the costs of production are so low in China?'

While the intricacies of the cement manufacturing process were beyond my comprehension, I was surprised to learn that their key import, coal, comes all the way from South Africa. And because the Nepal Electricity Authority was yet to construct a dedicated 132 KV transmission line to supply 40 MW of electricity to the plant, Hongshi had begun generating 12 MW of power through waste, and the rest via captive diesel generators.[15] The Hongshi brand had already captured a significant market share; its advertisements dotted villages along the highways and on billboards within the cities. And I was intrigued by the corporate practices the company had put in place here.

The first was the speed with which the plant had been constructed. Work began on the site in May 2016, and within sixteen months, the plant was ready for production. 'In Nepal, building a cement plant normally takes around three to four years; Hongshi did it in half,' Agrawal said. I asked him whether there had been any local opposition. In October 2018, another USD 140 million joint venture, Huaxin Cement Narayani, was accused of flouting environmental impact assessment (EIA) norms and of encroaching upon public land during its construction. Although the Public Accounts Committee of the Nepal Parliament ordered the local municipality to cancel the land lease agreement in July 2019, the Investment Board of Nepal (IBN) said the plant could go ahead with construction and that the investment was not 'under threat'.[16] With Hongshi, too, a 2016 report suggested that locals who lived near the limestone quarry had halted construction, seeking better compensation. Agrawal told me that the company handled such issues well. 'The locals knew that once the industry came up, the area would get developed, so they supported the construction.' A more recent report highlighted how a local economy had come up around the plant, and that land prices had jumped to NPR 4 million a kattha[17] from NPR 15,000 a few years ago.

A second element that the association with the Chinese had brought into Nepali corporate culture was the periodic review all employees had to undergo. In Hongshi, employees were evaluated weekly, monthly and annually, and their salaries rose as per their performance. 'Seventy per cent of the salary is fixed, while 30 per cent is a variable component, which increases as the employees' performance gets better,' Agrawal said, adding that Hongshi implements an 'anti-bribery' clause in their contracts with suppliers. 'You cannot gift cash or in kind to any of our employees.'[18]

These practices are new to Nepali corporate culture, signalling a subtle shift in how local employees adapt to foreign practices. For example, while Nepali companies generally adopt a fixed number of leave days an employee can take annually, at Hongshi, the number of leave days depend on how many years an employee has spent in the company.

Hongshi's massive investment—by Nepali standards—has allowed the company's Nepali partners a ringside view of how Chinese companies operate and become successful across the world. The partnership between Nepali and Chinese companies offers us a glimpse into real-time Chinese engagement in the country beyond the state. The joint venture will now buy out the stake of Indian-owned Ambuja

Cement in a plant that had been out of operation for sixteen years at a cost of NPR 32 billion, which will be funded by foreign loans.[19]

'If you look at it from a macro level, Chinese influence in Nepal has tremendously risen. Even customs clearing in Nepal is today done by Chinese agents. Although they can't get a licence from the Nepali customs agents, they have got the contract to handle it. For example, whatever Hongshi imported into the country, the imports were all handled by CJ Cargo, a Chinese company. Plus, the Chinese are eager to learn. They keep on learning,' Agrawal said. He was certain this would translate into more investments in Nepal, either through loans backed by local banks or a direct injection of foreign funds, and lead to a technology transfer. But Nepal needed to ease its FDI rules if it wanted to attract more investments, he thought, not just in regulatory approvals and labour rules, but also in how foreign investment was perceived. 'You have to be positive towards China, or you have to be negative. You can't be both. If you want to bring in investment, you have to be clear on what needs to be done, and you have to support that,' Agrawal said.

✦

As in other developing countries, there is awe at the pace of Chinese growth in the last two decades, its infrastructural capability, its economic surplus and its poverty reduction among Nepali policymakers, government officials, private-sector participants and the general public. The economic rise of China manifests as a potent weapon in diplomacy and other engagements, such as tourism, especially in developing countries where the shortage of capital (and resultant economic weaknesses) is seen as the biggest deterrent to growth and development. Nepal also expects that its participation in the BRI will pave the way for several infrastructure and connectivity projects, especially now that such projects have been brought under the 'Trans-Himalayan Multi-Dimensional Connectivity Network' umbrella. Although the cross-Himalayan railway is at the heart of Nepal's aspirations, the paradigm shift is notable. The new Connectivity Network, for example, envisions 'six economic corridors between Nepal and China with enhanced border facilities and advanced transport infrastructure'.[20] BRI is viewed variously as a development tool that is 'a viable alternative to previous international schemes', as a method to extricate Nepal from India's economic hold and as a future vision of a more developed Nepal.[21]

However, new concerns over 'debt-trap diplomacy' emerged after several countries, like Sri Lanka, Malaysia and Pakistan, were unable to pay back the loans or reviewed their original agreements with China. In Nepal, charges of Chinese 'debt-trap diplomacy' were dismissed as coming from a 'negative attitude towards China' aimed at 'instilling psychological fear' in Nepal by the foreign minister himself,[22] amid larger debates in 2019 that hinted at political divisions on the question of Chinese engagement. Nonetheless, Chinese investment is welcomed across the board; there is little opposition to it, even if very little qualitative studies exist on how it has performed.

A recent perception survey on BRI found Nepali respondents to be among the most optimistic to see the initiative as an opportunity. 'At the country level, the more positive views on the BRI's long-term promise were found in South Asian nations such as Nepal (57.5%), Bangladesh (57.0%), and Pakistan (51.2%).'[23] This finding matches other perception polls about China's role in the world among developing countries. A Pew Research poll found 'views of China tend to be most negative in countries with the highest per capita gross domestic product. At the opposite end of the spectrum, countries with lower GDP per capita are less negative [towards China] . . . In many emerging economies, more people today are saying China's growing economy is a good thing for their nation compared with five years ago.'[24]

While Pew Research did not poll Nepali respondents, its findings matched what I found to be a near-universal view among Nepali politicians, policymakers and private sector players. In September 2019, the chief ministers of six provinces pitched for Chinese investments in their respective provinces at an investment forum organised by the Chinese embassy and a Chinese business committee. Agni Sapkota, the current speaker from the NCP and former Maoist leader, told me, 'China's economic growth is worthy of emulation . . . China has been increasing its influence without irritating anyone.' Similarly, a global credit rating agency's market intelligence wing said, 'Chinese investments will be a strong driver of growth in Nepal over the coming years . . . All these projects point to a likely surge in foreign direct investment from China over the coming decade, which will deliver a strong thrust to the Nepalese economy should these projects indeed proceed as planned.'[25]

China was the largest foreign investor in 2019–20 by a fair distance; of the 227 new FDI projects approved in the fiscal year, 176 were backed by Chinese investors, at an estimated investment value of NPR 26 billion.[26] The Department of Industry's statistics showed a rising number of Chinese investments in construction and related activities, cargo handling practices, software development and manufacturing, especially electric vehicle (EV) assembling. At least seven Chinese companies will begin assembling EVs in Nepal in the near future, with two more approved in FY 2019–20. According to its ambassador, Chinese companies received engineering contracts worth USD 1 billion in 2019, an increase of 13 per cent on the previous year. Similarly, Chinese investment in non-financial assets in Nepal increased to USD 98.7 million, rising by nearly 100 per cent over the previous fiscal year.[27] Bilateral trade rose in volume by 37.9 per cent, although the trade balance is heavily in China's favour.[28] More Chinese companies are now looking to do business in Nepal. Of the forty-one companies that showed interest in a government procurement tender for 300 electric buses in September 2020, thirty-four were Chinese brands.[29]

But beyond the qualitative analysis about Chinese investments and the strategic influence China can wield through economic largesse, there is the question of whether these companies are indeed more successful than other bilateral partners. Besides the two hydropower projects discussed above, the Chinese contractor China Railway exited the Melamchi drinking water project in 2012 after building 6.5 km of tunnels in four years instead of the targeted 27.5 km. In November 2019, the Chinese company North-West Civil Aviation Airport Construction, which is building the Bhairahawa international airport in the plains of Nepal, was accused of bringing in fake lighting systems for the runway, taxiway and terminal building. Nepal's state airline has been saddled with six Chinese aircraft since 2012: two of these were gifts, while the others were financed by a loan from the China EXIM Bank worth 218 million RMB. However, because of a lack of pilots and spare parts, the state airline finally grounded them for good in June 2020. The airline faced an annual loss of NPR 60 crore on the aircraft; from 2020 onwards, the public sector enterprise will have to pay NPR 250 million annually to pay back the loan. In December 2020, the airline finally came up with options to get rid of the aircraft: to ask the manufacturers to buy back the aircraft (the manufacturers refused to do so); to lease it to other Nepali operators or to other Chinese and international operators; or to auction them off.[30]

Even Hongshi was listed among eight cement companies said to be manufacturing substandard cement in early 2020.[31] 'More than Nepal's needs, China pushes its own self-interests while executing projects,' declared a 2019 magazine story,[32] while the energy minister asked the Chinese ambassador, 'Chinese companies have been performing excellently in other countries. Why can't they do it here too? What are the reasons for the delay?'[33]

There is also the question of how much employment is generated for locals by Chinese investments. At Hongshi Shivam, at least 500 Chinese nationals are employed, and the company was willing to be part of the Phase III trials of the COVID-19 vaccine developed by the Chinese company Sinovac by testing it on its employees (the details of the trials are not public yet). The Pokhara international airport employed 200 Chinese and 120 Nepali workers. According to the Department of Labour, at least 4,541 Chinese nationals are employed in Nepal, more than 70 per cent of all foreign workers in the country, excluding India.[34] While there are no accurate numbers for employment in foreign-owned small and medium enterprises (SMEs), anecdotal evidence suggests that most Chinese companies bring in Chinese workers at higher skill levels, while Nepalis are employed at low-skill jobs. A qualitative analysis of technology and skill transfer through Chinese investments is yet to be conducted.

This is not to say that Chinese companies should be held to a higher standard than others. The delays, the lack of transparency in the contract process, the low conversion of pledges to on-ground investments and the formidable loan structures are equally a consequence of Nepali negotiating skills and project execution abilities, as well as Nepal's laborious bureaucratic processes that are not conducive to foreign investors, and private business in general. Going by the current evidence in Nepal, however, the belief that Chinese companies can execute projects better than other bilateral partners is unwarranted. Although profiteering is an inescapable element of capitalism, questions have been raised about the quality standards of Chinese companies even within China. This was further highlighted during the COVID-19 crisis, when several countries pointed out flaws in Chinese testing equipment.

Needless to say, not all Chinese companies have underperformed in Nepal. The Bheri-Babai Diversion Multipurpose project, an irrigation-cum-hydropower scheme in western Nepal whose contractor was China

Overseas Engineering Group Co. Ltd, completed the construction of its 12.4 km-long tunnel in April 2019—a year before the deadline. Similarly, contractor China National Aero-Technology International Engineering Corporation completed the rehabilitation of the runway at the Kathmandu international airport more than four months before schedule. And the Pokhara international airport is held up as a model exemplar of Chinese engineering.

There is also the fact that Nepal is yet to follow up on its many agreements with China, including the one to supply petroleum products. Despite China offering duty-free access to more than 8,000 Nepali products, exports have been declining, and imports rising, leading to a significant trade deficit that is second only to the one Nepal has with India. While the possibility of exporting Nepali agricultural produce has been repeatedly highlighted by both countries, Chinese dissatisfaction over Nepali quality standards has resulted in disruptions, and Nepal has done little to address such issues.

Chinese investments in Nepal today can be broken down into a few specifics that shape the bilateral discourse in unique ways. The first are the government-to-government high-value investments in infrastructure and hydropower projects, with Chinese state-backed companies like Gezhouba, Three Gorges and CAMC Engineering forming the vanguard of Chinese diplomatic engagements in Nepal. Such engagements are almost all opaque in nature, but hold tremendous political value even if all have not been a shining beacon of success so far.

Although the projects listed under BRI have seen little progress, it is evident that Chinese economic engagements have significantly increased in Nepal in the past few years—certainly an outcome of the closer government-to-government relationship. While much of the political focus has been on connectivity—a broad term that emphasises physical connectivity as much as economic and cultural connections—projects have also been used to send across subtle messages about the ease of doing business in Nepal. Beyond the controversies surrounding hydropower projects, one instance of Chinese 'displeasure' at Nepal's way of functioning was expressed in the delay of the second phase of the Kathmandu ring road expansion project. After issues with land acquisition in the first phase, the Chinese delayed phase two by not submitting the designs on time. 'According to the consensus reached by China and Nepal . . . the Nepali side should first complete the land acquisition and demolition work in order to create necessary conditions for the successful completion of the project,' a Chinese official told a newspaper when asked about the delay.[35] As the Chinese ambassador said in an interview, 'I believe that the speed and effectiveness of the projects are also affected by political stability, policy continuity, government coordination, business environment, financing capacity and other factors of the country.'[36]

The second sphere is in the large private sector, where apart from the two cement companies, Huawei, the state-backed company at the centre of the US–China trade war, might be part of a telecom network that could usher in Nepal's first 5G network. The Chaudhary Group, more famous for their Wai Wai instant noodles, has recently inked a USD 100 million deal with Huawei to set up a 4G network that can be upgraded into a 5G network in Nepal.

That said, despite the print space devoted to how Chinese companies are leading the way in pledging FDI, high-value private investments are in fact rare. A distinction also needs to be made about whether the FDI is backed by loans from Nepali banks, as part of the Hongshi investment was, or whether it involves transfer of capital and technology. Most Nepali private-sector players who deal with China import finished products such as FMCG goods, clothing, furniture, electronics or automobiles—a continuation of the trading mindset of the Nepali private sector.[37] The opacity of the Nepal–China Chamber of Commerce and Industry and similar bodies, which ought to ideally take the lead in private-sector participation, and their limited role in policymaking, has also played a part in this.[38]

Chinese investment today is most visible to the average Nepali in SMEs that form the largest share of FDI in the country. The hotels and restaurants in Thamel and other tourist districts, agro-businesses like Xiang's and the many stores that sell to the Chinese tourist and expatriates—these enterprises shape the interactions and perceptions of Nepalis towards China, its companies and its people. But that brings separate challenges.

While its low-cost production methods are a boon to the Nepali consumer because of low prices, the scale of Chinese investments— even at SME levels—can overwhelm the Nepali entrepreneur. It is also apparent that Chinese companies have a tendency to remain as silent partners in private ventures while orienting the business to Chinese nationals. In Thamel, for example, I visited a traditional ayurvedic medicine store that marketed to the Chinese tourist: the prices were in RMB, most of the salespeople were Chinese and even the billing system was in Mandarin. I asked the Nepali cashier, who had only joined a month ago and was visibly struggling with the computer's Mandarin user interface, about the company. She told me the products were Indian, the investment was Chinese but the owner was a Nepali. I finally paid her in the Nepali rupees equivalent of 28 RMB, i.e. NPR 470. The invoice was in Mandarin too.

Such an enterprise raises questions about outward capital flow and the loss of state revenue through the circumventing of local taxation systems. At the moment, there is little regulatory oversight, especially over digital payment mechanisms. It is clear that there is an urgent need for Nepal to update its financial and taxation system and widen its net in the years to come. Chinese digital wallets such as Alipay and WeChat have now been permitted to operate in the country, but their use was ubiquitous for years among Chinese tourists and stores catering to them without an official policy mechanism in place for such wallets. Travellers were paying for goods and services acquired in Nepal through the Chinese financial system, which prevented Nepali authorities from registering Chinese spending as foreign income since the money never entered the Nepali financial system. 'This has also enabled Chinese businesspersons to repatriate earnings without paying any taxes here because the domestic authority has no evidence to substantiate that those transactions have taken place in Nepal.'[39] It was only after the issue was discussed widely on social media that Nepal first banned them—a reactive and anachronistic policymaking approach when digital wallets have become the norm across the world—and then approved their use.

Then there is the larger question about how increasing economic engagements with China will affect Nepal's worldview, besides the fear that they might lead to an extension of Chinese state power, as the debt-trap argument suggests. Because there are limited interactions with the Chinese private sector, in scale as well as numbers, the Nepali imagination of its northern neighbour is shaped by state-backed enterprises at the moment. Such interactions, when successful—as with the Pokhara international airport—will shape positive opinions towards

China; when unsuccessful—as with the hydro-power projects—will force China to be looked upon as just another foreign player in a long history of Nepali interactions with bilateral donors. In either case, unless the awarding of contracts follows a transparent and accountable process, a charge that has been levied on Chinese infrastructure investments globally, such projects will continue to be scrutinised at a variety of levels.

As more and more Chinese entrepreneurs and private sector players like Xiang and Hongshi enter the market, the Nepali private sector will be forced to either step up their game, possibly by artificial market manipulations through lobbying, or be forced out by the competition, as has been the fate of several small businesses in Thamel. But there is also a severe need to learn from the Chinese new economy, which will not occur if opaque government-to-government interactions are the only force shaping the economic relationship, as opposed to direct interactions with Chinese private sector leaders. Private participation and inflow of foreign funds, along with technology transfer, will remove some of the artificial distortions in the market, but unless the Nepali private sector is encouraged to break out of its inward-looking mentality, such distortions will only be magnified as Chinese private sector participation increases.

Ultimately, Nepal needs to resolve its own dilemmas before it can fully absorb the transforming potential of Chinese economic engagements. A shift towards transparency and accountability in contracts will allow not just Chinese private sector players but also global players to enter the market. A regulatory authority that provides oversight, creates opportunities and removes market distortions will allow Nepali entrepreneurs to compete with Chinese entrepreneurs in the same market. A financial system that grasps the import of the shift towards digital currency will be able to raise much-needed state revenue. And finally, only a government willing to engage with the Chinese people, and not just its unitary government system, can fully realise the potential of Nepal's budding economic relationship with the country.

10

All Roads Lead North

On most evenings, Ramesh Bishwokarma, also known as San-Dai, can be found in the kitchen. There is an orchestral quality to the chaos inside his Sichuan restaurant New Chong Qing Wei's cooking bay; the floor is slippery, and the air is heavy with the waft of timur, the Sichuan peppercorn. San-Dai relays the instructions for wafer-thin potato crisps and Dou Ban Yu, a whole fish cooked in spicy bean sauce, to his two sous-chefs—one of them his older brother. Meanwhile, he is busy getting the taste just right for Chicken La Zi Jhi, tender chicken pieces fried crisp and served on a bed of timur and dried red chilli, garnished with scallions. His wife and father take down the orders from customers. The used plates are stacked in a corner. On one stove, the water for steamed rice is not boiling; the flame is weak. San-Dai shouts at the serving boy to replace the LPG cylinder. 'Didn't I tell you to do it in the morning?' Then he walks into a private section, where six travellers from Beijing are eating Cold Buff in Mala Sauce. He talks to them in fluent Mandarin, asking them how they learnt about his place ('friends who had visited before' and 'Baidu'), and how long they plan to stay in Nepal ('one month'). 'How did you learn to cook Sichuan food without going to China?' one of them asks. San-Dai beams with pride. For that indeed is the question: how does a Nepali chef who has never been to China speak Mandarin with flair and cook authentic Sichuan cuisine in Kathmandu?

One winter afternoon, I arrived at New Chong Qing Wei to find San-Dai and his brother with meat cleavers in their hands. Three or four bamboo poles lay on the ground in a narrow alley that one needs to walk past to arrive at the restaurant, a blink-and-you-miss-it sort of place. The only signboard advertising the restaurant is now hidden amid the many glittering neon boards advertising Chinese medicine shops, restaurants, hotels, handicrafts, jewellery, sportswear and Chinese tea. Thamel is a cornucopia of visual delights, a tourist district replete with live music bars, hotels promising the best facilities at the lowest of prices, restaurants advertising global cuisines and mountaineering gear stores. But signs in the Mandarin script stand out, with its smooth type and bright colours, and for their novelty. There is an almost cyberpunkish ambience when the neon signs begin to light up as the mist of the winter evening starts to descend over Kathmandu's tourist district, a few blinking, a few glittering, in various shades of red, purple, yellow fluorescence.

At San-Dai's restaurant, the zinc sheet awning had begun to leak when it rained a few days previously, and he now wanted to cover the awning with a plastic sheet that would be tied to the bamboo poles. Here he was, once again relaying instructions to his brother on how to split the pole. As the cleaver went down hard—did he use the same one to chop meat in the kitchen?—the pole split with precision. Again the cleaver struck, and again the bamboo split. San-Dai is an excellent chef, a gastronome's delight, but on that day I realised the import of what he had said about becoming a chef by accident. Originally from a village in Gorkha, a five-hour drive west from Kathmandu, San-Dai was enrolled in a bachelor's degree in education and also learning Japanese, when he took up a job to do the dishes at a restaurant in Thamel in 2007. It was the beginning of the Chinese tourist boom in Nepal.

✦

This is based upon personal observation and interviews, so I hesitate to speak in absolutes, but it would not be wrong to say that the Nepali tourism industry has been the most affected by the new China–Nepal relationship. Tourism has always been a crucial sector, and has shaped the global perception of the country over the years. When Nepal opened its doors to the world in the 1950s, the first travellers were diplomats and aid workers. There were few tourists at the time. Then came the conquest of Everest, and Nepal became an explorer's dream. For the flower generation, Kathmandu became the last stop in the South Asian counterculture trail, before anti-narcotic policies politely compelled them to stop dropping out and tuning in. Nepal repositioned itself as a

Himalayan destination: full of treks to unexplored valleys, base camps and remote villages. Natural, untouched beauty became the buzzword, and Thamel was the centre of this universe of base-camp treks, its lanes occupied by stores selling trekking equipment or Nepali handicrafts and pubs blaring live music, allowing those who returned from the silence of the mountains to immerse themselves in the cacophony of urbanity before flying back home.

Then came the Chinese.

China sends the highest number of travellers abroad today, and Chinese tourists are consistently the biggest spenders. Naturally, Nepal has always wanted a slice of it. In 2002, it became the first South Asian country to receive 'approved destination status' from China, which allowed Chinese nationals to travel to the country in groups. But the escalation of the Maoist war and the 2006 People's Revolution severely affected the business, and it was not until 2008–09 that Chinese tourists started visiting in greater numbers. The 2015 earthquake once again devastated the industry, and Nepal then decided to offer free visas on arrival to Chinese tourists to help the sector rebound.

Today, Nepali tourism has reoriented itself for the Chinese visitor. And why not? Between 2009 and 2019, Chinese arrivals increased from 32,272 visitors to 169,543, a more than five-fold jump. Even in November 2019, when tourist arrivals dipped by 17.5 per cent—the worst-ever in a month since 2001—Chinese arrivals increased by 18.25 per cent.[1] Before the COVID-19 crisis threw everything down the sink, Nepal had projected around 500,000 Chinese visitors during Visit Nepal Year 2020.

The magnitude of change Chinese travellers have brought to the Nepali tourism industry has been immense. But that is only one part of the story. As relations grow friendlier and China is more assured of a partnership with Nepal, ordinary Nepalis have begun to believe in China's potential to transform their country. Long held captive by the dreams of 'bikas', China has come to represent many things at once for the ordinary Nepali. No longer are its consumer and industrial goods derided; and no longer is it the closed Communist state of yore. Instead, this is a China replete with the wealth to buy, consume and travel. And the Nepali entrepreneur, like San-Dai, wants to cash in on that.

His story, and those of others like him, is about opportunity, transformation and a cultural synergy that was absent between Nepal and China through the better part of history. And unlike Beijing's interactions with the Kathmandu establishment, these engagements do not shy away from the public gaze and create a new outlook towards China in Nepal.

San-Dai started doing the dishes at a restaurant run by Wang Chu Wei from Chongqing sometime around 2009. Within a few days, he was chopping vegetables and learning Mandarin. 'Wang taught me a few words, and I taught him some English,' San-Dai recalled. He still cannot read Mandarin, but he is a fluent speaker, conversing with all his Chinese customers in the language (and practising with his wife on the side). This was around the time Chinese travellers started coming to Nepal in groups. Nepali tourism had seen group tours before—most Indian tourists travel to Nepal in groups, usually for pilgrimages—but not at this scale. More importantly, there was the willingness to spend. A few Chinese entrepreneurs like Wang had already taken the jump, and now San-Dai would see the potential for himself.

A year into the job, Wang fell ill, and he wanted to shut down the restaurant. San-Dai asked him to keep it open. 'A customer asked for Fish in Pickled Cabbage—Suan Cai Yu—and I wasn't fully sure of the recipe. But [while cooking] I kept tasting the dish, adding spices as I thought it should be. That was the first Chinese dish I ever served.' On that first day, he handed Wang NPR 42,000 in earnings. Trust and goodwill are important factors in small businesses, and Wang now trusted San-Dai enough to let him run the show. He then asked Wang to teach him more Sichuan dishes. 'He taught me for three years. I noted down the recipes he followed, and worked on the dishes according to my taste. Finally, when he thought I had learnt enough, he told me I could now open my own restaurant. He taught me when I didn't know anything about food, and now I can call myself a cook because of him. The man treated me like a son.' When he started out on his own and opened New Chong Qing Wei in 2011, San-Dai named it after Wang's hometown.

✦

Bamboo poles split, San-Dai and I go to Jialin Pavilion, another Sichuan restaurant across the road from his. I want to speak to Xian Tang, who runs the restaurant with her husband, and San-Dai, by virtue of knowing the couple well and because he knows Mandarin, is my interpreter.

The Jialin's husband-and-wife team arrived in Kathmandu in 2013 from Shandong province when friends told them, 'Kathmandu was a nice place without too many problems'. And just like that, they started a new restaurant in a foreign land.

The difference between Jialin's decor and New Chong Qing Wei's is stark. Jialin *feels* like a restaurant—with tablecloths, napkins, sauce-dispensers, a stocked bar, even an aquarium stocked with live fish. Here, the tablecloth is protected with a transparent plastic sheet, and chopsticks are placed on a holder neatly. Back at San-Dai's, rexine-covered benches and bare tables make up the seating area, while the bar shelf is mostly bare. Red Chinese lanterns drop from the ceiling at Jialin, and San-Dai takes photos of the laminated menu. 'I should get menus like this too,' he says.

San-Dai is a work-in-progress entrepreneur. He has the culinary skills, but that alone does not make a restaurant. Over the years, he has tried to get better at the art of it. He obsesses over the plating; he is careful to wipe the stains from his plates, and loses his cool when one of his servers misses a detail like that. He fusses over what other restaurants do and he is not doing. He runs his restaurant like a mom-and-pop store, and seeks to improve the customer's experience as much as he can, within the means he has. For him, the restaurant is not an investment. It is his life.

On the other hand, it is not difficult for Chinese entrepreneurs to open a business in Nepal, as witnessed by Xian Tang's belief in word-of-mouth recommendation. Initial investments are relatively low. Nepal offers five-year business visas on low rates in a bid to encourage foreign investments. Although the Chinese are the largest foreign investors in the country, the true scale of Chinese investment in Nepal emerges in tourism, where seventy-three out of the eighty-nine approved FDI projects in the sector in FY 2019–20 had come from China.[2] The previous year, seventy-two out of the 131 approved projects came from the country.[3] Of the NPR 32.8 billion FDI pledged in tourism since 2015, Chinese investors had committed to NPR 23.2 billion, nearly 71 per cent of the total. Even in 2020, when the pandemic severely affected the Nepali economy, Chinese investors led the way in pledging nearly 97 per cent of the NPR 5.5 billion foreign investment in tourism.[4]

A spatial transformation is already evident in Jyatha, the Thamel lane where San-Dai's restaurant is, where neon signs in Mandarin advertise all sorts of wares and services for the Chinese traveller, where Chinese cargo offices promise to bring in or send goods to all parts of the world, where hotels advertise their rates in Mandarin and noodle makers from Gansu have set up shop; in short, where a 'Chinatown' is in the making. A study found Mandarin to be the second-most used language in signages in this lane, after English.[5] Chinese investors are also perceived to have more money, and it is widely known that Thamel landlords prefer to rent out to Chinese nationals because they pay higher rents.

For the Nepali entrepreneur, this competition can be the death knell. As San-Dai knows only too well.

A few years ago, the New Chong Qing Wei was located on prime Thamel property: a ground-floor shutter on the street itself, across from a popular hotel. Business was excellent, but San-Dai's landlord wanted to rent out the space to a Chinese-backed restaurant for twice the rent San-Dai was paying. 'There had been an electrical fire in my kitchen, so the landlord had been looking for a reason to kick me out. I still had a year left on my agreement, but the landlord stopped my electricity and water supply. Finally, I quit, but not before taking him to court,' San-Dai told me. The court, unfortunately, ruled in favour of the landlord.

San-Dai seems bitter about the resolution, but there was little he could do. It is common to hear of smaller Nepali business owners in Thamel being displaced by Chinese businesses that offer much higher rents. Such anxieties create a 'fundamentally unequal' relationship between Chinese and Nepali businesses: 'the Chinese have more startup capital with which to procure better signs and marketing. In the general perception of Nepalis, Chinese investors—whether out of ignorance or economic frivolousness—are willing to pay exorbitantly higher rents for commercial space. They can buy larger quantities of merchandise, giving them more advantageous profit margins. They can buy goods in advance and weather longer commercial droughts, offering them greater market flexibility than their Nepali counterparts.'[6] There is also the cultural and linguistic advantage Chinese entrepreneurs have over Nepalis; when Chinese travellers visit, who better than Chinese locals to help them negotiate fares, hotels, food bills and handicraft prices?

Once upon a time, Thamel was an outpost for the seekers of the Western world: 'it wasn't designed for Nepalis, not as they were then'.[7]

The Nepalis who visited Thamel belonged to the urban, higher-income categories. Thamel has undergone several waves of transformation from its original roots of Thabahi, the site of an eleventh-century Newar Buddhist monastery. So the change that has accompanied the Chinese arrivals is not new. But there is a difference. Chinese entrepreneurs have adapted their businesses solely for the Chinese visitor, such as at the Chinese pharmacy I visited, which is remarkably exclusive for this cosmopolitan tourist district. 'Thamel has always adapted through waves of development in the past. The question is whether the scale of the Chinese wave is too much for a smallish place like Thamel,' Nepali writer Rabi Thapa, who has documented the history of the tourist district, told me.

Outbound tourism from China is soon expected to touch 200 million travellers—more than 135 million Chinese travelled abroad in 2016, the highest numbers by nationality.[8] Chinese outbound tourism has consistently grown at 16 per cent on average since 2000.[9] China has also realised the potential of soft-power projection through its citizens travelling abroad—what it calls 'tourism diplomacy'—as an 'important and indispensable' tool of China's foreign policy.[10] In Nepal, Beijing pays close attention to tourism and the perceived benefits for Nepal. President Xi's 2019 visit, for example, had left 'a deep impression on the Chinese people, and more of them began to pay close attention to Nepal', according to the Chinese ambassador.[11] The joint statement issued after Xi's visit said China would support the Visit Nepal Year 2020 programme, and the Chinese ambassador to Nepal posted her pictures on Twitter to further publicise the tourism year.

Chinese outbound tourism is also influenced by political outcomes, as it is with all other influential nations. The sheer scale of it, however, makes an impression. 'Just as Chinese tourism can win friends, so its curtailment can be used to show displeasure.'[12] China had suspended group tours to South Korea after Seoul decided to deploy four American-made Terminal High Altitude Area Defense (THAAD) missile systems in early 2017. More than half of all Chinese outbound tourists—55 per cent—travel in groups,[13] and the ban cost the South Korean travel economy USD 6.8 billion. Seoul decided to freeze the deployment, and as political tensions clawed back to normalcy, Chinese tourists once again returned to South Korea.[14] Other tourist economies that have suffered Chinese displeasure include New Zealand, Turkey, Japan, the

Philippines and the tiny island nation of Palau—all due to political reasons. A United Nations World Tourism Organisation report on Chinese tourists lists several dos and don'ts to welcome them; among the don'ts is: 'Don't raise politically sensitive issues such as human rights or independence without great care.'[15]

In Nepal, which has faced no political repercussions, local business operators concede that their businesses would face massive losses without the Chinese. Even as Nepal strives to increase the number of tourists visiting the country, there has been a fall in the daily average spend. In 2014, the average tourist spent USD 48 per day in the country. In 2015, despite the earthquake, the spend went up to USD 68, which fell to USD 53–54 in 2016 and 2017. In 2018, it was USD 44, a seven-year low. Tourism operators suggested that, besides the fact that Nepal attracts low-spending travellers, tourists were spending fewer number of days in the country, and did not have sufficient avenues to spend money. Thus, the Chinese are that much more important to the trade. The Chinese tourist is already the highest spender in the world, spending about a thousand dollars on average every trip abroad.[16]

The transformation wrought by the Chinese tourist in Nepal was best (or worst) seen during the COVID-19 pandemic. Tourist arrivals dropped by 21 per cent in February, even before international flights were completely halted due to a nationwide lockdown. Most hotels had already seen a 50 per cent reduction in occupancy, and ordinary businesses had been hit hard. In Pokhara and Sauraha, where Chinese tourists made up 60 per cent of the business in a typical February, the tourist areas were completely shut down. In June 2020, the World Bank estimated that losses from the sector would cost the Nepali GDP at least USD 460 million, with 230,000 jobs at risk and more than 2,600 trekking agencies closed.[17] The decision to welcome new tourists continued to be delayed as the number of Coronavirus cases rose, and by mid-November, although tourists were welcomed in after following health guidelines, the numbers continued to be disappointing. With only 230,085 tourists in 2020, the year recorded the worst numbers for tourism since 1986—worse than during the insurgency years and after the earthquake, and less than a fifth of the 1.2 million who visited in 2019.[18]

One evening in early March 2020, I was in Thamel for dinner. San-Dai's restaurant was shut, as were several other eateries, hotels and stores. 'Chinatown' wore a deserted look. No neon lights flashed and blinked Mandarin characters. No Chinese visitors walked the streets in a group, holding up mobile phones and live-streaming products that they could sell back at home. The stores had their shutters down. The silence was eerie, even frightening, for Thamel is never quiet in the evenings. It felt like a return to the years of the insurgency, when tourists, and hope, were both in short supply.

✦

Every summer in the Himalayan highlands, thousands of Nepalis—men, women and children—camp out and dig the newly thawed grounds for yarsagumba, *Ophiocordyceps sinensis*, a fungus that emerges from a caterpillar and is colloquially known as 'Himalayan viagra' for its supposedly aphrodisiac properties. Skyrocketing Chinese demand for yarsa in recent years has created new opportunities both for rural Nepali collectors and the more urban middlemen, and the country now earns at least USD 50 million from yarsa, primarily from China. In recent years, however, overharvesting has impacted yarsa numbers, but trade has continued—the returns are too high for an impoverished family to ignore. A yarsa collector can earn as much as NPR 2–3 lakh in one season alone.

There are numerous stories of individuals who have benefited from and got rich off the Chinese, not just from yarsa, but also other herbs and natural produce used in traditional Chinese medicine. But in Timal, an entire village has been transformed—all because of a Buddhist master's gift and a newfound Chinese demand for seeds that promise divinity but look surprisingly ordinary.

Timal, 80 km to the east of Kathmandu, is a nondescript lower-Himalayan village. To the south are rolling hills that descend to the Indo-Gangetic Plains; mighty peaks dominate the skyline to the north. It sits on a ridge that overlooks a fertile valley, but the soil on the peak allows only for corn, and little else (and there is a divine reason for that). It may have once been on a trade route; an old paati, a resthouse, carved in traditional Newari architecture still stands en route to Timal. Its Tamang people, one of the hundred-plus ethnicities in Nepal, are slowly reclaiming their own histories in the new republic. Newly erected busts of the Tamang king, Rhinjen Dorje, said to be defeated by Prithvi Narayan Shah while unifying Nepal, and his consort greet visitors on a recently excavated road, still traversable only by four-wheel drives or lorries.

It was also in Timal that Padmasambhava, the eighth-century Buddhist teacher, hurled his vajra into a sandalwood forest to kill demons. A local myth calls the adversary a demon who hated creation and even killed unborn babies in the womb. Padmasambhava 'crush[ed] their dark yaksha lords to dust',[19] but inadvertently, the Buddhist master vapourised all local water sources. When the residents pleaded with him to save them, he scattered a few seeds around and told them the seeds would bring their descendants a bounty. This was the gift of bodhichitta.

The bodhichitta seed, a variety of buckthorn called *Ziziphus budhensis* unique to this region, is a pea-sized brown seed enclosed in a sponge-like layer of flesh. It is not much to look at; the tree does not grow too tall either, and its thorns are a deterrent too. When I visited Timal in the winter, the trees were barren and leafless. They grew everywhere—in the wild, along the dusty unpaved road, on cliffs with a sheer drop, and in plantations too, where goat dung served as fertiliser. But come harvest time in May–June, and Timal turns into a fortress. Villagers installed CCTVs and employed local boys to guard the trees all night long. Entire trees were reserved with payments in advance; the lease for one particular tree was NPR 1 crore 70 lakh. In 2018, a chartered helicopter had flown all the way to a hill across from Timal to buy seeds; in another instance, a convoy of seven SUVs was escorted by the police. In June 2020, at the peak of the pandemic, seeds worth NPR 90 lakh were robbed one night; the robbers carried SMGs, pistols and khukuris, and blocked off the road to a nearby village. All this, for a seed that is Padmasambhava's gift, and is worth its weight in gold—a single seed, a puny little fulvous bead that looks like a child's marble, can cost NPR 6 to 7 lakh.

Timal's people grew corn and painted thangkas previously; occasionally, they would sell the bodhichitta seeds to Tibetan monks, who used them as prayer beads. A mala consists of 109 such seeds. The seed has always been holy; like the rudraksha, which Hindus consider to be born of the tears of Lord Shiva, the bodhichitta is a physical manifestation of divinity here on earth. It was bought and sold in lesser quantities, and at lesser prices. A mala cost NPR 20 in 1990, local journalist Gyanzo Lama told me. 'The price had declined to as low as NPR 5 a mala. Nobody cared about the business of bodhichitta.'

Until Timal residents discovered that the Chinese were interested in the seeds.

✦

Sixty-four-year-old Tirtha Lama took us to his backyard in Timal, where a row of bodhichitta trees stood forlorn. He had demarcated his land with corrugated zinc sheets; bodhichitta trees grew everywhere. Mounds of manure and goat-dung pellets sat at the base of the trees; it had been a tough winter, and Tirtha hoped he would make more money this year. 'Last year, I earned less than a lakh,' he said, picking up a seed from the ground and showing it to us in his palms. His trees were six to seven years old, and his first sale had come four years ago. The seeds had brought him NPR 4 lakh, then NPR 7 lakh and NPR 3 lakh respectively, before the last harvest of less than a lakh. The good times had been worth it. 'I grew maize earlier. What am I to do with maize now when one bodhi seed can get me NPR 2,000–3,000?'

Tirtha had arrived late to the bodhichitta boom. The prices for the seeds started increasing sometime in 2009–10, when Chinese tourists began to buy the seeds in bulk. Stores selling bodhichitta seeds started popping up in Thamel, and by 2016, annual tax revenue from the sales were estimated to be NPR 30 million, with more than fifteen Nepali suppliers being listed on Alibaba.[20] An illegal supply network that operated without the requisite licences was up by 2017; a Chinese man was caught with nearly 50 kg of seeds worth NPR 10 million in July that year.

Although the primary use of bodhi seeds is as rosary beads, a study found they had multiple uses in China, including as traditional medicine.[21] In Timal, the end use did not matter. 'The Chinese are ready to buy anything,' a farmer told us as we sat on the grounds of a local government school. Then the tales began—and with that I too began to get a clearer idea of the impact Chinese demand (and the subsequent increase in incomes) can have on Nepali small-scale farmers and producers.

Kancha Tamang, who wore a blue down jacket and a gold watch, chewed on some grass and told me a Chinese buyer named Gao had bought all his seeds for two years in a row. He did not know whether the man would return this year, but he certainly hoped so. 'Because of the Chinese demand, there has been an oversupply in the past few years, and the prices have come down,' he said. A few moments later, however, he told me someone had assured him NPR 50 lakh for one of his trees. 'I would be paid the sum no matter what the harvest was, but I didn't go ahead with it. What if nothing grows at all?' It was hard to miss the boisterousness in his voice. Nobody challenged him. He seemed to be one of the more 'connected' farmers, with a bodhichitta store in the Bouddha stupa complex. When we began asking locals about the business, everybody looked at him.

Kancha Tamang broke down the trade in greater detail. He had worked in Saudi Arabia for ten years before returning to Timal. The bodhichitta had transformed his village, he said. 'Earlier, the trade was purely religious. Only Buddhist priests would buy it.' The commercialisation was the result of Chinese demand. Several locals said the Dalai Lama had recommended Timal's bodhichitta seeds as the best, which also had an effect on the demand (although I found no evidence of this recommendation). 'The market believed that if you were a true Buddhist, you would keep a bodhichitta mala at home,' Kancha said.

The seeds were adjudged in a method similar to rudraksha seeds. In both, there was the notion of a mukh, lines, that determined the value of a seed. For rudraksha seeds, the lesser the number of lines, the more valuable a seed was (the rarest was considered the one-mukhi seed—'excellent for business-class people and useful for heart patients', as an advertisement in a Nepalgunj hotel read). However, for bodhichitta seeds, the more lines there were, the greater the value. If a seed had seven–eight lines (saat–aath mukhi), it could cost NPR 6–7 lakh. 'Earlier, seeds with three–four mukhs were in demand. Now the demand is for five–six mukhi seeds,' Kancha said. The diameter of the seed too held value. Seeds less than 10 mm wide were the most expensive, and those between 20–24 mm also commanded reasonable prices. The rest were considerably cheaper.

Several locals had cashed in on the transformation of what had been a subsistence-level trade into a mass-scale commercial enterprise. Everybody I met in Timal—the boy who ran a teahouse along the way, our driver Nima, and Gyanzo Lama, the journalist—had cashed in on the trade in some form or the other. Gyanzo had sold his harvest for NPR 3 lakh the previous year. 'If I had been growing maize, I wouldn't have received even NPR 3,000.' Some simply made money through serendipity. 'We had eight plants in our lands since our grandfather's time, which we've now increased to thirty–thirty-five plants,' Nima, our driver, said. He has earned NPR 15–16 lakh a year on average for the past few years; he preferred selling off entire trees to buyers. 'The buyers come around April to see the plants. They cannot harvest the seeds until they pay us the entire sum in cash.' Gyanzo told me that, although Chinese buyers came to check out the trees themselves, they always dealt with the farmers via middlemen.

The incentive in the trade is too great for anybody from Timal to resist. But the rewards have also brought their fair share of ills. Beyond the almost surreal imagery of buyers coming in helicopters with suitcases full of cash, and farmers guarding their trees with CCTVs and round-the-clock protection, Timal residents also reported that farmers would pour acid into the roots of others' trees in case there was discord. 'Timal has completely changed because of the trade,' Kancha said, and the others agreed. Gyanzo listed the effect of the trade on Timal, saying, 'Timal's religious and cultural value is now widely known, and the trade has raised the poor's incomes. There is a sense of economic security because of the trade,' he said. 'But at the same time, because of a lack of foresight and long-term vision, and coupled with the easy availability of cash at harvest time, farmers have also spent heavily and ended up in debt. The trade has reduced the culture of working hard among the youth.'

✦

China today has the highest number of Buddhists in the world, with nearly a fifth of its population professing the religion. And of the nearly 170,000 Chinese travellers who visited Nepal in 2019, 21,269 visited Lumbini, the birthplace of Buddha. While not all of them may have been religious, there is an emerging trend of Chinese nationals visiting sites of Buddhist importance in Nepal. Balaram Adhikari, a guide who has worked with Chinese tourists since 2013, told me about the Buddhist circuit the Chinese traveller follows. Beyond the popular Swayambhu and Bouddha stupas in Kathmandu and Lumbini itself, the Namo Buddha monastery outside the valley, where a bodhisattva sacrificed himself to feed a starving tigress and her cubs, is a popular destination; another is the Pharping cave, where Padmasambhava meditated (which the Chinese actor Jet Li also visited in 2017); and the Halesi Mahadev caves in Khotang, another site associated with Padmasambhava. 'Religious tour packages are designed by travel agencies. The Chinese are increasingly coming to Nepal to learn yoga and meditation,' Adhikari said. 'Chinese travellers think Nepal is beautiful and mysterious, and its people are happy.' This view is built upon the 2013 Chinese film *Up in the Wind*, a coming-of-age story that was shot in Kathmandu, Pokhara and Chitwan (and got Chinese travellers to Pokhara interested in paragliding, much like the protagonist of the film).

The growth in this sort of religious tourism is consistent with Beijing's push towards a people-to-people approach built on shared heritages. Buddhism is but one of the instruments of its soft-power focus, even as Beijing seeks to wean the religion away from the Tibetan variety led by the Dalai Lama. It is now anticipated that there will be two Dalai Lamas in the future—one approved by China and one chosen by the Tibetans in exile—and that Beijing will seek the support of states like Nepal for their candidate, perhaps making it as inalienable a part of its joint statements as the 'One China' declaration.

The geopolitical struggle over Buddhism reached its peak in 2011, when a Chinese proposal to invest USD 3 billion in Lumbini appeared out of nowhere. The project was the brainchild of the Asia Pacific Exchange and Cooperation Foundation (APECF), an NGO of dubious origins, said to be backed by the Chinese government.[22] In Nepal, the project received high-level political attention until it was suddenly dropped, reportedly after India expressed displeasure at a Chinese project close to its borders. Regardless, Lumbini continues to matter. As a senior editor with the official CCP newspaper *People's Daily* wrote, 'Lumbini, in addition to being a spiritual site, is also a political one. It could provide important clues for us to know present-day Asia . . . Does it mean China and India will shake hands at the birthplace of Buddhism if the two ancient civilizations are linked via Nepal?'[23]

The geopolitical use of Buddhism is, however, just one part of the story. In recent years, as its ambitions have soared, so has China's desire—and need—to have its story heard. To that end, one of the avenues its diplomacy has consistently focused on is to expand people-to-people contact with other countries by building on both historical legacies as well as contemporary possibilities, as seen in Nepal. Xi Jinping himself had written in his op-ed, 'It is important that we encourage more exchanges and cooperation in such areas as education, youth and tourism ... China will give more government scholarships to outstanding young Nepalis and help train more professionals needed in Nepal's development endeavor. China welcomes more Nepali students to China.' Previously, the focus had been on security and connectivity. However, Xi's visit would 'improve people-to-people relationship', Sudheer Sharma said.

This new focus on developing relations with Nepal's youth is most evident in the scholarships—both government and privately funded—at Chinese universities and cultural institutes like the Confucius Institute, as well as greater interactions with the Nepali people through language training. An increasing number of Nepalis now study in the country. This is in line with the rest of South Asia: from 15,395 South Asian students in China in 2011–12, the number rose to 37,592 in 2016-17, with Pakistan sending the highest among all South Asian nations. 'China now receives approximately the same number of students from South Asia compared to India.'[24] Although India still remains one of the primary educational destinations for Nepalis, more than 3,000 Nepalis have received Chinese scholarships, and at least 6,400 Nepalis currently study in China.[25]

'When I went to study in China [in 2018], I didn't know anyone who had studied there. But now, when I come back to Nepal for breaks, many people ask me about the admission process and scholarships in China,' Siddhartha Mainali, a PhD student at Peking University told me. We were in one of the many Kathmandu cafes one evening, together with two other Nepalis—Aneka and Raunab—who are at Peking University too. 'Ten years ago, it was rare to see Nepalis studying anything except medicine and engineering in China. Even now it's rare, but the numbers are increasing in other streams. It's the same trend in universities other than Peking too. More courses are being offered in English, and people are realising that China also has world-class institutions. The Chinese embassy holds [promotional] events from time to time too.'

Outside the cafe, the evening rush-hour traffic has begun to pick up. Inside, unbeknown to us, the cafe owners were getting ready for their weekly Ethiopian dinner buffet. I wanted to know why Nepali students chose to go to China. In recent years, Nepalis have preferred the US and Australia for higher-education goals; in both countries, Nepali students are among the top ten foreign students. Raunab, who is pursuing a master's degree in economics, told me he too had been thinking of going to study in the US. When a British professor he had worked with at an international non-governmental organisation (INGO) told him to look at China as a possible alternative, he started checking out the universities and 'made up my mind to go to China'.

It is not just young Nepali students who go to China to study. From government officials to journalists, China offers several scholarships for Nepali professionals, besides training programmes in Nepal itself. More than 850 Nepali bureaucrats will study in China under a new programme, a dramatic rise from the twenty seats it offered in 2004. Further, although the exact number of journalists who have visited China on exchanges and training programmes could not be confirmed, the Nepal Journalists' Association has led delegations to China since 1980. Sudheer Sharma told me that journalists from his newsroom get frequent invitations from the Chinese side for different programmes. 'This is a new phenomenon. They would earlier get such invitations mostly from India or the West.'

Further, there is also now a focus on expanding Chinese-language training programmes, either through the Confucius Institute, or through other language institutes across Nepal. Several private Nepali schools— at least eighty to eighty-five schools, according to a report in *Record Nepal*—now offer Chinese language classes as a mandatory subject, with the teachers being funded by the Chinese embassy.[26] A memorandum to expand the 'Volunteer Chinese Teachers' Program' was exchanged during Chinese Foreign Minister Wang Yi's Nepal visit in September 2019. State broadcaster China Radio International's Nepali service airs regular Chinese-language classes. Although the Confucius Institute was set up in 2007, and is in many ways similar to cultural institutes set up by other powers, say, the American Center or the British Council, there has been a new focus on them because of their rising numbers across the world, and because the US has alleged that the Confucius Institute is a proxy for the Chinese government.

Although there is a difference between such Chinese government-funded programmes and the ordinary Nepali student pursuing a course at a Chinese university, both contribute to how China itself is perceived by Nepalis. 'It's too early to tell whether Chinese soft power is working in Nepal, but from what I hear from African students, there are a lot of people in decision-making posts who've studied in China,' Mainali said.

Providing scholarships to foreign students is a familiar soft-power approach by global powers, starting from the Cecil Rhodes scholarship that was built on an edifice of British imperialism to the Fulbright programme of the Americans. In China, the preference for students from the BRI countries has been clear. While the number of foreign students grew four times between 2004–16, those from BRI countries grew eight times. By 2016, 61 per cent of all Chinese government scholarships were given to students from BRI countries, with 10,000 scholarships being reserved annually for such students.[27] While strengthening of ties and a familiarity with Chinese governance and value systems would be a natural outcome of such a rise in numbers, another goal is to negate the deep-rooted 'Western bias against China's political system'. '. . . [O]utside views on China can be easily influenced by negative Western reports that play up China's weakness and exaggerate its potential as a regional threat. International students can gain a better understanding of the Chinese political system, culture, economic model and values and so on by studying in the country, and act as a bridge between China and their home countries, offering a new channel for people in their own countries to know the true picture of China.'[28]

✦

China certainly wants the world to acknowledge its position and narrative, as seen in its geopolitical claims over Buddhism. Nepal's history with China began from Tibet, but in the first decades of the twenty-first century, this is no longer true. Rather, as the two states have grown closer, so have its people. From cross-border trade and profiting off Chinese demand, to reorienting entrepreneurial skills and cultural outposts for the Chinese traveller, or simply using newfound bilateral bonhomie to import more consumer goods, more Nepalis are now involved in dealing with China in some way or the other. Similarly, while Nepal may not present a massive market for Chinese firms that are used to operating on scale, Chinese entrepreneurs and state-backed enterprises have capitalised on several opportunities within the Nepali market, even if some of it is directed at Chinese presence and projects.

What these sorts of commercial and social engagements do is shift the narrative away from the corridors of power and ground them in everyday discourse. While the popular perception of China among Nepalis is that of a neighbour who has helped Nepal in its time of need, such unidimensional views will change once more Nepalis study in China, or more Nepalis sell to the Chinese, or if the Chinese give stiff competition to Nepali business owners. The past will matter, but the future will not always be shaped by it.

At any rate, in the present, Nepalis have benefited in a host of different ways. We have seen how Chinese investment is shaping Nepal's approach to infrastructure and industry, and how Nepali business owners and entrepreneurs are gearing up to supply to the Chinese market or visitors. In the Himalaya, China's push for development has presented Nepali communities with an alternative to the Nepali state. In the cities, new interactions are reshaping the perceptions of urban Nepalis about the Chinese. And in Nepal's villages, livelihoods depend on Chinese demand, even if it is the middlemen and large farmers who benefit most from the export of natural products like yarsa and bodhichitta seeds. As Nepal becomes more entwined in Beijing's worldview, several other spheres will open up and provide a host of opportunities. Besides Kathmandu playing catch-up in terms of export standards, reducing the trade deficit, shifting to the digital economy and finding its own place in the global state of affairs during a time of US–China competition (while addressing both its neighbours' concerns), there is also the risk of being overwhelmed by the Chinese scale, which local tourism entrepreneurs have already got a whiff of. This will especially matter if China sees Nepal as a transit state in its pursuit of the populous north Indian market; if Nepal is to become an assembly-line state, what are the returns it can expect?

Throughout history, China had been part of Nepal's imagination, an amorphous idea more than a reality, a 'card' against India than an actual hand. It was only in the twenty-first century that China became 'real' for Nepal. As China's economic potential grew, so did its ambitions—and they came to include Nepal. China's status as a world power means that it has its own view of what the world will look like, and how the current Chinese system will enable such a world. Chinese expectations from Nepal have also changed since the days it saw a smooth border demarcation with Nepal as a riposte to the Indian challenge and the abrogation of the Nepal–Tibet treaty as essential for its sovereignty project in Tibet.

China is many things at once in Nepal today. It is a superpower, a beneficent aid-giver, a friend in need, an essential provider, a demanding neighbour, an older brother, a competitor, a model of development and growth, and a vision of a developed future. China is changing regional and global dynamics in unprecedented ways, and no other South Asian nation has witnessed modern China's abilities and limitations in a starker way than Nepal. As China declares itself on the world stage, Nepal wants to tag along for the ride. Relations have never been better than in the contemporary era, but they need to be sustained, nurtured and developed as they evolve. It is in Nepal's interest to do so, and imperative to do it in a way that acknowledges its own aspirations.

At Kora La in Mustang, I marvelled at the under-construction immigration and customs building on the Chinese side. On that cold, wind-swept plain, 16,000 feet high, there was little imagination required to understand why Nepalis held a dramatic view of China as a superpower, a stark contrast to the view of India as an interfering, unsympathetic neighbour. In Limi, entire villages relied on Chinese goodwill and were dependent on Chinese goods to sustain their livelihoods. In Rasuwa, locals were in awe of the unyielding Chinese capacity to build. In the tourist district of Thamel, entrepreneurs grumbled about the influx of Chinese investment, yet their businesses were sustained on Chinese arrivals. In Pokhara, I met Tibetans who lived in anger, both at Nepal for bending over backwards for China, and at the latter for chasing them even beyond its borders. In Timal, a village had changed because of the Chinese capacity to consume. And in Patan, I met students whose views will shape the future of China in Nepal.

The road to the north has been built; it is now up to Nepal to decide how smooth the ride will be.

EPILOGUE
Future Tense

In May 2020, as the rest of Nepal remained home during the COVID-19 lockdown, social-media savvy Chinese ambassador to Nepal, Hou Yanqi, had been busy. She first met with Prime Minister K.P. Sharma Oli, who had been asked to resign by two leaders within the NCP—Prachanda and Oli's old-time UML rival, Madhav Kumar Nepal. The three had been at loggerheads over several issues: the US-backed MCC grant; Oli's insistence on retaining both the prime ministership and the chairmanship of the party; and his push to promulgate two presidential ordinances that made it easier to split political parties. The NCP looked like it was on the verge of a split only two years after the merger.

Ambassador Hou then met with the two other leaders and called for unity within the ruling party. A political crisis was averted thanks to Beijing's intervention, with a ceasefire that hinged on Oli's willingness to share power. A few days previously, Nepali President Bidya Devi Bhandari had had a long chat with Chinese President Xi Jinping. The sum of the conversation was Nepal's continued support for Chinese efforts to control the pandemic at a time when the international community had been accusing China of underplaying the disease's spread. But there was another critical assessment: in China's own words, the current Nepali leadership was crucial in the fight against COVID-19.

A week later, Indian Defence Minister Rajnath Singh inaugurated the road to the Himalayan pass of Lipu Lekh, nearly 500 km to the west of Kathmandu. The road went through a thin triangular sliver of land Nepal considers its own. A territorial dispute erupted. India–Nepal relations once again went into a freefall, one with lesser physical ramifications than the 2015 blockade, but perhaps even more damaging because of the legacy of that blockade. Kathmandu brought out a new political map claiming the disputed territory, and Indian policymakers saw a Chinese hand behind it. Oli rallied the people in his anti-Indian narrative of Delhi encroaching upon Nepali sovereignty once again. The Indian media first asked whether Nepal was now a Chinese puppet state, and then spun an imaginary (and misogynist) tale about Oli being honeytrapped by the Chinese ambassador. A former Indian diplomat called for activating Indian 'assets' in Nepal to 'get rid' of the prime minister on live television. Nepali cable operators in turn banned Indian news channels.

Then, one night in June, Indian and Chinese troops fought each other at Galwan Valley in Ladakh with baseball bats studded with nails and other crude, homemade weapons. It was the first loss of lives on the Sino–Indian border in forty-five years. And just like that, relations between the two Asian giants, which had been dedicated to trade and economy for the past two decades, collapsed like a house of cards. South Asia watched keenly, especially Nepal. Several analysts recalled the adage 'When two elephants fight, it is the grass that gets trampled', even as Nepal counselled peace. But Kathmandu still could not convince Delhi to talk about its territorial dispute.

In July, the ceasefire negotiated by Ambassador Hou came crashing down—if you follow Nepali politics, this was only to be expected. Petty personal ambition is the hallmark of Nepal's ruling class. Oli was convinced India was trying to remove him as prime minister through the offices of Prachanda and Nepal. Prachanda retorted with loud rhetoric: it's not India that wants Oli gone; it's us. Once again, the ambassador had to resume her meetings. Once again, a split was averted. Beijing had put far too much political capital into the merger of the two Left parties to let it split.

But domestic squabbles are often the most difficult to resolve, as the ambassador would discover. In October, the old differences between the NCP leaders resurfaced (and the ambassador had to resume her meetings), but this time, the discord erupted against a background of international push-and-pulls. As India sent a series of officials—its external intelligence head, its army chief and, finally, its foreign secretary—in a signal that Delhi was finally revisiting ties with Kathmandu, China was caught on the backfoot. Although its defence minister countered the Indian visits with his own day-long stay in

Kathmandu, Oli seemed to have made peace with the fact that internal differences within his party were non-resolvable, and was believed to have told the Chinese ambassador that he was open to a split in the NCP.

By December, Beijing's fears came true. Oli dissolved the parliament and called for mid-term elections. The NCP was vertically split between the camps of Oli and Prachanda and Nepal, respectively. The twists and turns of Nepali domestic politics had once again left their imprint on international affairs; China, which so far had been comfortably ensconced in the Kathmandu worldview, found itself being scrutinised in greater detail with these manoeuvres and open plays with Nepali politicians. On the other hand, a rapprochement was underway with India after the war of words and maps, as had happened so often in the past. When India issued a statement after Oli's dissolution of parliament saying it was Nepal's internal affairs, one wondered whether the New Delhi mandarins had got a better sense of the bickering between Nepali politicians than Beijing had. As it had done with the monarchy, had China once again invested too much political capital in one particular section of the Nepali establishment?

China's visible involvement in trying to prevent a split in the NCP were a stark contrast to its conduct in previous years. China had prided itself on its quiet diplomacy and working behind official channels so far. But it seemed Beijing no longer cared; it now wanted to get its message across. China had been increasing its presence in Kathmandu; the past three ambassadors had broken tradition and spoken in English at public forums, a signal that China wanted its message to Nepal and to the world delivered clearly, keeping in line with their new world-power status. But this was the first time a Chinese ambassador and leaders were visibly doing the rounds of Nepali politicians as Indians had done in the past. Beijing was no longer the non-meddling neighbour. Nepalis now began to ask, is China the new India, controlling Nepali political leaders from behind the scenes?

Far away, in Delhi, one could imagine a chuckle in the corridors of South Block. Nepal's politics, and its politicians, are a quagmire. Its leaders play each other and its neighbours constantly in the struggle for power. India had long waded into the puddle, played the game and lost. Now, it was China's turn.

✦

Nepal's newfound friendship with its northern neighbour can perhaps be best described with a verse by classical Chinese poet Qu Yuan—'a great joy it is to make friends anew'. As difficult as it is to escape a worldview in which India has little role to play in Nepal, the new reality is that China is now Nepal's primary bilateral partner, the special relationship with India notwithstanding. The irony is unmissable: when China first appeared as a neighbour, Nepali leaders were hesitant, and it was Nehru who convinced Kathmandu (and the world) that it was essential to recognise communist China and the new status quo. Until 1962 happened. Then, in 2006, Delhi once again brought several Nepali actors, including the Maoist insurgents, together in an anti-royal alliance, lending its weight to the agenda of a republic state. Fast-forward to a decade later, and India once again has come out worse off. Today, an entire generation of young, urbane and globally connected Nepalis will grow up with the 2015 blockade as their first substantive political memory—cementing their view that India does not have Nepali interests at heart, as Pasang had told me at Kora La.

Delhi may continue to emphasise the socio-cultural connections between the two countries, but a shared religion and culture may not be adequate to overcome the deep animosity towards India prevalent across society and institutions, not least the influential Nepali media. The visibility of Chinese largesse also stands in stark contrast to India's faltering aid projects; as Westad has written, '[c]ompeting with China cannot be done on the cheap'.[1] And even though Indian policymakers point towards new infrastructure and connectivity projects to show that Delhi is still keen to invest in people-to-people relationship with Nepal, it may have missed the bus.

Indian foreign policy overreach was the ammunition, but the desire to break away from India existed long before the blockade. More importantly, the China that greeted Nepal in the twenty-first century was no longer the old closed-door nation; it was a China willing to embrace the world and shape it.

Today, across the length of Nepal, it is the friendly neighbour. China's soft diplomacy approach emphasises the importance of Nepal in Beijing's worldview; at the November 2020 Beijing international photo exhibition, Nepal was chosen as the theme country. China's diplomatic mission in Kathmandu has charmed ordinary Nepalis and the influential crowd alike with its ambassador's rendition of Nepali songs and her social media posts promoting Nepali tourism. When the new height of Everest was announced, the Chinese foreign ministry spokesperson said, 'No matter how high Mt. Qomolangma is, it can be climbed. No matter how great the difficulty is, it can be overcome . . . As long as countries work together in good faith as China and Nepal do, we will finally defeat the [Corona]virus.'[2] Relations between the two are held up as a shining beacon of neighbourly goodwill.

Chinese largesse is also visible across the capital: a sparkling new school built out of the rubble of Nepal's oldest; a renovated eighteenth-century palace in the heart of the old city; an eight-lane carriageway smoother than any of Nepal's roads. Chinese investment is transforming not just Nepali cities, but also the rugged Himalayan borderlands. All of these underline China's ability in spatial transformation. They allow Nepalis to dream big—to think of monorails, new airports, better roads, increased trade and new opportunities. There's the promise of the train from Tibet, the ultimate vision of bikas for Nepali policymakers, even if the country does not know how to pay for it. Then there is the message of respecting Nepal's sovereignty, even if the events of 2020 throw doubt on those claims, and the question of Tibetan exiles is always on the slow burner.

Dig further, and one begins to understand not just what Nepalis think and want out of China, but also what China wants from Nepal.

✦

In July 2020, Nepali Foreign Minister Pradeep Gyawali participated in a video conference organised by Chinese Foreign Minister Wang Yi. The foreign ministers of Pakistan and Afghanistan, too, participated, leading analysts to call it a 'Trans-Himalayan Quad', in a nod to the grouping of the US, Australia, Japan and India, which has been seen as a move to counter China's military rise and influence in the Indo-Pacific.[3] A second such conference with foreign ministry officials was held in October, this time with Sri Lanka and Bangladesh joining in, while Afghanistan did not participate. Both conferences were said to focus on coordinating efforts in the fight against COVID-19; both, however, also emphasised cooperation on BRI, with the July conference 'exploring ways to synergize the China-Pakistan Economic Corridor (CPEC) and the Trans-Himalayan Multi-Dimensional Connectivity Network'.[4]

The official statements, however, also tell us more than this being a story about simple strategic gains. In a post-COVID world, where China's early management of the pandemic was severely critiqued by other nations, Beijing now wants its neighbours, including Nepal, to align with its views on the international stage. During the pandemic, Nepal supported the Chinese management of COVID-19. By rejecting the 'politicisation' of the pandemic, China had targeted US-led accusations about mismanagement, even though it utilised 'COVID medical diplomacy' to the fullest.

Optics matter in international relations. China has projected its rise as a peaceful one, based on mutual interest and growth. It has opened its purse strings and made its beneficence known. But it has also asked for support on issues that matter to it. Nepal's support for the One-China policy is as important to China's sovereignty project in Tibet today as it was in the past. It is no surprise that all joint statements between the two nations explicitly state this (and include references to Taiwan being a part of China). It is also expected that Nepal will support the next Beijing-approved candidate for the Dalai Lama. In recent times, Nepal has also supported China's policies in Xinjiang at the United Nations, and was among the fifty signatories that spoke out against a letter by twenty-two nations condemning China's human rights abuses in Xinjiang. Nepal also welcomed the new Hong Kong security laws.

Kathmandu has similarly been co-opted in Beijing's attempts to wrest control of the narrative over Everest. Beyond China's arguments that the name of the peak itself is a colonial relic (which it is—the indigenous name of the peak is Chomolungma), it finalised the height of the peak according to its own measurements, before the two countries jointly announced the new height—the peak had grown by nearly three feet—in December 2020. But Nepal's Survey Department had been measuring Everest's height for two years, and it was not consulted before the agreement to jointly announce the height was signed during Xi Jinping's October 2019 visit, even though it was nearly done with the measurements.

This last incident brings the current state of bilateral relations into sharp focus. The relationship is driven by partisan political decisions from the Nepali side, resulting in a lack of coherent national agenda, and sometimes the weakening of its own institutions. For Beijing, however, the agreement on Everest is vital in its quest to shape international perception, as is outlined under the term 'huayuquan', translated as 'speaking rights' or 'international speaking rights'.[5] China seeks not just to speak and be heard on the international stage; like any great power, it wants 'to influence others' perceptions of China, and eventually to shape the discourse and norms that underpin the international order'.[6]

The semantics of the Nepal–China relationship are equally revealing. Over the years, China has consistently lent 'firm support' to upholding Nepal's territorial integrity and sovereignty; the historical baggage of an overbearing India is evident here. Chinese aid in Nepal, although yet to replicate the 'gift of development' vocabulary as seen in Tibet—'a series of acts of altruism and generosity, bringing benefit and generating positive sentiment'[7]—revolves around talk of a long-lasting friendship. At the Kalanki underpass built as part of the Kathmandu ring road expansion grant project, bold red letters in Mandarin and Nepali, carved in concrete, tell commuters, 'Let the eternal friendship between Nepal and China remain forever.' As scholars Austin Lord and Galen Murton have documented in Rasuwa, Chinese aid in Nepal is '[p]redicated on alliances made on the basis of bilateral agreements between Nepali and Chinese leaders and "gifts"[;] these relationships provide soft loans to Nepal, construction contracts to Chinese firms, and political capital increasingly leveraged by Beijing in Kathmandu in exchange for Chinese support of Nepal's own state-making projects'.[8]

Beijing has also framed its relationship with Nepal as that of a sibling caring for another. 'China and Nepal are good brothers who always stand alongside each other,' wrote Xi in his op-ed before the October 2019 visit, listing out the Chinese relief, rescue and reconstruction efforts post the 2015 earthquake as 'shining examples of how China and Nepal look out for each other like brothers do'.[9] By framing its foreign policy within the ambit of kinship ties, and subsequently an imagined community, Beijing allows for a closer—and yet a more hierarchical—imagination of the relationship.

For Nepali policymakers, the expectation from Beijing has been that it would assist Kathmandu against Indian incursions on its sovereignty. While historically, moral and verbal support had been forthcoming, China's limitations allowed it to do little more. But even today, there are indications that China's outlook towards Nepal is overshadowed by Beijing's relations with Delhi. One instance of this is in the Kalapani territorial dispute. The Indian road to Lipu Lekh is a result of the 2015 trade agreement between India and China, to which Nepal had raised objections. But China has been silent, arguing the dispute is Nepal's bilateral issue with India. Nepali ministers and ambassadors have also rushed to China's defence at accusations of territorial encroachment in the Himalaya, showing a willingness to align with China's view irrespective of the national interest (and without the official report being made public).

Further, even as Nepali expectations about Chinese infrastructure investments bringing about a transformation, not just in the physical space but also in the accompanying economic arenas, continue to rise, Kathmandu's view must be tempered by reports of China scaling down on BRI investments in the post-pandemic era. In 2020, loans from the China Development Bank and the China EXIM Bank fell to USD 4 billion, from a peak of USD 75 billion in 2016.[10] This is not just because Beijing seems to have grown warier over reports of debt traps, and is now committed to the viability of BRI projects, but also because of rising domestic debt and the post-pandemic economic uncertainties. Till October 2020, new contracts signed by Chinese firms in sixty-one BRI countries fell by 29 per cent as compared to 2019.[11]

At the same time, the sharpening war of words between the US and China had led to sanctions and countersanctions on officials of the two countries in December 2020, signalling that, despite a new president taking over, the US will continue to view China as the primary challenge in the years to come. As calls grow for a reimagination of Nepali foreign policy, Kathmandu needs to prepare for a period of great power shifts. A shift in its policy of non-alignment is immediately visible, with the tilt towards China more noticeable than Nepal would like to admit. But the fissures of such a vision are already apparent, and will become even more prominent in the years to come, especially when it comes to balancing the demands of its two neighbours and pressures from powers like the US.

Through Nepal's modern history, its rulers have been driven by survival instinct, and have deftly balanced the two neighbours in their quest for sovereignty. These tactics were instinctively founded on an anti-Indian approach (because Beijing was too far away in the past). Such adversarial politics may have been useful in extending the rule of whatever dispensation was in power at a given point in time, but inevitably, they will come up short. Nepal's inability to convince Delhi to come to the table for talks on Kalapani is evidence of this. Kathmandu's determination to stand up to what it calls Indian 'bullying' has been partially driven by the weight of a newly resurgent China behind it. And China will only become stronger from hereon, and Delhi's ability and influence within the Kathmandu establishment will continue to weaken if it does not swiftly recognise and address the foundational shortcomings in the bilateral relationship.

✦

Beyond the corridors of power, however, it is in the Himalayan borderlands that China's relationship with Nepal will come to be best understood. As we have seen, communities in the Himalaya are coming under state jurisdiction for the first time in their history, partly due to the Nepali push towards infrastructure, but mostly through Beijing's economic initiatives in Tibet, which Nepali nationals have capitalised upon. In the years to come, as these regions become better connected due to infrastructure and state-building processes from both sides, they will be vital links in the bilateral relationship. State power becomes most visible (or invisible) on the peripheries; territorialisation is as much a function of how citizens feel empowered by the centre as it is about the centre establishing claims on a periphery. Nepali citizens have capitalised on the blurred sovereignties that arises out of living in the border regions. But such overlaps will also weaken Nepal's own state-building project, especially when it comes into conflict with China's rising ambitions in the mountains.

As China faces growing adversarial relationships with other powers, such as the US and India, it will continue to secure its Himalayan frontier as much as possible. Old questions about Tibetan self-determination and Beijing's treatment of minorities will come up again, and the scrutiny over China's soft spots of Tibet, Xinjiang and Hong Kong will intensify. The US has already signalled it will do so by passing the Tibet Policy and Support Act (TPSA) in December 2020. Beyond the TPSA making the selection of the next Dalai Lama contingent upon the current Dalai Lama's wishes, the US will now sanction Chinese officials who appoint their own Dalai Lama. But most significantly for Nepal, under the TPSA, the US will 'urge' Nepal to honour the gentlemen's agreement, and provide USD 6 million every year between 2021 and 2025 as support to Tibetan communities in India and Nepal, as well as for 'the next generation' of leaders from the Tibetan exile community.[12]

With new Chinese intentions to drive investments and state authority in Tibet to quell restiveness—as Xi Jinping said in August 2020, to turn it into an 'impregnable fortress' to prevent 'splittism'[13]—and enhance its presence, Nepal and its citizens will certainly feel the impact as global focus turns on Tibet once again.

Forty years after the CIA switched off funds to Tibetan guerrillas in Mustang, Nepal is once again in the geostrategic spotlight, even if the old imperial paradigm of being a buffer state is no longer of much use. Once again, the US conceives of China as its primary adversary. Washington will continue to hold this view under its new president. Delhi predicates that a negative global sentiment towards China will allow it to be seen as an alternative for investments (and as a natural ally for Western democracies), but sooner or later, India will have to determine whether it has aligned itself with American foreign policy goals of limiting China's rise. For Beijing, India remains the greatest challenge, even if it does not like to say so. It had long sought a relationship based on trade and economy, but it has also been wary of Indian infrastructure gains in the Himalaya. It cannot afford to have a giant neighbour grumbling at its back door as it attempts to gain supremacy over its eastern coast. Unless China can overcome its distrust of Delhi, the two Asian giants will continue to remain, if not at loggerheads, at least competitors for influence within the subcontinent and beyond. The old dictum of being a yam between two boulders will come to haunt Nepal once again as tensions between India and China rise. In Beijing's view, India seeks to be part of the US-led anti-China alliance; the old issues of the LAC are a convenient stick to beat Delhi with. For India, China's belligerence is proof that Beijing does not wish to see India's rise, and by cultivating its neighbours like Nepal, China seeks to entrap India within the subcontinent. As for Nepal, regardless of its claims of non-alignment, there is an undeniable tilt to the north, assisted by a politically expedient wariness of Delhi.

Although the three neighbours do not share many commonalities, all three now boast of a cult of personality around their leaders (Narendra Modi in India, Oli in Nepal and Xi in China), and have witnessed the centralising and authoritarian tendencies that grow out of such a cult. In this, they are not alone; democracies across the world are headed in the same direction. But the greater the turn of major democracies towards authoritarianism, the more it incentivises smaller nations to turn away from democratic values and multilateral commitments, and allows Beijing to exemplify the existing international order as unjustifiable and unequal. 'According to the CCP, Western talk about democracy is simply a pretext for robbing poorer countries of their sovereignty and economic potential.'[14] A turn towards authoritarianism is also antithetical to countering an already authoritarian China's rise. China is not eroding the international liberal order's foundations; rather, countries who are said to represent the liberal order are doing it themselves. China is simply picking up the pieces and making friends as those who once argued for globalisation now pitch for isolationism. This also ties in with Beijing's belief that national sovereignty, rather than international responsibilities, is the 'fundamental principle on which the international order should rest'.[15] For post-conflict and politically unstable countries like Nepal, where a commitment to the existing multilateral system also means answering tough questions on human rights, individual freedoms and war crimes, the isolationism and turn towards autocracy of bigger powers can be a boon.

Countering authoritarianism may be a domestic choice, but if the international mood is centred on the rise of a 'strong' leader, Nepal will not be far behind. The challenge before its policymakers in the years to come, however, will be to balance the demands that the great powers make on Kathmandu. The challenge will also be to steer the country away from the debris of the collision between those powers even as it seeks to drive its citizens towards economic prosperity. But can it overcome the partisanship and kleptocracy that has come to exemplify post-conflict Nepal? And does it have the necessary wherewithal to deftly negotiate the backdrafts of global power flux? Or will it falter along and be reduced to domestic power struggles that act as proxy for other nations even as its own institutions continue to wither?

On the eve of the 1814 war with the East India Company, the Qing amban in Lhasa curtly told the petitioning Gorkhas that it was not China's custom to give money or weapons to other countries. As hard as the Kathmandu durbar tried to convince the Qing court that the British would march on to Tibet after Nepal, the amban refused to entertain such a notion. The Gorkhas had to go to war alone with the British. Ninety years later, at the peak of the Himalayan 'Great Game', Rana Prime Minister Chandra Shamsher ignored Nepal's previous treaty with Tibet and offered support in various forms to Francis Younghusband's

Tibet expedition, intending to bring Kathmandu closer to the Calcutta durbar and preserve Rana rule in the country. By doing so, Chandra was also successful in negating the dying Qing empire's claims of suzerainty over Nepal with the help of the British.

More than a hundred years later, once again Kathmandu finds itself being drawn to a great power during a time of shifting loyalties and ideologies. Histories can help us make sense of the present, but they do not determine the future. Nepal must now decide how it wants to write its own.

Notes

Introduction: A Fine Balance

1. Theodore Riccardi Jr., 'Translator's Introduction to Sylvain Levi's *The History of Nepal*', Part I, *Kailash Journal*, vol. 3, No. 1, 1975. https://www.repository.cam.ac.uk/bitstream/handle/1810/227202/kailash_03_01_01.pdf?sequence=2.
2. Andras Hofer, 'On Re-reading *Le Nepal*: What We Social Scientists Owe to Sylvain Levi', *Kailash Journal*, vol. 7, No. 3 & 4, 1979. http://himalaya.socanth.cam.ac.uk/collections/journals/kailash/pdf/kailash_07_0304_01.pdf.
3. Sylvain Levi (trans. S. Mitra, eds. Harihar Raj Joshi and Indu Joshi), *Nepal: A Notebook of Sojourn*, The Nepal Studies: Past and Present, Kathmandu, 2006, p. 8.
4. Ibid, p. 21.
5. Ibid, p. 33.
6. Ibid, p. 23.
7. Sylvain Levi, 'Nepal: Chinese and Tibetan Documents', *Ancient Nepal*, vol. 27, April 1974. The English translation of *Le Népal* by the Department of Archaeology, Nepal, was published in forty-four instalments in the *Ancient Nepal* journal starting in 1973. http://himalaya.socanth.cam.ac.uk/collections/journals/ancientnepal/pdf/ancient_nepal_27_07.pdf.
8. Vijay Kumar Manandhar, *A Comprehensive History of Nepal-China Relations up to 1955 AD, Vol. 1*, Adroit Publishers, New Delhi, 2004, p. 30.
9. Levi, 'Nepal: Chinese and Tibetan Documents'.
10. Songtsen Gampo is also said to have wed Princess Wencheng of the Tang dynasty.
11. Mary Shepherd Slusser, *Nepal Mandala: A Cultural Study of the Kathmandu Valley*, Princeton University Press: 1982, p. 281.
12. Other regions in the Nepali Himalaya, such as those of Mustang, are also recorded in seventh-century Tibetan Dunhuang chronicles. See David P. Jackson, 'Notes of the history of Se-rib, and nearby places in the upper Kali Gandaki valley', *Kailash Journal*, vol. 6, No. 3, 1978. http://himalaya.socanth.cam.ac.uk/collections/journals/kailash/pdf/kailash_06_03_03.pdf.

(Note: URLs in the notes were last accessed on 1 December 2020.)

13. Levi, 'Nepal: Chinese and Tibetan Documents'.
14. Ibid.
15. Sylvain Levi (trans. S.P. Chatterjee), *The Mission of Wang Hiuen-Tse in India*, Indian Geographical Society: Calcutta, 1967, p. 9.
16. Ibid., p. 10.
17. Xigaze in Chinese.
18. Slusser, *Nepal Mandala*, p. 71.
19. Ibid.
20. Ramesh K. Dhungel, 'Nepal-Tibet Cultural Relations and the Zhva-Dmar-Pa (Shyamarpa) Lamas of Tibet', *CNAS Journal*, vol. 26, No. 2, July 1999.
21. D.S. Kansakar Hilker, *Syamukapu: The Lhasa Newars of Kalimpong and Kathmandu*, Vajra Publications, Kathmandu: 2005, p. 87.
22. Levi, 'Chinese and Tibetan Documents'.
23. Kanchanmoy Majumdar, *Political Relations Between India and Nepal*, 1877–1923, Munshiram Manoharlal, New Delhi, 1973, p. 190–191.
24. Jawaharlal Nehru's speech to Indian Parliament on India's Policies, 6 December 1950, reproduced in *Selected Works of Jawaharlal Nehru* (hereafter *SWJN*), vol. 15, Part II, p. 432.
25. See Mark Liechty, *Far Out: Countercultural seekers and the Tourist Encounter in Nepal*, Martin Chautari, Kathmandu, 2019.
26. Some prominent recent examples include Probal Dasgupta's *Watershed 1967: India's Forgotten Victory over China*, Juggernaut, 2020; Shiv Kunal Verma's *1962: The War That Wasn't*, Aleph, 2016 and Pravin Sawhney and Ghazala Wahab's *Dragon on our Doorstep: Managing China through Military Power*, Aleph, 2017.
27. Also known as 'Dram' in Tibetan and 'Khasa' in Nepali.
28. Known as 'Kyirong' in Tibetan, 'Jilong' in Pinyin and 'Kerung' in Nepali.
29. Jianying Zha, 'China's Heart of Darkness', *China Heritage: The Wairarapa Academy for New Sinology*, 14–22 July 2020. Available here: http://chinaheritage.net/journal/chinas-heart-of-darkness-prince-han-fei-chairman-xi-jinping-part-ii/.
30. Xi Jinping, 'Toward Greater Progress of China-Nepal Friendship across the Himalayas', Full text republished in *Xinhua*, 14 October 2019. http://www.xinhuanet.com/english/2019-10/11/c_138463745.htm.
31. Bhikkhu Amritananda, *Buddhist Activities in Socialist Countries*, New World Press, Peking: 1961, p. 20. Any scholar familiar with Nepal will notice the emphasis on Buddha's birthplace, a sensitive topic vis-à-vis India and Nepal.
32. See Satya Mohan Joshi, *Kalakar Arniko: The Well Known Nepali Architect*, Vijay Gajanand Vaidya, Kathmandu, 1982 edition.
33. 'Chinese Ambassador Hou Yanqi Visit and Extend Birthday Wishes to Satya Mohan Joshi', Chinese Embassy in Nepal, 17 May 2019. http://np.china-embassy.org/eng/News/t1664509.htm.

1. Traders on the Silk Road

1. Radhika Iyengar, 'In 1952, Hindi Film Songs were banned on All India Radio', *Live Mint*, 13 July 2018. https://www.livemint.com/Leisure/XUjIcb1XdO60gXOrHCyH2H/In-1952-Hindi-film-songs-were-banned-on-All-India-Radio.html.
2. Nepal's ethnic diversity has often been downplayed by its rulers who have subscribed to a more uniform Nepali identity, but there are over a hundred ethnic groups and over a hundred languages in the country. The current nationalist history overshadows the histories of ethnic groups such as the Gurungs, Magars and Tamangs. The Nepali identity has come under much debate in recent years, especially when discussing the role of the Shah kings in its unification, the imposition of Nepali as a national language to the detriment of others and the incorporation of Brahminical Hindu caste rules within its constitution, leading to legal sanction for gender inequalities. See works of Richard Burghart, Pratyoush Onta and Seira Tamang for more.
3. Nyalam Pass in Chinese and Tibetan.
4. Jahar Sen, 'India's Trade with Central Asia via Nepal', *Bulletin of Tibetology*, 1971, pp. 21–40. https://www.repository.cam.ac.uk/bitstream/id/637465/bot_08_02_03.pdf/.
5. Mahesh Chandra Regmi, 'The Kathmandu Valley Entrepot Trade', *Regmi Research Series* (hereafter RRS), Year 11, No. 12, 1 December 1979, pp. 189–90. The *Regmi Research Series* was a privately distributed historical journal initiated by Nepali historian Regmi in 1969. It ran for twenty-one volumes, and published translations of Nepali historical documents.
6. For more details on the treaty and Nepal's economic and political ties with pre-1950 Tibet, see Prem R. Uprety, N*epal-Tibet Relations 1850-1930*, Ratna Pustak Bhandar, Kathmandu, 1998; Regmi, *An Economic History of Nepal, 1846–1901*, Nath Publishing House, Varanasi, 1988; Regmi, 'The Kathmandu Valley Entrepot Trade'.
7. Charles Bell, *The People of Tibet*, Motilal Banarasidass Publishers, New Delhi, 1994 edition, p. 118.
8. Filippo de Filippi (ed.), *An Account of Tibet: The Travels of Ippolito Desideri of Pistoia, S.J. (1712-1727)*, George Routledge & Sons, London, 1937, pp. 309–312.
9. Perceval Landon, N*epal, Vol. II*, Constable and Co. Ltd, London: 1928, p. 34.
10. Kamal Ratna Tuladhar, *Caravan to Lhasa: A Merchant of Kathmandu in Traditional Tibet*, Lijala & Tisa, Kathmandu: 2011, p. 37.
11. Chittadhar 'Hridaya', *Letter from a Lhasa Merchant to His Wife* (originally published in Nepal bhasa as *Mimanah Pau* ('The Unburnt Letter'), translated by Kesar Lall, Robin Books, New Delhi: 2002, p. 21. Hridaya wrote, '[On] occasion a porter in a hurry would get into [the basket] while a man pulled him to the other side. Sometimes the [latter] got tired while pulling the rope or the rope slackened, and the basket plunged down to the water.'

12. Landon, *Nepal, Vol. II*, p. 41.
13. Alex McKay, "The British Invasion of Tibet, 1903–04." Inner Asia 14, No. 1 (2012): 5–25. http://www.jstor.org/stable/24572145.
14. Ibid.
15. 'A Petition from Nepalese merchants in Lhasa to the Nepalese government (VS 1949)', eds. and trans. by Bal Gopal Shrestha, Ramhari Timalsina and Rabi Acharya, in *Documents on the History of Religion and Law of Pre-modern Nepal*, Heidelberg Academy of Sciences and Humanities, Heidelberg, Germany, 2018; courtesy of the National Archives, Kathmandu. https://abhilekha.adw.uni-heidelberg.de/nepal/editions/show/26554.
16. Tuladhar, p. 46.
17. One possibility was that the soldiers were buying the watches to sell them in Beijing, since there were no taxes in Tibet at this time. See David G. Atwill, 'Himalayan Asia', in *Islamic Shangri-La: Inter-Asian Relations and Lhasa's Muslim Communities, 1600 to 1960*, University of California Press, Oakland, California, 2018, pp. 65–91. www.jstor.org/stable/j.ctv941r61.8.
18. Ibid.
19. 'A Petition from Nepalese merchants in Lhasa to the Nepalese government (VS 1949)'.
20. Albert Terrien de Lacouperie, 'The Silver Coinage of Tibet', *The Numismatic Chronicle and Journal of the Numismatic Society*, vol. 1, 1881, pp. 340–353. http://www.jstor.org/stable/42679461.
21. Ibid.
22. Uprety, *Nepal-Tibet Relations, 1850-1930*, p. 24.
23. Ibid, p. 26.
24. Charles Bell, *Tibet: Past and Present*, Clarendon Press, Oxford, 1924, p. 238. Under Chandra Shamsher, Nepal disregarded the 1856 treaty's terms by not coming to the aid of Tibet during the 1904 Younghusband expedition by insisting Tibet make peace with the British; instead, he aided Younghusband by supplying material. Chandra had previously, it is rumoured, come to power with the support of Lord Curzon.
25. Ibid, pp. 234–240.
26. 'A petition from the merchant Harṣapati of Tuṃche to the government of Nepal regarding the plundering of his shop in Lhasa (VS 1940)', Timalsina, Shrestha and Acharya, *Documents on the History of Religion and Law of Pre-modern Nepal*.
27. Uprety, *Nepal-Tibet Relations*, pp. 94–96
28. David G. Atwill, 'How Half-Tibetans Made Tibet Whole', in *Islamic Shangri-La: Inter-Asian Relations and Lhasa's Muslim Communities, 1600 to 1960*, University of California Press, Oakland, California, 2018, pp. 34–64. www.jstor.org/stable/j.ctv941r61.7.
29. D.S. Kansakar Hilker, *Syamukapu: The Lhasa Newars of Kathmandu and Kalimpong*, Vajra Books, Kathmandu: 2005, p. 138.
30. Translation mine. Video of Heera Nani Tuladhar, *Women, Wives and Daughters: Newa Traders in Lhasa*, ImPACT! Productions, 2020.

Available here: https://www.facebook.com/ImpactProductions2011/videos/249846216064404/?v=249846216064404.
31. Atwill, 'How Half-Tibetans Made Tibet Whole'.
32. Ibid.
33. Lucette Boulnois, 'Nepalese traders in Lhasa', *European Bulletin of Himalayan Research*, Vol. 15 & 16, 1998–99, pp. 32–33. Available here: http://himalaya.socanth.cam.ac.uk/collections/journals/ebhr/pdf/EBHR_15&16_17.pdf.
34. Atwill, 'How Half-Tibetans Made Tibet Whole'.
35. Tirtha Prasad Mishra, 'Nepalese in Tibet: A case study of Nepalese half-breeds (1856-1956)', *CNAS*, Vol. 30, No. 1 (January 2003), pp. 1–18.
36. Ibid.
37. Todd T. Lewis, 'Newar-Tibetan Trade and the Domestication of "Siṃhalasārthabāhu Avadāna"', *History of Religions*, 33, No. 2, 1993, pp. 135–160. http://www.jstor.org/stable/1062932.
38. Dor Bahadur Bista, 'Nepalis in Tibet', *Contributions to Nepali Studies*, vol. VIII, No. 1, December 1980, pp. 1–20. The 1956 bilateral note on trade in Tibet, too, outlined children of mixed parentage who had reached the age of eighteen 'may, according to their own will, choose the nationality' of the PRC for themselves as well as for their children who were under the age of eighteen. See 'Notes on trade and intercourse between Tibet Region of China and Nepal', reproduced in A.S. Bhasin (ed.), *Documents on Nepal's Relations with India and China, 1949-66*, Academic Books, Delhi, 1970, p. 189–191.
39. Siegfried Lienhard, *Songs of Nepal: An Anthology of Nevar Folksongs and Hymns*, Centre for Asian and Pacific Studies, University of Hawaii Press, Honolulu, Hawaii, 1974, p. 84. The epigraph to this section quotes from the song.
40. Lewis, 'Newar-Tibetan Trade and the Domestication of "Siṃhalasārthabāhu Avadāna"'.
41. Lienhard, *Songs of Nepal*, p. 51–60.
42. In the previously cited documentary, *Women, Wives and Daughters*, a Tuladhar man says Tibetan wives were useful since they 'didn't shy away from hard work'. Domestic quarrels were common in families where there was a second wife; Heera Nani talks about how her mother would do the kora at Swayambhu when she was overcome by sadness.
43. Indeed, it was hurtful for the Newar wife, who feared her husband's travel to Lhasa. The documentary *Women, Wives and Daughters* recollects how Heera Nani hid her husband's passport when she learnt he was leaving for Lhasa. Her father had a Tibetan wife, and her mother had suffered a lot on this account. Heera Nani recalls how the women often sold their jewellery to fund their children's education when the husbands refused to return. Her husband Anand Siddhi says other Newars were scared to give their daughters in marriage to Lhasa traders.
44. Atwill, 'How Half-Tibetans Made Tibet Whole'.

45. Lewis, 'Newar-Tibetan Trade and the Domestication of "Siṃhalasārthabāhu Avadāna"'.
46. David G. Atwill, 'The Tibetan Muslim Incident of 1960.' In *Islamic Shangri-La: Inter-Asian Relations and Lhasa's Muslim Communities, 1600 to 1960*, pp. 92–122. Oakland, University of California Press, California, 2018. http://www.jstor.org/stable/j.ctv941r61.9.
47. Bell, *Tibet: Past and Present*, p. 233.
48. Mishra, 'Nepalese in Tibet'.
49. Todd T. Lewis, 'Buddhist merchants in Kathmandu: The Asan Twah Market and Uray social organization' in David N. Gellner & Declan Quigley (eds.), *Contested Hierarchies: A Collaborative Ethnography of Caste Among the Newars of the Kathmandu Valley, Nepal*, Oxford University Press, India, 2003, pp. 38–79. Fiction often addresses these stories in a more comprehensive way. See Chittadhar Hridaya's *Mimanah Pau* (The Unburnt Letter) and Dharma Ratna Yami's *Reply from Lhasa*, the latter an ode to the poet's romance with a Tibetan girl while he was in Lhasa.
50. Melvyn Goldstein, 'In the Eye of the Storm: 1957–1959', *A History of Modern Tibet, Vol. 4*, University of California Press, Oakland, California, 2019, p. 446.
51. Goldstein, *A History of Modern Tibet, Vol. 4*, p. 443.
52. Ibid., p. 448.
53. Ibid., p. 452. Goldstein notes that Beijing sent back a reply at 11 a.m. saying, 'Do not take action.' 'When Mao Zedong found out that Tan Guansan had disrupted his plan, being angry, [Mao] said, Tan Guansan is becoming more and more stupid (Ch. Hutu). However, since the battle has already begun, it would leave the PLA in a disadvantaged situation if [the PLA] stopped halfway; [so] they had to win. So Mao sent a telegram back, replying that he agreed that [PLA] could continue the battle, but instructed Tan Guansan that [the PLA] must win. It meant that, if Tan Guansan lost the battle, he would be punished by Mao Zedong.'
54. Sulmaan Wasif Khan, *Muslim, Trader, Nomad, Spy: China's Cold War and the People of the Tibetan Borderlands*, University of North Carolina Press, Chapel Hill, North Carolina, 2015.
55. Pragya Ratna Tuladhar's letter to Karuna Ratna Tuladhar, dated 28 August 1959, private collection of Kamal Ratna Tuladhar.
56. I am grateful to Kamal Ratna Tuladhar for access to his private collection of letters and telegrams from Ghorasyar. Kamal Ratna also wrote *Caravan to Lhasa*, a highly popular account of the trade between Nepal and Tibet. Ghorasyar was owned by his father, Karuna Ratna Tuladhar. All letters and telegrams hereafter quoted are from his private collection.
57. Wasif Khan, *Muslim, Trader, Nomad, Spy*.
58. David G. Atwill, 'Himalayan Asia', in *Islamic Shangri-La: Inter-Asian Relations and Lhasa's Muslim Communities, 1600 to 1960*, University of California Press, Oakland, California, 2018, pp. 65–91. www.jstor.org/stable/j.ctv941r61.8.

59. Atwill, 'The Tibetan Muslim Incident of 1960'.
60. Ibid.
61. Figures for Nepali-owned businesses in Lhasa quoted from Lucette Boulnois, 'Nepalese traders in Lhasa', *European Bulletin of Himalayan Research*, vol. 15 & 16, 1998–99, pp. 32–33. Boulnois in turn attributes the figures to a 1961 Chinese survey whose results were published in a 1993 paper by Long Xijiang, 'Investigating the History of Nepalese Traders in Lhasa', published in *Zhongguo Zhang Xue* (Chinese Journal of Tibetology), ed. by Chinese Center of Tibetology, No. 3, pp. 41–51.
62. Atwill, 'The Tibetan Muslim Incident of 1960'.
63. Ibid.
64. Wasif Khan, *Muslim, Trader, Nomad, Spy*.
65. Atwill, 'The Tibetan Muslim Incident of 1960'.

2. Neither Nepal nor China

1. See https://www.asianart.com/articles/Waltse/index.html. I've spelt the town as 'Burang' unless it has been spelt otherwise in a reference. For more on the historical switch in the monastery's allegiances, see http://www.kailashzone.org/pages/limi/rinchen.html.
2. Emily T. Yeh, 'The land belonged to Nepal but the people belonged to Tibet: Overlapping sovereignties and mobility in the Limi Valley Borderland', *Geopolitics*, June 2019, pp. 1–27, DOI: 10.1080/14650045.2019.1628018. The long history of dual taxation indicates the valley has come under both Nepal and Tibet at different times. There is also a record of the Waltse monastery being built in the reign of a fourteenth-century local Khas-Nepali ruler, while oral histories also suggest that a noted lama from Tibet had been given the Limi valley as a land grant by another local ruler.
3. See 'History of Limi People', http://www.kailashzone.org/pages/limi/history.php.
4. CIA, Central Intelligence Bulletin, 15 December 1959. https://www.cia.gov/library/readingroom/docs/CENTRAL%20INTELLIGENCE%20BULL%5B15787730%5D.pdf.
5. Melvyn C. Goldstein, 'A report on Limi Panchayat, Humla District, Karnali Zone', *Contributions to Nepalese Studies*, vol. 2, No. 2, 1975.
6. Christoph von Fürer-Haimendorf, *Himalayan Traders*, St. Martin's Press, New York, 1975, pp. 251–252.
7. Yeh, 'The land belonged to Nepal but the people belonged to Tibet'.
8. Fürer-Haimendorf, *Himalayan Traders*, p. 286.
9. Interview with Tsewang Lama, member of Parliament from Humla. Also see Goldstein, Furer-Haimendorf and Yeh.
10. Goldstein, 'A report on Limi Panchayat'.
11. In 2012, Nepal and China signed a cross-border grazing agreement that allowed for grazing within 30 km of the border. When I visited Limi,

however, no locals took their animals across the border to graze. A copy of the agreement in Chinese can be found here: http://np.china-embassy.org/chn/zngxs/zywj/t1059643.htm. Translated via Google Translate Firefox extension.
12. For more on how iodised salt contributed to the collapse of the salt caravans in Humla, see Martin Saxer, 'Between China and Nepal: Trans-Himalayan Trade and the Second Life of Development in Upper Humla', *Cross-Currents: East Asian History and Culture Review*, E-Journal No. 8, September 2013. http://cross-currents.berkeley.edu/e-journal/issue-8.
13. As of writing, a Humla MP from the Nepali Congress claimed China had indeed encroached upon Nepali territory; however, both Kathmandu and Beijing have repeatedly denied this.
14. In the winter of 2020, however, Nepali APF officials stayed on at the Hilsa border outpost for the first time. The APF border outpost had been set up earlier in the summer.
15. Yeh, 'The land belonged to Nepal but the people belonged to Tibet'.
16. Ibid.
17. See my interview with him here: https://www.recordnepal.com/perspective/its-difficult-to-govern-a-place-if-you-dont-understand-its-ecology/.
18. Martin Saxer, 'New Roads Old Trades' in *The Art of Neighbouring: Making Relations Across China's Borders*, eds. by Martin Saxer and Juan Zhang, Amsterdam University Press, Amsterdam, 2014, p. 88–91.
19. Ibid. p. 89.
20. Interview with Mangal Lama, 4 April 2019.
21. Although this could also be particular to the time we visited, as outsiders had gathered in the valley for the trade fair. See Yeh, 'The land belonged to Nepal but the people belonged to Tibet', who experienced something similar.
22. Sara B. Shneiderman, 'Himalayan border citizens: Sovereignty and mobility in the Nepal–Tibetan Autonomous Region (TAR) of China border zone', *Political Geography*, vol. 35, 2013.
23. Narjan Tamang, 'Limi ka Basindalai Sahajai Mulyama Chamal (Limi residents get rice at subsidised rates)', *Naya Patrika*, 17 October 2020. Available here: https://nayapatrikadaily.com/news-details/53206/2020-10-17.
24. Yeh, 'The land belonged to Nepal but the people belonged to Tibet'.
25. Fürer-Haimendorf, *Himalayan Traders*, p. 294.
26. Tina Harris, *Geographical Diversions: Tibetan Trade, Global Transactions*, University of Georgia Press, Athens, Georgia, 2013, p. 88.
27. Ibid, p. 129–132.
28. See Yeh, 'The land belonged to Nepal but the people belonged to Tibet'.
29. Shneiderman, 'Himalayan border citizens'.
30. Hongyi Harry Lai, 'China's Western Development Program: Its Rationale, Implementation, and Prospects', *Modern China*, vol. 28, 2002.
31. Andrew Fischer, 'The great transformations of Tibet and Xinjiang: A comparative analysis of rapid labour transitions in times of rapid growth in

two contested minority regions of China', paper presented at the conference *Challenging the Harmonious Society: Tibetans and Uyghurs in Socialist China*, Nordic Institute of Asian Studies, Copenhagen, 20–21 May 2011. For more on *xibu da kaifa*, also see H. Holbig, 'The emergence of the campaign to open up the West: Ideological formation, central decision-making, and the role of the provinces', *The China Quarterly*, 2004, No. 178, pp. 335–357.
32. Emily T. Yeh, *Taming Tibet: Landscape Transformation and the Gift of Chinese Development*, Cornell University Press, Ithaca and London, 2013, p. 344.
33. Jay Bahadur Rokaya, 'Humla Locals Happy to Work in Taklakot', *Kathmandu Post*, 4 August 2018. https://kathmandupost.com/money/2018/08/04/humla-locals-happy-to-work-in-taklakot.
34. Matrika Dahal, 'Taklakot bata tatkal uddhar asambhav' (Rescue from Taklakot impossible right now), *Kantipur*, 14 March 2020. https://ekantipur.com/news/2020/03/14/15841490335529330.html.
35. Both Nepal and China are today exploring a road that connects Burang to Nepalgunj on the Indian border. See https://english.onlinekhabar.com/chinese-team-in-humla-for-feasibility-study-of-road-connecting-india-and-china.html.
36. Yeh, 'The land belonged to Nepal but the people belonged to Tibet'.
37. Ibid. Also, in September 2019, US Congressmen wrote to Nepali authorities after six Tibetans were sent back to China from Humla. See https://www.phayul.com/2019/11/21/41991/.
38. Emma Austin, *The Mountain People of Northern Humla*, Recordnepal.com, 24 February 2018. https://www.recordnepal.com/wire/the-mountain-people-of-northern-humla/.
39. Ibid.
40. Goldstein, 'A report on Limi Panchayat'.
41. Saxer, New Roads Old Trades, p. 78.
42. Saxer, 'Between China and Nepal'.
43. Basanta Pratap Singh, 'Smuggling of medicinal herbs, wildlife parts rampant via Urai border point, Bajhang', *The Kathmandu Post*, 11 November 2020. https://kathmandupost.com/sudurpaschim-province/2020/11/11/smuggling-of-medicinal-herbs-wildlife-parts-rampant-via-urai-border-point-in-bajhang.

3. A Fence in the Himalaya

1. Name changed.
2. Michel Peissel, *Mustang: A Lost Tibetan Kingdom*, Futura, London, 1979, p. 89.
3. More than 2,000 yaks, dzos and sheep died in Mustang alone in the winter of 2018, a police officer who prepared the final report told me. Villagers were still reporting more deaths till April 2019, when I visited.
4. Galen Murton, 'Border Corridors: Mobility, Containment, and Infrastructures

Notes

of Development between Nepal and China', PhD Dissertation, Department of Geography, University of Colorado, Boulder, 2017, p. 187. Thesis available here: https://www.academia.edu/34173508/BORDER_CORRIDORS_Mobility_Containment_and_Infrastructures_of_Development_between_Nepal_and_China.
5. Ibid., p. 189.
6. A December 2019 picture showed the building as nearly ready. See Thomas Heaton, 'The Free Wheeling Woman Who Defied Society's Motorbike-Based Stigma', *Kathmandu Post*, 5 December 2019. https://kathmandupost.com/travel/2019/12/05/the-free-wheeling-woman-who-defied-society-s-motorbike-based-stigma.
7. Emily T. Yeh, *Taming Tibet: Landscape Transformation and the Gift of Chinese Development*, Cornell University Press, Ithaca, 2013, p. 63. Yeh writes: 'The state farms encapsulated the dominant environmental imaginary of the Maoist period, in which land without agriculture was seen as empty, uninhabited, and desperately in need of civilization.' Barren land in Tibet was converted to fields by PLA soldiers, and their efforts 'celebrated as patriotic and heroic'.
8. The Kali Gandaki corridor is a 435-km road under construction that will connect the Kora La border to Bhairahawa in the south of Nepal, providing a transit route for products between China and India. The shortest road route between the two countries, it currently needs to be expanded and black-topped, and requires several bridges on the Kali Gandaki river as of writing. However, commercial and passenger traffic up to Jomsom is regular. For more, see: https://kathmandupost.ekantipur.com/news/2017-07-09/kaligandaki-corridor-becomes-operational.html and http://ssrn.aviyaan.com/assets/docs/Schematic%20Diagram%20of%20SSRN%20Model%202017-18.pdf.
9. Isabel Hilton, 'Flight of the Lama', *New York Times*, 12 March 2000. https://www.nytimes.com/2000/03/12/magazine/flight-of-the-lama.html.
10. The film can be viewed at https://www.youtube.com/watch?v=onRbwRZP3dA&t=655s. It was produced by Yoichi Shimatsu, former editor of *Japan Times*.
11. 'Escape From Tibet,' https://kagyuoffice.org/in-india/the-karmapas-great-escape-december-28-1999-january-5-2000/.
12. Isabel Hilton, 'Flight of the Lama.'
13. Barbara Cossette, 'Buddhist's Escape from Tibet, by Car, Horse and Plane', *New York Times*, 31 January 2000. https://www.nytimes.com/2000/01/31/world/buddhist-s-escape-from-tibet-by-car-horse-and-plane.html.
14. 'Tibet's Stateless Nationals: Tibetan Refugees in Nepal', Tibet Justice Center, Berkeley, California: 2002, p. 74. http://www.tibetjustice.org/reports/nepal.pdf.
15. B. Raman, 'The Karmapa Controversy,' *Outlook India*, 1 February 2011. https://www.outlookindia.com/website/story/the-karmapa-controversy/270296.

16. Suhasini Haidar, 'Karmapa Kept India in the Dark', *The Hindu*, 27 December 2018. https://www.thehindu.com/news/national/karmapa-kept-india-in-the-dark/article25843227.ece
17. Murton, *Border Corridors*, p. 144.
18. See Yeh, *Taming Tibet*, p. 5. 'Rather than a preconstituted, naturalized geographical unit or container of social, cultural and political-economic relations, state territory is the product of an ongoing process of territorialization through which the "spatial relations" that make a given state-society ensemble hegemonic are worked out. Territory is the fundamental form of space of the modern nation-state . . . Territorialization is a deeply material and embodied process that involves the transformation of both subjectivities and landscapes.'
19. Galen Murton, 'A Himalayan Border Trilogy: The Political Economies of Transport Infrastructure and Disaster Relief between China and Nepal', *Cross-Currents: East Asian History and Culture Review*, March 2016. https://cross-currents.berkeley.edu/e-journal/issue-18.
20. 'Traders: Access to China's ports not a magic bullet', *The Kathmandu Post*. https://kathmandupost.com/money/2018/09/09/traders-access-to-chinas-ports-not-a-magic-bullet. The six crossing points are: Pulan–Hilsa, Jilong–Rasuwa, Zhangmu–Kodari, Riwu–Olangchung, Lizi–Nyichung and Chentang–Kimathanka.
21. Sanjeev Giri, 'Korala Port Process Gathers Momentum', *The Kathmandu Post*. http://kathmandupost.ekantipur.com/printedition/news/2017-07-23/korala-port-process-gathers-momentum.html. Also see http://kathmandupost.ekantipur.com/printedition/news/2018-03-05/bids-called-for-feasibility-study-for-korala-dry-port.html. The foundation stone for the APF border outpost was laid in November 2020.
22. When Murton visited the border and took photographs, 'a Chinese Armed Police Force SUV quickly appeared upon the horizon' (Murton, *Border Corridors*, p. 117). Chinese forces may particularly be looking out for foreigners along this border due to its sensitivity.
23. Murton, *Border Corridors*, p. 147.
24. Ibid. p. 157
25. Peissel, *Mustang*, p. 128–129. The Chushi Gangdruk (Four Rivers, Six Ranges) movement is colloquially known as the Khampa movement, since a majority of its fighters were from the Kham region in eastern Tibet.
26. Ibid, p. 87.
27. Carole McGranahan, *Arrested Histories: Tibet, the CIA, and Memories of a Forgotten War*, Duke University Press, Durham and London, 2010, p. 138.
28. Kenneth Conboy and James Morrison, *The CIA's Secret War in Tibet*, University Press of Kansas, Lawrence, Kansas, 2002, p. 151.
29. Ibid., p. 158.
30. Peissel, p. 231. A declassified CIA weekly summary from January 1959 states that the US was planning to build nine airfields for Nepal, including one in

Mustang. 'This last may become a target for Chinese Communist propaganda regarding "American air bases" in the Himalayan Area.' See https://www.cia.gov/library/readingroom/docs/CIA-RDP79-00927A002300030001-4.pdf.
31. Conboy and Morrison, p. 147.
32. Carole McGranahan, *Arrested Histories*, p. 181. In 1950, Tribhuvan was the king; his son Mahendra ruled for most of the period during which the resistance operated out of Mustang.
33. Tsering Shakya, *The Dragon in the Land of Snows: A History of Modern Tibet Since 1947*, Pimlico, London, 1999, p. 284. McGranahan also makes note of this visit in an interview with Yeshi, who claims that even Mahendra's son, Birendra, visited them.
34. CIA, 'Central Intelligence Bulletin', 15 December 1959. https://www.cia.gov/library/readingroom/docs/CIA-RDP79T00975A004800380001-7.pdf.
35. Sam Cowan, 'The Curious Case of the Mustang Incident', *Record Nepal*, 17 January 2016. https://www.recordnepal.com/wire/curious-case-mustang-incident/.
36. Until August 1970, India maintained anywhere between seventeen and twenty checkposts on the northern border of Nepal. The Intelligence Bureau, under B.N. Mullick, recommended such checkposts along India's northern frontier and in the neighbouring countries of Nepal, Bhutan and Sikkim. As to why Nepal agreed upon them, a retired army officer was quoted as saying, 'the Indians just did it and there was nothing Nepal could do about it'. For more on this, see Sam Cowan, 'The Indian Checkposts, Lipu Lekh and Kalapani', *Record Nepal*, 14 December 2015. https://www.recordnepal.com/wire/indian-checkposts-lipu-lekh-and-kalapani/. The checkpost at Kalapani, at the heart of the 2020 India–Nepal dispute, was one of these; as to why it was not disbanded when the other checkposts were, the answer is not in the public domain. There is also new evidence that the Kalapani checkpost was uniquely set up before the other Indian Army outposts. See Cowan, 'The Gorkha War and its Aftermath', *The Record*, 14 November 2020. https://www.recordnepal.com/category-explainers/the-gorkha-war-and-its-aftermatth/.
37. Cowan, 'The Curious Case of the Mustang Incident'.
38. Quoted in Cowan, 'The Curious Case of the Mustang Incident'.
39. Sulmaan Wasif Khan, *Muslim, Trader, Nomad, Spy*.
40. CIA, 'The Sino-Indian Border Dispute', p. vi, (first published 19 August 1963, approved for release in May 2007). https://www.cia.gov/library/readingroom/document/5077054e993247d4d82b6a65.
41. Sulmaan Wasif Khan, *Muslim, Trader, Nomad, Spy*.
42. Ibid.
43. CIA, 'The Sino-Indian Border Dispute', p. 59.
44. 'B.P. Koirala's reply to Chou En-Lai, 24 July 1960', reproduced in R.K. Jain (ed.), *China-South Asian Relations: 1947-1980*: vol. 2, Radiant Publishers, New Delhi, 1981, p. 336.

45. Leo E. Rose, *Nepal: Strategy for Survival*, University of California Press, 1971, p. 229.
46. Sulmaan Wasif Khan, *Muslim, Trader, Nomad, Spy*.
47. Conboy and Morrison, *The CIA's Secret War in Tibet*, p. 146.
48. Cowan, 'The Curious Case of the Mustang Incident'.
49. Report by Yuri Andropov, 'On the Situation in Tibet', 31 March 1959, History and Public Policy Program Digital Archive, TsKhSD, f. 5, op. 49, d. 238, ll. 42–48 (R. 8929); trans. from Russian by David Wolff. Published in CWIHP Working Paper No. 30. https://digitalarchive.wilsoncenter.org/document/118751.
50. Sam Cowan, addendum to 'The Mustang Incident', *Essays on Nepal: Past and Present*, Himal Books, Kathmandu, 2018, p. 294–298. In the addendum, Cowan also dismisses claims that Chinese forces collaborated with Nepali forces in 1964 to eliminate the Khampas. Beyond the oral recollection of one Chinese diplomat, there is no evidence that any Chinese forces entered Nepal on such a mission, nor were the Khampas eliminated in 1964.
51. CIA, 'The Sino-Indian Border Dispute', p. 59.
52. Sulmaan Wasif Khan, *Muslim, Trader, Nomad, Spy*.
53. Ibid.
54. Manjushree Thapa, *Mustang Bhot in Fragments*, Himal Books, Kathmandu, 2008 (3rd edition), p. 89.
55. 'Press Release on Solar Power Handover Ceremony held in Mustang', Ministry of Foreign Affairs, 11 September 2015. https://mofa.gov.np/press-release-on-solar-power-handover-ceremony-held-in-mustang/. The Tibetan Autonomous Region government provided RMB 10 million each year as grant assistance to fifteen districts bordering China under an agreement that stipulated RMB 50 million for a period of five years. The agreement has now been renewed, with the newly set up China International Development Cooperation Agency now responsible for projects. See here: http://kathmandupost.ekantipur.com/news/2019-03-30/chinese-development-agency-to-aid-15-northern-nepali-districts.html.
56. Ramchandra Pokhrel, 'The road to Lo Manthang', *Himal Khabarpatrika*, 14–28 January 2002, Issue 80. http://archive.nepalitimes.com/news.php?id=6251. Another report from the time states a grant under the 'Aafno Gaun Aafai Banau' ('Build your village yourselves') initiative of the then The Communist Party of Nepal (Unified Marxist–Leninist) government also funded the road. See: http://archive.nepalitimes.com/news.php?id=3802. There have also been unconfirmed reports that the Chinese had funded the road.
57. Pokhrel, 'The road to Lo Manthang'.
58. Ramesh Dhungel, *The Kingdom of Lo (Mustang): A Historical Study*, Tashi Gaphel Foundation, Kathmandu, 2002.
59. Peissel notes that a nobleman told him the yearly tribute was Rs 896 and two horses until 1962, whereupon Mustang no longer gave two horses but an additional Rs 80. Peissel, *Mustang*, p. 230.

60. Dhungel, p. 140.
61. Dilip Poudel, 'Drastic increase in Chinese aid surprises Mustang locals', *Republica*, 19 November 2015. http://archive.myrepublica.com/2015-16/society/story/31284/drastic-increase-in-chinese-aid-surprises-mustang-locals.html. In May 2020, local Mustang authorities refused to accept Chinese aid saying the health and relief material had been sent without permission, and feared the material could be infected by coronavirus. See https://english.khabarhub.com/2020/20/97322/.
62. Murton, *Border Corridors*, p. 246.
63. 'NA Concerned Over China's Suspicious Activity in Mustang', *Khabarhub*, 6 January 2020. https://english.khabarhub.com/2020/06/66748/.
64. As it turned out, the livestock that had died in the 2018 winter had not been insured. 'Farmers are eligible for 75% subsidy on premiums on livestock insurance; Mustang farmers get additional 12.5% subsidy from ACAP (Annapurna Conservation Area Project).' See https://myrepublica.nagariknetwork.com/news/not-a-single-farm-animal-that-died-during-mustang-snowfall-was-insured/.

4. War and Peace

1. Colonel William Kirkpatrick, *An Account of the Kingdom of Nepaul: Being the substance of observations made during a mission to that country in the year 1793*, Manjusri Publishing House, New Delhi, 1969 (first edition 1811), p. 348. https://archive.org/details/in.ernet.dli.2015.49850/page/n3.
2. Ibid, p. 350.
3. Xiaoyuan Liu, *To the End of Revolution: The Chinese Communist Party and Tibet, 1949–1959*, Columbia University Press, New York, 2020, p. 65.
4. Matthew W. Mosca, *From Frontier Policy to Foreign Policy: The Question of India and the Transformation of Geopolitics in Qing China*, p. 136, Stanford University Press, Palo Alto, California, 2013.
5. Sabine Dabringhaus, 'The Ambans of Tibet—Imperial Rule at the Inner Asian Periphery', in *The Dynastic Centre and the Provinces: Agents and Interactions*, Dabringhaus Sabine and Duindam Jeroen (eds.), Brill, Leiden, Boston, 2014, pp. 114–126. http://www.jstor.org/stable/10.1163/j.ctt1w8h2x3.12.
6. The 'Golden Urn' has been controversial since its inception. There are debates on its neutrality, as well as the number of times it was used for choosing high-ranked reincarnations. Most recently, the Communist Party of China has said it will choose the next reincarnation of the Dalai Lama using the urn, a claim rejected by Tibetans in exile.
7. Elliot Sperling, 'Awe and Submission: A Tibetan Aristocrat at the Court of Qianlong', *The International History Review*, 20:2, 1998, pp. 325–335. https://doi.org/10.1080/07075332.1998.9640826.
8. When the Qing made this claim in the last days of their empire, Nepal's Rana prime minister, Chandra Shamsher, vehemently refused it, and wrote to

the British, 'This claim so lightly made by China is not only an unwarranted fiction, but is also a damaging reflection on our national honour and independence.' The British in turn told the Chinese clearly, 'His Majesty's Government cannot allow any administrative changes in Tibet to affect or prejudice the integrity of Nepal . . . and they are prepared, if necessary, to protect the interests and rights of these three states [of Nepal, Sikkim and Bhutan].' See Vijay Kumar Manandhar, *A Comprehensive History of Nepal-China Relations*, Vol. II, Adroit Publishers, New Delhi, 2004, p. 123–129.

9. Samuel Turner, *An Account of an Embassy to the Court of the Teshoo Lama in Tibet, Containing a Narrative of a Journey Through Bootan and Part of Tibet*, Bulmer, London, 1800, p. 372. https://books.google.co.in/books?id=tJjajE8_6VUC&dq=teshoo+lama&source=gbs_navlinks_s.

10. 'An Official Nepali Account of the Nepal-China war: King Ran Bahadur Shah's letter to officials sent for the conquest of Kumaun Garhwal', Dhana Bajra Bajracharya and Gnyan Mani Nepal (trans. M.C. Regmi), *RRS*, Vol. 2., January 1970, pp. 177–188. The original letter was published in *Aitihasik Patra Sangraha* ('A Collection of Historical Letters'), Nepal Samskritic Parishad, Kathmandu, 1957. http://digitalhimalaya.com/collections/journals/regmi/. (Hereafter, Regmi Research Series citations will be referred to as RRS.)

11. Ibid. Some historians suggest the Shamarpa had misappropriated funds.

12. Fr. Ludwig Stiller, *The Rise of the House of Gorkha: A Study in the Unification of Nepal 1768-1816*, Patan Jesuit Society, Kathmandu, 1975, p. 163.

13. Ibid., p. 164. The deputy to the chief amban was also addressed as 'amban'. See Dabringhaus, 'The Ambans of Tibet'.

14. W.W. Rockhill, 'The Dalai Lamas of Lhasa and Their Relations with the Manchu Emperors of China: 1644-1908', *T'oung Pao*, Second Series, 11, No. 1, 1910, pp. 1–104. www.jstor.org/stable/4526129.

15. Stiller, *The Rise of the House of Gorkha*, p. 170.

16. Schuyler V. Cammann, *Trade through the Himalayas: The Early British Attempts to Open Tibet*, Princeton University Press, Princeton, New Jersey, 1951, p. 123–124.

17. 'An official account of the Nepal-China war', *RRS*, Vol. II, p. 180.

18. Stiller, *Rise of the House of Gorkha*, p. 170.

19. 'An official account of the Nepal-China war', *RRS*, Vol. II, p. 179.

20. 'An official account of the Nepal-China war', *RRS*, Vol. II, p. 180.

21. Stiller, *The Rise of the House of Gorkha*, pp. 173–174.

22. 'An official account of the Nepal-China war', *RRS*, Vol. II, p. 181.

23. Ibid. p. 181.

24. A chronicle by Wei Yuan, reproduced in Perceval Landon's *Nepal*, Vol. II, p. 275.

25. Tibet had incited Sikkim to attack in the east, while some hill principalities in the west had revolted against the Gorkhalis at this time. Gorkha forces were also tied up with the military campaigns in Kumaon, which couldn't

be pulled back. Mosca writes that Fuk'anggan had written to Jumla, Bhutan and the British to join his campaign against the Gorkhalis.
26. 'An official account of the Nepal-China war', *RRS*, Vol. II, p. 181.
27. Manandhar, *A Comprehensive History of Nepal-China Relations*. However, the Chinese did not come to Nepal's aid during its war with the British, with the ambans refusing to forward Nepal's missive to Beijing. 'It is not China's custom to give money or weapons to other countries. Therefore we ambans cannot send your request to the emperor': Stiller, *The Silent Cry: The People of Nepal, 1816-1839*, Sahayogi Prakashan, Kathmandu, 1976, p. 96.
28. 'An official account of the Nepal-China war', *RRS*, Vol. II, p. 187.
29. Galen Murton, Austin Lord and Robert Beazley, 'A handshake across the Himalayas: Chinese investment, hydropower development, and state formation in Nepal', *Eurasian Geography and Economics*, 2016, 57:3, pp. 403–432. http://dx.doi.org/10.1080/15387216.2016.1236349.
30. Kyirong in Tibetan, Kerung in Nepali.
31. Murton, Lord and Beazley, 'A handshake across the Himalayas'.
32. L. Boulnois, 'Chinese Maps and Prints on the Tibet-Gorkha War of 1788-92', *Kailash Journal*, vol. 15, 1989.
33. The Gyirong Zangbo (zangbo means 'river', from the Tibetan word 'tsangpo') is colloquially known as Bhote Koshi in Rasuwa and Kyirong Tsangpo in Tibet; the same river is known as Trishuli downstream. The Trishuli's headwaters in Nepal are believed to be the holy lake of Gosainkunda.
34. The bridge came into operation in May 2019. http://kathmandupost.ekantipur.com/news/2019-06-07/friendship-bridge-in-rasuwagadhi-comes-into-operation.html. Its construction began in September 2018.
35. Name changed.
36. Sam Cowan, 'All Change at Rasuwa Garhi,' *Himalaya: the Journal of the Association for Nepal and Himalayan Studies*, vol. 33, No. 1, Article 14, 2013. http://digitalcommons.macalester.edu/himalaya/vol33/iss1/14.
37. A similar scenario would take place in late 2019, when India banned the export of onions, and China exported onions to Nepal. Unfortunately, not many took to the change in taste. See https://myrepublica.nagariknetwork.com/news/after-india-ban-chinese-onions-take-local-market/.
38. Dram in Tibetan, Khasa in Nepali.
39. In June 2019, Rasuwa container operators blocked trucks from crossing over into China. They demanded truck crossings on a first come, first served basis and a regulation of the queues. See https://www.kantipurdaily.com/news/2019/06/11/156022847956539141.html.
40. Ramesh Kumar, 'New China-Nepal rail corridor', *Nepali Times*, 5 June 2020. https://www.nepalitimes.com/latest/new-china-nepal-rail-corridor/.
41. Hou Yanqi, 'Friendship across Mount Zhumulangma: A bond for shared prosperity', *Republica*, 1 November 2020. https://myrepublica.nagariknetwork.com/amp/friendship-across-mount-zhumulangma-a-bond-for-shared-prosperity.

42. 'Chin sanga aapurti khalbaliyo, vyapar siddhant viparit aayat ma quota' ('Supply of goods from China disrupted, Import quotas applied irrespective of trade principles'), *Online Khabar*, 11 October 2020. https://www.onlinekhabar.com/2020/10/902577. A trader reportedly committed suicide because of mounting debts and his goods being stuck at Gyirong for over eight months. See https://shilapatra.com/detail/44416.
43. Transport costs per container from Rasuwagadhi to Kathmandu were reported to be NPR 85,000 during the second half of 2020. However, transport costs from Birgunj to Kathmandu per container were anywhere between NPR 45,000–50,000. See Rishiram Paudyal, 'Chin ko Asahayog le Uttari Naaka ajhai asahajh' ('Northern borders still erratic after China's lack of support'), *Kantipur*, 23 Mangsir 2077, 8 December 2020. https://ekantipur.com/news/2020/12/08/16073939600382821.html.
44. Name changed.
45. Murton notes that Rasuwa male residents sometimes 'rent' out their border cards to licensed cargo truck drivers and can earn up to NPR 50,000 per month doing so. Murton, 'Border Corridors', p. 155.
46. Abrahm Lustgarten, *China's Great Train: Beijing's Drive West and the Campaign to Remake Tibet*, Henry Holt and Company, New York, 2008, p. 49.
47. See Emily Yeh, *Taming of Tibet*. Also see 'The Qinghai-Tibet Railway: China's new instrument for assimilation', Jamestown Foundation, 9 May 2007. https://jamestown.org/program/the-qinghai-tibet-railway-chinas-new-instrument-for-assimilation-2/.
48. David P. Nickles (ed.), 'Foreign Relations of the United States: 1969-1976', vol. XVIII: China 1973-1976, Department of State, Washington, D.C., 2007, p. 888. https://2001-2009.state.gov/documents/organization/100316.pdf.
49. 'Tibet: Tourism, The Train and Migrant Labour,' WikiLeaks, 7 March 2008. https://wikileaks.org/plusd/cables/08CHENGDU43_a.html.
50. 'Tibet Vice Governor: Slams Dalai Lama, Denies Political Oppression, Outlines Chinese Government Efforts To Improve Living Standards,', WikiLeaks, 9 November 2009. https://wikileaks.org/plusd/cables/09CHENGDU251_a.html.
51. Anil Giri, 'China Assures Rail Link with Nepal', *Kathmandu Post*, 28 December 2014. https://kathmandupost.com/miscellaneous/2014/12/28/china-assures-rail-link-with-nepal.
52. 'Joint Press Statement Between the People's Republic of China and Nepal,', Ministry of Foreign Affairs, 23 March 2016. https://mofa.gov.np/joint-press-statement/.
53. Anil Giri, 'Foreign Minister Heads to China on Monday', *Kathmandu Post*, 14 April 2018. http://kathmandupost.ekantipur.com/printedition/news/2018-04-14/foreign-minister-heads-for-china-on-monday.html. Also see: 'Nepal-China railway govt's priority: Gyawali', *Himalayan Times*, 21 April 2018. https://thehimalayantimes.com/nepal/nepal-china-railway-govts-priority-minister-for-foreign-affairs-pradeep-kumar-gyawali/.

240   Notes

54. 'Nepal Team in China to Discuss Rail From Kyirong to Kathmandu', *The Himalayan Times*, 1 May 2018. https://thehimalayantimes.com/business/nepali-team-in-china-to-discuss-rail-from-kyirong-to-kathmandu/.
55. 'Joint Statement Between Nepal and the People's Republic of China,' Ministry of Foreign Affairs, 21 June 2018. https://mofa.gov.np/joint-statement-between-nepal-and-the-peoples-republic-of-china/. Also see Akhilesh Upadhyay, 'PM Oli winds up Beijing visit on high note', *Kathmandu Post*, 22 June 2018. http://kathmandupost.ekantipur.com/printedition/news/2018-06-22/pm-oli-winds-up-beijing-visit-on-high-note.html.
56. Anil Giri, 'Kathmandu-Kerung Railway Chugs Ahead as China Tables Report', *Kathmandu Post*, 11 December 2018. http://kathmandupost.ekantipur.com/printedition/news/2018-12-11/kathmandu-kerung-railway-chugs-ahead-as-china-tables-report.html.
57. Anil Giri, 'Rs 35 billion and Two Years is What it Takes to get Detailed Project Report of Kathmandu-Kerung Rail', *Kathmandu Post*, 18 March 2019. https://kathmandupost.com/national/2019/03/18/rs35-billion-and-2-years-is-what-it-takes-to-get-detailed-project-report-of-kathmandu-kerung-railway.
58. Anil Giri, 'China Pledges Rs 2 Billion in Grant for Railways but Where will it Go?', *Kathmandu Post*, 7 June 2019. http://kathmandupost.ekantipur.com/printedition/news/2019-06-07/china-pledges-rs-2-billion-in-grant-for-railways-but-where-will-it-go.html.
59. Sangam Prasain, 'China to Extend Tibet Rail to India Border Via Nepal', *Kathmandu Post*, 14 September 2018. https://kathmandupost.ekantipur.com/news/2018-09-14/china-to-extend-tibet-rail-to-india-border-via-nepal.html.

5. Communism Comes by Road

1. 'Nepal: Robin Hood of the Himalayas', *Time*, 5 August 1957. http://content.time.com/time/subscriber/article/0,33009,867789,00.html.
2. B.P. Koirala, *Atmabrittanta: Late Life Recollections* (trans. by Kanak Mani Dixit), Himal Books, Kathmandu, 2001, p. 166.
3. Ibid. Also see Leo E. Rose, *Nepal: Strategy for Survival*, p. 200; and David Atwill, 'Himalayan Asia'.
4. Jawaharlal Nehru, *SWJN, Vol. 15, Part II*, p. 381–82, Jawaharlal Nehru Memorial Fund, New Delhi, 1993.
5. Ibid.
6. Jawaharlal Nehru, *SWJN, Vol. 27, Part II*, Jawaharlal Nehru Memorial Fund, New Delhi, 2000, pp. 19–20.
7. David G. Atwill, 'Himalayan Asia', pp. 65–91.
8. Ibid.
9. Leo E. Rose, *Nepal: Strategy for Survival*, p. 163.
10. Stuart R. Schram, *The Political Thought of Mao Tse-tung*, Praeger Publishers, New York, 1969, p. 375. https://archive.org/details/politicalthought0000unse_k1v5/page/n5/mode/2up.

11. CIA, 'Summaries of trends and developments', 21 November 1950, p. 7-8. https://www.cia.gov/library/readingroom/docs/CIA-RDP79-01090A000300040003-2.pdf.
12. M.D. Gurung, 'Communist Movement in Nepal', *Economic and Political Weekly*, 12, No. 44, 1977, 1849–852. http://www.jstor.org/stable/4366057.
13. Ibid.
14. 'Nepalese Rebel Said to Plan New Attack', *New York Times*, 9 May 1952. https://timesmachine.nytimes.com/timesmachine/1952/05/09/84314906.pdf.
15. 'CIA, Chinese and Nepalese Communist Activities Along the Indian Border', August–October 1952. https://www.cia.gov/library/readingroom/docs/CIA-RDP80-00809A000700210057-1.pdf.
16. CIA, Information Report, 24 December 1953. https://www.cia.gov/library/readingroom/docs/CIA-RDP80-00810A003200120003-0.pdf.
17. Atwill, 'Himalayan Asia', p. 79.
18. Ibid., p. 80.
19. Nehru, SWJN, vol. 27, p. 73.
20. Available here: https://www.gettyimages.in/detail/news-photo/kakmandu-nepal-dr-k-i-singh-stands-in-a-jeep-as-his-fellow-news-photo/517251946.
21. CIA, Current Intelligence Bulletin, 31 July 1957, p.7 https://www.cia.gov/library/readingroom/docs/CURRENT%20INTELLIGENCE%20BULL%5B15757404%5D.pdf.
22. Nehru, Note to Secretary General, MEA, and Foreign Secretary on 14 May 1956, *SWJN*, Vol. 33, p. 446.
23. 'Nepal: Robin Hood of the Himalayas', *Time*.
24. Sulmaan Wasif Khan, *Haunted by Chaos: China's Grand Strategy from Mao Zedong to Xi Jinping*, Harvard University Press, Cambridge, Massachusetts, 2018, p. 1. Here, 'different forms of power' can be defined as how states use various means to achieve their national objectives—via hard military power, soft cultural power or economic influence.
25. Odd Arne Westad, *Restless Empire: China and the World Since 1950*, Vintage Books, London, 2013, p. 324.
26. Khan, *Haunted by Chaos*, p. 68.
27. Westad, *Restless Empire*, 2013, p. 328.
28. Khan, *Haunted by Chaos*, p. 100.
29. 'Record of Conversation of N.S. Khrushchev with CC CCP Chairman Mao Zedong, Deputy Chairman Liu Shaoqi, Zhou Enlai, Zhu De, Lin Biao, Politburo Members Peng Zhen and Chen Yi, and Secretariat Member Wang Jiaxiang', David Wolff (trans.), History and Public Policy Program Digital Archive, APRF, copy on Reel 17, Volkogonov Collection, Washington, DC: Library of Congress, 2 October 1959. https://digitalarchive.wilsoncenter.org/document/118883. In the same conversation, Khrushchev talks about how the Soviets did not send an ambassador to Nepal for a long time to respect Nehru's wishes.
30. CIA, 'Intelligence Report: Ten Years of Chinese Communist Foreign Policy, Section II: South and Southeast Asia, Reference Title: POLO XXVII',

9 April 1968, Directorate of Intelligence, p. 94. https://www.cia.gov/library/readingroom/docs/polo-18.pdf.
31. Quoted in Westad, *Restless Empire*, p. 343.
32. J.W. Garver, *China's Quest: The History of the Foreign Relations of the People's Republic of China*, Oxford University Press, New York, 2016, p. 185.
33. Westad, *Restless Empire*, p. 328.
34. Interview with the author on 8 January 2020.
35. CIA memorandum, 'The Royal Coup in Nepal', 25 January 1961, pp. 4–5. https://www.cia.gov/library/readingroom/docs/CIA-RDP79R00904A0007000 10026-8.pdf.
36. Ibid.
37. CIA report, 'Ten Years of Chinese Communist Foreign Policy', p. 92.
38. P.K.S. Namboodiri, 'China's Aid to Nepal in Perspective', *India Quarterly*, 35, No. 2, 1979, pp. 223–232. www.jstor.org/stable/45070926.
39. Eugene Bramer Mihaly, *Foreign Aid and Politics in Nepal: A Case Study*, Oxford University Press, New York, 1965, p. 151.
40. Ibid., p. 153.
41. All three projects were delayed. The shoe factory was started in 1965, a paper mill funded by the Chinese only started in 1986, while the cement factory never took off.
42. 'Record of Conversation following Pakistani Ambassador to the PRC Raza's Presentation of Credentials to Liu Shaoqi's', 1 September 1962, History and Public Policy Program Digital Archive, PRC FMA 105-01801-02, pp. 28–34. Obtained and translated by Christopher Tang. https://digitalarchive.wilsoncenter.org/document/121571.
43. 'Interview granted by Mr. B.P. Koirala to Mr. Wilson, the correspondent of Far Eastern Economic Review (Hong Kong), Kathmandu, May 26, 1960 (Excerpts)', reproduced in A.S. Bhasin (ed.), *Documents on Nepal's Relations with India and China, 1949-66*, Academic Books Ltd, Delhi, 1970, p. 210.
44. Rose, *Nepal*, p. 239.
45. Khan, 'Muslim, Trader, Nomad, Spy'.
46. 11 December 1961 motion in Rajya Sabha, *SWJN*, vol. 73, p. 537.
47. Quoted in Sam Cowan, 'A Worried Monarch', *The Record*, 14 January 2020. https://www.recordnepal.com/perspective/a-worried-monarch/.
48. Fr. László Ladányi, *China News Analysis*, vol. 402, 5 January 1962. http://www.ladanyi.ch/china-news-analysis/.
49. Rose, *Nepal*, p. 264. Also see 'The Road to Lhasa', *Economic and Political Weekly*, 5, No. 21, 1970, p. 834. http://www.jstor.org/stable/4360011.
50. Quoted in Cowan, 'A Worried Monarch'.
51. CIA report, 'Ten Years of Chinese Communist Foreign Policy', p. 94.
52. Ibid.
53. M.D. Gurung, 'Communist Movement in Nepal', *Economic and Political Weekly*, 12, No. 44, 1977, pp. 1849–1852. http://www.jstor.org/stable/4366057 (last accessed on 30 April 2020).

54. David N. Gellner and Mrigendra Bahadur Karki, 'KP Oli's Early Life and Influences', *The Record*, translation published on 26 August 2018. https://www.recordnepal.com/perspective/interviews/kp-oli-early-life-and-influences/.
55. Julia Lovell, *Maoism: A Global History*, The Bodley Head, London, 2019, p. 387.
56. The road allowed for the import of Chinese literature because India had banned its imports.
57. Lovell, *Maoism*, p. 388.
58. Aditya Adhikari, *The Bullet and the Ballot Box: The Story of Nepal's Maoist Revolution*, Aleph Book Company, New Delhi, 2014, p. 6.
59. Gellner, David, and Mrigendra Bahadur Karki, 'The Sociology of Activism in Nepal: Some Preliminary Considerations', in H. Ishii, D.N. Gellner & K. Nawa (eds.), *Social and Political Transformations in North India and Nepal* (Social Dynamics in Northern South Asia, vol. 2: Japanese Studies on South Asia vol. 7), pp. 361–397, Manohar, Delhi, 2007. https://www.academia.edu/11780714/The_Sociology_of_Activism_in_Nepal_Some_Preliminary_Considerations
60. Quoted in Gellner and Karki, 'The Sociology of Activism in Nepal'.
61. Adhikari, *The Bullet and the Ballot Box*, p. 155.
62. Ina Zharkevich, 'A New Way of Being Young in Nepal: the Idea of Maoist Youth and Birth of a New Man', *Studies in Nepali History and Society*, 14(1), June 2009, pp. 67–105. https://www.academia.edu/3242219/A_New_Way_of_Being_Young_in_Nepal_the_Idea_of_Maoist_Youth_and_Birth_of_a_New_Man.
63. Ibid.
64. Adhikari, *The Bullet and the Ballot Box*, p. 126.
65. Declassified CIA special report, Chinese Communist Influence in Nepal, dated 7 May 1965. https://www.cia.gov/library/readingroom/docs/CIA-RDP79-00927A004900010003-7.pdf.
66. Ibid. p. 3.
67. Declassified CIA report, Red China Escalate Infiltration of Nepal, undated, p. 3–8. https://www.cia.gov/library/readingroom/docs/CIA-RDP69B00369R000100200003-0.pdf.
68. Ibid.
69. Ibid.
70. Adhikari, *The Bullet and the Ballot Box*, p. 1.
71. CIA report, 'Ten Years of Chinese Communist Foreign Policy', p. 95.
72. Adhikari, *The Bullet and the Ballot Box*, p. 2. Also quoted in Rose, *Nepal*.
73. CIA report, 'Ten Years of Chinese Communist Foreign Policy', p. 97.
74. Garver, *China's Quest*, p. 268.
75. Westad, *Restless Empire*, pp. 354–355.
76. Garver, *China's Quest*, p. 196.
77. Bertil Lintner, *China's India War: Collision Course on the Roof of the World*, Oxford University Press, New Delhi, 2017.

78. First published as an editorial in *People's Daily*, organ of the Central Committee of the Communist Party of China, on 5 July 1967. It was reproduced in *Liberation*, vol. I, No. 1, November 1967. https://www.marxists.org/subject/china/documents/peoples-daily/1967/07/05.htm.
79. Bappaditya Paul, *The First Naxal: An Authorised Biography of Kanu Sanyal*, Sage India, New Delhi, 2014. All subsequent quotes by Sanyal are attributed to this volume.
80. Bertil Lintner, 'Burma and its Neighbours', paper presented at a conference in February 1992 at the Nehru Memorial Museum and Library, New Delhi. Also published in Surjit Mansingh (ed.), *Indian and Chinese Foreign Policies in Comparative Perspective*, Radiant Publishers, New Delhi, 1998. Also available here: http://www.asiapacificms.com/papers/pdf/burma_india_china.pdf.
81. Quoted in Westad, *Restless Empire*, p. 362.
82. Khan, *Haunted by Chaos*, p. 118.
83. Sino–US Joint Communique, 28 February 1972. https://www.fmprc.gov.cn/mfa_eng/ziliao_665539/3602_665543/3604_665547/t18006.shtml.
84. Declassified CIA report, 'India's Postwar Foreign Policy', 5 April 1972, p. 14. https://www.cia.gov/library/readingroom/document/cia-rdp79r00967a000500010007-2.
85. Declassified CIA report, 'South of the Himalayas: The View from Peking', 26 February 1973, p. 7.https://www.cia.gov/library/readingroom/document/cia-rdp85t00875r001100160037-9.
86. Peter Francon-Smith, 'Kathmandu-Bhaktapur Trolley Bus', *The Nepali Times*, 4 May 2018. https://www.nepalitimes.com/banner/kathmandu-bhaktapur-trolley-bus/ The project is now defunct.
87. Declassified CIA report, 'The Chinese View Of The Crisis In Southwest Asia: Past Relations, Current Policy, Prospect', 7 March 1980, pp. 15–16. Available at: https://www.cia.gov/library/readingroom/document/cia-rdp85t00287r000100840002-9.
88. Khan, *Haunted by Chaos*, p. 137.
89. 'Teng Hsiao-Ping Visit to Nepal', Wikileaks, 7 February 1978. https://wikileaks.org/plusd/cables/1978KATHMA00683_d.html.
90. Ibid.
91. 'Indian Reaction to Teng's Visit to Nepal', WikiLeaks, 10 February 1978. https://wikileaks.org/plusd/cables/1978NEWDE02248_d.html.
92. Teng Hsiao-Ping Visit to Nepal, Wikileaks, 7 February 1978. https://wikileaks.org/plusd/cables/1978KATHMA00683_d.html.
93. Quoted in Deepak Thapa and Bandana Sijapati, *A Kingdom under Siege: Nepal's Maoist Insurgency, 1996 to 2004*, The Printhouse, Kathmandu, 2004, p. 45.

6. Ghosts: Tibetan Exiles in Nepal

1. Carole McGranahan, *Arrested Histories: Tibet, the CIA, and Memories of a Forgotten War*, note no. 67, Duke University Press, Durham, 2010, p. 263.
2. All names of Tibetan exiles and representatives have been changed or withheld on request. Several individuals told me this was because Chinese authorities kept track of the names that appear in news stories and articles.
3. McGranahan, *Arrested Histories*, p. 188. Also see Elliot Sperling, '"Orientalism" and Aspects of Violence in the Tibetan Tradition', *Imagining Tibet—Perceptions, Projections, and Fantasies*, Wisdom Publications, Boston, 2001. http://elliotsperling.org/orientalism-and-aspects-of-violence-in-the-tibetan-tradition/#22.
4. Tsering Shakya, 'The Myth of Shangri-La', originally published in *Lungta*, Special Issue: Tibetan Authors, 1991, pp. 20–23. https://info-buddhism.com/Myth_of_Shangri-Ia_Tsering_Shakya.html.
5. Xiaoyuan Liu, *To the End of Revolution*, pp. 774–778.
6. See McGranahan, *Arrested Histories* for more on how the Khampas lived.
7. Ibid. Quoted on p. 149. The details of the operation that led to the seizing of documents are in Conboy and Morrison, *The CIA's Secret War in Tibet*, pp. 160–163.
8. Conboy and Morrison, *The CIA's Secret War in Tibet*, p. 199. Also see Sam Cowan, 'Raid into Tibet', *Essays on Nepal: Past and Present*, Himal Books, Kathmandu, 2018. Cowan writes that Mahendra told British officials the film would be 'a big headache for us and for you'. After 1964, however, there were few Khampa ops, especially as the Chinese had increased surveillance on the fighters. Also, the joint India–US effort after the 1962 war focused on inserting Tibetan fighters into Tibet itself by raising a separate unit, Establishment 22, today known as the Special Frontier Force.
9. Conboy and Morrison, *The CIA's Secret War in Tibet*, p. 233. McGranahan says Yeshi returned to Mustang to find Wangdu had taken 'unilateral control' of the forces rather than waiting for Yeshi to officially hand over the position.
10. Foreign Relations of the United States, 1969–1976, Volume XVII, China, 1969–1972, Washington, DC: United States Government Printing Office, 2006, editorial note on p. 1140. https://history.state.gov/historicaldocuments/frus1969-76v17.
11. Conboy and Morrison, *The CIA's Secret War in Tibet*.
12. Foreign Relations of the United States, 1969–1976, p. 1146. Memorandum Prepared for the 40 Committee, dated 11 January 1971.
13. John Masko, 'CIA Operations in Tibet and the Intelligence-Policy Relationship', *American Intelligence Journal*, 31, No. 2, 2013, pp. 127–132. www.jstor.org/stable/26202084.
14. Sam Cowan, 'A Secret Nepal File', *Essays on Nepal: Past and Present*, Himal Books, Kathmandu, 2018, p. 347.
15. Ibid., p. 348. The same essay quotes another November 1963 telegram in which the Indian ministry of external affairs denied supplying the Khampas.

However, India had begun raising Establishment 22, a tactical unit made up of Tibetan exiles intended to serve behind Chinese lines, with the help of the CIA by end-1962. By September 1963, a joint ops centre directing Tibetan operations opened in Hauz Khas, Delhi. Also see Conboy and Morrison, *The CIA's Secret War in Tibet*.
16. Sam Cowan, 'The Mustang Incident', *Essays on Nepal: Past and Present*, addendum, pp. 296–297.
17. Ibid. Garver argues a joint Chinese–Nepali military operation against the Khampas took place in 1964. However, this claim has since been debunked.
18. Prem Singh Basnyat, *Nepal-Chin: Vaad-vivaad ra Samvaad*, p. 131. Translations mine.
19. Although the Mustang camps were mostly known because of their numbers, Khampas had positioned themselves across most of the northern border, albeit in smaller numbers, such as in Manang, Dolpa and Olangchung in the east.
20. 'Disarming of Khampas', WikiLeaks, 17 July 1974. https://wikileaks.org/plusd/cables/1974KATHMA02903_b.html.
21. Office of the Historian, Bureau of Public Affairs, United States Department of State, 'Documents on South Asia, 1973–1976', Foreign Relations of the United States, 1969–1976, vol. E–8. https://history.state.gov/historicaldocuments/frus1969-76ve08/d251.
22. Thondup is known to have had covert links with the CIA in the founding of the resistance movement.
23. Mikel Dunham, 'Mustang: Royal Nepal Army's Defeat of the Tibet Freedom Fighters', 17 September 2009. https://www.mikeldunham.com/mikeldunham/2009/09/the-royal-nepal-armys-defeat-of-the-tibetan-freedom-fighters-in-mustang-new-information.html. In *Arrested Histories*, McGranahan notes Wangdu's terms for surrender: a) release of Lhamo Tsering, another Khampa operative who had been arrested in Pokhara earlier; b) Rs 2 million per month; c) the Khampas could continue to live in Nepal; d) land for their settlement; e) weapons to be handed over in three stages. The Nepali government accepted all but the last. As time passed and Tsering was not released, Wangdu decided to flee. Note 60, p. 158.
24. Conboy and Morrison, *The CIA's Secret War in Tibet*, p. 251.
25. Mikel Dunham, 'Mustang: Royal Nepal Army's defeat of the Tibetan Freedom Fighters—New Information', 17 September 2009. https://www.mikeldunham.com/mikeldunham/2009/09/the-royal-nepal-armys-defeat-of-the-tibetan-freedom-fighters-in-mustang-new-information.html.
26. Basnyat, *Nepal-Chin*, p. 140. The figure of 150 Khampas Basnyat provides is not confirmed in other sources.
27. 'Disarming of Khampas', WikiLeaks, 2 August 1974. https://wikileaks.org/plusd/cables/1974STATE169259_b.html.
28. 'GON Efforts to Disarm Khampas', WikiLeaks, 12 July 1974. https://wikileaks.org/plusd/cables/1974STATE151507_b.html.

29. The numbers were inflated. Although exact figures are not available, not more than 2,000 Chushi fighters and their families were eventually resettled in Jampaling and Paljoling camps in Pokhara. See McGranahan, *Arrested Histories*, and Tibet Justice Center's 2002 report, 'Tibet's Stateless Nationals'. 'Resettlement Assistance for Khampas', Wikileaks, 16 January 1975, https://wikileaks.org/plusd/cables/1975KATHMA00261_b.html and the 1971 memorandum to the 40 Committee.
30. 'Resettlement Assistance for Khampas', WikiLeaks, 9 December 1974. https://wikileaks.org/plusd/cables/1974STATE270009_b.html.
31. 'Resettlement Assistance for Khampas', Wikileaks, 20 December 1974. https://wikileaks.org/plusd/cables/1974KATHMA05227_b.html.
32. 'Resettlement Assistance for Khampas', Wikileaks, 31 January 1975. https://wikileaks.org/plusd/cables/1975STATE023112_b.html.
33. Tibet Justice Center, 'Tibet's Stateless Nationals', p. 20.
34. Jawaharlal Nehru, 'To Mahendra: Grievances', 12 May 1964, *SWJN*, vol. 85, pp. 322–323.
35. Tibet Justice Center, 'Tibet's Stateless Nationals', p. 34.
36. A conical basket woven out of bamboo used across Nepal.
37. School-Leaving Certificate Examinations, equivalent to the tenth-grade exams. It has now been replaced by the Secondary Education Examination.
38. Tibet Justice Center, 'Tibet's Stateless Nationals', p. 36.
39. Ibid., pp. 38–39.
40. Ibid., p. 3.
41. Apart from Tibet Justice Center report, also see International Campaign for Tibet's 'Dangerous Crossing: Conditions Impacting the Flight of Tibetan Refugees', 2011 update; Human Rights Watch's 'Under China's Shadow: Mistreatment of Tibetans in Nepal', 2014; and Saferworld's 'China and Conflict-affected States: Nepal Case Study', 2012, all available online. While a senior journalist suggested the reports could 'exaggerate' facts and numbers, a cross-examination with news reports and leaked US cables suggests a high degree of truth in the human rights reports. Some officials deny that Nepal entered into a 'gentleman's agreement'.
42. Tibet Justice Center, 'Tibet's Stateless Nationals', pp. 58–62.
43. Human Rights Watch, 'Under China's Shadow: Mistreatment of Tibetans in Nepal', p. 14.
44. Ibid., p 5.
45. International Campaign for Tibet, 'High-level Chinese Visit to Nepal Highlights Difficulties for Tibetan Community', 28 August 2017. https://savetibet.org/high-level-chinese-visit-to-nepal-highlights-difficulties-for-tibetan-community/#23.
46. Kunsang Tenzin, 'Nepal Deports 6 Tibetan Asylum Seekers to China', 10 September 2019. https://tibet.net/nepal-deports-6-tibetan-asylum-seekers-to-china/.
47. Bhrikuti Rai, 'Nepali citizens detained during Xi Jinping's visit for Tibetan signage on clothes and accessories', 17 October 2019. https://kathmandupost.

com/national/2019/10/17/nepali-citizens-detained-during-xi-jinping-s-visit-for-tibetan-signage-on-clothes-and-accessories.
48. Vivek Kumar Shah, *Maile Dekheko Durbar* ('The Palace as I Saw'), Yeti Books, Kathmandu, 2010, p. 235. Translations mine.
49. Note that the Army had not been mobilised against the Maoists at this time.
50. 'Police Cancel Dalai Lama Birthday Events in Kathmandu', WikiLeaks, 9 July 2002. https://wikileaks.org/plusd/cables/02KATHMANDU1332_a.html. Gyanendra visited China in July that year.
51. 'Chinese Pressure Stifles Tibetans in Nepal', WikiLeaks, 1 October 2002. https://wikileaks.org/plusd/cables/02KATHMANDU1903_a.html.
52. 'Tibetan Refugee Deportation: Post Mortem', WikiLeaks, 5 June 2003. https://wikileaks.org/plusd/cables/03KATHMANDU1042_a.html.
53. 'Nepal's Man in Tibet Discusses Refugee, Arms and Flood Issues', WikiLeaks, 19 December 2005. https://wikileaks.org/plusd/cables/05KATHMANDU2866_a. html. Also see: 'Nepal shuts down Tibetan offices', BBC, 28 January 2005. http://news.bbc.co.uk/2/hi/south_asia/4214933.stm.
54. The US also made similar proposals in 2011, but the Nepali authorities did not respond. See http://www.phayul.com/news/article.aspx?id=30938&t=1.
55. 'Ambassador Raises Reported Shootings of Tibetans with Vfm Yang Jiechi', WikiLeaks, 12 October 2006. https://wikileaks.org/plusd/cables/06BEIJING21638_a.html.
56. 'Nepal's Man in Tibet Discusses Refugee, Arms and Flood Issues', WikiLeaks, 19 December 2005. https://wikileaks.org/plusd/cables/05KATHMANDU2866_a. html.
57. 'American Climbers Fired Upon Near Tibet Border', WikiLeaks, 26 September 2002. https://wikileaks.org/plusd/cables/02KATHMANDU1872_a.html.
58. 'AMCIT Climber Discuss Shooting Incident,' WikiLeaks, 30 September 2002. https://wikileaks.org/plusd/cables/02KATHMANDU1902_a.html.
59. 'Refugees Confirm Details of Shooting Incident at Nepal-Chinese Border', WikiLeaks, 7 October 2002. https://wikileaks.org/plusd/cables/02KATHMANDU1933_a.html.
60. Ibid.
61. Ibid.
62. For more details on the Nangpa La shooting, see 'Himalayan climbers witness shooting', Al Jazeera, 10 October 2006, https://www.aljazeera.com/news/2006/10/10/himalayan-climbers-witness-shooting and 'The Nangpa Pass Incident', International Campaign for Tibet, 16 January 2007, https://savetibet.org/the-nangpa-pass-incident-september-2006/. The video of the incident is available on *YouTube*.
63. 'Chinese Shooting Spree Results in One Dead Tibetan,' WikiLeaks, 10 October 2006. https://wikileaks.org/plusd/cables/06KATHMANDU2677_a. html.
64. Forty-three of the seventy-six refugees who crossed the pass made it to Kathmandu.

Notes

65. 'Tar Fao responses on September 2006 Shooting at Natula Pass', WikiLeaks, 29 March 2007. https://wikileaks.org/plusd/cables/07CHENGDU86_a.html.
66. 'Tibetan woman deported by Switzerland jailed in Nepal', *Phayul*, 24 February 2017. https://www.phayul.com/2017/02/24/38707/.
67. Dinesh Bhatarai, 'Seize the Moment', 19 June 2018. https://myrepublica.nagariknetwork.com/news/seize-the-moment-1/.
68. Anil Giri, 'Nepal has Reassured it would Continue to Protect Rights of Tibetans in Our Country', *Kathmandu Post*, 19 March 2019. http://kathmandupost.ekantipur.com.np/news/2019-03-19/nepal-has-reassured-it-would-continue-to-protect-rights-of-tibetans-in-the-country-us-secretary-of-state.html.
69. The Human Rights Watch, 'The Costs of International Advocacy', 5 September 2017. https://www.hrw.org/report/2017/09/05/costs-international-advocacy/chinas-interference-united-nations-human-rights#page.

7. Between Two Boulders

1. Report of the Chinese Foreign Ministry, 'Some Existing Issues in and Suggestions for the Asia-Africa Conference', 1955, History and Public Policy Program Digital Archive, PRC FMA 207-00004-06, 59-62. Obtained by Amitav Acharya and translated by Yang Shanhou. https://digitalarchive.wilsoncenter.org/document/113179.
2. Report of the Chinese Foreign Ministry, 'List of Problems Between China and Other Asian-African Countries', 1955, History and Public Policy Program Digital Archive, PRC FMA 207-00073-01. Obtained by Amitav Acharya and translated by Yang Shanhou. https://digitalarchive.wilsoncenter.org/document/114718.
3. The text of the seventeen-point agreement can be accessed here: http://www.china.org.cn/english/zhuanti/tibet%20facts/163877.htm.
4. V.K. Manandhar, *A Comprehensive History of Nepal-China Relations until 1955 AD*, vol. II, Adroit Publishers, New Delhi, 2004, p. 220.
5. 'Telegram, Mao Zedong to CCP CC and CCP Northwest Bureau, 10 January 1950 (Excerpt)', 10 January 1950, History and Public Policy Program Digital Archive, Jianguo yilai Mao Zedong wengao [Mao Zedong's manuscripts since the founding of the People's Republic], vol. 1, Central Press of Historical Documents, Beijing, 1987, pp. 226–227; translation from Shuguang Zhang and Jian Chen (eds.), *Chinese Communist Foreign Policy and the Cold War in Asia*, 136. https://digitalarchive.wilsoncenter.org/document/112677. As an aside, it is interesting to note the UK only recognised Chinese direct rule over Tibet in 2008.
6. 'Memorandum of Conversation, Soviet Ambassador N.V. Roshchin with CC CCP Secretary Liu Shaoqi', 6 May 1951, History and Public Policy Program Digital Archive, AVP RF f. 0100, op. 44, por. 13, pap. 322, ll, pp. 17–22. Translated by David Wolff. https://digitalarchive.wilsoncenter.org/document/118734.

7. Rose, *Nepal*, p. 204.
8. Manandhar, *A Comprehensive History of Nepal-China Relations*, vol. II, p. 221.
9. Rose, *Nepal*, p. 109–110.
10. Prem R. Uprety, *Nepal-Tibet Relations 1850-1930*, pp. 74–75. The Tibetans, on the basis of this clause, asked for assistance from Nepal when the Chinese came in 1950. 'As might be expected, Nepal's interpretation of this clause was flexible, depending upon the circumstances': Rose, *Nepal*, p. 117.
11. Quoted in Atwill, 'Himalayan Asia', pp. 65–91. www.jstor.org/stable/j.ctv941r61.8.
12. Letter to Matrika Prasad Koirala, 23 March 1954, *SWJN*, vol. 25, pp. 456–459.
13. Letter to Matrika Prasad Koirala, 29 June 1954, *SWJN*, vol. 26, p. 488.
14. Nehru's address in Indian Parliament, 'India's Policies', reprinted in *SJWN*, vol. 15, Part II, p. 433.
15. B.P. Koirala, Kanak Mani Dixit (trans.), *Atmabrittanta: Late Life Recollections*, Himal Books, Kathmandu, 2001, p. 176.
16. Ibid., p. 177.
17. Note to Secretary General, Foreign Secretary and Joint Secretary, MEA, 18 June 1954, *SWJN*, vol. 26, pp. 476–480. This note also clearly outlines Nehru's position on Tibet: 'We must remember that our interests in Tibet derive largely from our inheriting certain British interests . . . Our policy thus should be an observance, in letter and spirit, of our agreement with China.'
18. Rose, *Nepal*, p. 206.
19. Letter to King Tribhuvan, 11 September 1954, *SWJN*, vol. 26, pp. 497–501.
20. Minutes of talks with Zhou Enlai, 21 October 1954, *SWJN*, vol. 27, p. 30. The Chinese Foreign Ministry Archives, however, adds to this conversation in its minutes: Nehru also said, '[The US] carried out anti-Indian propaganda campaigns in Nepal. We once lodged protest with the United States and the United Kingdom, although the United Kingdom is less to blame and does not interfere in Nepal's internal affairs. I said to them, they must recognize India's special position in Nepal, but they were undermining India's reputation in Nepal.' See 'Minutes of the Third Meeting between Premier Zhou Enlai and Nehru', 21 October 1954, History and Public Policy Program Digital Archive, PRC FMA 204-00007-09, 62-80. Obtained by Chen Jian and translated by 7Brands. https://digitalarchive.wilsoncenter.org/document/121748. The Soviets also, in fact, deferred to Nehru's wishes of not appointing an ambassador to Nepal, despite Kathmandu's desires to have one. See 'Record of Conversation of N.S. Khrushchev with CC CCP Chairman Mao Zedong, Deputy Chairman Liu Shaoqi, Zhou Enlai, Zhu De, Lin Biao, Politburo Members Peng Zhen and Chen Yi, and Secretariat Member Wang Jiaxiang', 2 October 1959, History and Public Policy Program Digital Archive, APRF, copy on Reel 17, Volkogonov Collection, Library of Congress, Washington, DC. Trans. David Wolff. https://digitalarchive.wilsoncenter.org/document/118883.

21. Situation in South East Asia (Minutes of talks between Nehru and Zhou Enlai), 21 October 1954, *SWJN*, vol. 27, p. 31.
22. 'Minutes of the Fourth Meeting between Premier Zhou Enlai and Nehru', 26 October 1954, History and Public Policy Program Digital Archive, PRC FMA 204-00007-16, 130-134. Obtained by Chen Jian and translated by 7Brands. https://digitalarchive.wilsoncenter.org/document/121749.
23. Nehru's note on 14 November 1954, *SWJN*, vol. 27, p. 122. The note also lays down Nehru's thoughts on Nepal's sovereignty prior to Indian independence: 'Nepal was far from independent, that is, before India became independent. There was no interference in internal matters, but otherwise the United Kingdom was the suzerain power. Independent India had accepted the full independence of Nepal, and had not claimed some of the rights the British had exercised.'
24. A former foreign minister close to the monarchy claimed India was not pleased with Mahendra's 'decision' to establish bilateral relations with China (Ramesh Nath Pande, *Kootniti ra Raajniti* [Diplomacy and Politics], Sangrila Books, Kathmandu, 2018, p. 267). However, a closer reading of Nehru's letters suggests otherwise.
25. Translations mine. Dr Bipin Adhikari, 'Ajhai Samjhiine Raja' ('A King Remembered'), *Kantipur Daily*, 23 September 2017, Koseli weekend supplement. https://www.kantipurdaily.com/koseli/2017/09/23/20170923112344.html.
26. Declassified CIA report, 'The Royal Coup in Nepal', 25 January 1961. https://www.cia.gov/library/readingroom/document/cia-rdp79r00904a000700010026-8.
27. 'Nepal's Cabinet is Ousted by King', *New York Times*, 16 December 1960. https://timesmachine.nytimes.com/timesmachine/1960/12/16/99979270.pdf.
28. Letter to K.D. Malviya, 16 December 1960, *SWJN*, vol. 65, p. 567.
29. Ibid., Appendix 42, p. 751.
30. Rose, *Nepal*, p. 212. Rose also suggests it was during Zhou's February 1957 visit to Nepal that China first proposed a road between Tibet and Kathmandu.
31. Ibid., p. 220.
32. 'Speech of the Nepalese delegate Mr S.P. Upadhyaya on the draft resolution on the question of Tibet and the violation of human rights and fundamental freedoms in the UN General Assembly, New York, October 20, 1959', reproduced in ed. A.S. Bhasin, *Documents on Nepal's Relations with India and China*, p. 199-201
33. Sinicized to Zhumulangma.
34. Ramakant, 'The Mount Everest Controversy between Nepal and China', *South Asian Studies*, vol. 10, No. 1 & 2, January–July 1975. https://www.cia.gov/library/readingroom/docs/CIA-RDP08C01297R000200050001-6.pdf.
35. While the Tibetan name for Everest is Chomolongma, which is what locals of the Khumbu region called it, there was no Nepali name for the peak until 1938, when Nepali historian Baburam Acharya gave it the name 'Sagarmatha'.

36. Koirala, *Atmabrittanta*, p. 227.
37. Ramakant, 'The Mount Everest Controversy between Nepal and China'.
38. Ibid.
39. Ibid.
40. Koirala, *Atmabrittanta*, p. 224.
41. CIA report, 'The Sino-Indian Border Dispute, Section 2: 1959-61', pp. 42–43, 19 August 1963. https://www.cia.gov/library/readingroom/docs/polo-08.pdf.
42. Koirala, *Atmabrittanta*, p. 226.
43. Ibid., p. 228.
44. Ibid., p. 229.
45. Letter to B.P. Koirala, 31 March 1960, *SWJN*, vol. 59, pp. 351–352.
46. Ibid., letter to Bidhan Chandra Roy, 3 April 1960, p. 353–354.
47. Laszlo Ladany, *China News Analysis*, vol. 294, 25 September 1959, p. 7.
48. B.P. Koirala, *Atmabrittanta*, p. 254. B.P. narrated his life story in 1981 after being diagnosed with throat cancer.
49. 'Nepalese King escapes unhurt as explosive is thrown at car, palace says', *New York Times*, 24 January 1962. https://timesmachine.nytimes.com/timesmachine/1962/01/24/89831642.pdf (last accessed on 30 April 2020).
50. Letter from Mahendra Bir Bikram Shah Dev: Nepal's Grievances, 3 February 1962, *SWJN*, Appendix 2, vol. 75, p. 642. Nehru wrote to his ambassador in Nepal, 'It is not a pleasant letter to read by us and I have not enjoyed reading it.' Letter to Harishwar Dayal, 9 February 1962, *SWJN*, Appendix 2, vol. 75, p. 642.
51. Ibid. Letter to Mahendra Bir Bikram Shah Dev, 9 February 1962, pp. 609–611. However, as seen after the 1962 war, Nehru could indeed direct the Nepali Congress activists to stop violent acts.
52. Ibid. Letter to Rajendra Prasad, 19 October 1962, Vol. 79, pp. 279–282.
53. 'Cable from the Chinese Embassy in India, "Overview of India's Foreign Relations in 1961"', 1 January 1962, History and Public Policy Program Digital Archive, PRC FMA 105-01519-01, 1–14. Trans. Anna Beth Keim. https://digitalarchive.wilsoncenter.org/document/116482.
54. Shen-Yu Dai, 'Peking, Katmandu and New Delhi', *The China Quarterly*, No. 16, 1963, pp. 86–98. http://www.jstor.org/stable/651574.
55. Nehru's thoughts on Chen Yi's statement reproduced from *National Herald*, 17 October 1962, *SWJN*, vol. 79, p. 279. His thoughts on Nepal's pro-China stance are in a letter to Indian President Rajendra Prasad dated 19 October 1962 in the same volume, pp. 279–282.
56. McGranahan, Carole. 'From Simla to Rongbatsa: The British and the "Modern" Boundaries of Tibet.' *The Tibet Journal* 28, no. 4 (2003): 39–60. http://www.jstor.org/stable/43302541.
57. Note to Secretary-General, Foreign Secretary and Joint Secretary T.N. Kaul, 25 October 1953, *SWJN*, vol. 24, p. 597.
58. Conversation between Jawaharlal Nehru and Zhou Enlai, 31 December 1956 & 1 January 1957, *SWJN*, vol. 36, pp. 598–600.

Notes 253

59. Zhou Enlai's letter to Nehru, 23 January 1959, *SWJN*, Appendix II, vol. 47, p. 557.
60. Khan, *Haunted By Chaos*, p. 101.
61. 'Report from the PLA General Staff Department, "Behind India's Second Anti-China Wave"', 29 October 1959, History and Public Policy Program Digital Archive, PRC FMA 105-00944-07, 84–90. Trans. 7Brands https://digitalarchive.wilsoncenter.org/document/114758. The other reasons were: to force China to accept the McMahon Line; internal contradictions within Indian politics; the Tibet dispute; to strike down the Indian communist party and to flatter the US for aid.
62. John W. Garver, *Protracted Contest: Sino-Indian Rivalry in the Twentieth Century*, University of Washington Press, Seattle, London, 2001, p. 149.
63. Quoted in 'Agnew's Royal Host in Nepal', *New York Times*, 5 January 1970. https://timesmachine.nytimes.com/timesmachine/1970/01/05/80012639.pdf.
64. 'A King 'For the People', *New York Times*, 29 April 1960. https://timesmachine.nytimes.com/timesmachine/1960/04/29/105430313.pdf.
65. 'South of the Himalayas: A View from Peking', CIA memorandum, p. 2, 26 February 1973. https://www.cia.gov/library/readingroom/docs/CIA-RDP85T00875R001100160037-9.pdf.
66. Ibid., pp. 4–5.
67. Ibid, p. 10.
68. 'Record of Conversation between French Prime Minister Jacques Chirac and Vice Premier of the People's Republic Deng Xiaoping', 12 May 1975, History and Public Policy Program Digital Archive, Ministère des Affaires Etrangères, la Courneuve (MAE), Série Asie-Océanie, Sous-série Chine 1973-1980 (AO), 2174. Archival Reference Code ('Côte'): 752INVA/2174. Obtained and translated for CWIHP by Martin Albers and included in CWIHP e-Dossier No. 45. https://digitalarchive.wilsoncenter.org/document/118650.
69. 'Telegram from L.L Mehrotra, Charge d'Affaires in Beijing', 17 September 1975, History and Public Policy Program Digital Archive, File No: PP(JS)3(9)/75—vol. I. Obtained by Ryan Musto. https://digitalarchive.wilsoncenter.org/document/133960.
70. CIA, 'Chinese-Indian Relations, 1972-1975', September 1975, p. 13. https://www.cia.gov/library/readingroom/docs/CIA-RDP86T00608R000600170014-4.pdf.
71. Memorandum of Conversation, Document 97, in David P. Nickles (ed.), Edward C. Keefer (general ed.), *Foreign Relations of the United States, 1969–1976*, vol. XVIII, China, 1973–1976, United States Government Printing Office, Washington, D.C., 2007, p. 615-617. https://history.state.gov/historicaldocuments/frus1969-76v18.
72. Ibid, Document 136, p. 888.
73. 'King With a Sense of Mission', *New York Times*, 24 February 1975. https://www.nytimes.com/1975/02/24/archives/king-with-a-sense-of-mission-birendra-bir-bikram-shah-dev.html
74. CIA Intelligence Assessment, 'Nepal: Continuity and Change in a Himalayan

254   Notes

Monarchy', p. 2, November 1983. https://www.cia.gov/library/readingroom/docs/CIA-RDP84S00927R000200030003-7.pdf.
75. Maharaja Krishna Rasgotra, *A Life in Diplomacy*, Viking, New Delhi, 2016.
76. 'Telegram from L.L. Mehrotra, Charge d'Affaires in Beijing', 30 April 1975, History and Public Policy Program Digital Archive, File No: PP(JS)3(9)/75—Vol. I. Obtained by Ryan Musto. https://digitalarchive.wilsoncenter.org/document/133959.
77. 'Telegram from L.L Mehrotra, Charge d'Affaires in Beijing', 17 September 1975, History and Public Policy Program Digital Archive, File No: PP(JS)3(9)/75—vol. I. Obtained by Ryan Musto. https://digitalarchive.wilsoncenter.org/document/133960.
78. Rose, *Neoal*, p. 273. It has been argued that Mahendra agreed to the defence agreement to mollify Indian concerns arising out of the Lhasa–Kathmandu road.
79. 'Nepalese Interest in Air Defense Equipment', Wikileaks, 30 May 1975. https://wikileaks.org/plusd/cables/1975STATE126276_b.html.
80. Cable, 'Nepalese Interest In Air Defense Equipment', 29 September 1975. https://wikileaks.org/plusd/cables/1975KATHMA04307_b.html.
81. On Kathmandu approaching New Delhi for anti-aircraft weapons, see John W. Garver, 'China-India Rivalry in Nepal: The Clash over Chinese Arms Sales', *Asian Survey*, 31, No. 10 (1991), doi:10.2307/2645066, pp. 956–975.
82. Cable, 'Nepalese Interest In Air Defense Equipment', 17 October 1975. https://wikileaks.org/plusd/cables/1975STATE247219_b.html.
83. Zorawar Daulet Singh, 'Twists and Turns in the India-China Border Saga', *Outlook*, 26 May 2015. https://www.outlookindia.com/website/story/twists-and-turns-in-the-india-china-border-saga/294406.
84. CIA, Near East and South Asia Review, p. 5, 25 April 1986. https://www.cia.gov/library/readingroom/docs/CIA-RDP87T00289R000200850001-4.pdf.
85. Ibid, p. 7.
86. Singh, 'Twists And Turns In The India-China Border Saga'.
87. CIA, 'Near East and South Asia Review', p. 28-29, 21 October 1988. https://www.cia.gov/library/readingroom/docs/DOC_0000633372.pdf.
88. Ibid, p. 29.
89. John W. Garver, 'China-India Rivalry in Nepal'.
90. Lok Raj Baral, 'India-Nepal Relations: Continuity and Change', *Asian Survey* 32, No. 9, 1992, doi:10.2307/2645073, pp. 815–829.
91. Garver, 'China-India Rivalry in Nepal'. Former Foreign Minister Pande also attributes three other underlying causes of the dispute: Sonia Gandhi being denied permission to enter Pashupati as a non-Hindu; Rajiv Gandhi's wish that his Sri Lankan adventure be supported during the third SAARC summit; and a cancelled breakfast meeting between Birendra and Rajiv at the fourth SAARC summit in Islamabad. See Pande, *Kootniti ra Raajniti*, pp. 241–245.
92. Garver, 'China-India Rivalry in Nepal'.

93. CIA, 'India-Nepal-China: Implications of the Trade Impasse', 8 May 1989. https://www.cia.gov/library/readingroom/docs/DOC_0000633366.pdf.
94. Uttam Sengupta, 'Nepal faces mounting crisis since the lapse of trade and transit treaties with India', *India Today*, 15 May 1989. https://www.indiatoday.in/magazine/special-report/story/19890515-nepal-faces-mounting-crisis-since-the-lapse-of-trade-and-transit-treaties-with-india-816083-1989-05-15.
95. 'Nepal's Economy is Gasping as India, its Huge Neighbor Squeezes it Hard,' *New York Times*, 11 April 1989. https://www.nytimes.com/1989/04/11/world/nepal-s-economy-is-gasping-as-india-a-huge-neighbor-squeezes-it-hard.html.
96. Garver, 'China-India Rivalry in Nepal'.
97. Pande, *Kootniti ra Raajniti*, p. 287.
98. Nayan Bahadur Khatri, 'Chaar Dashak Pachi Cheen ma Rajdoot' (An ambassador in China after four decades) in Bishnu Rijal (ed.), *Nepal ko Kootnitik Abyaas* (Nepal's Diplomatic Efforts), Institute for Foreign Affairs, Kathmandu, 2019, p. 118. Nepal also asked China whether the Soviets could assist in improving relations with India. See 'Diary of Teimuraz Stepanov-Mamaladze, 17 May 1989', 17 May 1989, History and Public Policy Program Digital Archive, Hoover Institution Archive, Teimuraz Stepanov-Mamaladze Papers: Diary No. 9. Trans. Sergey Radchenko. https://digitalarchive.wilsoncenter.org/document/12178.1.
99. Garver, 'China-India Rivalry in Nepal'.
100. M. Taylor Fravel, *Strong Borders, Secure Nation: Cooperation and Conflict in China's Territorial Disputes*, Princeton University Press (Project MUSE), Princeton, New Jersey, 2008, p. 157. muse.jhu.edu/book/30390.
101. Biswas Baral, 'India's "Blockade" Has Opened the Door for China in Nepal', *The Wire*, 2 March 2016. https://thewire.in/diplomacy/indias-blockade-has-opened-the-door-for-china-in-nepal.
102. CIA, 'India-Nepal-China: Implications of the Trade Impasse', p.3.

8. 'A Friendship Across the Himalayas'

1. Borrowed from Chinese president Xi Jinping's essay before his October 2019 state visit to Nepal.
2. Rajan Pokhrel, 'Man Labelled Dalai Lama's Agent, Deported to US', *Himalayan Times*, 25 June 2019. https://thehimalayantimes.com/kathmandu/man-labelled-dalai-lamas-agent-deported-to-us/.
3. Ibid. The number '6' is Nepali type shorthand for the word 'cha', which means something like 'is' or 'there is'.
4. Anil Giri and Tsering D. Gurung, 'China Asked Nepal to Ban a Tibetan Official From Entering the Country, Nepali Officials Got the Wrong Man', *Kathmandu Post*, 27 June 2019. https://kathmandupost.com/national/2019/06/27/china-asked-nepal-to-ban-a-tibetan-official-from-entering-the-country-nepali-officials-got-the-wrong-man.
5. I did not hear back from the US embassy on whether the Nepal government

had responded to their queries. Also see: Roshan S. Nepal, 'American embassy seeks clarification', *The Himalayan Times*, 28 June 2019. https://thehimalayantimes.com/nepal/american-embassy-seeks-clarification/.

6. China's 'security interests' is an umbrella term, but here, it primarily refers to visible political activity by Tibetan exiles against Chinese occupation of the plateau, and the flight of Tibetan nationals across the Himalaya into Nepal.

7. 'China Ambassador Calls for International Cooperation to help Nepal Fight Maoists', WikiLeaks, 16 May 2002. https://wikileaks.org/plusd/cables/02KATHMANDU953_a.html.

8. 'Chinese Ambassador Denies Commercial Weapons Sales to Nepal', WikiLeaks, 18 November 2005. https://wikileaks.org/plusd/cables/05KATHMANDU2516_a.html.

9. 'Government Restricts Tibetan Refugee Movement', WikiLeaks, 29 November 2005. https://wikileaks.org/plusd/cables/05KATHMANDU2633_a.html. Gyanendra's attempts to involve China within SAARC further alienated the Indian establishment.

10. 'Nepal's Man in Tibet Discusses Refugees, Arms and Flood Issues', WikiLeaks, 19 December 2005. https://wikileaks.org/plusd/cables/05KATHMANDU2866_a.html.

11. 'PRC/Nepal: China Encouraged by King's Speech but Taking a "Wait and See" Approach', WikiLeaks, 25 April 2006. https://wikileaks.org/plusd/cables/06BEIJING7838_a.html.

12. 'PCR/Nepal: Beijing Assessing How to Engage with Nepal's Interim Government', WikiLeaks, 20 June 2006. https://wikileaks.org/plusd/cables/06BEIJING13004_a.html.

13. Ibid.

14. 'DDG Luo On China-South Asia Developments', WikiLeaks, 22 September 2006. https://wikileaks.org/plusd/cables/06BEIJING20223_a.html.

15. 'MFA: China Supports Constituent Assembly Election: Will Continue to Intervene on "Core Interest" of Tibet', WikiLeaks, 14 March 2008. https://wikileaks.org/plusd/cables/08BEIJING969_a.html.

16. 'China Tries to Adjust to Nepal's New Political Landscape', WikiLeaks, 15 May 2008. https://wikileaks.org/plusd/cables/08BEIJING1876_a.html.

17. Bhojraj Bhat, 'Cheers! Naya Naata' ('Cheers to a new relationship'), *Nepal Magazine*, 3 Asar 2064, 17 June 2007. Prachanda had also written to the Chinese president separately in 1999, he said in an interview, while the Maoists had reached out to China after the People's War began. Nothing came out of these attempts either.

18. Ibid.

19. 'Chinese Ambassador Worried about the Maoists', WikilLeaks, 27 September 2006. https://wikileaks.org/plusd/cables/06KATHMANDU2619_a.html.

20. 'DDG Luo on China-South Asia Developments', WikiLeaks, 22 September 2006. https://wikileaks.org/plusd/cables/06BEIJING20223_a.html.

21. A mainstream offshoot of the Communist movement, the UML's trajectory was marked by both an acquiescence to royal rule as well as opposition to it.
22. Tanka Prasad Acharya, however, was the first Nepali prime minister to visit China in 1954.
23. Editorial, 'Prachanda problem', *Indian Express*, 26 August 2008. http://archive.indianexpress.com/news/prachanda-problem/353207/0.
24. Bhojraj Bhaat, 'Mao ko gharma Prachanda' ('Prachanda at Mao's home'), *Nepal Magazine*, 22 Bhadra 2065, 7 September 2008.
25. Saroj Raj Adhikari, 'Tibet ko Tanav' ('Tibet's Tensions'), *Nepal Magazine*, 29 Baisakh 2065, 11 May 2008.
26. 'A new torch controversy: the battle for Everest', *The Independent*, 2 May 2008. https://www.independent.co.uk/news/world/asia/a-new-torch-controversy-the-battle-for-everest-819737.html.
27. Nepal had already banned any climbing on the world's highest peak between 1–10 May that year, when the Beijing Olympic torch was to reach the summit.
28. Several protestors, however, were based out of Nepal.
29. 'Calling the Shots', *Economist*, 17 March 2012. https://www.economist.com/asia/2012/03/17/calling-the-shots.
30. Three Tibetans living in Kathmandu protested Chinese rule in Tibet by self-immolating in the wave of such protests that wracked the Tibetan plateau from 2009 onwards. Of the three, two died in their attempts. For more information, see https://savetibet.org/tibetan-self-immolations/#inexile.
31. 'MFA: China supports Constituent Assembly Election; Will continue to intervene on "core interest" of Tibet', Wikileaks, 14 March 2008. https://wikileaks.org/plusd/cables/08BEIJING969_a.html. The official was Zhao Lijian, today more noted as the 'Wolf Warrior' diplomat.
32. Human Rights Watch, 'Under China's Shadow: Mistreatment of Tibetans in Nepal', 2014, p. 6. https://www.hrw.org/sites/default/files/reports/nepal0314_ForUpload_2.pdf.
33. Santosh Acharya and Upendra Pokharel, 'Andolan Tataune Tayari' ('Time to Heat Up the Revolution'), *Nepal Magazine*, 28 Asar 2066, 12 July 2009.
34. Chudamani Bhattarai, 'Seema ma Doot Haru (Ambassadors at the Border)', Nepal Magazine, 22 Kartik 2066 (8 November 2009) issue. China was also worried about possible cooperation between Uighur and Tibetan activists in Nepal. See Santosh Acharya, 'Uighur ko Dar' ('The Fear of Uighurs'), *Nepal Magazine*, 22 Kartik 2066, 8 November 2009.
35. 'Exclusive Interview with Nepal's Deputy Inspector General of Police: "Tibetan Pro-independence Elements" Won't Be Able to Stir Up Trouble in Nepal', *Huanqiu Shibao*, 29 March 2009. Quoted in Human Rights Watch, 'Under China's Shadow', Appendix II, p. 94.
36. Saferworld, Nepal case study, 'China and conflict-affected states: Between principle and pragmatism', January 2012, p. 10. https://www.saferworld.org.uk/resources/publications/612-china-and-conflict-affected-states.

37. Human Rights Watch, 'Under China's Shadow', p. 27–32.
38. Rewati Sapkota, 'Chinese Rider on Tato Pani', *Himalayan Times*, 14 January 2018. https://thehimalayantimes.com/nepal/chinese-rider-tatopani/.
39. China has been asking Nepal to sign an extradition treaty since at least 2010. See 'Nepal: China pressure but Nepalis say refugee policy hasn't changed', Wikileaks, 18 February 2010. https://wikileaks.org/plusd/cables/10KATHMANDU144_a.html.
40. There are also questions over whether the agreement violates international laws prohibiting refoulement in instances where torture is possible. Both China and Nepal have signed the UN Convention against Torture.
41. See Saferworld, Nepal case study; Human Rights Watch, 'Under China's Shadow'; International Campaign for Tibet, 'Dangerous Crossing'.
42. ICT, 'Dangerous Crossing', p. 50.
43. Ibid., pp. 100–102. Also see Human Rights Watch, 'Under China's Shadow', pp. 68–73.
44. Pande, *Kootniti ra Raajniti*, p. 660. Another ex-Home Ministry official said the same to me.
45. Yeshe Dorje and Rajani Tamang, 'Nepalese Journalists Pushed to Avoid Reporting on China, Tibet', VOA News, 29 June 2019. https://www.voanews.com/south-central-asia/nepalese-journalists-pushed-avoid-reporting-china-tibet.
46. From 1990 onwards, New Delhi had, until Gyanendra's 2005 coup, pursued diplomacy in Nepal based on two pillars: constitutional monarchy and multiparty democracy. Subsequent to the coup, India facilitated the 12-Point agreement between the Maoists and seven leading political parties.
47. Sudheer Sharma, *Prayogshala: Nepali Sankraman ma Dilli, Durbar ra Maobadi* ('The Laboratory: Delhi, the Palace and the Maoists during Nepal's Conflict'), p. 294, Fineprint Books, Kathmandu: 2013.
48. Mukul Humagain, 'Chin ko Prastaav' (China's Proposal), *Nepal Magazine*, 2 Chaitra 2065, 15 March 2009. In 2020, a former ambassador to China highlighted the need for revising the treaty with China in light of the upgraded strategic ties during Xi Jinping's 2019 visit. See Leela Mani Paudyal, 'Sajha Bhavishya ka laagi Sahakarya' ('Cooperation for a better future'), *Kantipur*, 16 Shrawan 2077, 31 July 2020. https://ekantipur.com/opinion/2020/07/31/159616299432512980.html?author=1.
49. Sudheer Sharma, *Prayogshala*, p. 293.
50. An Indian embassy official quoted in Prashant Jha, *Battles of the New Republic: A Contemporary History of Nepal*, p. 128, New Delhi: Aleph Book Company, 2013. See Jha for more details on this tricky period of the Nepali political transition.
51. Sapkota would also tell me firing Katuwal three months before his retirement was another mistake on their part.
52. 'India Boosts Ties on Nepal, Keeps as Eye on China', WikiLeaks, 28 August 2009. https://wikileaks.org/plusd/cables/09NEWDELHI1801_a.html.

53. B. Raman, 'China wants Prachanda to stay in Nepal', 4 May 2009. https://www.rediff.com/news/column/guest-b-raman-china-wants-prachanda-to-stay-in-nepal/20090504.htm.
54. International Crisis Group, 'Nepal's Future: In Whose Hands?', Asia Report no. 173, 13 August 2009, p. 20. https://d2071andvip0wj.cloudfront.net/173-nepal-s-future-in-whose-hands.pdf.
55. Sudheer Sharma, *Prayogshala*, p. 314.
56. The Jhalanath Khanal Foundation, chaired by Khanal, is known to have close links with China. In 2018, it signed a memorandum of cooperation with the China International Council for Multinational Corporations; at a November 2018 meet of international MNCs in Tianjin, China, the foundation represented Nepal.
57. A 2010 report alleged Indian intelligence operatives had called up a Nepali MP and threatened to have his daughter's admission into the embassy-run Kendriya Vidyalaya revoked if he didn't vote to keep Prachanda out of power. Siddharth Varadarajan, 'The Danger in India's Nepal Policy', *The Hindu*, 16 August 2010. https://www.thehindu.com/opinion/columns/siddharth-varadarajan/The-danger-in-Indias-Nepal-policy/article13101110.ece.
58. David Gellner and Mrigendra Bahadur Karki, 'K.P. Oli's early life and influences', *The Record*, 26 August 2018. https://www.recordnepal.com/perspective/interviews/kp-oli-early-life-and-influences/
59. Suhasini Haider, 'Supporter turned antagonist', *The Hindu*, 31 May 2020, https://www.thehindu.com/news/international/supporter-turned-antagonist-the-problem-posed-by-oli/article31715944.ece. An analyst told me Oli had mainstreamed the conservatism of Nepali society in the post-conflict era as a counter against liberal ideals such as secularism and federalism that had come to dominate the public narrative.
60. For more on the violence amid Nepal's constitution-making process, see Human Rights Watch, 'Like We Are Not Nepali: Protest and Police Crackdown in the Terai Region of Nepal', October 2015. https://www.hrw.org/report/2015/10/16/we-are-not-nepali/protest-and-police-crackdown-terai-region-nepal.
61. 'Statement on Situation in Nepal', Ministry of External Affairs, India, 20 September 2015. https://www.mea.gov.in/press-releases.htm?dtl/25821/Statement+on+the+situation+in+Nepal.
62. 'Nepal's Divisive New Constitution: An Existential Crisis', International Crisis Group, Asia Report Number 276, 4 April 2016, pp. 16–17. https://www.crisisgroup.org/asia/south-asia/nepal/nepal%E2%80%99s-divisive-new-constitution-existential-crisis.
63. Ibid., p. 20.
64. Sudheer Sharma, *Prayogshala*, p. 315
65. Prashant Jha, 'HT Analysis: Nepal PM Oli's Departure Marks and Indian Comeback', *Hindustan Times*, 24 July 2016. https://www.hindustantimes.com/analysis/prime-minister-oli-s-departure-marks-indian-comeback-in-nepal/story-SlfKmL3xkCWZDHO0IPDPwI.html.

66. Zhang Shubin, 'Will Nepal's PM repair Ties with China?' *Global Times*, 20 March 2017. http://www.globaltimes.cn/content/1038667.shtml.
67. Xu Liang, 'Nepal Risks Missing Chance with China', *Global Times*, 19 September 2016. http://www.globaltimes.cn/content/1007091.shtml.
68. However, he was not the first to do so. Former Chinese ambassador to Nepal, Yang Houlan, had pushed the idea in 2012. See http://np.china-embassy.org/eng/EmbassyInfo/asaa/t970295.htm.
69. CIA Intelligence Report, 'The International Liaison Department of the Chinese Communist Party', p. i-vi, December 1971. https://www.cia.gov/library/readingroom/docs/polo-33.pdf.
70. Neil Thomas, 'Proselytizing Power: The Party Wants the World to Learn from Its Experiences', Macro Polo, 22 January 2020. https://macropolo.org/international-liaison-department-ccp/.
71. 'Xi Jinping: Let the Sense of Community of Common Destiny Take Deep Root in Neighbouring Countries', Ministry of Foreign Affairs of China, 25 October 2013. https://www.fmprc.gov.cn/mfa_eng/wjb_663304/wjbz_663308/activities_663312/t1093870.shtml.
72. Anil Giri, 'Beijing recalibrating its Nepal policy as political situation unfolds fast', *The Kathmandu Post*, 30 December 2020. https://kathmandupost.com/national/2020/12/30/beijing-recalibrating-its-nepal-policy-as-political-situation-unfolds-fast-in-kathmandu.
73. 'Xi Jinping Meets with President of Nepali Congress Party Sher Bahadur Deuba', Ministry of Foreign Affairs of China, 13 October 2019. https://www.fmprc.gov.cn/mfa_eng/zxxx_662805/t1707861.shtml.
74. 'National Security Strategy of the United States of America', The White House, Washington, D.C., December 2017. https://www.whitehouse.gov/wp-content/uploads/2017/12/NSS-Final-12-18-2017-0905-1.pdf.
75. Binod Ghimire, 'Why the MCC Compact Courted Controversy in Nepal', *Kathmandu Post*, 9 January 2020. https://kathmandupost.com/national/2020/01/09/why-the-mcc-compact-courted-controversy-in-nepal.
76. 'A Free and Open Indo-Pacific: Advancing a Shared Vision', Department of State, US Government, 4 November 2019. https://www.state.gov/wp-content/uploads/2019/11/Free-and-Open-Indo-Pacific-4Nov2019.pdf.
77. See details of the MCC compact here: https://hr.parliament.gov.np/uploads/attachments/ns1zpda2uw3x2odp.pdf. Nepali opponents of the MCC have alleged in the event of a dispute in the project, New York laws will apply. However, the treaty makes no mention of it.
78. Akhilesh Upadhyay, 'In Nepal, how domestic politics is colliding with geopolitics', *Hindustan Times*, 23 November 2020. https://www.hindustantimes.com/analysis/in-nepal-how-domestic-politics-is-colliding-with-geopolitics/story-rn13tL5lzGKnZTWVZ5rGYK.html.
79. In fact, Wei's November visit was intended to deepen the military-to-military relationship, with the resumption of military aid and training programmes on the cards. There was also a suggestion that domestic political turmoil had led China to view the Nepal Army as a 'permanent establishment' in

the country. See Kamal Dev Bhattarai, 'Chiniya Rakshya Mantrile Jangi Addama Dui Ghanta Bitaunu ko Artha' ('The meaning behind the Chinese defence minister spending two hours at Nepal Army headquarters'), *Online Khabar*, 29 November 2020. https://www.onlinekhabar.com/2020/11/912436.
80. Phanindra Dahal, 'Wei Fenghe Nepal Bhraman: Chin Nepali sena sanga kasto sambandha chahancha' ('Wei Fenghe's Nepal visit: What sort of relationship does China want with Nepal Army?'), *BBC Nepali*, 2 December 2020. https://www.bbc.com/nepali/news-55134776.
81. Interview with Chinese ambassador Hou Yanqi: 'China wants trilateral ties involving India also for Nepal's development', *Online Khabar*, 10 November 2020. https://english.onlinekhabar.com/china-wants-trilateral-ties-involving-india-also-for-nepals-development-ambassador-hou.html.
82. These nine projects are: upgrading the Rasuwagadhi–Kathmandu road; the Kimathanka–Hile road; a road from Dipayal to the Chinese border; the Tokha–Bidur road; the Galchhi–Rasuwagadhi–Gyirong 400kv transmission line; the Gyirong–Kathmandu railway; the 762MW Tamor hydroelectricity project; the 426MW Phukot Karnali hydroelectric project; and the Madan Bhandari Technical Institute.
83. Krishana Prasain, 'Local traders fear they may miss the winter shopping season too', *The Kathmandu Post*, 27 November 2020. https://kathmandupost.com/money/2020/11/27/local-traders-fear-they-may-miss-the-winter-shopping-season-too.
84. 'Nepal-Chin Seema baare boleko bhandai Humla ka sahayak CDO lai griha ko 24 24-ghante spashtikaran' ('Humla assistant CDO asked to submit clarification within 24 hours by Home Ministry for speaking about the Nepal-China border'), *Pahilopost*, 24 September 2020. https://pahilopost.com/content/20200924112422.html.
85. Amrit Raj Kaphle, 'Interview: I feel threatened for my findings that China encroached land in Humla – NC leader Shahi', Khabarhub, 22 November 2020. https://english.khabarhub.com/2020/22/143664/.
86. 'Congress lai Chin ko chitthi: Seema samasya samadhan ma BP ko thulo yogdaan cha' ('China's letter to Congress: BP greatly assisted the resolution of any border disputes'), *Online Khabar*, 5 December 2020. https://www.onlinekhabar.com/2020/12/913456.

9. Chinese Capitalism with Nepali Characteristics

1. Jeffrey Wasserstrom, 'From the Little Red Book to the Big White one', *Times Literary Supplement*, https://www.the-tls.co.uk/articles/little-red-book-big-white-one/. Chinese reviews were more positive, however.
2. Ritu Raj Subedi, 'Xi's book is an intellectual bridge with Nepal', 31 January 2017. http://www.china.org.cn/opinion/2017-01/31/content_40179128.htm.
3. Editorial Committee (Trans. Saurav Dhakal, Saroj Dhakal, Anup Timilsina), *Chiniya Soch ra Sanskritika Pramukh Awadhaarnaharu-4* (Key Concepts

in Chinese Thought and Culture—4), Foreign Language Teaching and Research Press, Current Publications Pvt. Ltd, Bhaktapur, 2018.
4. People's Daily Commentary Department (Trans. Dr. Pradeep K.C.), *Xi Jinpingle Sunayeka Kathaharu: Yuwa Sanskaran* (Stories told by Xi Jinping: Youth edition), Current Publications Pvt. Ltd, Bhaktapur, 2019.
5. People's Daily Commentary Department (Trans. Luo, J.), *Narrating China's Governance: Stories in Xi Jinping's Speeches*, Springer, Singapore, 2020. https://www.springer.com/gp/book/9789813291775.
6. Ibid., p. 120.
7. Ibid., pp. 134–135.
8. Kunda Dixit, 'Pokhara: Nepal's New Aviation Gateway', *Nepali Times*, 21 December 2019. https://www.nepalitimes.com/banner/pokhara-nepals-new-aviation-gateway/.
9. Disclosure: my father, Ananda Raj Mulmi, is among those who have lobbied for an international airport in Pokhara.
10. Sangam Prasain, 'Pokhara's new international airport to be equipped with wide area multilateration', *Kathmandu Post*, 23 December 2019. https://kathmandupost.com/29/2019/11/15/pokhara-s-new-international-airport-to-be-equipped-with-wide-area-multilateration. 'As per the agreement, 25 per cent of the loan from China EXIM Bank is interest-free. Interest on the rest of the loan has been fixed at 2 per cent per annum. The loan repayment period has been fixed at twenty years, including a grace period of seven years when no interest will be charged. The government will bear any risk from fluctuations in the foreign exchange rate.'
11. Also see Josie Wang, 'Chinese Farmer Strikes Roots in Nepal', *Nepali Times*, 10 January 2020. https://www.nepalitimes.com/here-now/chinese-farmer-strikes-roots-in-nepal/.
12. 'Nepal expects more Chinese investment in infrastructure to boost development', *Global Times*, 24 December 2018. http://www.globaltimes.cn/content/1133460.shtml. In August 2020, a Sichuan-based metallurgical laboratory declared the commercial viability of iron mines in Dhaubadi, western Nepal. The mine is currently owned by a state enterprise.
13. Department of Industry, Nepal Industrial Statistics 2019–20. https://drive.google.com/file/d/1b93dI7XXn765K-PpeQsWfcF4yjOaYspN/view.
14. Yubaraj Ghimire, 'China Eyes Exit, Nepali's West Seti Hydroproject in Jeopardy', *South China Morning Post*, 30 August 2018. https://www.scmp.com/week-asia/geopolitics/article/2161968/nepals-west-seti-hydropower-project-jeopardy-china-eyes-exit. One report suggested Three Gorges pulled out because its Nepali agent asked for a 20 per cent stake in the project. See https://kathmandupost.com/national/2020/08/25/implementation-of-projects-under-investment-board-is-drawn-out-process.
15. Agrawal told me the NEA would build the transmission line by 2019 at the latest. However, the line had not been completed by December 2020.
16. Prahlad Rijal and Harihar Singh Rathore, 'Investment Board says Huaxin Cement Narayani's investment not under threat', *The Kathmandu Post*, 23

July 2019. https://kathmandupost.com/money/2019/07/23/investment-board-says-huaxin-cement-narayani-s-investment-not-under-threat. The plant will now start production from February-March 2021.
17. 1 *kattha* equals 3,645 sq. ft.
18. The variable component is a common feature among Chinese companies. See https://www.china-briefing.com/news/salary-structuring-and-payment-of-employees-in-china/.
19. Krishna Rijal, '16 Barsa dekhi rokiyeko Dang Cement Chin kai thulo Hongshi Cement le aghi badhaune, sadhe 32 arab lagani' ('China's large manufacturer Hongshi cement to take forward Dang Cement project halted for 16 years, NPR 32.5 billion investment'), Naya Patrika, 17 Asar 2077, 1 July 2020. https://nayapatrikadaily.com/news-details/46482/2020-07-02.
20. Galen Murton and Nadine Plachta, 'China in Nepal: On the Politics of Belt and Road Initiative Development in South Asia', BRI Handbook (to be published 2021). https://www.academia.edu/44552671/China_in_Nepal_On_the_Politics_of_Belt_and_Road_Initiative_Development_in_South_Asia.
21. Ibid.
22. Anil Giri and Sanjeev Satgainya, 'Nepal Conducts an Independent Foreign Policy but Does Not Mean We Want to Remain in Isolation', *Kathmandu Post*, 25 February 2019. https://kathmandupost.com/interviews/2019/02/25/nepal-conducts-an-independent-foreign-policy-but-this-does-not-mean-we-want-to-remain-in-isolation-foreign-minister-pradeep-gyawali and https://www.nepalitimes.com/here-now/nepal-is-now-seen-and-heard/.
23. Pradumna B. Rana, Chia Wai-mun and Ji Xianbai, 'China's Belt and Road Initiative: A Perception Survey of Asian Opinion Leaders', S. Rajaratnam School of International Studies, Singapore, 25 November 2019. https://www.rsis.edu.sg/wp-content/uploads/2019/11/WP325.pdf.
24. Pew Research Center, 'China's Economic Growth Mostly Welcomed in Emerging Markets, but Neighbors Wary of Its Influence', December 2019. https://www.pewresearch.org/global/wp-content/uploads/sites/2/2019/12/PG_2019.12.05_Balance-of-Power_FINAL.pdf.
25. 'Nepalese Economy to Gain Significantly from Strong Chinese Investment', Fitch Solutions, 28 November 2019. https://www.fitchsolutions.com/country-risk-sovereigns/economics/nepalese-economy-gain-significantly-strong-chinese-investment-28-11-2019.
26. Department of Industry, Ministry of Industry, Commerce and Supplies, Industrial Statistics, Fiscal year 2076/77 (2019–20). https://drive.google.com/file/d/1b93dI7XXn765K-PpeQsWfcF4yjOaYspN/view.
27. Purushottam Poudel, 'An interview with Chinese ambassador to Nepal Hou Yanqi', *Annapurna Express*, 30 August 2020. https://theannapurnaexpress.com/news/an-interview-with-chinese-ambassador-hou-yanqi-2751.
28. Interview with Chinese ambassador, 'China wants trilateral ties involving India also for Nepal's development: Hou Yanqi', *Online Khabar*, 10

November 2020. https://english.onlinekhabar.com/china-wants-trilateralties-involving-india-also-for-nepals-development-ambassador-hou.html. In FY 2018–19, Nepal exported goods to China worth NPR 2.1 billion, while importing goods worth NPR 205 billion, resulting in a negative trade balance of NPR 203.4 billion. See 'Nepal Foreign Trade Statistics FY 2075-76 (2018/19)', Trade and Exports Promotion Centre. http://www.tepc.gov.np/tepc_pub/Nepal%20%20Foreign%20Trade%20Statistics%202075_76.pdf.

29. 'Nepal lai 55 model ka bijuli bus bechna 41 aapurtikarta tayaar' ('41 importers ready to sell 55 models of electric buses to Nepal'), *Online Khabar*, 1 Ashwin 2077, 17 September 2020. https://www.onlinekhabar.com/2020/09/897056.

30. Sangam Prasain, 'Fed up of losses, Nepal Airlines comes up with options to get rid of six Chinese aircraft', *The Kathmandu Post*, 1 December 2020. https://kathmandupost.com/national/2020/12/01/fed-up-of-losses-nepal-airlines-comes-up-with-options-to-get-rid-of-six-chinese-aircraft.

31. Krishana Prasain, 'Quality watchdog cites 13 cement and steel factories for violations', *The Kathmandu Post*, 7 February 2020. https://kathmandupost.com/money/2020/02/07/quality-watchdog-cites-13-cement-and-steel-factories-for-violations.

32. Yogesh Dhakal, 'Chiniya khelanchi ka 17 drishtant' ('17 examples of Chinese frivolity'), *Nepal* magazine, 10 Baisakh 2076 issue, 23 April 2019. https://nepalmag.com.np/miscellaneous/2019/04/23/20190423124139. (Translation mine).

33. 'Urja mantri le rajdoot lai sodhe: "Chiniya company le Nepal ma kina dhilo kaam garcha?"' ('Energy minister asks ambassador: "Why are Chinese companies slow in Nepal?"'), *Kantipur*, 10 Asar 2076, 25 June 2019. https://ekantipur.com/news/2019/06/25/1561464897555623.html.

34. Official statistics on work permits issued for non-Nepalis between 2017 and 2020, Department of Labour and Occupational Safety, Ministry of Labour, Employment and Social Security. https://dol.gov.np/en/site/workpermit?type=all.

35. Bibek Subedi, 'China's Design Plan Delays Ring Road Phase Two Project', *Kathmandu Post*, 31 January 2019. https://kathmandupost.com/valley/2019/01/31/chinas-design-plan-delays-ring-road-phase-two-project. The project is being executed by Shanghai Construction Group, a state enterprise.

36. Interview with Chinese ambassador Hou Yanqi, Online Khabar, 10 November 2020.

37. See Sujeev Shakya's *Unleashing the Vajra* (Penguin Random House, New Delhi, 2019) for an explainer on Nepal's private sector.

38. The current chairman of the body refused to speak to me, as did the previous chairman.

39. Rupak D. Sharma, 'Use of Chinese wallets banned in Nepal', *The Himalayan Times*, 21 May 2019. https://thehimalayantimes.com/business/use-of-chinese-digital-wallets-banned-in-nepal/.

10. All Roads Lead North

1. Sangam Prasain, 'Fall in Arrivals by Aid During Peak Tourist Season Does Not Bode Well for Visit Nepal 2020', *Kathmandu Post*, 27 December 2019. https://kathmandupost.com/money/2019/12/27/fall-in-arrivals-by-air-during-peak-tourist-season-does-not-bode-well-for-visit-nepal-2020.
2. Department of Industry, Ministry of Industry, Commerce and Supplies, Industrial Statistics, Fiscal year 2076/77 (2019–20). https://drive.google.com/file/d/1b93dI7XXn765K-PpeQsWfcF4yjOaYspN/view. Hotels and restaurants are classified under 'Tourism' under Nepali industry laws.
3. Department of Industry, Ministry of Industry, Commerce and Supplies, Industrial Statistics, Fiscal year 2075/76 (2018–19). Available here: https://drive.google.com/file/d/12qWtJWscgFyB38nejCX10Oj2n3Y9NvKV/view.
4. 'FDI pledges from China in Nepal's tourism sector amounts Rs 5.35 billion in the first two months of the current fiscal year', *Republica*, 24 September 2020. https://myrepublica.nagariknetwork.com/news/fdi-pledges-from-china-in-nepal-s-tourism-sector-amounts-rs-2-50-billion-in-the-first-two-months-of-the-current-fiscal-year/.
5. B. Linder, '"This Looks Like Chinatown!": Contested Geographies and the Transformation of Social Space in Jyatha', Kathmandu: *City & Society*, 31, 2019, pp. 164–187. https://www.researchgate.net/publication/334006923_This_Looks_Like_Chinatown_Contested_Geographies_and_the_Transformation_of_Social_Space_in_Jyatha_Kathmandu_This_Looks_Like_Chinatown.
6. Ibid.
7. Rabi Thapa, *Thamel: Dark Star of Kathmandu*, New Delhi: Speaking Tiger Books, 2016, p. 42.
8. Zigor Aldama, 'How Chinese Tourists are Changing the World', *Post Magazine*, 1 October 2017. https://www.scmp.com/magazines/post-magazine/long-reads/article/2113116/how-chinese-tourists-are-changing-world.
9. World Tourism Organization, 'Guidelines for the Success in the Chinese Outbound Tourism Market', UNWTO, Madrid, 2019. https://doi.org/10.18111/9789284421138.
10. 'China's High Spending Tourists Bring Political Clout', *Economist*, 23 February 2019. https://www.economist.com/china/2019/02/23/chinas-high-spending-tourists-bring-political-clout.
11. Huang Ge and Li Xuanmin, 'China-Nepal Economic Relations Enter Fruitful Year', *Global Times*, 5 January 2020. http://www.globaltimes.cn/content/1175764.shtml.
12. 'China's High Spending Tourists Bring Political Clout', *Economist*.
13. World Tourism Organization, 'Guidelines for the Success in the Chinese Outbound Tourism Market'.
14. Qi Xiija, 'Tourists Return to South Korea as Relations Warm Up', *Global Times*, 24 December 2019. http://www.globaltimes.cn/content/1174684.shtml. For more on the China–South Korea tensions, see https://foreignpolicy.

15. World Tourism Organization, 'Guidelines for the Success in the Chinese Outbound Tourism Market'.
16. Ibid.
17. Louise Twining-Ward and Jessie F. McComb, 'COVID-19 and Tourism in South Asia : Opportunities for Sustainable Regional Outcomes', World Bank brief, June 2020. https://openknowledge.worldbank.org/handle/10986/34050.
18. Sangam Prasain, '2020 was the worst year for tourism since 1986', *The Kathmandu Post*, 3 January 2021. https://kathmandupost.com/money/2021/01/03/2020-was-the-worst-year-in-terms-of-tourist-arrivals-in-the-country-since-1986.
19. Padmasambhava's biography in Nepal is based upon readings from Nekhor, the Treasury of Lives, and the Lotsawa House online repositories. All translations of 'Barché Lamsel, the Prayer that Removes All Obstacles on the Path', from https://www.lotsawahouse.org/tibetan-masters/chokgyur-dechen-lingpa/barche-lamsel.
20. Pralad Rijal, 'Bodhichitta Biz Booms Amid Rising Demand', *Kathmandu Post*, 24 July 2016. https://kathmandupost.com/money/2016/07/24/bodhichitta-biz-booms-amid-rising-demand.
21. F. Li, J. Li, B. Liu, J. Zhuo and C. Long, 'Seeds used for Bodhi beads in China', *Journal of Ethnobiology and Ethnomedicine* 10, No. 15, 2014. https://doi.org/10.1186/1746-4269-10-15.
22. Ananth Krishnan and Prashant Jha, 'Chinese Foundation Plans $3 Billion Project in Nepal', *The Hindu*, 17 July 2011. https://www.thehindu.com/news/international/chinese-foundation-plans-3-billion-project-in-nepal/article2233492.ece.
23. Ding Gang, 'Buddha's Birthplace Hints at Asian Century', *Global Times*, 27 November 2019. https://www.globaltimes.cn/content/1171403.shtml.
24. Constantino Xavier, Aakshi Chaba and Geetika Dang, 'Is India Still the Neighbourhood's Education Hub?', Brookings India Policy Brief, 032020-02, March 2020, Brookings Institution India Center. https://www.brookings.edu/wp-content/uploads/2020/03/Is-India-still-the-neighbourhood%E2%80%99s-education-hub-1.pdf.
25. 'Over 100 Nepali students to study in China under government scholarship', Xinhua, 28 August 2019. http://www.xinhuanet.com/english/2019-08/28/c_138343188.htm.
26. Abha Lal, 'Ni Hao, Nepal', *Record Nepal*, 19 September 2019. https://www.recordnepal.com/wire/features/ni-hao-nepal/. Also see https://thehimalayantimes.com/nepal/mandarin-made-mandatory-in-many-schools/.
27. 'Silk Rhodes: Why is China lavishing money on foreign students', *Economist*, 26 January 2019. https://www.economist.com/china/2019/01/26/why-china-is-lavishing-money-on-foreign-students.
28. Yu Jincui, 'China should continue to enroll more foreign students', *Global Times*, 14 July 2019. https://www.globaltimes.cn/content/1157835.shtml.

Epilogue: Future Tense

1. Odd Arne Westad, 'The Sources of Chinese Conduct: Are Washington and Beijing Fighting a New Cold War?', *Foreign Affairs*, September/ October 2019. https://www.foreignaffairs.com/articles/china/2019-08-12/sources-chinese-conduct.
2. 'Foreign Ministry Spokesperson Zhao Lijian's Regular Press Conference on December 9, 2020', Ministry of Foreign Affairs of the People's Republic of China. https://www.fmprc.gov.cn/mfa_eng/xwfw_665399/s2510_665401/2511_665403/t1838915.shtml.
3. Jagannath P. Panda, 'The Trans-Himalayan Quad, Beijing's Territorialism, and India', *China Brief*, vol. 20, Issue 20, Jamestown Foundation. https://jamestown.org/program/the-trans-himalayan-quad-beijings-territorialism-and-india/.
4. 'Wang Yi on the Five-point Important Consensus Reached at the Video Conference of Foreign Ministers of China, Afghanistan, Pakistan and Nepal on COVID-19', China's Ministry of Foreign Affairs, 27 July 2020. https://www.fmprc.gov.cn/mfa_eng/zxxx_662805/t1801954.shtml. The October conference's official statement can be found here: http://lk.china-embassy.org/eng/xwdt/t1831592.htm.
5. Nadège Rolland, 'China's Vision for a New World Order', National Bureau of Asian Research, Special Report No. 83, January 2020. https://www.nbr.org/wp-content/uploads/pdfs/publications/sr83_chinasvision_jan2020.pdf.
6. Ibid., p. 7.
7. Emily Yeh, *Taming Tibet: Landscape Transformation and the Gift of Chinese Development*, p. 14, Cornell University Press, Ithaca and London, 2013.
8. Galen Murton, Austin Lord and Robert Beazley, 'A handshake across the Himalayas: Chinese investment, hydropower development, and state formation in Nepal, Eurasian Geography and Economics', 2016, https://www.tandfonline.com/doi/full/10.1080/15387216.2016.1236349.
9. 'Full text of Xi's signed article on Nepali newspapers', Xinhua, 11 October 2019. http://www.xinhuanet.com/english/2019-10/11/c_138463745.htm. The irony here of chafing at India's 'big brother' attitude in South Asia must be noted.
10. 'China curtails overseas lending in face of geopolitical backlash', *Financial Times*, 8 December 2020. https://www.ft.com/content/1cb3e33b-e2c2-4743-ae41-d3fffffa4259.
11. Cissy Zhou, 'China debt: Beijing may cut belt and road lending due to domestic pressure, to ensure future of project', *South China Morning Post*, 24 November 2020. https://www.scmp.com/economy/china-economy/article/3111052/china-debt-beijing-may-cut-belt-and-road-lending-due-domestic.
12. International Campaign for Tibet, 'Congress passes key legislation supporting Tibetans' aspirations, rights', 21 December 2020. https://savetibet.org/congress-passes-key-legislation-supporting-tibetans-aspirations-rights/.

13. 'Xi says China to step up efforts to fight "splittism" in Tibet', Reuters, 29 August 2020. https://www.reuters.com/article/us-china-tibet/xi-says-china-to-step-up-efforts-to-fight-splittism-in-tibet-idUSKBN25P0E0.
14. Westad, 'The Sources of Chinese Conduct'.
15. Yan Xeotong, 'The Age of Uneasy Peace: Chinese Power in a Divided World', *Foreign Affairs*, January/ February 2019. https://www.foreignaffairs.com/articles/china/2018-12-11/age-uneasy-peace.

Bibliography

BOOKS

A.S. Bhasin (ed.), *Documents on Nepal's Relationship with India and China 1949-66*, Academic Books Ltd, New Delhi, 1970.

Abrahm Lustgarten, *China's Great Train: Beijing's Drive West and the Campaign to Remake Tibet*, Henry Holt and Company, New York, 2008.

Aditya Adhikari, *The Bullet and the Ballot Box: The Story of Nepal's Maoist Revolution*, Aleph Book Company, Delhi, 2014.

B.N. Mullik, *My Years with Nehru: The Chinese Betrayal*, Allied Publishers, Delhi, 1971.

B.P. Koirala (tr. Kanak Mani Dixit), *Atmabrittanta: Late Life Recollections*, Himal Books, Kathmandu, 2001.

Bappaditya Paul, *The First Naxal: An Authorised Biography of Kanu Sanyal*, Sage India, New Delhi, 2014.

Barry C. Bishop, *Karnali Under Stress: Livelihood Strategies and Seasonal Rhythms in a Changing Nepal Himalaya*, University of Chicago, Chicago, 1990.

Bertil Lintner, *China's India War: Collision Course on the Roof of the World*, Oxford University Press, New Delhi, 2017.

Bertil Lintner, *The Costliest Pearl: China's Struggle for Indian Ocean*, Context/Westland, Chennai, 2019.

Bhikkhu Amritananda, *Buddhist Activities in Socialist Countries*, New World Press, Peking, 1961.

Bishnu Rijal (ed.), *Nepal ko Kootnitik Abyaas* ('Nepal's Diplomatic Efforts'), Institute for Foreign Affairs, Kathmandu, 2019.

Bruno Macaes, *Belt and Road: A Chinese World Order*, Viking, Delhi, 2019.

Buddhi Narayan Shrestha, *Border Management of Nepal*, Bhumichitra, Kathmandu, 2003.

Carole McGranahan, *Arrested Histories: Tibet, the CIA, and Memories of a Forgotten War*, Duke University Press Books, Durham, 2010.

Charles Bell, *The People of Tibet*, Motilal Banarasidass Publishers, New Delhi, 1994.

Bibliography

Charles Bell, *Tibet: Past and Present*, Clarendon Press, Oxford, 1924.

Chittadhar 'Hridaya' (tr. Kesar Lall), *Letter from a Lhasa Merchant to His Wife* (Originally published in Nepal bhasa as *Mimanah Pau* ['The Unburnt Letter']), Robin Books, New Delhi, 2002.

Christoph von Furer-Haimendorf, *Himalayan Traders*, St. Martin's Press, New York, 1975.

Clements R. Markham, *Narratives of the Mission of George Bogle to Tibet and of the Journey of Thomas Manning to Lhasa*, Trubner and Co, London, 1879.

Colonel William Kirkpatrick, *An Account of the Kingdom of Nepaul: Being the substance of observations made during a mission to that country in the year 1793*, first edition 1811, Manjusri Publishing House, Delhi, 1969.

Corneille Jest, *Monuments of Northern Nepal*, UNESCO, 1981.

D.R. Regmi, *Ancient Nepal*, K.L. Mukhopadhyay, Calcutta, 1960.

D.S. Kansakar Hilker's *Syamukapu: The Lhasa Newars of Kathmandu and Kalimpong*, Vajra Books, Kathmandu, 2005.

David G. Atwill, *Islamic Shangri-La: Inter-Asian Relations and Lhasa's Muslim Communities, 1600 to 1960*, University of California Press, Oakland, California, 2018.

David N. Gellner & Declan Quigley (eds.), *Contested Hierarchies: A Collaborative Ethnography of Caste Among the Newars of the Kathmandu Valley, Nepal*, Oxford University Press, Delhi, 2003.

Deepak Thapa and Bandana Sijapati, *A Kingdom under Siege: Nepal's Maoist Insurgency, 1996 to 2004*, Himal Books, Kathmandu, 2004.

Dharma Ratna Yami (tr. D.B. Gurung), *Reply from Tibet*, Vajra Books, Kathmandu, 2018.

Dor Bahadur Bista, *Report from Lhasa*, Sajha Prakashan, Kathmandu, 1979.

Emily T. Yeh, *Taming Tibet: Landscape Transformation and the Gift of Chinese Development*, Cornell University Press, Ithaca and London, 2013.

Eugene Bramer Mihaly, *Foreign Aid and Politics in Nepal: A Case Study*, Oxford University Press, New York, 1965.

Evan Osnos, *Age of Ambition: Chasing Fortune, Truth, and Faith in the New China*, Farrar, Strous and Giroux, New York, 2014.

Ezra F. Vogel, *Deng Xiaoping and the Transformation of China*, Harvard University Press, Cambridge, MA, 2013.

Filippo de Filippi (ed.), *An Account of Tibet: The Travels of Ippolito Desideri, S.J. (1712-1727)*, George Routledge & Sons, London, 1937.

Fr. Ludwig Stiller, *The Rise of the House of Gorkha: A Study in the Unification of Nepal 1768-1816*, Patan Jesuit Society, Kathmandu, 1975.

Fr. Ludwig Stiller, *The Silent Cry: The People of Nepal, 1816-1839*, Sahayogi Prakashan, Kathmandu, 1976.

Galen Murton, *Border Corridors: Mobility, Containment, and Infrastructures of Development between Nepal and China*, Dissertation, University of Colorado, Boulder, 2017.

George Patterson, *God's Fool*, Faber and Faber, London, 1956.

Greg C. Bruno, *Blessings from Beijing: Inside China's War on Tibet in Exile*, Speaking Tiger Books, Delhi, 2019.

Heinrich Harrer, *Seven Years in Tibet*, Rupert Hart-Davies, London, 1953.

Human Rights Watch, *Under China's Shadow: Mistreatment of Tibetans in Nepal*, 2014.

Ian Johnson, *The Souls of China: The Return of Religion after Mao*, Pantheon, New York, 2017.

International Campaign for Tibet, *Dangerous Crossing: Conditions Impacting the Flight of Tibetan Refugees*, 2011 update, 2012.

J.W. Garver, *China's Quest: The History of the Foreign Relations of the People's Republic of China*, Oxford University Press, New York, 2016.

J.W. Garver, *Protracted Contest: Sino-Indian Rivalry in the Twentieth Century*, University of Washington Press, Seattle, London, 2001.

James C. Scott, *The Art of Not Being Governed: An Anarchist History of Upland Southeast Asia*, Yale University Press, New Haven, 2010.

James F. Fisher, *Trans-Himalayan Traders: Economy, Society & Culture in Northwest Nepal*, University of California Press, Berkeley, 1986.

John Keay, *China: A History*, Harper Press, London, 2009.

John Kenneth Knaus, *Orphans of the Cold War: America and the Tibetan Struggle for Survival*, PublicAffairs, Perseus Books Group, New York, 1999.

Julia Lovell, *Maoism: A Global History*, The Bodley Head, London, 2019.

Julia Lovell, *The Opium War: Drugs, Dreams and The Making of China*, Picador, London, 2011.

Kamal Ratna Tuladhar, *Caravan to Lhasa: A Merchant of Kathmandu in Traditional Tibet*, Lijala & Tisa, Kathmandu, 2011.

Kanchanmoy Mojumbdar, *Political Relations between India and Nepal, 1877–1923*, Munshiram Manoharlal, New Delhi, 1973.

Kenneth Conboy and James Morrison, *The CIA's Secret War in Tibet*, University Press of Kansas, Kansas, 2002.

Kesar Lall, *The Newar Merchants in Lhasa*, Ratna Pustak Bhandar, Kathmandu, 2001.

Laxmi Prasad Devkota, *Muna Madan*, Sajha Prakashan, Lalitpur, 2009.

Leo E. Rose, *Nepal: Strategy for Survival*, Center for South and Southeast Asia Studies, University of California Press, Berkeley, California, 1971.

Ludwig F. Stiller, *Nepal: Growth of a Nation*, Human Resources Development Research Center, Kathmandu, 1993.

M. Taylor Fravel, *Strong Borders, Secure Nation: Cooperation and Conflict in China's Territorial Disputes*, Course Book ed. Princeton University Press, Princeton, 2008.

Ma Jian, *Red Dust: A Path Through China*, Vintage, London, 2006.

Maharajakrishna Rasgotra, *A Life in Diplomacy*, Viking, New Delhi, 2016.

Mahesh Chandra Regmi, *An Economic History of Nepal 1846-1901*, Nath Publishing House, Varanasi, 1988.

Manjushree Thapa, *Mustang Bhot in Fragments*, Himal Books, Kathmandu, 2008 (3rd edition).

Martin Saxer, Juan Zhang (eds.), *The Art of Neighbouring: Making Relations Across China's Borders*, Amsterdam University Press, 2017.

Mary Shepherd Slusser, *Nepal Mandala: A Cultural Study of the Kathmandu Valley*, 2 vols., Princeton University Press, Princeton, New Jersey, 1982.

Matthew W. Mosca, *From Frontier Policy to Foreign Policy: The Question of India and the Transformation of Geopolitics in Qing China*, Stanford University Press, Stanford, 2013.

Melvyn Goldstein, *A History of Modern Tibet, Volume 4: In the Eye of the Storm 1957-1959*, University of California Press, Oakland, California, 2019.

Michael Hutt, *Himalayan Voices: An Introduction to Modern Nepali Literature*, Indian Book Company, Dehradun, 1993.

Michel Peissel, *Mustang: A Lost Tibetan Kingdom*, Futura, London, 1979.

Mikel Dunham, *Buddha's Warriors: The Story of the CIA-Backed Tibetan Freedom Fighters, the Chinese Communist Invasion, and the Ultimate Fall of Tibet*, Tarcher Perigee, Penguin Publishing Group, New York, 2004.

Min Bahadur Shakya, *Princess Bhrikuti Devi: The Life and Contributions of the Nepali Princess to Tibetan History*, Book Faith India, Delhi, 1997.

Odd Arne Westad, *Restless Empire: China and the World Since 1750*, Vintage Books, London, 2013.

Odd Arne Westad, *The Global Cold War: Third World Interventions and the Making of Our Times*, Cambridge University Press, Cambridge, 2005.

Patrick French, *Younghusband: The Last Great Imperial Adventurer*, HarperCollins, London, 2004.

Perceval Landon, *Nepal*, 2 vols., Constable, London, 1928.

Peter Hessler, *Country Driving: A Chinese Road Trip*, Harper Perennial, New York, 2011.

Peter Hessler, *Oracle Bones: A Journey Through Time in China*, Harper Perennial, New York, 2007.

Prashant Jha, *Battles of the New Republic: A Contemporary History of Nepal*, Aleph Book Company, Delhi, 2013.

Prem R. Uprety, *Nepal-Tibet Relations 1850-1930: Years of Hopes, Challenges and Frustrations*, Ratna Pustak Bhandar, Kathmandu, 1998.

Prem Singh Basnyat, *Nepal-China: Vaad-vivaad ra Samvaad ('Nepal-China: Discords and Dialogues')*, Brother Books, Kathmandu, 2017.

R. Dhanalaxmi, *British Attitude to Nepal's Relations with Tibet and China (1814-1914)*, Bahri Publications, Chandigarh and New Delhi, 1981.

R.K. Jain (ed.), *China-South Asian relations 1947-1980*, vol. 2, Humanities Press Inc., New Jersey, 1981 (New Delhi edition).

Rabi Thapa, *Thamel: Dark Star of Kathmandu*, Speaking Tiger Books, Delhi, 2016.

Ramesh Dhungel, *The Kingdom of Lo (Mustang): A Historical Study*, Tashi Gaphel Foundation, Kathmandu, 2002.

Ramesh Nath Pande, *Kootniti ra Raajniti* ('Diplomacy and Politics'), Sangrila Books, Kathmandu, 2018.

Sam Cowan, *Essays on Nepal: Past and Present*, Himal Books, Kathmandu, 2018.

Sam Van Schaik, *Tibet: A History*, Yale University Press, London and New York, 2011.

Samuel Turner, *An Account of an Embassy to the Court of the Teshoo Lama in Tibet, containing a Narrative of a Journey through Bootan and part of Tibet*, W. Bulmer & Co, London, 1800.

Sanjay Upadhya, *Nepal and the Geo-Strategic Rivalry between China and India*, Routledge Books, London (special Nepal edition), 2012.

Satya Mohan Joshi, *Kalakar Arniko: The Well-Known Nepali Architect*, Vijay Gajanand Vaidya, Kathmandu, 1982.

Schuyler V. Cammann, *Trade through the Himalayas: The Early British Attempts to Open Tibet*, Princeton University Press, Princeton, 1951.

Selected Works of Jawaharlal Nehru (ed. various), 80 volumes, Ministry of Culture, India.

Sheldon Pollock, Benjamin Elman (eds.), *What China and India Once Were: The Pasts That May Shape Global Future*, Viking, New Delhi, 2018.

Shree Bhakta Khanal, *Apthyaro Baato: Tibbati Sharanarthi ko Sangharsha Katha ('A Difficult Road: The Struggles of Tibetan Refugees')*, Sangrila Books, Kathmandu, 2017.

Siegfried Lienhard, *Songs of Nepal: An Anthology of Nevar Folksongs and Hymns*, Centre for Asian and Pacific Studies, University of Hawaii Press, Hawaii, 1974.

Sudheer Sharma, *Prayogshala: Nepali Sankraman ma Dilli, Durbar ra Maobadi* ('Laboratory: Delhi, the Royal Palace and the Maoists in Nepal's Conflict'), Fineprint Books, Kathmandu, 2013.

Sulmaan Wasif Khan, *Haunted By Chaos: China's Grand Strategy from Mao Zedong to Xi Jinping*, Harvard University Press, Cambridge, MA, 2018.

Sulmaan Wasif Khan, *Muslim, Trader, Nomad, Spy: China's Cold War and the People of the Tibetan Borderlands*, The New Cold War History series, University of North Carolina Press, North Carolina, 2015.

Sylvain Levi (ed. Harihar Raj Joshi and Indu Joshi), *Nepal: A Notebook of Sojourn*, The Nepal Studies: Past and Present, Kathmandu, 2006.

Sylvain Levi (tr. S.P. Chatterjee), *The Mission of Wang Hiuen-Tse in India*, Indian Geographical Society, Calcutta, 1967.

T.R. Ghoble, *China-Nepal Relations and India*, Deep & Deep Publications, New Delhi, 1991.

Tenzin Dickie (ed.), *Old Demons New Deities: Contemporary Stories from Tibet*, Navayana, New Delhi, 2017.

Tibet Justice Center, *Tibet's Stateless Nationals: Tibetan Refugees in Nepal*, Berkeley, 2002.

Tina Harris, *Geographical Diversions: Tibetan Trade, Global Transactions*, University of Georgia Press, Athens, Georgia, 2013.

Todd Thornton Lewis, *The Tuladhars of Kathmandu: A Study of Buddhist Tradition in A Newar Merchant Community*, Dissertation, Columbia University, New York, 1984.

Tsepon D. Shakabpa, *Tibet: A Political History*, Yale University Press, New Haven and London, 1967.

Tsering Shakya, *The Dragon in the Land of Snows: A History of Modern Tibet since 1947*, Pimlico London, 1999.

Tsering Woeser (tr. Kevin Carrico), *Tibet on Fire: Self-Immolations Against Chinese Rule*, Verso Books, London, 2016.

Tsering Woeser and Wang Lixiong (ed. and tr. Violet S. Law), *Voices from Tibet: Selected Essays and Reportage*, Hong Kong University Press, Hong Kong, 2014.

V.K. Manandhar, *A Comprehensive History of Nepal-China Relations up to 1955*, 2 vols., Adroit Publishers, New Delhi, 2004.

V.K. Manandhar, *A Documentary History of Nepalese Quinquennial Missions to China 1792-1906*, Adroit Publishers, New Delhi, 2001.

Vikram Seth, *From Heaven Lake: Travels Through Sinkiang and Tibet*, Chatto & Windus, London, 1983.

Wang Hui, *China's Twentieth Century: Revolution, Retreat and the Road to Equality* (ed. Saul Thomas), Verso Books, London, 2016.

Wang Hui, *The End of the Revolution: China and the Limits of Modernity*, Verso Books, London, 2011.

Wang Lixiong and Tsering Shakya, *The Struggle for Tibet*, Verso Books, London, 2009.

Warren W. Smith (ed.) (tr. Min Ratna Bajracharya), *Mythological History of the Nepal Valley from Svayambhu Purana*, Avalok Publishers, Kathmandu, 1978.

Xiaoyuan Liu, *To the End of Revolution: The Chinese Communist Party and Tibet, 1949–1959*, Columbia University Press, New York, 2020.

Yu Hua (trans. Allan H. Barr), *China in Ten Words*, Anchor Books, New York, 2012.

JOURNALS

American Intelligence Journal
Ancient Nepal
Asian Survey
Contributions to Nepalese Studies
Economic and Political Weekly
European Bulletin of Himalayan Research
Himalaya
India Quarterly
Journal of Asian Studies
Kailash
Modern Asian Studies
Proceedings of Indian History Congress
Regmi Research Series
The China Quarterly
China News Analysis

ONLINE PORTALS, NEWSPAPERS AND MAGAZINES

Caixin
Caravan
China Neican
Economist
Foreign Affairs
Foreign Policy
Global Times
High Peaks Pure Earth
Himal Khabarpatrika
Himal Southasian
India Today
Kantipur
Los Angeles Review of Books: China Channel
Naya Patrika
Nepali Times
Nepal magazine
Online Khabar
Outlook
South China Morning Post
The Record

The Hindu
The Indian Express
The Kathmandu Post
The New York Times
The Wire
Times of India
Xinhua

ONLINE RESOURCES

Academia.edu
CIA declassified files
Jawaharlal Nehru Memorial Fund
Jstor
Pahar
Project MUSE
Researchgate
US State Department archives
Wikileaks
Wilson Center

Index

Acharya, Madhu Raman, 115
Acharya, Tanka Prasad, 123
Adhikari, Manmohan, 92
Adhikari, Rabindra, 177
Afghanistan, Soviet occupation of, 136
aid by Beijing to Nepal, increase in, 89–90, 128
Aksai Chin, 24, 91, 132
Amshuverman, xiii
Andropov, Yuri, 56
anti-Beijing Olympics protests in Kathmandu, 115
Armed Police Force (APF), 114
arms supply to Nepal by China in 1988, 138–139
Arniko Highway, 89–91, 92, 93, 95–96

Bahadur, Jung, xx, 10–11, 112, 121. *See also* Rana dynasty
Bandung Conference (1955), 85, 120
Bangladesh war (1971), 133
Basnyat, A.B., 20
Beijing international photo exhibition (2020), Nepal as theme country, 214–215
Beijing Olympics (2008), 114, 146, 150, 157
Bell, Charles, 11, 18
Belt and Road Initiative (BRI), xxi, 75–76, 163, 168, 188, 215, 218
  Nepal participation in, 184–185
Bhandari, Bidhya Devi, 166, 211
Bheri-Babai Diversion Multipurpose project, 187–188
Bhrikuti, xiv, 119

Bhutan, xviii, 10, 83
bikas (development), 77, 194
bilateral relationship between India and China, 95, 124
  India–China war of 1962, 24, 55, 87, 131–133, 152
  LAC, 220
  Panchsheel Agreement between India and China 1954, 85, 122–123
bilateral treaties of Tibet, abrogation of previous, 121
BIMSTEC military exercise (2018). *See under* Nepal
Bingde, Chen, 153
Bishwokarma, Ramesh (San-Dai), 192–196, 199–200
Bista, Dor Bahadur, 13–14
bodhichitta seed/trees, 201–203
bodhisattva Manjushri, xiv
border citizen cards, 36
Bouddha (the ancient stupa), xvi, 18, 203
Boundary Management System treaty, 154
BRICS, 163
Bright Red Star (Li Xintian), 93
British recognition of Nepal through 1923 treaty, xviii
Buddhabhadra, xxiv
Buddhism/Buddhists, xxv
  connection invoked by modern leaders, xiv
  geopolitical struggle over, 205–206, 208

Index

Kagyu school of Tibetan Buddhism, xvi
Nepali, xvi
population in China vs world, 204
revival in Tibet, 26
romanticism, 102
and Tibetan monks, xvi
Tibetan monks and Nepali traders, relationship between, xvi–xvii
Vajrayana, xiv, xvi
Budhi Gandaki project, 180
Burang, 27, 30, 33–34, 36, 38–41, 42, 58, 73
Burma. *See* Myanmar.

Calcutta–Lhasa trade route, 7–8
cement imports in Nepal, 182–183
Central Intelligence Agency (CIA), xxiii, 52–55, 84–85, 89, 94, 125, 127–128
  arsenal given to Tibetan Khampas, 100
  Project ST Circus, 102
  rehabilitation funds, 110
  switched off funds to Tibetan guerrillas, 220
  Tibetan guerrillas funded by, 78
  Tibetan resistance programme, 98
Central Tibetan Administration (CTA), 101, 103, 113, 117, 145–146
Chhosar village, 43, 50
China CAMC Engineering, 76, 176
China EXIM Bank, 176, 186, 218
China Gezhouba Group Corporation (CGGC), 180
China Great Western Development Strategy (*xibu da kaifa*), 36–37, 42, 141, 148, 152
  'Open up the West' campaign, 36–37, 141
China International Water and Electric Corporation, 69
China Liberation Day (1 October), 97
China-Pakistan Economic Corridor (CPEC), 215

China Radio International, 207
China Study Centre, Kathmandu, 149
China's Tibet-Nepal trade fair, 118, 174
Chinese communist entry, 93
Chinese Communist Party (CCP), xx, 47–48, 90, 92, 95–96, 205, 221
  International Liaison Department (ILD), 164–165, 168
Chinese missions, post Arniko, xvi
Chin Sachitra (China Pictorial), 93
Chushi Gangdruk, 8, 51–53, 102–107, 110, 137
Cold War, 78, 84, 102
Communist government in Nepal, China's preference for, 165–166
Communist Party of India (Marxist-Leninist), 96
communism in Nepal
  Communist Party of Nepal (CPN), 84, 94
  Communist Pachik Prachar Patra (Communist Fortnightly Bulletin), 84
  establishment in 1949, 84
  Communist Party of Nepal (Unified Marxist Leninist (UML)), 150, 158
  -Maoist coalition, 161
  Communist Party of Nepal (Maoist), 100
Comrade Rohit, 93
Confucius Institute, 206–207
Congyong, Wu, 147
construction sector, contribution to Nepal GDP, 181–182
COVID-19 pandemic, xxiii, 35, 72, 155, 167, 170–171, 187, 199, 211, 215–216
Cuban Missile Crisis (1962), 87
Cultural Revolution, xxv, 93, 95–96, 99, 105, 111, 133, 137

Dalai Lama, 2, 11, 27, 34, 46, 63, 65, 87, 107, 112, 115, 122, 140, 147, 152–153, 203, 205, 216, 219

Index

emissary arrived in Kathmandu in 1952, 121
escape from Lhasa in 1959, 102
Gyatso, Tenzin (14th Dalai Lama), 190–20
  urged to stop tiger and leopard skin robes, 42
debt-trap diplomacy of China, 185
Delhi Agreement (1950), 81–82, 84
Desideri, Ippolito, 6
Deuba, Sher Bahadur, 115, 163, 166, 180
Dev, Narendra, xv–xvi
Dharamsala, India, 47, 104
Dorje, Ogyen Trinley (known as the Karmapa), 47–48, 101–102, 117
  Karma Kagyu sect of Tibetan Buddhism, 47
  non-recognition as 17th Karmapa Lama by India government, 48
Drikung Kagyu sub-sect of Tibetan Buddhism, 26

earthquake in Nepal (2015), 59, 68–70, 73, 75, 159–161, 179, 181, 194, 199, 217
East India Company, xvii, 64
economic rise of China, 184
Enlai, Zhou, 54–55, 82, 85, 105, 122–124, 127
  east-west swap solution, 137
  mutual non-aggression pact with Nepal, 128
  visit to India in 1957, 132
environmental impact assessment (EIA), 183
Everest
  Base Camp, 151
  Chomolungma, 6, 216
  Mt. Everest, 126–127, 151–152, 174, 215–216
  Mt. Kailash, 27, 30, 39
  Mt. Qomolangma, 215

Felter, Joe, 168
Fenghe, Wei, 168–169

Ford, Gerald, 75, 134–135
foreign investor in Nepal, China as largest, 185–186
foreign policy failure of India, in Nepal, 147, 150–151, 153, 156–157, 158–172
Fürer-Haimendorf, von Christoph, 28–29, 36, 95, 225

Galwan Valley clash in Ladakh, 212
Gandhi, Indira, 98, 133–134
geopolitical ambitions of Beijing in South Asia, 75, 86–87, 91–92, 133–134, 137, 156–169, 172
Ghorasyar trading house, 4, 20–22, 23
Global Times, 163, 171
Golden Urn, 63
Goldstein, Melvyn, 28–29, 41
Gongsu, Yang, 97
Gorkha/Gorkhas, 221
  circulation of their own coins in Tibet, 10
  Gorkhali military expansionism in Nepal, 63–68
  Malla king wars with, 10
  Shahs, 58, xvi
  territorial expansion, 10
Gosains, 5, 10
Great Leap Forward, 74, 103
Guansan, Tan, 20
Gyalpo, 12
Gyangdrag monastery, 27
Gyatso, Thinley, 151
Gyawali, Pradeep, 167, 215
Gyirong–Kathmandu railway line, 76, 166
Gyirong town, xxiii, 33, 65, 68, 70–74

Hambantota Port deal, 168
Hien, Fa, xxiv
Hilsa border, 35, 38
  illicit wildlife trade in crossing of, 42
Himalayan borderlands, 22, 24, 29, 31–35, 42, 52, 55, 57

China's international development agency, financing by, 59
Nepali limited capacity in, 31
Hodgson, Brian, xii, xvi
Hongshi cement plant/Hongshi Shivam Cement, 174, 181–184, 187
Hridaya, Chittadhar, 6
Huaxin Cement Narayani, 183
huayuquan, 216–217
Humla/Humla community, 28, 35, 41, 57, 59
　border identity cards for resident of, 38
　Nepalis inflow in, 39
　UN agency World Food Programme in, 41

Indian National Army, 81
Indo-Pacific Strategy (IPS), 167
Indo-Soviet friendship treaty (1971), 133
infrastructure development in Nepal by China, xxi, 31, 68–69, 76–78, 176, 178, 180–181, 184, 188, 191, 209, 219
International Committee of the Red Cross, 109
Investment Board of Nepal (IBN), 183
investments by China in Nepal, 39, 59, 68–69, 115, 168, 171, 176, 178, 180–186, 188–190, 196, 209–210, 215, 218, 220

Jaishankar, S., 160–161
Jampaling Tibetan Settlement Camp, 101, 112, 119
Jelep La, 8
Jiabao, Wen, 153
Jiechi, Yang, 115
Jinping, Xi, xxiv, 72, 154, 163, 165, 170, 175–176, 198, 211, 216, 220
　consciousness of incorruption, 175
　Governance of China, The, 173–174
　improve people-to-people relationship, 206
　visit to Kathmandu, 166
Jintao, Hu, 151
Ji Waya, 14
Jomsom, 54, 60, 106–108
Joshi, Satya Mohan, xxv

Kagyu School of Tibetan Buddhism, xvi, 64
Kalanki underpass, 217
Kalapani territorial dispute, xii, 166, 218
Kali Gandaki corridor, 43, 46–47
Kalikasthan (earlier known as Dhaibung), 66, 77
Kalimpong, 7–8, 16
Kashmiri Muslim merchants, 5
Kathmandu–Kuti route in Himalayan range, 6
Kathmandu valley, xi, xvii, 4–5, 7, 10, 13, 28, 33, 35–36, 69, 96, 104, 108, 113–114, 118, 121–122, 132–133, 137, 163, 139, 147, 149, 151–152, 161–162, 212–214, 216–217, 221–222. *See also* Tibet
　battleground for world powers, 78
　current political establishment, 168
　customs duties imposed on articles, 5
　encompassing three-city states, 4
　goods arrival from China, 72
　policy of China, 95
　secret agreement with India on military equipment, 136
　trade missions by, 83
　views of Beijing under communists, 83–84
Kathmandu–Pokhara railway line, 76, 166
Kathmandu–Pokhara–Lumbini railway line, 166
Katuwal firing, 157
Kennedy, John F., 53
Kerung mountain pass (known as Gyirong), 5, 65, 67

Khanal, Jhalanath, 158
Khan, Kublai, xvi
King Birendra. *See under* Shah kings
  Zone of Peace proposal, 99, 135–136, 139
King Gyanendra. *See under* Shah kings
King Harshavardhana. *See under* Shah kings
King Langderma, xiv
King Mahendra. *See under* Shah kings
  bomb on motorcade in Janakpur, 130
King Prithvi Narayan Shah, 111, xvii
King Ran Bahadur. *See under* Shah kings
King Tribhuvan. *See under* Shah kings
King Yeshe, 26
Kirkpatrick, Colonel William, 63
Kissinger, Henry, 75, 108, 134
Kodari road project. *See* Arniko Highway
Koirala, B.P., 54–56, 81, 87, 89–91, 123–129, 172
Koirala, Girija Prasad, 152, 156
Koirala, Matrika Prasad, 122–123
Kora La border, 43, 48, 54, 61
  bilateral agreement of 2012, 50
  China on, 52
  geographical location of, 46–47
  represents restricted space, 50
Korean War, 103
  US entry into, 86
Kot Massacre, 84
Kunming Xinzhi Group, 173
Kuti mountain pass (known as Nyalam), 5, 65, 67

Landon, Perceval, 7
Lapcha Pass, 28–32, 35
  China agreed to open crossing of, 33
Lévi, Sylvain, xi–xiii, xvii
Lhasa, 3–5, 7, 89
  free-flowing trade, 22
  life in, 8
  uprising in 1959, 115, 126

Lhasa Consul General, 13–14
Lhasa Newars traders, xvii, 4–14, 16, 57
  issue of passports and visa by Chinese to, 24
    and Nepali traders to retain nationality and citizenship, 23
  PLA attack on, 20–21
  resident called nayo or vakil, 5
  romanticism of trade, 18–19
  Tibetan women, relationship with, 17
  Tibetan-Nepalis take Nepali citizenship after 1959, 18
  Urays caste, 17, 42
    alliances with Tibetan wives and lamas, 19
    etymology of surnames, 4
  wife/wives (Tibetan)
    called sem, 15
    China imposition of strict conditions on, 23
    second, 18
Lhasa River, 9
Lianyungang, 166
Licchavi dynasty, xiii–xiv
Limi valley, xxiii, 25, 60
  border identity cards, 38
  and China, 29–30, 40
  citizenship, 33, 34
  Darchula border use by, 33
  economic strategies employed by inhabitants, 41
  food shortage during Covid-19 pandemic, 35
  idea of belonging, 32
  maple-wood bowl/phuru trade, 39
  refuge for members of dissenting sects, 27
  slow pace of development from Nepali side, 34–35
  social sovereignty of community, 32
  solitary police post in, 31–33
  traders switched to modern consumer goods import, 37
  trade, 28–29

Index

Limi Valley Youth Club, 26
Lipu Lekh, 211–212, 217–218
Lo Manthang, 49–51, 58–60
Lord Cornwallis
 received missive from Dalai Lama, 62
Lord Curzon, xviii
Lovell, Julia, 93

Madhes movement, 159–161
Mahakali River, 64, 160
Mahara, Krishna Bahadur, 158
Mahindramalli, 10
Malinowski, Michael, 115, 147
Malla treaty, 10
Maoism, 89
McGranahan, Carole, 53, 131
McMahon Line, 131–32
Mehrotra, L.L., 134
Menon, V.K. Krishna, 82
Millennium Challenge Corporation (MCC), 167
Modi, Narendra, 163, 220
Mother, The (Maxim Gorky), 93
Muna Madan, 14
Murton, Galen, 48, 52, 217
Mustang region, 5, 43, 48, 50–53, 58, 104–108
 Beijing on India's advantage due to resistance, 56–57
 Chinese transgressions on, 53–56
 Chushi Gangdruk Tibetan armed resistance in, 101
 and earthquake in 2015, 59
 instruments of state authority, 60
 Mustang kings tasked to protect border with Tibet, 58
 Nepal-China economic linkage, 60
 primary location for Tibetan armed resistance, 53
 residents and Nepali mainland, difference between, 59
 susceptible to foreign intervention, 59–60
 and Tibetan armed resistance, 56
Mustang–Tibet border, Border citizenship at, 52
Mutual Legal Assistance treaty, 154
Myanmar policy of China, 81, 87, 95–96, 120, 128

Nangpa La, 116
 Khumbu region, American climbers shot down in, 116
Nathu La, 8, 21, 24
Naxalbari revolution/movement in India, 92–93, 96, 159–160
Nehru, Jawaharlal, xvii–xviii, 81–82, 87, 109, 123, 143, 214
 dream about South Asian subcontinent, 134
 foreign relations with Nepal, 122
 idealism on Indo-China relationship, 124
 ideal of Himalaya, 92
 on Indo-Tibetan frontier, 131–132
 interest to keep Nepal with India, 86–87, 122–125, 127–132, 214
Nepal
 agreement of 1950, 139
 aid mission of China in, 128
 and New Delhi, relationship between, 122, 132–133, 163
 and US, relationship between, 137
Nepal Army
 BIMSTEC military exercise (2018), 169
 China's aid package to, 169
 China's supply of weapons and ammunition to, 115–116
 Royal Nepal Army, 106, 115
Nepal–China Chamber of Commerce and Industry, 189
Nepal–China treaty on Tibet (1956), 13–14, 22
Nepal Communist Party (NCP), 163–165, 169, 180, 211–213
Nepal Congress (NC) party, xvii, 81–82, 84, 106, 125, 130, 133

Nepal Constituent Assembly (CA)
 first elections in 2008, 149–150, 156
 second elections in 2013, 162
Nepal–India agreement (1950), xviii
Nepali Maoists, 88, 93, 147–150, 156–157
Nepal, Madhav Kumar, 157, 164, 211
Nepal Survey Department, 216
Nixon, Richard, 98, 133
non-alignment, 168, 172, 218, 220
Norbulingka Palace, Lhasa, 19–20
Northern Region Border Development Programme, 59
nuclear test by India (May 1974), 134–135

Oli, Khadga Prasad Sharma, 75–76, 92–93, 159–166, 211–212, 220
 anti-Indian nationalism, 172
 dissolution of parliament in December 2020, 167, 213
One Belt One Road. *see* Belt and Road Initiative (BRI)
one-China policy, Nepal's support for, 118, 140, 155, 216
Opium Wars, xx, 64, 121, 175
outbound tourism from China, 194, 198–199

Pakistan-administered Kashmir, 91
Panchayat system of governance, 85, 138
Panchen Lama, 10, 63–64
Pande, Ramesh Nath, 155
Pant, Govind Ballabh, 82
Patan, xvii, 4, 10
Patterson, George, 103–104
Paudyal, Leela Mani, 115–116, 147–148
Peissel, Michel, 44, 52–53
Peng, Li, 140
People's Daily, 92, 96, 129, 205
People's Liberation Army (PLA), 20, 56, 102–103
 overran Indian positions in Arunachal Pradesh and Aksai Chin, 24
People's Republic of China (PRC), xxv, 8–9, 20, 57, 82–83, 86, 105, 120–121
 arrival in Himalayan plateau, 26
 established control over Tibet in 1951, 122
People's Revolution in Nepal (2006), 146, 148–149
Phādi (Phari or Pagri), 6–8
Pokhara, 46, 60–61, 75, 101, 104, 162, 176–179, 210
 international airport, 187–188, 190–191
 –Lumbini railway line, 76, 166
 –Naubise Highway (known as Prithvi Highway), 94–95, 101, 111
 Tibetan refugee camps in, 109
political map of Nepal, controversy over, 212
Pompeo, Mike, 167
post-Maoist conflict transition, xix
Prachanda (Pushpa Kamal Dahal), 148, 150–151, 157, 162–164, 211–213
Prasad, Subedar Bam, 54
Prithvi Chowk (Lakhan Thapa Chowk), 112
private Nepali schools, Chinese languages as mandatory subject in, 207

Qing dynasty/empire, 68, 83
 brokered treaty (1789), 62
 Emperor of China, 62–63
 forces entry into Tibet, 66
 political control over Tibet affairs, xx, 63
 reassertion of sovereignty, 11
Qing General Fuk'anggan, 64, 66–68
Qinghai-Tibet Railway (QTR), 37, 74–75

Rajiv Gandhi–Deng Xiaoping summit (December 1988), 138

Raksha Dal, 82
Raman, B., 47–48
Rana dynasty, xvii
　Shamsher, Chandra, 83, 221
　Shamsher, Dev, xi
　Shamsher, Mohan, 81
Rana, General Arjun, 136–137
Rana, Sachhit S.J.B., 106
Ranz, David J., 167
Rasgotra, M.K., 135–136
Rastriya Samachar Samiti, 155
Rasuwa, 68–71, 77–78, 217
　Rasuwagadhi, 67–69, 72, 74, 170
　Rasuwagadhi hydropower project, 77
　Rasuwagadhi-Kathmandu highway, 76
　Rasuwa-Gyirong border, 71
Ratnapura, 14
Rayamajhi, Keshar Jung, 92
Regmi, D.R., 123
Repentin, Thierry, 151
Research and Analysis Wing (R&AW), 157–158
Rinchenling monastery, 26
　era of fluid borders, 27
Roy, Bidhan Chandra, 129
rudraksha seeds, 203
Rumtek monastery, Sikkim, 47

SAARC, 147
Sagarmatha, 6, 126
Sakya, 6
San-Dai. *See* Bishwokarma, Ramesh (San-Dai)
Sanyal, Kanu, 96–97
Sapkota, Agni, 88–89, 93, 149–150, 156, 185
Seti Gandaki river, 101, 176
Shah kings
　Birendra, 58, 75, 135
　　Zone of Peace proposal, 99, 135–136, 139
　Gyanendra, 115, 147–148, 162
　Harshavardhana, xv
　Mahendra, 53–54, 88–92, 94–95, 105, 109, 124–125, 127, 133
　　bomb on motorcade in Janakpur, 130
　Prithvi Narayan Shah, xvii, 10–11, 64, 111, 133, 200–201
　Ran Bahadur, 2, 68
　Tribhuvan, xvii, 81–82, 123–124
Shakya, Tsering, 54, 102
Shamarpa Lama, 64, 68
Shangri-la, xx, 102
Shaohua, Xiang, 178–179
Shaoqi, Liu, 90, 121
Sharma, Sudheer, 115, 150, 152, 166, 169, 181
Shek, Chiang Kai, 63
Shenzhen, 166
Shigatse, xvi, 6, 64–65, 72, 82–83
Shigatse-Gyirong railway line, 74, 76
Shneiderman, Sara B., 36
Shrestha, Pushpa Lal
　elected as secretary, 92
　translated *Communist Manifesto* into Nepali, 84
Shringla, Harsh Vardhan, 166–167
Siddhartha Highway, 109–110
Sikkim, xviii, 7, 24, 65
　annexation in 1975, 134–135
Simhala/Simhalasarthabahu temple, 14, 20
Simla Convention (1914), 131
Singh, Kunwar Inderjit, 81–84, 86, 120
　communist credentials, 85
Singh, Manmohan, 152
Singh, Rajnath, 211
Sino-American friendship, 78
Sino-Soviet clashes, 98
Slusser, Mary, xiv, xvi
soft diplomacy approach of China, 118, 214
South Asia, China's foreign policy in, 75, 133–134, 158, 172
South Block, Delhi, 213
Soviet Union Illustrated, 93
Sri Lanka, 98, 134
　India's military intervention in, 138

Index

Stalin, 86
Swayambhu stupa, 204
Swiss Red Cross, 109

Tai, Hieun, xv
Taiping Rebellion, 64, 121
Tang dynasty, xv–xvi
Tarun Dal, 129
Tashilhunpo, 64–65, 68
Tatopani–Zhangmu border, 68, 71–73, 170
Terminal High Altitude Area Defense (THAAD) missile systems, 198
Thapa, Manoj, 149
Third World countries, 87–88
Third World solidarity, 85
Thondup, Gyalo, 106
Tibet, xi, xii, xiv, xvii, 5, 32–33, 36, 68–69, 71–72, 208, 217, 219–222.
  See also Kathmandu valley (Nepal)
  American relationship with, xxi–xxii
  British invasion of, 7
  as centre for Vajrayana Buddhism, xiv, xvi
  China's annexation in 1951, xx
  clashes between Chinese and Tibetan soldiers, 8
  entrepreneurs, 110
  food imports by western, 41
  Gorkhalis attacked, 62
  gravitated for Buddhist instruction, xiv
  Guge-Purang kingdom, 27
  Kathmandu war on Tibet in 1788, 65
  Nepal minted coins for, 10
  and Nepal, socio-political relationship between, 4–5
  and PRC, agreement on 1951, 8, 13
  Qing political control over, xx
  resistance guerrillas, 51
  rise in GDP, 37
  17-point agreement between China and, 120–121

Shangri-la, xx
treaties with Nepal, 86–87
Tibetan Autonomous Region, 37
Tibetan exiles in Nepal, 16, 40–41, 47, 53, 102–119, 140, 169, 215
  inability to get driving licence, 113–114, 118
  resettlement of refugees in US, Nepal rejection of US plan, 115
Tibetan–Nepali children and families, 19, 23–24
Tibetan resistance
  Nepali military operation in 1974, 104
Tibetan uprising of 1959, 19, 29
Tibet Fuli Construction Group Company Limited, 69
Tibet Justice Center report on Tibetan refugees, 111
Tibet–Nepal treaty (1856), 121–122
Tibet Policy and Support Act (TPSA) 2020, 219
Tibet Tinalu Company Ltd, 69
Tibet Work Committee, Lhasa, 20
Tinkar pass, 107
tourism-oriented economy of Nepal, 174, 193–199
trade war between US-China, 189, 209, 218
trans-Himalayan trade, 4–5
  decline of, 52
  infrastructural and colonial changes in, 6–7
  trade in Himalayan regions, 35–36
Trans-Himalayan Multi-Dimensional Connectivity Network, 184, 215
trans-Karakoram highway, 91
Trump, Donald, 167
Tsangpo River, 14
Tsering, Penpa, 145–146
Tsewang Lama, 33–34
Tsurphu monastery, 47
Tuladhars, 16, 20
Tuladhar, Kamal Ratna, 23–24
Tuladhar, Karuna Ratna, 21–22

Tuladhar, Pragya Ratna, 3–6, 8–9, 12, 18–21, 23
Tuladhar, Purna Man, 22
Tuladhar, Pushpa Ratna, 23

Udall, Tom, 146
Ukyab, Tamla, 17, 53, 105–107
United Nations (UN), 98, 126
　Convention Relating to the Status of Refugees (1951), 113
　High Commissioner for Refugees (UNHCR), 107–108, 113, 116
　Protocol Relating to the Status of Refugees (1967), 113
　World Tourism Organisation report on Chinese tourists, 199
Upadhyay, Surya Prasad, 53, 126
Up in the Wind Chinese film, 205
USAID, 109
US National Security Strategy 2017, 167
Ussuri River, 98

Vajpayee, Atal Behari, 137
Vajrayana, 4
Visit Nepal Year 2020 programme, 194, 198

Waltse village, 31, 40
　clash of cultures, 32
Wangdu, Gyato, 104
war between Nepal and Tibet
　first (1788-89), 64
　second (1792), 66
　Lord Cornwallis sent Colonel Kirkpatrick to mediate, 63
Westad, Odd Arne, 88
Western exoticisation, of Tibetan struggle, 102
World Bank, 199

Xiaoping, Deng, 99–100, 134–135, 137
Xinzhi Bookstore, Kathmandu, 173–175
Xuance, Wang, xv–xvi

Yadav, Ram Baran, 157
Yangpachen monastery, xvi
Yanqi, Hou, xxv, 168, 186, 189, 211–212, 214
yarsagumba, 200
Yat-Sen, Sun, 88
Yatung, 8
Yellow-Hat Gelugpas, 27
Yeshe, 26
Yeshi, Baba, 52, 104, 106
Yezhou, Guo, 168–169
Yi, Chen, 131
Yi, Wang, 215
Yongkang, Zhou, 153
Younghusband, 24
　Colonel Francis, 7, 221–222
　expedition, 64
Youth League, 129
youth scholarships for Nepali students, to study abroad, 206–207
Yuan, Qu, 143, 214

Zangpo, Rinchen, 26–27
Zedong, Mao, 83, 94, 100, 120, 126, 143, 151
　approaches to South Asia, 86
　brand of communism, 89
　China's claim over eastern Siberia, 87
　defeated Chiang Kai Shek Guomindang forces, 120
　economic programmes, 90
　little red book, 93
　quarrel with Soviets, 87
　Red Guards, 95
Zemin, Jiang, 140
　xibu da kaifa campaign, 141, 148, 152
Zhen, Yang, 175
Zili, Pan, 54

Acknowledgements

San-Dai's story was first published in a different version in Al Jazeera as 'In Kathmandu, the Nepalese Chef Making Authentic Sichuan Food'.

My *Kathmandu Post* columns have featured in shorter versions my views on the half-Tibetan children of Newar traders, Kanu Sanyal's clandestine China visit, Deng Xiaoping's Kathmandu visit, the modern Nepal–China border, the US–China contest in Nepal and the contemporary Nepal–China bilateral relationship. My views on China's influence in South Asia were featured in *Himal Southasian*. My ideas on developing Nepal's soft power potential through its history of Buddhist culture and crafts were published in more detail in the Institute for Foreign Affairs journal.

Travel to Humla was made possible by an ICIMOD grant.

Travel to Rasuwa was partly assisted by the Quixote's Cove's Book Bus programme.

No book such as this is possible without assistance. Across Nepal, various friends, acquaintances and fellow travellers helped me make sense of China in the country. My thanks to the many who I cannot name, and to those I can:

In Timal: Niranjan Shrestha, Nagendra Adhikari, Gyanzo Lama.

In Kathmandu: Balaram Adhikari, Aneka Rajbhandari, Sujeev Shakya, Satya Mohan Joshi, Prateebha Tuladhar, Kamal Ratna Tuladhar, Pragya Ratna Tuladhar, Agni Sapkota, Tamla Ukyab, Basanta Basnet, Akhilesh Upadhyay, Ajaya Bhadra Khanal, Sudheer Sharma, Ashok Gurung, Pramod Jaiswal, Anil Giri, Ramesh Bishwokarma (San-Dai), Vikas Agrawal, Singha Bahadur Shrestha, Nepal Bhushan Chand, Kamal Dev Bhattarai, Sworup Nhasiju, Aditya Adhikari, Mahendra Krishna Shrestha, Monica Shrestha, Mahima Shrestha, Prawin Adhikari, Nayan Sindhuliya, Avasna Pandey, Rabi Thapa, Peter Gill, Anju Joshi, Suman

Joshi, Anup Ojha, Austin Lord, Anagha Neelakantan, Gyanu Adhikari, Kabindra Dhakal, Prem Singh Basnyat, Raman Raut, Samrat Pandey, Nabin Pokharel, Rajesh Kaji Shrestha, Rupak Sapkota, Madhav Lal Shrestha, Sanjeev Satgainya, Vijay Kant Karna and the CESIF team, Bikas Rauniar.

In Humla: Amy Sellmyer, Maxim Shrestha, Neelima Vellangi, Tina Chen, Mangal Lama, Yonten Gyatso (Sagar) Lama, Tsewang (Chakka Bahadur) Lama, Bishnu Lama, Gyaltsen Lama, Yi Shaoliang, Jitendra Bajracharya, Janita Gurung and ICIMOD team.

In Rasuwa: Meghnath Ghimire 'Prabhakar', Kriti Adhikari and the Book Bus team.

In Mustang: Tul Bahadur Karki, Lotus Holiday Inn.

In Pokhara: Bishwa Palikhe, Krishna Chapagain, Pokhara Chamber of Commerce and Industry, Basu Tripathi, Xiang Shaohua (Sandesh).

Elsewhere: Shubhanga Pandey, Rohan Chhetri, Surabhi Pudasaini, Krish Raghav, Prakash Khanal, Suresh Neupane, Saif Khalid.

Gratitude to the Nehru Memorial Museum and Library in Delhi (and the India Ministry of Culture and Jawaharlal Nehru Memorial Fund's online collection of Nehru's letters), Martin Chautari in Kathmandu, the Digital Himalaya online collection of journals, WikiLeaks, the Wilson Center Digital Archive and the People's Association for Himalaya Area Research (Pahar) online database. In particular, the *Ancient Nepal* journal, the *Contributions to Nepali Studies* journal of the Centre for Nepal and Asian Studies, *Kailash* journal, the Regmi Research Series and *Purnima* are to be highlighted for their excellent work in Nepali historical studies. The *Nepali Times* online archive stands as an example to all Nepali news sites in its comprehensiveness. It needn't be said that there is a serious lack of historical studies in Nepal presently; Onta et al. have constantly argued for it. The assumption of history by Nepali nationalism has created a flawed template for all Nepalis inside or outside. This book is an attempt at a more measured reading of Nepal's history.

My travels in the Himalaya have been informed by the excellent works of Sara Shneiderman, Emily Yeh, Tina Harris, Martin Saxer, Dor Bahadur Bista, and Galen Murton. On Tibet, its complex political relationship with China, and to understand those who live in exile, I turned to Tsering Shakya, Melvyn Goldstein and Carole McGranahan. To James C. Scott, we owe the concept of 'zomia' (although coined originally by Willem Van Schendel), which has built my own understanding of the fourth world in the Himalaya, even if Scott didn't extend his thesis to South Asia.

My views on China's foreign policy during the Cold War are shaped by the works of Odd Arne Westad and Sulmaan Wasif Khan. On modern China, the works of Yu Hua, Peter Hessler, Ma Jian and Evan Osnos stand out. Sudheer Sharma, Akhilesh Upadhyay and Ajaya Bhadra Khanal have consistently broken down the evolution of China in Nepal, while Sam Cowan has single-handedly brought a new focus with the help of archives unavailable to Nepali researchers. On Newar traders, Kamal Ratna Tuladhar remains the one-man archive.

My deepest appreciation to the works of several Nepali writers and scholars. This work stands on the shoulders of giants such as Dor Bahadur Bista, Ludwig Stiller and Mahesh Chandra Regmi. In particular, Regmi's translations of Nepali historical papers in the Regmi Research Series have been of profound importance; until a new work of the scale and magnitude is published, the Regmi Research Series will remain the benchmark for Nepali historical research. Foreign scholars on Nepal, such as Mary P. Slusser, Mary Des Chene, Mark Turin and Mark Liechty, have immensely contributed to Nepal studies. I have noted my appreciation for Indologist Sylvain Levi in the introduction, while anthropologist Christoph P. Haimendorf was among the first to explore the trade dynamism of the Himalaya.

The book lacks women's voices or stories; it was not always easy to speak to ordinary women without the intervention of other men during my travels (also because it was difficult to speak to women, travelling as I was as a lone man), and a telling sign of the male domination in Nepali public affairs comes from the fact that there are few Nepali women historians, and fewer still women who have worked on the subject. Perhaps a future historian or writer will correct this gap. My apologies for the present.

Friends who've been with me through the journey: Dhrupad Das, Ankita Sharma, Samarth Dixit, Seema Dahiya, Harsimran Gill, Ankit Agarwal, Samriddha Rana, Aanchal Baranwal, Sujay Rajkhowa, Gaurav Shrestha, Utsab Shrestha, Saurav Shrestha, Prabesh Shrestha, Mohit Krishna Shrestha, Amy Sellmyer, Sworup Nhasiju, Prashant Jha, Pranab Man Singh, Suvani Singh, Ujjwal Prasai, Ruhi Tewari, Prawin Adhikari, Deepika Arwind and Ayeshea Perera.

Gratitude to Iona Liddell for poring over the draft in detail and for much more! Harsimran Gill and Prateebha Tuladhar both read portions and gave valuable inputs. Gaurav Shrestha was an early reader who suggested I needed to write more right till the book went to press!

Anushka Joshi and Kiran Dahal for research assistance.

Ajitha, my editor, for cutting through my clutter and shaping this into book form. And for reminding me that behind every book is an editor who has put her soul into the text.

Simar Puneet and Kalyani Gandhi for an invigorating edit.

Kanishka, friend, super-agent, lifeline—for patiently listening to my frustrated outbursts and being the foundation this work needed.

Our families, immediate and extended, both in India and Nepal for their support.

Neha, for being my muse and for continued inspiration, and being the centre of our universe. For the push I needed to write. Thank you for everything!